Scholar, Father, Soldier, *Wynot!*

Scholar, Father, Soldier, *Wynot!*

A Memoir

By

Frederick Joseph Burbach

Scholar, Father, Soldier, *Wynot!*
Copyright ©2018 by Frederick J. Burbach. All rights reserved.

No part of this book may be reproduced in any form or by any means, electronic, mechanical, digital, photocopying or recording, except for the inclusion in a review, without permission in writing from the publisher.

Published in the USA by:
Coulter-Burbach
905 Sheila Place
Apopka, FL 32703

Printed in the United States of America
ISBN   978-1-7322226-1-8 (paperback)
        978-1-7322226-0-1 (hardcover)
        978-1-7322226-2-5 (eBook)

Book & cover design and layout by Dan and Darlene Swanson • www.van-garde.com

Contents

Chapter 1	1932–1937 Preschool Years	1
Chapter 2	1937–1946 Elementary School Years	29
Chapter 3	1946–1952 Boarding School	85
Chapter 4	1952–1953 Creighton University	127
Chapter 5	1953–1954 Army Enlisted Time	137
Chapter 6	1954–1956 Fort Sill.	173
Chapter 7	1956–1958 Monterey & Fort Holabird	201
Chapter 8	1958–1960 The Pentagon	229
Chapter 9	1960 Creighton University	247
Chapter 10	1960–1961 Fort Sill – Fort Bliss	257
Chapter 11	1962 Korea	265
Chapter 12	1962–1966 Foreign Area Officer Training.	285
Chapter 13	1966–1967 Panama Canal Zone	303
Chapter 14	1968–1969 Vietnam	315
Chapter 15	1969–1971 Defense Intelligence Agency	325
Chapter 16	1971–1974 470th Military Intelligence Group . .	337
Chapter 17	1974–1975 St Bonaventure University	351
Chapter 18	1975–1976 InterAmerican Defense College. . . .	363
Chapter 19	1976–1979 United States Southern Command . .	375

Chapter 20	1979–1981 University of Mississippi	389
Chapter 21	1982–1990 Military Hospital to Retirement	399
Chapter 22	1990–2002 Sabbatical	421
Chapter 23	1992–2017 Retirement	471
Chapter 24	Thoughts & Memories	487
	When, What, Where	496

Preface

One would think that it would be easy for a soldier to write a personal history given his multiple assignments, frequent relocations, living abroad, meeting a constant array of people, etc.

And to some extent it is. That part almost writes itself, at least in draft form.

But I wanted my story to be more than that. It should be written for future generations of my family, for people who never met me but may be interested in getting to know me, how I think, how I feel about life in general, and what comparable experiences we may have shared.

I want to write a personal history of the type I wish my great-grandfathers (and mothers) had written as pioneers in Nebraska, or their grandparents who came over from Ireland during the famine or from Westphalia, Germany after the failed revolutions of 1848. I would want that each of them would tell me about others in the family whom they knew, from grandparents to grandchildren, thereby covering a century of our ancestry. With that in mind, I write this to give my descendants whom I shall never meet, a window into their ancestry spanning the Twentieth Century.

By necessity, the story will focus on my life. But the story is not solely about me but us—we the Burbach/Wieseler lineage (and of the Coulter family as you will note later). My story deals with the events of the world, the nation, our locality and family—how

I see these events and relate to them, and some thoughts on the issues of our time.

This story is also an accounting of how I spent my 80+ years on earth. It is about the family I was born into, and about friends and acquaintances. It tells how they influenced me to be who I am, how I lived, how this influenced my children and they, in turn, their children to be as they are and to live as they do. Thus, I hope to give descendants of our Burbach/Wieseler lineage an insight into their DNA and a better understanding of how my story became part of theirs as well.

I am grateful to the following who contributed in completing this book. My dear wife, Lucinda, was priceless from beginning to end. My cousin, Richard Burbach has researched the Burbach and Wieseler families and collected pictures and stories which he has graciously contributed and lent constant support. My daughter Susan got me started and for 12 years urged me on. Hannah Springer, Dr. Arthur Salmon, Dr. Gail Baker, and Teresa Green all helped.

Family Tree

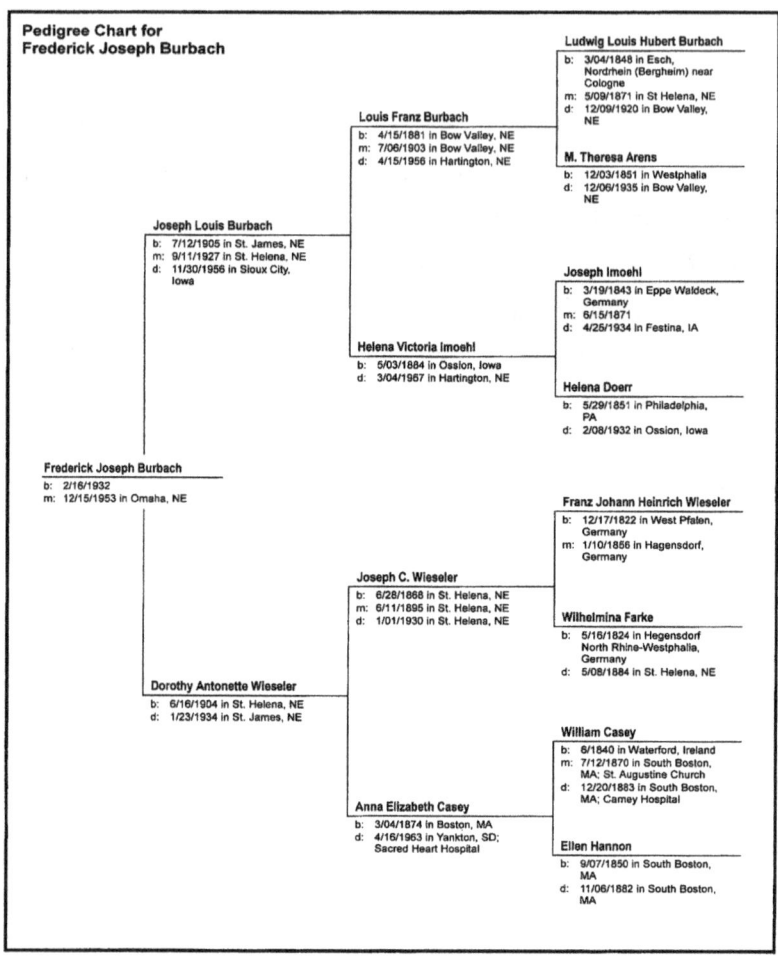

Chapter 1
1932-1937 Preschool Years

Creamed corn and mashed potatoes. That always made me feel happy and mischievous—happy because that was my favorite meal at Grandma Wieseler's, and mischievous translates to teasing my sister Yan, two years older than I am. Here is a flashback from the time I was three years old and sitting in the dining room of Uncle Mark's farmhouse. Grandma is cleaning the kitchen, so she fed us lunch in the dining room. Grandma has just finished cleaning the dining room but had not yet rearranged the furniture, so we are crowded into the center of the room, close to the open kitchen door, which is to my back. I am showing off to Yan by leaning back in my chair. Menfolk do that a lot when they finish eating. They tilt their chair back and balance it on the hind two legs. It's comfortable if you have a good sense of balance. Obviously, I don't. Yan, doing her usual tattling, is calling Grandma at about the time the chair and I crash to the floor. On my way down, I hit my head on the open door. Blood appears immediately and in quantity. That is one of those snippets I remember from my earliest years. Unfortunately, the memory leaves the tale at this point, but I am confident that it must be true since I have a prominent scar on the back of my skull.

Another flashback. About a month after the above incident I am home with Dad and a lady whom I do not know. He and she were very happy, doing a little hugging and kissing when Dad tells me to go out and count the horses in the barnyard. Now a five-year-old or older boy might have some second thoughts about that since the entire barnyard could be seen through the window in the kitchen. Also, the barnyard has a high wooden fence. Farmers do not go out to the barnyard and count their five horses just to be counting their five horses. But I am three years old, so this is a great privilege for me. Dad trusts me enough to give me a real job to do. When I get to the high barnyard fence, I have to step over some old boards from the old fence that had been torn down, and I climb up the fence as one would climb a ladder. About halfway up I slip and fall feet first. An upstanding nail punctures the sole of my shoe, my foot, and lodged its tip in a bone of my left foot. That hurt, and I tried to tell the whole world how much that hurt. Dad is having a hard time dislodging the board and nail from me. I don't think he likes being interrupted from what he had been doing. About this time Grandma appears on the scene, I know not from where. She insists that we go to the doctor in Wynot. That is the first form of punishment. I worry all the long four miles to the doctor's office. The second form of punishment comes at the doctor's office when I get a tetanus shot. Lesson learned: if you stick a nail in your body, someone will want to stick a needle in your body, so do not step on nails and do not go to doctors' offices. Again, the story must be true because I have a scar to prove it.

Another time I am in the kitchen looking through the keyhole of the outside door. I am looking to see if the goat is there; if not, I will go out to play. We do not know where the goat came from nor to whom it belongs. On the day it first appeared, it caught me outside and unaware. Every time I stood up, it butted me down. This happened for an awfully long time (probably a minute) until Grandma came out and chased it away. I guess the goat had so much fun playing with me it decided to hang around. It did a lot of damage to the flowers and shrubbery around the house. The day it got into Grandma's garden, Grandma was very angry and told Uncle Mark how angry she was. The next day the goat was gone. I guess animals know when people do not like them anymore.

One day when we lived for a short time in a house in Wynot, Uncle Art Burbach stopped by to see us. He had a buckboard pulled by a team of horses and loaded with sorghum stalks which he was taking to a processing plant where they squeeze the stalks real hard, and sorghum (it's like syrup only not as good on pancakes or Johnny cake as store-bought syrup) comes out of the stalks. He cut a piece off of a stalk for each of us. Yan told Uncle Art that it tasted just like candy. It was sweet, but to compare it to candy was too much of a stretch of the imagination. I told Uncle Art that I did not like it. Yan told me after he left that I should not have told him I did not like it. But I didn't like it!

These are my earliest memories save two. What I remember is as clear as if it happened last year, but each memory is an incomplete story. Also, our memories are not foolproof, even when we are certain of the facts as we remember them, which leads me to the final two. To comprehend the story, the reader needs to know that my mother died when I was almost two years old.

The following memory is probably not factual. It's a static scene. We are in front of a house on a farm (I choose to think it was my home on the farm). A five-foot square entry fronts the door of the house. These were common in cold, windy regions. It allows one to close the entry door behind oneself before opening the door to the house, hence not letting in the elements. There are a lot of cars and people around. A coffin has been removed from the hearse but will not fit through the entry. (I choose to believe that my mother's remains are in that coffin.)

I must have missed my mother terribly when I was very young. Over the years, whatever memories I had of my mother have all disappeared except this one. And I hang on to this scene tenaciously, and I always will. It is my connection to a person whom I loved without reserve, and she me. I know down deep in my soul that that is true even though I have no memory of her save this. And I intend to keep it just so.

Some have described Nebraska as mostly a sparsely populated, featureless plain. To me, it is a whole bunch of space with the finest people in the world. Rolling hills dominate along the Missouri River, which washes the shores of Nebraska on its eastern and northeastern limits. The dominating occupation in the rural areas is agriculture, and the dominant subject of conversation is the weather. The extremes of my experience have been 32 degrees below zero (Fahrenheit) in the winter and 106 degrees for several consecutive days in the summer. And wind, lots of wind. In Cedar County, there is enough rain for crops most years, although droughts and gully washers sometimes happen. In the last half-century, some farmers have installed irrigation systems. Earthquakes and hurricanes are not a worry, and tornadoes do occur but not with the frequency some nearby states experience. The most dangerous natural disaster here is the blizzard.

I have been in a couple but fortunately was not caught out in a wide, open area such as a pasture. Imagine stepping out of your house, walking twenty feet and being totally lost. The wind is howling so that you cannot hear anything else, and it is swirling; it isn't blowing in one direction but rather in all directions, so you have no sense of direction. The only view you have is grey haze with flying snowflakes. You are alone and disoriented. Also, the biting cold is affecting you. If you are in an open area and try to walk in one direction to reach cover or a recognizable feature, a fence or a ditch which you might then follow to some haven, you will invariably end up walking in a big circle. Soon you will have an irrepressible urge to lay down and rest. Your reasoning powers are exhausted, and your brain is no longer serving you well. You finally succumb to the urge of curling up for a little bit of rest. Days or weeks later your frozen body is discovered. It might be intact or possibly distorted by coyotes and other animals. A Nebraskan is well aware of all this; even most kids know not to go out in a blizzard. Yet, every once in a while, the blizzard captures another victim.

Well, February 16, 1932, did not bring a blizzard to Joe and Dora Burbach's farm in northeastern Nebraska in Cedar County, about three miles southeast of the small town of Wynot, but according to Aunt Gert, it did bring a snow-storm and a baby boy allegedly weighing thirteen pounds. Years later, after many occasions when I admitted to weighing 13 pounds at birth, which explained to many why I am six feet four inches tall and weigh over 200 pounds, Aunt Gert told me how country doctors were able to tell the weight of a newborn. They held the baby by the ankles, looked at the baby and pronounced its birth weight. According to her, I probably weighed nine or ten pounds at birth, "but you were a well-developed, plump little fella."

I was baptized in the St Peter and Paul Catholic Church in St. James about two miles from our farm. St. James had been a fair-sized village of a few hundred people about a mile from its present site, but that town had died out or been incorporated by Wynot. When I was growing up in Nebraska, St. James consisted of the church, a house for the priest, a house for the sisters, a grade school building, a cemetery, and a gas station/general store. It was picturesque and so small you felt a sense of possessiveness and protection about it. Years later Uncle Florenz built his retirement home next to the church. Today the church building is gone, and the grade school is closed. No priest is in residence; nor are the sisters. Florenz's house still stands, the graveyard has added a few tombstones, and the gas station/general store remains. To most of us, all that remains of St. James are memories.

I was christened Frederick Joseph Louis Burbach. My birth certificate has my name as stated. However, in keeping with the Catholic Church's practice at the time, my baptismal certificate has the names Latinized: Fredericus Josephus Ludovicum Burbach and LeAnn's is Helenam Anham Dorotheam Burbach. According to Aunt Gert, my Mom really liked the name Frederick. She thought it had a regal, powerful sound. Also, her oldest brother, Uncle Fritz, had that name. Joseph was my maternal grandfather's name and also my Dad's name. Louis was my paternal grandfather's name. When I was ten years old, I received the sacrament of Confirmation in the Catholic Church. It was customary to pick a saint's name and add it to one's name. On behalf of Grandma Wieseler's Irish heritage, I picked the name, Patrick. So, in some circles, my name is Frederick Joseph Louis Patrick Burbach.

When I was very young, I referred to myself as Febbie. That was my version of Freddy, the nickname that I went by for a while. Later I was called Fritz or Fred, the same as my Uncle, Fred Wieseler, who was my sponsor when I was baptized. There was a change when I went to live with my paternal grandparents. Grandma Burbach had it in her mind that my deceased mother wanted me to be called Frederick, and so I carried that name for nine years until I left her house to go to boarding school. I hated being called Frederick. I'm not sure why. Probably because it represented my move to live among the Burbachs, which I did not like. Burbachs called me Frederick and Wieselers called me Febbie or Fritz.

There is a lot of meaning in what a person is called.

Psychiatrists probably have a field day with the subject. People reflect how much they like a person by what they call him. Those who are close friends call him by a nickname or add the 'e' sound to the end of the name (e.g., Tommy, Jackie, Freddie). Those who have a favorable disposition toward a person but are not close, and members of the extended family, called him by his first name. Also in this group are those who try to tease or upset. They would call the person by his first name with a special emphasis or twist. Finally, there are those who keep one at arm's length or are strangers. They address a person by his surname. Over the years I've had many monikers: Mister, Private, Candidate, Lieutenant, Captain, Major, Colonel, (an endearing form often used by civilian employees is the rank followed by a letter (as in Captain B), Sir, Father, Dad, Old Man, Handsome (not really), Grandpa, Gramps, Pops, Papa, Love, Dear, Darling, Uncle, Bro, Brother, Cuz (for cousin), Slim, High Pockets, Hose Nose (yes, I have a large nose), Curly (yes, my hair is curly), Hey You and a few blankety blank names. . My cousin Don and I were classmates from fourth grade through part of college. He was shorter in stature than I, so at boarding school, he was called Little Bur and I was called Big Bur. Yes, there is a lot in how a person is addressed. When I was young, nicknames were common and often went a long way in defining a person.

My sister, LeAnn, was almost two years old when I was born. She was my "Yan." She was my best buddy, my faithful companion, and my nemesis. My earliest memories of her were when I was three. She was bossy, always wanted things her way, a tattletale, self-righteous, and smart. In other words, in my prejudicial mind, she was all girl. For a couple of years, she was also my rock, my defender, someone I could always lean on. Life threw us a few curves, so after a couple of years and for the rest of our lives, we seldom saw each other. To this day, down deep in my being is a very special attachment to my "Yan," whom today I address as LeAnn.

My sister, Della Rose, was born January 12, 1934, and then Mom got really sick. She was in isolation for a few days in the hospital in Yankton and then died. The cause of death was entered as scarlet fever. One rumor has it that before the doctor came to deliver Della, he called on a lady who later died of scarlet fever. In 1934 country doctors had little knowledge of contagion and sterile techniques, so it is credible that the doctor may have brought the disease to Mom. Aunt Gert told me of her belief. "Everyone in our family had had appendicitis, Dora probably died of an undetected ruptured appendix." The final word: Dad's wife, mother of three under the age of 4, died at the age of 30.

I blame Dad for what happened next to our family, splitting up and all. I loved that man unconditionally until the day he died at age 51. Life had dealt him many blows. He was a weak and selfish man in some respects, not all of which were his fault. From rumors I heard within the family; he was the family's black sheep, the misfit. He did not have a close relationship with his father, who I think genuinely disliked Dad, but in a quiet, disapproving way. According to the stories I heard, Dad was his mother's favorite. To know his mother, my Grandma Burbach, was to know that that was not good. He and his oldest sister, Rose, were in conflict since their childhood. According to his siblings, Dad was a drunkard, a woman chaser, and a party guy, very likable but unreliable.

My maternal grandfather, Joseph C. Wieseler (28 June 1868 - 1 January 1930) died two years before I was born, so I never knew him. My only sources about Grandpa were his daughter Gert and her husband Arthur Burbach, my father's brother. It was always a pleasure to query Gert because her eyes would light up, and there seemed to be a special joy set-aside just for her Dad. She mentioned a number of times that the happiest years of her life were the years she lived under the roof of her parents. Her Dad was a kind and happy man, and her mother and father were "very close and radiated good feelings."

Grandpa Wieseler loved to grow things on the hillside behind their house. He planted about every kind of fruit tree that would grow in Cedar County. According to Art, each time he went to the Wieseler farm Grandpa "had to take me to his orchard, show me the latest trees he had planted and the fruit that was ripening at that time. He was very proud of that orchard." The family also had a large vegetable garden with a great variety of edibles. Traditionally, the vegetable garden was maintained by the family children under the supervision of their mother.

In his later years, Joseph Wieseler suffered from cardiovascular problems, especially high blood pressure. Gert was his primary caregiver during those last months and said that it was a privilege taking care of her father. One of the outdated treatments for high blood pressure, which she witnessed, was allowing the patient to bleed under controlled conditions to relieve the pressure. I wish I could have known Joseph C. Wieseler. I am eternally grateful for having known his wife, my maternal grandmother.

Anna Elizabeth Casey Wieseler (4 March 1874–16 April 1963) personified love, compassion, and joy. I had the enviable privilege of living with her from age two through four. Today, at most any of our family gatherings, a half-century after her passing, she is a topic of conversation, and one after another of us will compete in telling stories of experiences with her. She was the consummate female in the family, and it is a delight to identify others in the family who are like her. The Grandma Wieseler gene is by no means extinct. Optimism and good humor were not her only characteristics. She also had memories of joy over the years beginning when she first met Joseph C. Wieseler, which she graciously shared with us, and memories of great sadness from earlier times, which she seldom talked about.

Joseph and Anna Casey Wieseler raised six children (Fritz, Otto, Dora, Mark, Gert, and Ruddy) on a farm located midway between the three villages of Wynot, St. Helena and Bow Valley, Nebraska. Their oldest was Fritz (Frederick Franz, 1898 - 1974) a fun-loving, hardworking family man who had a rich voice and a hearty laugh. He was married to Katie (Catherine Elizabeth Klug), a loving mother of strong character. My favorite place to visit, when I was a very young boy, was Fritz and Katie's farm. There I found camaraderie because they had many happy, fun loving kids (eventually nine). There was exploration because of all the buildings and fields, lots of great food, and very little supervision by the adults. The older kids who were ordered to "keep an eye on us younger ones" did not seem to pay us much attention.

Uncle Fritz was Grandma's oldest son; she leaned on him more, and in turn, he made a special effort to look after her, and by extension, LeAnn and me, until I moved in with my Burbach grandparents. After that disrupting experience, I saw less and less of my Wieseler relatives. My memories and opinions of them are mostly as seen through the eyes of a very young boy, except Gert with whom I had a close and lifelong friendship.

I made my first communion when I was eight years old and living among the Burbachs. This was a big event at that time for Catholic children, and I looked forward with great anticipation to Uncle Fritz coming to the ceremony and the dinner that followed. He sent me a card of congratulations and a gift, but he did not come. He was my godfather! And I was named after him! I was crushed. Later when the roles were reversed, and I was invited to some young relative's event, I was mindful of how insignificant the event may seem to me, but how much it might mean to him or her that I be there, so I made a special effort to attend. Admittedly, I probably didn't always try hard enough.

Uncle Otto (1902–1971) and Regina (Sudbeck, sister to Art Sudbeck) lived on the home place where Grandpa and Grandma had raised their family. Grandma seemed to enjoy going there since the place was filled with so many happy memories. I remember that we went there a lot when I lived with Grandma. When I no longer lived with her, I seldom saw members of Otto's family. I don't remember much about Otto; he always seemed older than his age - a silent man. Regina was ok but different. I think she had suffered a heat stroke once when she walked the long distance from the house to their mailbox, on a very hot day in the summer. I heard that Otto found her at the mailbox disoriented and sick.

Dora (Dorothy Antonette (1904–1934) was my mother. I do not remember her, yet I miss her in some inexplicable way even today. Maybe it is a subconscious retention of the trauma of her death, her absence after that, or the early bonding of the first two years of my life. Many well-meaning people constantly reminded me of this sad happening for years after that. When I was five years old and walking down Main Street in Hartington with Grandma Burbach, a lady came up to us and asked, "Is that the little boy who lost his mother? How sad!"

Strong emotions stirred in me: anger, sorrow, loneliness, and yearning. I did not lose my mother. She died! And it is nobody's business but mine and Yan's and Grandma Wieseler's and all the Wieseler's! And I want to go home to Grandma Wieseler! Then I remembered an exchange that Yan and I had earlier. (By the way, I am supposed to call her LeAnn, but she is still Yan to me. I just don't say 'Yan' out loud.) Yan scolded me. I said something like,

"I wish my Momma was here." Yan told me to stop saying that (I must have done this frequently), and never say it again. I seemed to know that what I was really trying to do was to get Grandma to react. She would smother me with pity and hugs which felt so good and were so reassuring. I believe I stopped saying it after that because of the admonition from Yan.

All that I know about Dora is what her sister, Aunt Gertrude, told me over the years. I sensed that there was some sibling rivalry between them, probably for the attention of their father. It was obvious that Gert (called Gerty when she was young, but later she was most often called Gert) loved her father very deeply.

According to Aunt Gert, Dora was quiet, pensive, and very religious. She was very intelligent but didn't like to read much. She preferred doing housework or working in the garden. She wanted to become a nun, but her father would not consider it. Neither Gert nor Dora were allowed to go to high school. Gert wanted to very badly, but her father could not see the point in a girl going on to school at that age when she should be learning to be a housewife and mother by helping around the house. Gert had the highest test score in Cedar County when she graduated from eighth grade. Her youngest brother, Rudy, became a physician, which suggests something positive about the intellectual capacities of this family. Imagine what Gert and Dora might have done with their lives if they had been born fifty years later.

Uncle Mark Bernard (1906–1973) was fun-loving and exciting. According to legend he, even more than his brothers, great conversationalist, loved to tell stories, and had a good sense of humor. Again, I knew him only when I was very young. The last memory I have of being around him much was when I was seven years old and had the privilege of spending a week's vacation on his farm.

Uncle Mark gave me a very important job. He had to be gone

during the day, so he told me to watch the cattle in the pasture, so they didn't get into the adjoining cornfield. He said the fence was not very good there. Later that day I saw the cattle in the cornfield. I felt guilty and scared, so I didn't say anything about it to anyone. When Mark came home and saw where the cattle were, he was very angry. Later, I overheard his wife (Aunt Mary Catherine) ask him if I could stay for another week. He said: "no" very emphatically even though She tried to plead my case. I was crestfallen because I was sure he did not like me because I let the cattle get in the corn.

On the positive side of our relationship is another memory when I was about seven. It might have been when Uncle Mark picked me up to spend the aforementioned vacation on his farm. This memory is very clear and extensive. I was riding with him in his car. It is late in a dark and rainy evening. We are on a very muddy road with deep ruts, and the road is very slippery and rough. We have a flat tire. Mark got out of the car, jacked up the left rear of the car, removed the inner tube, and got in the car while he repaired it, replaced it in the tire, pumped it up, reinstalled it on the car, tightened the lug nuts, removed the jack and got back in the car. He did all this in the dark, in the mud and foul, wet weather. When he got in the car, I was very quiet, expecting him to be in a very bad mood. Instead, he looked over at me, I think he had a slight smile, but I couldn't tell because it was so dark, patted me on the knee and quietly said, "Things are never as bad as they seem." I liked that! We continued driving down the road happily chatting with one another. The last contact I had with Mark was in the summer of 1951. I was 19 and in need of a summer job. He wanted to hire me to drive a delivery truck for him. He was then living in Yankton and owned a tavern. Grandma Burbach gave that idea an emphatic no. She said it would not look good, studying to be a priest while driving a beer truck.

Mark was married to Mary Catherine O'Donnell. She was a beautiful lady with real class, and I liked her very much. During the vacation with them when I was seven, I fantasized how great it would be if I could live with them and be their son too. They had four sons, all younger than I. All were lots of fun. Aunt Mary Catherine treated me like a son and would give me big-boy jobs to do. One day she asked me if I could ring a chicken's neck for her so we could have chicken for dinner. I went outside, caught a chicken and began doing the task. She came running out and pleasantly told me I was torturing the poor thing so we took it into the shed and she chopped its head off. I felt kind of squeamish about the whole affair, but I wasn't going to let it show. I wanted to appear as she did, unmoved by normal goings-on at a farm.

I remember that we ate well. Her greatest feat in my view was pineapple ice cream. She made in the ice trays in the freezer compartment of the refrigerator. I had never tasted anything like it before, and I loved it. I saw Mary Catherine only a few times over the years after that, but I remember that each time we met, she seemed genuinely happy to see me and always called me by my favorite name, Febbie. She and Gert were lifelong close friends.

Aunt Gert (Gertrude Wilhelmina 1909–2007) was her generation's version of Grandma Wieseler. To be with her was fun and exciting. She was optimistic, industrious, and always glad to see you. She had her share of trials and tribulations but didn't dwell on them or bring them out in the open. That is not to say that she couldn't be a bit feisty, as could her mother, if the situation called for it. She was my very close friend and confidant from the time I was a very little boy until her death. She was married to my Uncle Arthur. They had ten children.

Uncle Ruddy (Rudolph John 1913–1950) was a physician. During World War II he was a flight surgeon in the United States

Army Air Corps serving in the Pacific Theater. He survived a number of tragedies including a plane crash and malaria. After the war, he set up a practice in Sioux Fall, South Dakota but soon succumbed to cancer and died. I never knew him well, but I liked and respected him immensely. He was married to Louise Veronica O'Donnell, also a very beautiful lady with class and character, and sister of his brother Mark's wife, Mary Catherine.

Three of Grandma's nine children (Joseph, Mary, and Anna) died in infancy. They are buried in a small graveyard in the countryside, about 2 miles from St Helena. My mother is buried there, as are her parents and many other Wieseler relatives. On the grounds of the cemetery is a little wooden chapel that is beautiful in its simplicity. One senses that memories of events of several centuries reside therein. Throughout my adult life, I have visited Cedar County every couple of years and go down memory lane. My itinerary always includes a pilgrimage to this cemetery. I meditate and become one with the spirits that I sense reside there. I also acknowledge my brother the Indian who taught us the meaning of "sacred burial grounds."

When Mom died, we all moved in with Art and Gert. Imagine what that was like for them. They had a year-old son, Roman Donald; and Gert was pregnant with Gerald who arrived in September. They took baby Della when Mom was taken to the hospital. Grandma Wieseler, who was by then taking care of LeAnn and me, moved in to help Gert. Dad also moved in. Gert told me that he was drinking heavily then and would often come home drunk. She was afraid of him, so finally, Art had to ask him to live someplace else.

The year 1932 posed many other problems for this young married couple. The natural disasters included hot summers, cold winters, drought, dust bowls, diseases, locusts. It was a trying time economically — the Great Depression was upon us. A big challenge to the farmer was to accumulate enough cash money so he could pay the taxes on his farm and thus keep it and try again the next year to raise a crop. The nationally acclaimed journalist Tom Brokaw from South Dakota wrote a book about these people born between 1901 and 1924, and he titled them and his book "the Greatest Generation." Among this group were the veterans of World War II. And standing alongside the best of them were the Arts and Gerts of Cedar County, Nebraska.

Going to church was a big thing for me because it was much ado about something, and there were lots of people around. I liked being with people. Grandma and I went to mass almost every day. LeAnn was not with us. She went with her class, and they all sat together in the front pews. We sat in the middle of the church and on the right side. There weren't a lot of people in church on the weekdays, not like Sundays when the church was full. It was fun on Sundays to look behind me and see all the faces looking in my direction. Many of them were looking at me. The women would smile, and the men would make faces at me, which would make me smile. Grandma was constantly bothering me to turn around. Whenever everybody had to stand (at mass there was always a lot of changing positions: sit, stand, kneel, stand, sit, etc.), I was lost. Later in life, I would learn a phrase for this predicament: can't see the forest for the trees. In this case, I couldn't even see many trees. I wish every adult had to spend one day every year being 3 feet tall. The world is a much different place from that perspective.

During the weekday mass, Grandma made me stand on the kneeler whenever she had to kneel or stand. Standing on the kneeler, I could see over the pew in front of us. If I stood on the floor, I couldn't. When that happened, I'd fidget a lot until Grandma had to bother me again.

There are some really important rules of conduct when someone goes to church: no talking, humming or singing unless everyone else is singing, no looking back, and certainly no turning all the way around to face the back while standing on the pew, no stepping on and off the kneeler a lot, no putting up or letting down the kneeler (and most certainly not with a bang), no walking around and no sleeping. I wish there was one rule that Grandma had to observe: no bothering a fella when he is in church. I don't know why we went to church. I guess it was because everybody else did mostly on Sundays. It seemed to make everybody happy and very talkative when mass was over, and everyone got to go outside.

I found out what it was like to feel really bad but not be sick. Well, I did feel sick too. I broke Yan's arm. It was her fault! I told her I was the toll man and she had to pay to cross my bridge, just like when we go with Uncle Fritz across the bridge over the Missouri River to Yankton. She wanted me to let her alone while she rode her tricycle, and she wasn't going to pay the stupid toll either, so, I pushed her off the bridge. The bridge was two planks across a four-foot ditch between the road and our sidewalk. She and the tricycle went tumbling down followed by a wailing of the first order. Grandma came a running. Everybody paid a lot of attention to Yan including the doctor and nurse who wrapped her arm in some heavy white stuff and gave her a dish towel like thing to tie around her neck and carry her arm in. I kind of felt sorry for Yan, but she was supposed to (or, as I would have said it then "pose to") pay the toll man. Down deep though I knew I had done something really bad, and I felt terrible about it, for at least the rest of that day.

One Sunday morning, Uncle Otto and family stopped by our house after church. Grandma was upset. Whenever she got like that, which was very seldom, I kept my mouth shut and gave her my undivided attention. This time she was not upset with me. She was telling Uncle Otto that she needed money, that she had kids to feed, and he was supposed to give her some money. Of course, I did not know why or how much or anything about it except she needed money, did not have any, and Uncle Otto was going to give her some. When Uncle Otto was a little boy, he must have been a good boy like me. He kept his mouth shut and gave Grandma his undivided attention. He also gave her some money.

That is the only clear memory of one of the families of Grandma's sons or daughters at our house, which is misleading. According to custom, Otto and Mark and their families, who belonged to the St. Helena parish, would stop by after church most Sundays. Fritz and family went to church in Wynot, and Gert and family went to church in St. James, but they would often stop by after church as well. Usually one of the families took us home with them for Sunday dinner and a few afternoon hours. Then they would take us home before it was time to do the chores (mostly, feed the animals and milk the cows). In front of our house, we had a big apricot tree. I remember how much I liked apricots and apricot pie. Over the years it has been my practice to eat a lot of fresh apricots during the summer and recollect these days of my youth,

As one approaches St. Helena from the south, one can see the village from the top of a high hill. More stunning, though, is the panoramic view of a long curve of woods through which one catches, here and there, a glimpse of the Missouri River some 1 1/2 miles distant. Much of the intervening land is either croplands or woodlands. Just beyond the bottom of the hill the road curves sharply to the left and then right, to the main group of houses and shops that make up the village. On the far side of the road at that first curve was a gas station/general store. For me, that was the business end of the town. Here is where a generous uncle or neighbor would buy me a sack of candy or bottle of pop. Things were not packaged as they are today. Aside from canned or bottled goods, most things were packed in bulk (i.e., in bags, barrels or tins). The most memorable feature of the store was its odor coming up from the dark, dirty, stained, and worn wooden plank floor that, over the years, had absorbed great amounts of juices, fuels, fluids of many types, and above all else, beer. Once you encountered that smell a few times, especially if it were good times well remembered, you never forgot it. That delightful aroma can be found yet today in general stores in villages far from the cities and the turnpikes of America.

Grandma's house was across the street and beyond a small field to the south of the store. Across the street in front of her house to the west was the priest's house and beyond that the big, brick, stone and masonry Catholic church with stained glass windows and a high steeple topped by a cross. Its size and implied strength dominated the area, as did the religion for which it stood. Every few miles in the northern part of Cedar County there was a church and school like the one in St. Helena, surrounded by a few houses and maybe a general store and a shop or two (e.g., Menominee, Fordyce, Constance, Bow Valley, to name a few).

Farther south of our house was a car barn, filled from time to time with corn cobs used for heating the house in the potbellied stove in the front room. Beyond that to the south was a small field; next was "Grandma" Klug's house and, finally, her car shed. The term garage was too highfalutin for us at that time. Today, residents of Cedar County have garages.

There is a sad story connected with the Klug's car shed. A few years before my time, Grandpa Klug was working on his car in the car shed. He had the car running, maybe to warm up because it was a very cold day. He also had the shed doors closed. He probably never heard of carbon monoxide, but sadly, he became its victim.

Sometimes in the morning when Yan was at school, I would sneak over to Grandma Klug's house. She wasn't really my grandma like Grandma was, but she was somebody's grandma. Grandma told me that all little kids are supposed to call such people grandma even if they aren't our own grandma. Anyway, whenever I visited Grandma Klug, she always gave me one or two cookies to eat while I was there and then one to take home. She called it "one for the road" and laughed. Often Grandma would come walking up before I left. She would always remind me that I should not run off like that, but she never got mad about it. In fact, I think she kind of liked what I did because it gave her a reason to come looking for me, which would always end up with the two grandmas sitting in the kitchen drinking coffee, eating cookies, and telling each other things that made them both laugh. And that always made me feel good.

Our house was nice but not with all the things that houses have today. We did not have a bathroom, electricity, electronics of any kind, running water, telephone, radio, TV, air conditioner, refrigerator, furnace, carpets, garage or car. But we did not know about most of those things then so we did not miss them. Our kitchen was small. It had a coal oil stove. Beside the stove was a small table on which was a long-handled dipper and a bucket of water for drinking or cooking. Grandma got the water from the pump outside. Yan would sometimes pump the water; I was not big enough yet to do that. There were a lot of rules about that bucket of water. I just stayed away from it. If I wanted a drink, I would ask someone. Once I had found a toad outside who was thirsty, so I put him in the bucket. Boy! Did Grandma get excited! She almost drank the poor fellow. The dining room was too small for our big round table and all the chairs, so Grandma pushed the table in the corner, and we used only part of the table.

The living room or parlor was called the front room because that's what it was, a front room. Uncle Fritz once said that some of the fancy houses have the front room in other parts of the house. That did not make sense to him because if the front room is really a side room or a back room, it can't be a front room. He thought the front room should be the front room, and after saying all that, he would laugh. I would laugh too because I liked it when he talked to me, even when I did not understand why he laughed.

Grandma's rocking chair sat in the middle of the front room. She liked to rock. I did too, but I wasn't allowed to if she was in the room, or if Yan was in the room because she would tattle on me. It was fun rocking. I would go so fast that it felt like I was flying. Then Grandma would come rushing into the room and make me get out of the chair and tell me to stay out of her rocking chair. Several times I had rocked too hard and upset the chair and once I got hurt doing that. Worse yet, the last time I upset it something got broken on her chair, and she had to wait until Uncle Fritz fixed it.

The most valuable thing we had in the living room was the new glass lamp that Uncle Fritz and Aunt Katie gave us for Christmas. You could see the kerosene inside. It had a new type of wick, which made a lot more light than the old one. I think Grandma was kind of glad I broke the old one because she sure did like this one. During the winter, a potbellied stove sat in the middle of the room. You were not supposed to touch it because it was too hot, and you would burn your finger.

The bedroom was small and crowded. The bed became too small for the three of us, so Grandma made a bed for me at the top of the stairs in the attic. I was too scared to sleep up there alone, so she also made a bed up there for Yan too. I always went to bed first because Yan was older than I and so she got to stay up late. I was not scared because Grandma left the door to the attic open. But something was not fair about all this because every morning Yan was sleeping in Grandma's bed. She must have gotten up really early and made her bed because it was always as neat as when I had gone to bed.

When it was really cold outside or stormy, I got to sleep on Grandma's bed too. But I had to sleep crosswise at the foot of the bed like I used to when I was little. Aunt Gert kidded me for years about my complaining to her that I had to sleep with Grandma's "tinkin petes."

There came a time when I really began to worry. I had a feeling of pending disaster. Our parish priest was having a serious talk with Grandma. I only heard or understood bits and pieces of what they were saying. What I got out of their conversation was that he was going to be a priest someplace else so he would be leaving. Somehow, I was part of their talks, and the word adoption came up, but I was not sure exactly what that meant. It sounded like I would be living someplace else too. I put all of this together and came up with the idea that I was going to live with him in another place away from St. Helena, and he would be my Dad. I liked him. He and I were buddies; he even said so. But I did not want to leave Yan and Grandma.

And why would Grandma want to get rid of me? I had done a lot of bad things, well not really bad but kind of bad. But I did not think I had done anything to make Grandma want to get rid of me. I also overheard a conversation between Aunt Gert and Grandma in which it was said that some people thought I was too much for Grandma (she was 63 years old at the time) and the best thing to do was to put me up for adoption. I don't remember saying anything to anyone that I knew about all this, but I was afraid.

Many years later, after Grandma died, I found out that she had hired a lawyer, had gone to the County Court House in Hartington and had filed official documents that gave her legal guardianship of both LeAnn and me, and she refiled such papers every year for a number of years after that. I know that she loved us very much. I believe she wanted to ensure that neither of us had to repeat her experiences of being an orphan or losing the family we knew.

Grandma Wieseler had been an orphan-train child, as had her sister, Lizzie. William Casey, at the age of 16, had left Waterford Ireland in 1855 for New York City. He married Ellen Hannon Casey, daughter of Timothy and Julia Mahoney Casey in South Boston in 1871. William and Ellen had three daughters, Annie Elizabeth (Grandma Wieseler), Julia Elizabeth, and Catherine (Katie, who died in infancy). The parents contracted consumption (tuberculosis), and Ellen died. William, knowing he was sick and dying took his two daughters to the Catholic Home for Destitute Children in South Boston.

"You take my daughters. Their mother is dead, and I am dying," he told the Sisters. He died 11 days later in December of 1883.

Quickly, the two little girls, 8 and 4 were, like 94 others, put on a train to St. Bridget's Catholic Church near Yankton, South Dakota where they were placed out to farm families. The two sisters were not placed in the same home. Grandma was first placed with the Mines family, and then with the Goetz family who worked her "terribly hard." Then she ended up at the home of Franz and Wilhelmina Wieseler. In 1895, she married their son, Joseph. For the rest of her life as I knew her, she was always happy and didn't want to talk about the hard times. Our mother had died. Enough! Yet my fear came to pass on my fifth birthday, February 16, 1937.

Louis Franz Burbach and Helena Victoria Imoehl Wedding 1903

Joselph C. Wieseler and Anna Elizabeth Casey June 11, 1898

Wedding photo of Joseph L. Burbach and Dorothy A. Wieseler on right with attendants, Gertrude W. Wieseler and Florenz L. Burbach

1932–1937 Preschool Years

Front—Grandma and Grandpa Wieseler, My mother, Dora
Rear—Aunt Gert, Uncles, Mark, Otto, Fritz, Rudy

Fred, Della and LeAnn   about 1935

Fred First Communion

Chapter 2
1937-1946 Elementary School Years

Something was going on, and it frightened me. Uncle Art came to Grandma's to take me to Grandpa and Grandma Burbach's house in Hartington for my birthday. But my clothes and stuff, including Teddy Bear, my best buddy, were in paper bags and were put in the car. Grandma had tears in her eyes and gave me the biggest hug ever. Yan was not there. I guess she was in school. As we got in the car and drove away, I felt like crying, but I did not. I guess I just did not know why I should - but something was not right.

On the way to Hartington, Uncle Art told me how nice it would be at Grandpa and Grandma's. I didn't know why he kept saying that, but I was glad that my Dad lived there, and so I would be with him. I loved my Dad, a whole bunch. I got along OK without him, but I sure did miss being with him. Nobody in the Burbach family seemed to like him, but I did. After a while, I understood what Uncle Art was saying. I'd be living with my Dad at Grandpa and Grandma Burbach's for a while.

Living with my Dad lasted only a short time. At first, he and I shared the middle bedroom. We slept in the same bed, but Dad didn't like that at all. He said I kicked him too much and I ground my teeth. Dad worked during the day and went out with his friends a lot in the evenings and on weekends, so I didn't get to spend much time with him. Then he became a truck driver and was gone a lot. Soon he lived in another town, but he came and visited once in a while. When he didn't live there anymore, Grandma rented out our room, and I got a bed in Grandpa and Grandma's bedroom. I liked that better than sleeping alone in a room. I was very frightened of the dark and of being alone.

A few years later I moved back into the middle bedroom, and it was mine until I finished the eighth grade, but fear still held me in her grip at night. I fought it all I could but to no avail. I decided to defeat this awful nighttime fear by proving to myself that there was not a person or monster lurking in the dark. Once when I was about eight or nine years old, and after Grandpa and Grandma were most likely fast asleep—they usually went to bed about 8:30 p.m. and got up about 5:30 a.m., so it must have been about 10 p.m., I got out of bed.

It was pitch dark. I walked slowly down the hall to the front room. I could feel cold shivers up and down my spine. All the time I was reaching out to touch anyone that might be lurking about. I went to the couch, knelt on it and reached behind it to feel if any monster might be there. My back and neck and scalp were alive with fear. I felt most vulnerable to an attack from behind. After exploring the rest of the front room and the front bedroom, I hurried back to my bed, jumped in and pulled the blankets over my head. After this brave but traumatic exercise, I concluded that all was in vain. My fears had not diminished one iota so; I never did that again.

Grandma Burbach tried very hard to make me feel at home. I didn't like my new lot in life, but there wasn't much I could do about it. Above all else, Grandma tried to keep me busy starting the week after I moved in. Thus, came about the case of Cold Coffee.

Grandpa worked all day at Nedrow's gas station. He liked coffee, and the hotter, the better. I think Grandma had been bringing him coffee at ten in the morning once in a while. Now she could turn that task over to me provided I didn't get lost. Grandma showed me how to get to the gas station by walking the route with me several times. We started out by walking diagonally through an intersection to the front of the house where the Jews lived. Grandpa would talk about them to Grandma from time to time. He would always talk in German when he talked of the "Juden," and he would lower his voice to almost a whisper. From here we walked to the end of the block, turned left and two blocks ahead was the gas station. It was wintertime, and there was a lot of snow on the ground, but the sidewalks had been cleared, and snow piled along the sidewalks. The following Monday morning I got all bundled up in warm clothes; Grandma half-filled a metal pail (with lid and handle) with very hot coffee and off I went. I enjoyed these walks, except for the loud barking German shepherd at one house. Before the end of the week, Grandpa was complaining that the coffee was always cold when I got to the station. So, the next Monday morning, Grandma had me leave at exactly ten minutes to ten. I bet that Grandpa and Grandma had "synchronized their watches." That did not solve the mystery, but Grandpa did a couple of days later.

Triumphantly he explained to Grandma that at many places along the route there were round impressions in the snow the size of the bottom of a gallon pail. Solution: a very mild reprimand and, hereafter a towel would be wrapped around the pail. It had been fun setting the hot pail in the snow to see it melt. A neat imprint.

In the fall Grandma took me to the public school to enroll in kindergarten. My first impression of this place was not good. At some point in the enrollment process, a teacher took me in a classroom with three other boys. She had four names on the blackboard. She started out by pointing to my name and asking:

"Whose name is this?" I did not know anyone in the room, so naturally, nobody knew that was my name. Why was she doing this? The teacher waited a minute and then told me to go with her and wait in the hall while she talked to Grandma. She explained that I should not be in first grade because I don't even know how to write my name. I should be in kindergarten. Grandma told her that we had made a mistake. Was Grandma pulling a fast one, trying to get me enrolled in first grade rather than kindergarten? Did she really make a mistake?

My paternal grandfather, Louis Franz Burbach (1881 - 1956) was fifty-six years old when I moved into his house in 1937. He had a job that brought in some cash money, and he grew a large vegetable garden. But his greatest joy was to help his sons on their farms during planting and harvesting. He grew up on a farm and had been a farmer until a few years before. But at that time, he was trying hard to wean himself from going to the farm, even at planting and harvesting time, and to turn his agricultural talent to raising the biggest and best vegetable garden in the town.

Grandma Burbach was a fanatically religious, suspicious, insecure, industrious and creative person. I disliked her very much. According to legend, each of us is three persons in one: the person whom others see and know, the person one thinks he is, and the person he actually is, and the three can differ greatly. In the case of Grandma Burbach, she was respected but not very gregarious and therefore not well-known or popular. Most of us knew that she "ruled the roost" at home. Grandpa and Grandma did not socialize much outside the family. They neither went to other homes nor entertained others at their home. They were very frugal probably because money had been short most of their lives, as it was for most farmers in the first half of the 20th Century.

Once I helped Grandpa wash and wax an expensive car. The

owner paid him well and said he was adding a little for the little helper. When we were walking home, I asked Grandpa if I could put my money in my piggy bank. Grandpa told me to mind my own business and not to say anything about this money to Grandma.

I liked Grandpa, but I don't think he was very happy about me living with them. Maybe it was more that he wasn't particularly happy at home. He seemed to be a much different person when he was out and about. He obviously liked his children and grandchildren with the possible exception of my Dad. He always seemed uncomfortable when Dad visited. He seemed to have a tolerable relationship with his sons-in-law and daughters-in-law, polite but not close. He was very fond of his grandchildren.

Grandpa didn't pay much attention to me. We seldom talked. On the other hand, he never mistreated me, and when I got older, he helped me find jobs. He was a man of high principles and moral standards. He was a quiet, kind and gentle man.

My paternal grandmother, Helena Victoria Imoehl (1894-1967) was, in my view, very different from Grandpa. And yet they seemed to get along well together. Their morning moods seemed always to be in sync. If Grandpa was grumpy, Grandma was haughty; if Grandpa was in a good mood, Grandma was quiet and pleasant. Where Grandma had it all over Grandpa was her fanaticism and her control of me.

Grandma's sister, Julie, married a Cedar County farmer at the turn of the century, and they lived near Grandpa's farm where he lived as a bachelor. Grandma told me of visits she made to her sister Julie and of meeting "Louie." Grandpa liked to tell the story of the time he traveled to Grandma's home in Ossian, Iowa *to* seek her hand in marriage (and the permission of her parents). Grandma had gotten "all gussied up" and awaited his afternoon arrival. Late in the evening, when he had not arrived, she went to bed with a broken heart. She did not know that the train was running very late that day. Finally, late into the night, he arrived. Sheepishly, Grandma greeted her soon-to-be fiancé in her bathrobe with her hair in curlers. Louis Franz and Helena Imoehl Burbach raised six children, (Joseph, Rose, Arthur, Florenz, Irene, and Mary) on a farm about four miles south of Wynot, Nebraska about nine miles from where he had grown up on his Dad's farm which was located about a mile west of Bow Valley. Grandpa began living on this farm and working it when he was sixteen years old. He must have been very lonesome the first few years. Louis and Helena were married July 6, 1903. He was twenty-two years old. She was nineteen.

Their oldest was my father Joseph Louis (1905-1956), considered by his siblings to be the "black sheep" of the family. Allegedly he drank heavily, was a real party guy, chased women and was generally irresponsible. I loved him unconditionally.

When he was in his early twenties, he was in love with Helen Lubeley and wanted to marry her. His parents would have none of it They "put their foot down!" because "she was a nobody and the Lubeleys had no money." In keeping with the times, "one did as his parents told him." So, Joe "broke up" with her. He may have married my mother Dora, (Dorothy Antonette Wieseler,1904-1934) on the rebound; as at that particular time she was trying to distance herself from a young man from 'St. Helena who was chasing her but whom she "could not stand." For several years Joe farmed, in keeping with his father's desires, but without much enthusiasm for that way of life. When his wife died after giving birth to their third child, he "went to pieces." He drank heavily and was unable to care for his children. He eventually got a job driving a truck on a route between Niobrara, Nebraska, and Chicago. Later he moved to Sioux City, Iowa where he established a small interstate trucking company of his own. He was called into military service for six months during World War II, after which he resumed the trucking business and spent the rest of his life eking out a living.

His health deteriorated in his forties, yet he continued smoking cigarettes and drinking heavily. He told me that he had an advanced cardiovascular disease with these words: "The doc says my pipes are plugging up." During the Christmas holidays of 1951, I spent a week with him and his family as I usually did each December and each summer. He told me then that on the first of January he was going to quit smoking and drinking. He said his doctor told him he had no choice. To my surprise, he did just that; and, as far as I know, he neither smoked nor drank excessively until he died of a massive heart attack November 1956.

Rose (1908-1997) was a large woman, as creative and hardworking as her mother, but very different in some ways. Rose was direct, forceful, and long-suffering. She was married to Art Sudbeck, a gruff person whom I barely knew. He was obviously not very well liked by the Burbachs. I often heard said pitifully, "Rose has a tough life." I was aware of animosity between my Dad and her that went back to their childhood years. While Joe was his mother's favorite, Rose was her Dad's favorite. Rose resented me living with her folks because, as I heard her say (I would eavesdrop on my grandmother's conversations with her children), "My children are your grandchildren too. Frederick is only one of your grandchildren, yet he's getting a lot more from you than the others." At another time she told Grandma, with reference to the individual first communion pictures of each grandchild (all were 5x7 except mine which was 10x12) which were displayed on the baby grand piano in the living room, "I could take that damn picture of Frederick and throw it on the floor so it would shatter into a thousand pieces." These were two of a number of "damnations" she related to her mother on my behalf—all of which were probably based in part on her disdain for my father. I overheard criticisms of my father from each of his siblings, but seldom did their remarks involve me.

Art (1910-1993) and Florenz (1910-1995) were identical twins. Art was married to Gertrude Wieseler (Dora's sister and my lifelong confidant). Florenz was married to Veronica Lammers who treated me well but with whom I was never close. As a boy, I thought that even though they were identical twins, Art and Florenz differed greatly in their personalities. Art was intense and demanding, and Florenz was more laid back and compassionate. Art was a very dynamic person with a lot of "git up and go." He was intelligent, religious, outgoing, responsible, and an excellent businessman. Apparently, his heart was not in farming. I often heard it said that if you drove by the Burbach farms (Art and Florenz's farms were co-located), you could tell from a distance which was sitting on the horse-drawn cultivator. Florenz's horses would be tight-reined and walking smartly; Art's horses would be loose-reined and plodding.

Florenz was also intelligent, religious and the most hardworking man I have known. I worked for him for several summers during my high school years. He was a very intense, driven, and "in a hurry," farmer who took pride in everything he did.

Art shared some of those characteristics naturally, but not for farming. He farmed for about twelve years and then moved to Hartington. He worked for a few months at the lumber yard building hog sheds while he awaited the completion of the transaction of buying an implement shop. His father was very upset by all this. I truly believe that Grandpa felt that God meant for all of Grandpa's offsprings to be farmers as he was, and to enter into any other occupation was morally, economically and socially wrong. From the first day he heard that Art was moving his large family to town, and going to work there, and for months after that, I heard him say many times: "Art is a damn fool."

Grandpa did not use foul language, but on at least two occasions I heard him say: "Art is a God damn fool." He just knew that Art was headed for "the poor house," meaning severe poverty and taking his family down with him. This from a man who had lived through the depression, drought, locusts, etc. of the twenties and thirties and yet neither he nor his sons Art and Florenz had "lost their farms," a common occurrence among farmers at that time whose farms were foreclosed upon because they had failed to pay the taxes, but a source of great pride and satisfaction for those, such as Grandpa, who "managed to keep their farm."

All went well for Art, and later Grandpa became proud and delighted with his son's success. As World War II ended, there was a huge demand for manufactured items such as tractors, cars and farm equipment. Art acquired franchises for New Idea Machinery, GI Case tractors, and Pontiac cars. He became very successful as a businessman and as one of the leaders in his community—Hartington.

Meanwhile, Florenz remained on the farm. In a way, I believe he was envious of his brother but could not find a way to follow his lead. On the one hand, his wife made it clear that she was not moving to town. On the other hand, he had been his mother's favorite (of the twins), and he fell under her spell, which could steal a man's identity. Florenz was one of the kindest, generous and giving men I knew. Unfortunately, I did not realize how much of a friend, supporter, and teacher he had been for me until many years later.

I went to see him in the nursing home a year or so before he died. He had Alzheimer's. When he saw me in the waiting room his face lit up, and with a big, loving smile he said my name. I was overcome with joy that he recognized me, and then he asked. "How is Grandma?" (She had been dead for many years.)

We chatted for a while, but it was very difficult for me. As I sat in my car after leaving him, I was filled with heavy sorrow, and I cried. I realized that even though he still looked like Florenz, there was no Florenz there. I had wanted so much to tell him that I loved him and to thank him for the many kindnesses he had bestowed on me, but it was too late. Why do we wait until it is too late to tell someone "thanks" or "I am sorry," and above all, "I love you?"

Irene, (1914-1997) the fifth of the Burbach's six children, was good to me and took an interest in what I did and said. I liked her very much.

She was pretty, and a real lady with class, although she tended to be overweight. Her daughter, Jolene, was like a sister to me and we played together often during the years I lived with my grandparents. Jolene seemed to have a very close relationship with both her mother and her father, Clarence Suing. He was a quiet, gentleman, short in stature, a successful farmer, and a man of character.

I don't think Irene liked living on the farm. Their house was very small and simple, and she had to store food in a cave a few yards away from the house. I thought the cave was neat. I believe Irene really missed living in Harrington, and as a result, she and Jolene often spent the day with Grandma when school was out. I regret that I did not maintain close contact with them over the years.

Mary (1916-1988) was a tall, slender, good-looking lady married to a tall, thin, handsome man, Henry Heine (1911). They seemed to have one of the best marriages around. Both of them were very bright and great parents. When I lived with my grandparents, they lived on a farm in a neighboring county, not far in miles but enough distance that they visited Harrington less frequently than her siblings.

As a young boy, I had the idea that they were not very interested in people because they did not pay much attention to me. Henry Heine never talked to me, and Mary was somewhat brusque. Today I laugh at an exchange that took place in their car as we all were riding together on our way to their farm. Mary said that we would stop in Crofton and buy some pop if anyone wanted some. All four of us kids gave an enthusiastic affirmative. She then asked what kind we wanted. I did not know that her kids were limited to one of two choices, orange or grape soda. When it became my turn, I said root beer. Mary stated emphatically that that was not one of the choices; I could have either orange or grape. I sulked and said I wanted neither. Mary then said to Grandpa and Grandma, "First orange or grape pop isn't strong enough, so they have to have root beer, then it's real beer, then it's whiskey, and before you know it they're drunkards." Yes, sir! That Joe's boy needs some strong parenting." These uncles, aunts, and cousins (excluding Uncle Art, Aunt Gert, and their family, and Uncle Florenz and Jolene) made up what I privately labeled the Burbach clan. They differed greatly from the Wieseler clan. At the time, I did not recognize why I liked the one much more than the other. Later, as my understanding of the world broadened from high school studies, such as European history, I found at least a partial explanation, although some may say that this is merely prejudice.

Our Burbach ancestors were heavily influenced by Prussian culture, in which the rigorously trained and disciplined army had a strong and deep influence on the rest of the population who came to respect and adopt for themselves the character of the Prussian soldier. They were tightly organized, strictly disciplined, fanatical in obedience to law and commands, and stern. Wieselers seemed more relaxed and happy. Like the Burbachs, the Wieselers, for the most part, were industrious, but they seemed to enjoy life more. Yes, Wieselers also came from Westphalia in Germany as the Burbachs did, but I believe the Irish blood of Anna Casey overpowered any Prussian fanaticism that might have been present in the genes of the Wieseler lineage.

My good fortune was that the two cultures were combined into one family, and I was a welcome guest in that family. As I saw it, Uncle Art was the strength and discipline of the Burbach clan. Although I was a bit afraid of him in my younger years, we became good friends as I grew up and remained close after that. Aunt Gert was her generation's equivalent to Grandma Wieseler. She and I were birds of a feather and great friends. They had ten children, and I felt as close to each of them as though we were siblings. Don (Roman Donald Burbach 1933-1997) was a year younger than I, but we were in the same grade in school and were classmates from the fourth grade through the first year of college. Don was a great guy, low keyed, a good friend, and reserved. Della (Della Rose Burbach 1934-2007), my biological sister, was as a cousin to me in earlier years but we were always good friends. Jerry (Gerald Joseph Burbach (1934-2007) was most like his father, intelligent, ambitious, and very active. Art junior, (Arthur Cyril Burbach 1936-2011) was quiet, kind, and gentle. Gene (Eugene Francis Burbach (1938-2015) was a well-rounded guy. He was intelligent, active, compassionate and dependable. Romaine (Romaine Burbach 1940-) was overwhelmed by her older siblings but had spirit and tried to keep up. Claudia (Claudette Marie 1942-) had some of Grandma Wieseler's genes including a mischievous bent and a fun-to-be-with personality. Chuck, (Charles Rudolph 1943-) was an unknown to me as a child because our paths crossed so seldom. As an adult, Chuck is a lot like Don in many ways. I think Gert saw a lot of herself in Karen, (Karen Ann Burbach-1946-2005) in whom some of her hopes and dreams were fulfilled including not only a high school diploma but a college degree. Richard (Richard Clarence Burbach 1950) was a bright, industrious and thoughtful boy. He and I were close friends as far back as I can remember even though there are eighteen years between us. Today we readily refer to each other as brothers.

Public school kindergarten was great fun. I decided I liked school. Starting first grade in the Catholic school was a big change, and I was not happy. The nuns who taught me were different from my kindergarten teachers. The schoolhouse was a two-story, old, brick building. Our classroom had twice as many big, old desks as we needed, and the teacher was an old nun who scared me. The first and second grades were in this classroom with lots of kids, all of whom I did not know. We were forbidden to go upstairs which bothered me because a huge pipe extended out of a second story window angling down along the side of the building to within two feet above the ground. It was called a fire escape. I just had to see it upstairs. So, one day, two classmates and I snuck upstairs and opened the door to the fire escape. There was no point in passing up this opportunity, so we slid down the escape. It was fast and scary—in other words, it was great fun, which ended abruptly at the bottom as we came face to face with Monsignor Lordeman. He was our pastor and the man ultimately responsible for our care. He was very calm and pleasant. Mother Superior, the principal of our school, took an entirely different view. Much later I learned a phrase in the US Army, that appears on all army commendations: "brought great credit on himself, his unit and the United States Army." Mother Superior, in her inimitable way, got across to us that we had brought great discredit on ourselves, our class and the Holy Trinity School. This was a heavy cross for a first grader to carry. Shortly after this, we moved to the new school at the other end of the block which had four classrooms, two grades per classroom.

Second grade was noteworthy for several reasons. Probably the most important event was the first communion. It is a Catholic ceremony in which a class of Catholic boys and girls who have finished two years of religious study and demonstrated that they are worthy and sincere believers, receive for the first time the consecrated host that is believed to be the body and blood of Jesus Christ who is God. It is usually a family affair. Relatives and friends gather at a big dinner and give gifts, mostly religious, to the new communicant. Boys dress up in coat and tie, and girls wear white veils and dresses for the occasion. Traditionally a professional photographer captures the clean-cut innocence of the child, and the family displays the framed photograph in a prominent place in their home.

I do not remember my first communion except for the fact that Uncle Fritz did not come. He was my idol. I was named after him, and he was my sponsor when I was baptized, which is the first of the three, major events in an average Catholic's life. The other two are Holy Matrimony and funeral. As for the traditional photograph, I still have mine.

During second and third grades a boy learns the prayers and responses he must know in Latin to be an altar boy. The altar boy participates in the celebration of the mass by various services to the Celebrant (priest), such as moving the Bible from one side of the altar to the other or taking him cruets of water and wine. For that reason, he is called a server. An altar boy may participate in other ceremonies. For example, he may carry a candle or the crucifix (usually my job because I was tall) at processions, at the Lenten Stations of the Cross, or at a funeral. I liked being an altar boy because of the attention I got when carrying out my duties. I seemed to need that. Also, there was a sense of doing something important and meaningful.

Once in a while, something unusual happens in the life of an altar boy. One morning I was lighting the tall candles on a side altar that had a large number of lighted votive candles on a table in front of it. I was using a candle extinguisher, which is a five-foot-long handle with an extinguisher and a lit taper on one end for lighting candles. I had to reach high and over the table of lighted votive candles to light the tall center candles. Suddenly one of the nuns came rushing up with a shawl and began beating a flame under my arm. The sleeve of my white surplice had caught on fire. The commotion was quickly over, and I went into the sacristy and put on a clean surplice and mass began. When we got to the classroom, my classmates were telling those who had not been in church about the fire. I was treated as a hero, and I loved it.

Serving a visiting priest was unusual. He would always be very focused before mass, but after mass, he would talk to me, kid around a little, and give me a tip for serving, usually 25 cents. More fodder for my bank.

Third grade was really the first grade of my academic life. The nun who taught first and second grades was a kind and grandmotherly type. We had lots of fun activities in her classes. In third grade (and after that) the teacher was more dedicated to teaching and didn't put up with much nonsense in class. There also was a clear distinction between the two classes in the room. We on the left side would listen to the teacher talking to only our class, while the right side of the room, the fourth graders, did an assignment or read. Later, the teacher would go to their side, and we would read or do assignments.

Father Kaup became our assistant pastor when I was in the third grade. He was young and very likable. Sometimes he would come to noon recess at school and give us tips on baseball. When I had a problem and needed to talk to an adult, I could always go to him. He listened and would give me advice that always made sense.

On rare occasions, he played golf, and I was his caddy. Every few months he would spend the weekend with his parents on their farm near West Point, Nebraska, and he would take me along. His father taught me how to play checkers, and we got to be great friends. He would never just let me win. He'd beat me, but then he would tell me what moves I should have made. I got interested in checkers and made a checker set at home and practiced a lot. Finally, I began to tie him often and beat him occasionally. He never let anybody else play when I was there. Only he and I played.

He loved to carve wood and had a lot of carvings on the walls of his house that looked like altars. I thought Father Kaup had a great family, and he had lots of friends in Hartington. Everybody liked him. I wanted to be like him someday.

The worst thing I did in third grade was to write a private note to a friend. Four of us good friends hung around together at school and gossiped and talked. More often than not we talked about that which we knew least. We either wanted to know more, or we wanted to convince the other three that we knew a lot more than we did. We had been talking about girls. How and why are they so different from boys? I knew hardly anything about girls. Two of the guys had sisters so they could tell us some things. The fourth guy had an older brother who clued him in on some anatomical stuff. He said his brother used the f-word a lot when he talked about girls. All four of us had heard that word being used by older boys when no adults or girls were around. We tried to figure out what it meant and eventually concluded that it meant "talking about the differences between boys' and girls' bodies."

Our favorite meeting place was behind the church where no one would come when school let out. We usually talked for ten or fifteen minutes and then headed home in different directions. Of late we had been keeping one another informed on an older kid who was probably going to go to reform school. We had pretty well exhausted that subject.

I was curious about what one of the guys had said the last time about girls. His desk was in the row to my right and two desks foreword. I wrote him a note, folded it three times and whispered until I caught the attention of the girl that sat behind him. I handed her the note and motioned for her to give it to him. The note said: "After school let's go behind the church and talk about the differences between boys' and girls' bodies." However, in place of the last nine words, I put in the f-word.

When the girl began to unfold the note, I panicked, and in apparently too loud a whisper I said: "No! Don't read it!" The teacher heard the commotion, walked to the girl, extended her hand and said: "Let me have that." She began reading the note, and suddenly, her face exploded into deep red as she became flustered and quickly headed out the door. She did take the time to glance back on her way out and say "Everybody keep your seats and read." In a few minutes, a nun stuck her head in the doorway and said: "Frederick come out here!"

As I walked out, my teacher was beside the door ready to walk in, but when I appeared, she turned her head up and away so as not to look at me. The other sister said to me, "You come with me. We are going to the principal's office!"

Only now did I begin to worry. Everybody knows that when

you hear those words "go to the principal's office" you are in really bad trouble. Grandma is really going to be upset. First, she'll have to scold me, then lecture me about how embarrassed she is and what will people think, then keep a closer eye on me and make sure that I am always busy and that I pray a lot. Oh well, I guessed it could be worse, but I didn't know how.

The meeting with the principal was not good. Almost immediately I started to cry. I was terribly scared and very embarrassed, and I had a hard time looking at her. She kept saying: "Look at me, Frederick!"

I would look at her for a moment and then back at the floor. I admitted writing the note. She thought I wrote the note to the girl who had it, which seemed to bother her until I told her it was for the boy in front of her. She asked me if I knew what the f-word meant. I said: "Yes. It means to talk about how girls are made differently than boys." I guess she knew that because she stopped asking questions and told me it was a sin to talk about such things.

I should stop doing it. And writing notes and whispering in class is wrong. I shouldn't be doing that either. I should pay attention to the teacher and do my studying. She told me I should be a good boy and try to be a nice boy. Then she sent me back to my classroom.

I dreaded to go back to the classroom, but I did. Everyone looked at me when I walked in and sat down. The teacher told us to pay attention to what she was saying because we would have a test on it tomorrow. I tried to relax in my seat, and the whole world seemed to settle down to the normal routine. After a week of not hearing anything from Grandma about the visit with the principal, I concluded that what she didn't know was a blessing. Thank God!

In the third grade, I began a double life, religious and criminal. The religious was evident in all aspects of my life. My bedroom, now mine alone, was adorned with a life-sized picture of the boy Jesus in the temple, with a picture of the Sacred Heart, and a picture of the Blessed Virgin Mary, and with a crucifix. The dresser had a miniature version of the chalice and associate paraphernalia used by the priest in saying mass. I was often encouraged to stand before the dresser and practice saying mass.

When I had memorized the Latin prayers and responses which an altar boy is expected to know, I became an altar boy and served at mass and other religious ceremonies as often as I could or as often as Grandma could arrange it. When I was a couple of years older, she made a commendable effort to get me up and on my way to the convent to serve at the 6 a.m. mass that Monsignor Lordeman said there each weekday. Grandma knew a priest who, as a boy my age, had done that. I am sorry to say that in this endeavor I was a total failure. In the few times that she got me on my way, I was either too late because mass had already begun, or I dozed off during mass.

What Grandma did not know was that when she and Grandpa went to bed, I would wait until I thought they were asleep, and then I would pull the sheet and blanket over my head and read with the light of my Boy Scout Morse code device, a battery mounted on a telegraph key and flashlight bulb. The top had a button which, when depressed, would light the bulb. Boy scouts learn the Morse code and then learn how to send messages with this device. She knew I had the device and was using it to practice so that I could learn Morse code for when I got to be a Boy Scout. What she didn't know was why my battery seemed to wear out so quickly, and she had to replace it. "It costs too much money!"

I liked to read, and I was not tired enough to go to sleep as early as they did. I first tried to use the room light to read by, but that didn't work. In the wall between my bedroom and theirs was a common heat vent, and Grandma could see the light and tell me to turn off my light. This new method under the blanket was working out fine except every few minutes I had to come up for air. The negative side was that I just couldn't get moving in the early morning hours after only five hours of sleep.

At some point, the good sisters or Monsignor Lordeman convinced Grandma that Jesus would be far more pleased for me to get a good night's sleep than to come to the convent so early in the morning. Furthermore, I was attending the 8:15 mass every weekday morning and two masses on Sunday mornings and practically all religious ceremonies except those during school hours, and that was as much or more than even Monsignor Lordeman was doing.

A close association with religious persons was very important to Grandma. From the first grade on, she had volunteered me to help the good sisters Saturday mornings after the 8:15 mass. They cleaned the church, the school, and part of the convent where outsiders were allowed, specifically the kitchen which was large, warm (important in winter) and well stocked with milk and cookies. But herein laid a conundrum. The sisters didn't get much work out of me. In fact, I was probably mostly a babysitting job for them. But when they spoke with Grandma, they would sing my praises which encouraged Grandma to see to it that I spend more time with them. That was part of her solid resolution that I would not grow up to be bad. She was going to make sure that I associated only with good Catholic boys, no girls, and preferably with priests and nuns which would help me avoid temptations and sin. Her role in my upbringing would be to keep a close eye on me so that I followed "the rules of association" and also that I would be kept busy at all times since idleness is the devil's workshop. She was going to make sure that I followed the path of others she knew who became priests—a calling she knew was meant for me.

After the first year, things changed. I unwittingly helped solve the problem for me and the nuns without disturbing Grandma. Originally, I stayed with the sisters until noon and then went home. The second year, they told me after I had been with them an hour or so and had some milk and cookies that they were almost done and I could leave. I gladly left, and occasionally stopped at Jack Dendinger's house and played for an hour or so. Jack's Mom was good to me and invited me to come and play anytime I wished. I think she knew more about my situation than she let on.

This began the Saturday that I was walking to serve at the 8:15 mass on the coldest day I ever experienced. As I passed the Dendinger house, Mrs. Dendinger called out to me to get in her house. For all I knew, she may have been watching for me. In a scolding voice, although I knew she wasn't scolding me, she said I had no business being out in that kind of weather. After breakfast with Jack and playing for a while she sent me home with the advice that I didn't have to tell Grandma about this.

We prayed a lot at home. I said morning prayers when I got up and said a prayer before and after breakfast and also dinner and supper. We said prayers and the rosary in the evening while I was on my knees. I went to confession every Saturday. Grandma got a book entitled "The Lives of the Saints" or something like that from some priest and I had to learn and recite stories of the saints to her. I also had to memorize the Baltimore Catechism.

I had some real problems with some things in that book. For example, according to the Catechism and as it was explained to me, all sins of the flesh are mortal. In other words, if you thought, said, or did anything remotely related to sex, you were as bad as a human could be, and you would be punished forever in hell. You would never see God, and you would never get to heaven. All in all, I had the same curiosities as any healthy boy, and as a result, I had one huge guilt complex throughout my youth.

My social life suffered from all this religious indoctrination. Other guys my age didn't seem to be as committed to all this religion as I was. Furthermore, Grandma would not let me play with non-Catholic boys. I referred to them as publicans because they went to the public school. Then I heard the word "republican" and assumed that was what it meant—non-Catholic. So, for a brief period, it was the Catholics against the Republicans. But then Grandma explained that it had something to do with bad company, the devil, and bad habits. I think Grandma kept a close eye on me to ensure that I didn't get into bad company, so she isolated me, much as she had seen her children grow up on the farm.

There was no gallivanting around by farm boys. There were only two things: pray and work; or as the Benedictine monks expressed their motto in Latin: "*Ora et Labora.*" I bet Grandma felt great joy and exoneration when she learned that from one of Uncle Matt's boys.

Uncle Matt was Grandpa's brother. He had moved his family to Conception, Missouri when his oldest son entered the seminary at the local Benedictine monastery. Uncle Matt and Aunt Frances had three sons and two daughters. The three sons became Benedictine monks, and the two daughters became nuns.

Being restricted to Catholics only cut out any group activity such as going to the picture shows (movies) parties or getting on any sports teams in town. I had the reputation of being a "very churchy guy," and others were very careful what they talked about when I was around. Why? Why did I have to be so churchy and they didn't?

Girls were another forbidden source of playmates, except for relatives. I did not know why. Katherine Haley and her Mom were organizing a zoo party for Saturday afternoon. Everyone was to bring an image of their favorite animal, and there would be games and ice cream and cake. I thought everyone in my class who lived in town would go. When I asked Grandma if I could go, her immediate response was "no." I frequently asked "why?" but always got the same answer: "you have plenty to do here at home." I soon learned that I could not go to any gathering with girls because I had work to do. I got even with Grandma in a way. I'd make up a question such as "Mary Ellen is having a party Saturday; may I go?" Grandma would give that good ole German guttural response "Achhh!" A child psychologist might say that I felt vindicated. To the reader, all this may sound far-fetched, and maybe it is but that's the way I remember it.

My criminal specialty was theft. I did quite well from the very beginning, but later on, my conscience bothered me and the fear of getting caught was overwhelming until I found the perfect victim, myself. After that, the thrill was every bit as great as before, but the guilt and fear were merely spices in the capers.

My first theft happened much earlier when I was in kindergarten. I stole a candy bar from Rueben Bird's grocery store. When I got home, I knew the candy bar was hot because there was no way I could legitimately have a candy bar. I wouldn't hide it in my room or anywhere in the house for fear Grandma would find it—perish the thought! I went to the side of the house where nobody went except to mow the lawn. Grandma didn't bother to grow flowers on that side, although she had plants everywhere else, including lots of plants in tan painted tin cans in the sunny side of the dining room. I knew because watering all the plants once a week was one of my many chores. Anyway, a window well (that dug-out area in front of a ground level basement window) looked like a good place to stash my cache.

I found a cigar box in the basement and some wax paper in the kitchen. I wrapped the candy bar with wax paper, put it in the cigar box then in the well and covered it with sticks and grass. What a thrill! In my little mind, I didn't feel guilty. It would be stealing if I ate the candy bar, but I wasn't going to do such a sinful thing. I was just putting it in my place rather than Rueben Bird's store. The fear that Grandma would find out was just something I'd have to live with. It was the thrill of outwitting her.

Over the following months, I stole five more candy bars, and put each one in my cache. And then it happened. Grandpa came into the kitchen carrying my loot saying: "What in the world is this?" From there, Grandma took over. After listing all the sins of which I was guilty, she told me to march down to Rueben Bird, give the candy bars back and tell him I was sorry for stealing and will never steal again. She said she was going with me to make sure I did what I was told. I was dumbfounded. To face up to Grandma was one thing, but I never expected to have to face up to Rueben Bird.

When I was face to face with Rueben Bird, I thought I was going to pee in my pants. Once he understood that I was telling him I had stolen the candy bars, he said, gruffly, that I had to pay for them. I told him I didn't have any money. He said that they were no good to him. What could he do with them? He couldn't sell them. I said: "Well, can I have them then?" His face got fatter and real red, as he shouted and pointed to the door: "Get out of here you little thief, and don't you ever come in my store again!" Frightened and embarrassed, I began to cry as I ran out of the store as fast as I could. I caught up with Grandma who was walking towards home. All the way home I wished I could tell Grandma to shut up.

We got our mail by going to the post office where one wall was covered with little square, brass doors with a combination lock built into each one and a number on the front. Behind these doors were little square boxes for letters and the like. If you had a package too big for the box, there would be a card in the box telling you to see the clerk at the window. If you took this card to the clerk, he would give you your package. This clerk also sold me savings stamps.

Grandpa usually wanted to get the mail. There was always worry at the beginning of the month when we got the water and electricity bills. The minimum for each was 80 cents. If the electric bill was high (e.g., $1.10), we had to be sure to turn off the lights if they were not in use. Grandpa liked to listen to the radio that Dad had given them for Christmas. At these times of ultra-conservatism, he would turn the radio volume real low so it wouldn't use much electricity. If a water bill were more than the minimum, Grandpa's right upper lip would twitch just as it did when he got mad. He would warn Grandma that we were "headed for the poor farm." Then, for the next couple of weeks, we would use more cistern water rather than city water.

I had seen Uncles Art, and Florenz dig a big hole and build a concrete tank that was bigger than they were, which they called a cistern. They finished it at ground level with a heavy iron lid. Rainwater collected from the newly shingled roof and flowed down the eaves into the cistern. My uncles and Dad shingled the roof at the same time they built the cistern. A kitchen corner had a big sink with a faucet for city water. Grandpa built a platform next to the sink with a hand operated pump on it so we could pump soft water right from the cistern. I did not like to drink the cistern water. It tasted funny; not like city water or even like well water out at my uncles' farms. But Grandma really liked this soft water, especially for cooking and washing.

People were a lot older at sixty then than they are today. Grandpa Burney who lived in the house at the end of the street was usually sitting on his porch when I came home from school if it was a warm day. At first, he would wave to me and have a cheery word. He was sixty-two, and since he was an old man I guessed that he was waiting to die. He lost interest in waving and talking to me after a while, and when he was sixty-four, or so he died of old age, at least that's what Grandma said. Poor guy also was almost blind; he had cataracts.

My Grandpa also was an old man, but by the standards of my youth, he lived to be really old—75 years. According to him, his longevity was because he never went to the doctor. He said that he did not believe in modern medicine and doctoring stuff and that your body would heal itself if you were careful. He said that doctors first give you a bunch of medicines, then want to put you in the hospital and operate. Once you are good and sick, they send you home to die.

About six months before Grandpa died he was so sick he relented and went to the doctor. The doctor gave him some medicine, put him in the hospital and did some exploratory surgery. He found that Grandpa's body was overrun with cancer from the prostate and sent him home to die, which he did on his 75th birthday. His prophecy was fulfilled.

Grandpa was shy but fond of people and liked talking with almost anyone. He seemed happiest when he was out and about meeting people. Grandma was just the opposite. When she talked with people other than family members she held her head sideways and talked real nicety nice. I think she thought people didn't like her, and she was trying hard to be liked. In other words, she tried to be a people pleaser rather than just being herself. At home, when she was correcting me for something I said or did in public which was not acceptable, the phrase "what will the neighbors think?" always crept into the criticism.

Grandma was very frugal. I suspect that she and Grandpa had saved very little money and were living off their earnings. For years she rented out the front bedroom. We always had nice tenants. One summer our roomer was a young man who became my friend. He gave me my first model airplane kit and showed me how to put the parts together. Of special note was our Bad Bird Attacker project. A big bird had taken up residence in a tree in the front yard and would fly low and frighten people who came by. My friend decided that we would do something about it

I don't remember what we did, but one day the bird left. I was proud the next Thursday when there on the front page of our weekly newspaper, The *Cedar County News*, was a short report of our feat, and my name was mentioned as the main character. But my friend was disappointed with the article because he had expected the paper to print my picture. Frankly, I was very pleased with my fifteen minutes of glory.

Mr. and Mrs. Polei lived next door beyond the vacant lot that Mr. Polei owned. The front half was lawn and the back half, together with much of the back half of the lot he lived on, plus Grandpa's adjoining garden formed one huge garden. He and Grandpa loved working in their respective gardens. They also talked with each other. I liked that. Grandpa and Grandma didn't seem to have any friends except for family. Seldom did anyone come to our house just to visit, and seldom did Grandpa and Grandma visit anyone.

The Poleis had a daughter who lived in Chicago. She would visit for a few days in the summer and then let her daughter who was my age stay for a week or two. Grandpa Polei was very proud of his granddaughter. Each summer he would invite me to spend an afternoon with him and his granddaughter at his jewelry shop. He would show us a lot of the things in his shop. The most interesting was using an eyepiece to see the inner workings of a pocket watch and seeing how a grandfather clock works with the pendulum, weights, wheels, and chimes. Mr. Polei was a very quiet and private man, but he was nice to me.

My crime career had a new twist. This time it was helping the farm kids dispose of the excess food they brought to school. About 1:30 in the afternoon I would get hungry and get the teacher's permission to go to the bathroom. Once in the hallway, I would ensure that "the coast was clear." Then I would head to the storage room which was used to store the students' coats and galoshes. The many shelves were for storage of books, backpacks and, most important to me, lunch bags and buckets. I became an expert at quickly identifying the bag that would hold my quest - a peanut-butter-and-jelly-on-store-bought-bread sandwich. At home, we had only home-made bread and very seldom peanut butter. If a banana were perchance spotted, I'd also help dispose of it. I did this once or twice a week for about a month. There wasn't much thrill or guilt in it, and I was getting quite lackadaisical until the following advisory was read by the teacher for all the class to hear (and I believe it was also read in the other classrooms).

"Someone has been stealing food from the lunch bags. We think we know who it is. If it happens one more time, the thief will have to see the principal. His or her parents will have to see the principal, and the stealer will not have any recess for a month, will have extra homework and will have to stay after school for one month. Whoever is stealing, stop it!" I resolved immediately to give up storage room snacks.

Generally, I felt in the way and looked down upon by most of the Burbach clan. For that reason, I constantly plotted to escape. When I was in the third grade, I thought I had a sure thing. Dad, his new wife, Mary Olive (1915-1976), and I were riding back to Hartington from my vacation in Sioux City, and Mary Olive said: "Maybe next year you can come live with us." I was speechless and overjoyed. Nothing more was said about it, but for the next year, I fantasized about living in Dad's house, and—more importantly, getting out of Grandma's world.

A year later, when I brought up this idea, my Dad said: "I work all the time. You'd see me less than you do now." I knew that was not true, but I also knew that any chance of living with my Dad was dead. I came to realize that I was not as important to him as he was to me. I cried about that a few times, but I still loved him till the day he died.

Over the years I created several schemes to remove myself from Grandma's world. Several of them saw me ending up in Boys Town near Omaha which was well known throughout Nebraska. Father Flanagan had started it as a home for wayward boys living on the streets of Omaha, or others who didn't have a place to live. And that was me! I figured I could get there one of two ways.

Two boys who were two years ahead of me in grade school hid in the clothing store downtown before the owner locked up for the night. Then they stole a bunch of stuff. They got caught when they tried to sell some of the loot. One of the boys, who was a bully around school and a generally bad boy was sent to reform school. The other one, who was being raised by a single mom, was not a bad guy, but I guess his mother couldn't control him, so he went to live in Boys Town. That sounded like an easy way to get to Boys Town, but my conscience just wouldn't allow me to commit a serious crime.

The other option was to hitchhike to Boys Town and ask them to let me in. I assumed that they would, but it could all backfire, and maybe I would end up back with Grandma. I thought to myself: if things are bad now, think of how much worse they could be. So, I pondered long and hard as the years went by, and finally, the opportunity to escape fell into my lap when I was in the eighth grade. Grandma got Father Maur to talk to me about going to high school at the seminary run by his Benedictine Abbey in Missouri. Since I figured I was going to be a priest anyway, this sounded like a great idea. I am quite sure that for her own reasons, she was as happy to see me go there as I was happy to leave.

As I saw it, she was trying to make me like she was: fanatical about sin and church stuff, very distrustful of people, almost too paranoid about what people thought of her, single-minded and a loner. Whether consciously or unconsciously, she tried hard to make me into an image of herself. And I'm sorry to admit, to some extent she may have succeeded. So, as I grew into manhood, I found that in a sense I had two personalities, the one molded by Grandma Wieseler, an open-minded extrovert, and an uncomfortable introvert like Grandma Burbach.

Of all my Burbach relatives, I always thought I was most like my Uncle Art. When I was in my forties and having a private conversation with Aunt Gert, she told me how much Art disliked his mother, and said it was sad that a son felt that way about his mother. Subsequently, Art and I talked about Grandma and found that we shared experiences and feelings. Grandma was dead by then, and I guess we both felt guilty speaking badly of her. Art showed that when he said, "In her own way she was probably a very good person. The way you and I feel about her is sad but justified. But we don't know what she was like down deep, nor do we know why she was the way she was."

Fourth grade is the most memorable of my elementary school years. A young, beautiful, Ursuline nun who was happy, gentle and fun was our teacher. I was her pet, or at least she let me think so. So was Mary Ann Dendinger who was living in the convent during the school week for this year, during which she would make her first communion. Her family lived near Coleridge where she went to public school. She and I would stay after school and help our teacher, Mother Dorothy, clean up the classroom before they would walk to the convent. Mary Ann and I became great friends. After that year I saw her twice, each time very briefly at the annual county fair. My heart did flip-flops each time, and I decided that she was my girlfriend, and if I married, it would probably be to her. She was my sweetheart in absentia for the next eight years.

About the third week of school, we received our textbook. When I opened mine, I was stunned and then began to laugh. Others came to my desk to see what was so funny. Even Mother Dorothy did. I was speechless as I pointed to the large round picture with details about the earth, continents, oceans, mountains, rivers, etc. It had never occurred to me that this huge world could be gathered up on a piece of paper. It was nothing less than a miracle. And so, began my life-long love affair with geography, but not that two-bit, simplistic version that entails not much more than knowing the names and locations of physical features of the earth. True geography is the study of the distribution and its cause and effect of any phenomenon throughout the surface of the earth or a given region, and the study of the resultant integration of part or all phenomena. For the next few years, my hobby was learning the geography of a site; although I did not know there was such a thing. Site geography is the study of the cause and effect of the phenomena at a specific spot such as a city or small area. I ended up studying ten sites. The most complete study involved Bend, Oregon. It is still my desire to visit there someday. My study would begin with data that was readily available in the maps, books, and encyclopedias in the library. Next, I would write the city chamber of commerce and the state tourist office and get whatever they were giving away. From the materials gathered, new leads would arise, and I would seek information from them. Occasionally I would tell a fib or two in my letter if it were necessary. For example, if I were writing to realtors, I would begin with "I am planning on moving to Bend, Oregon shortly." That brought an immediate response with a big envelope filled with data which would keep coming for weeks. Nothing was considered useless; bus or train schedules, telephone book, local newspapers, sales fliers, advertisements, etc. It was a great education in its own right, and a superb, although unwitting, preparation for my ultimate profession as a foreign area officer.

Music had never been a friend of mine. Grandpa and Grandma did not listen to music on the radio, nor did they have a record player. In grade school, I did not excel in music and therefore lacked interest or motivation. In the first few grades in elementary school, I was in the rhythm band. After demonstrating a remarkable void of talent and lack of timing on the tambourine, triangle, and drumsticks, I was "advanced" to the flute. My success with the flute is suggested by the advice I got from Sister Beatrice at the school-wide musical festival which Holy Trinity Grade and High School held in the city auditorium. The general public was invited by a note that each child would (or should) take home. At the recital, as the Rhythm Band took its place on stage, Sister Beatrice came to me, took me by the hand and placed me at the very end of the back row. Then she whispered in my ear: "Now Frederick, I want you to play very, very quietly." At report card time, my two worst grades were in music and art. Since no one seemed to mind, I didn't do anything to improve.

Years later in boarding school, I was offered six weeks of free violin lessons, and the school furnished the instrument. I liked the idea of playing it but did not practice enough. At the end of the six weeks, the instructor encouraged me to continue, but I would have to begin paying for lessons and for renting the instrument. Since I had no money, the lessons ended. But all was not lost. I could take free piano lessons. After a month of that, the instructor got me to agree with him that since I was not practicing enough, I should quit wasting my time and his. After that, throughout my six years at boarding school, I was in chorus, as were all of my classmates since chorus was required for all. Years later, I regretted not having developed some musical competence both for my enjoyment and as an inspiration for my children.

It is strange that I had so little interest or encouragement in appreciating music, yet my father and his siblings had a lot of fun with music. They formed a band and played at parties. The three girls played the piano; Dad played the fiddle, Art the trumpet and Florenz the drums. They filled a real need in Cedar County since commercial music was very scarce in rural Nebraska in the 1920's and 30's.

I don't know why I wasn't taught to play the piano when I was in elementary school. There was a baby grand in the living room which Irene often played, and she would have been willing to teach me. Anyway, modern music and the playing thereof were not meant for me. The only music I heard and appreciated by the time I left school was Gregorian chant and classical.

One year, I think it was 1942, during the week before Christmas, Dad's truck driver who delivered freight to the Cedar County area, brought a big box with all kinds of unwrapped presents for me: baseball glove, baseball, football, tennis racket and a can of tennis balls, and two model airplane kits. Grandpa hid the stuff and then put it under the Christmas tree Christmas morning. I was surprised and thrilled when I saw all the stuff. And I knew that Dad would be here again this year for a couple of hours in the afternoon. Then Grandpa told me that the driver told him that Dad couldn't visit us this Christmas. I was very sad and cried. I wished he would take back all these presents.

I never used the tennis racket. Grandma said the tennis courts at Ferber Park were too far away (about five blocks) for me to "go traipsing up there." The baseball glove I took to school on occasion; both to show it off and to use during recesses. Even though I lived with Grandpa and Grandma for nine years, I never did get to play a game of baseball (excepting what we played at school during recesses). The various boys' baseball teams that were formed in Hartington practiced at Ferber Park - "too far away, and anyway, they are mostly non-Catholics who play there." According to Grandma, I didn't have time for such "frolicking" around.

My nefarious, secret, criminal career took a turn for the better once I had developed some mechanical and analytical skills. The driving force in my secret career wasn't food. Look how easily I had stopped the storage room operation; and as for the candy bar caper, I didn't take even one bite of the stuff. No. My real motivation was twofold: to have the power to acquire and possess desirable things, and to be a contrarian against Grandma's fanatical goodliness. Conclusion—money. And where was there lots of money? In the bank; or more specifically, in my piggy bank.

The first step is to break into the bank and the best time is when Grandma is gone to a church thing, and Grandpa is talking to Mr. Polei and working in the garden. The bank is about three inches tall, designed like a barrel (with staves), and made of stainless steel. On the bottom is a key slot and Grandma keeps the key hidden, so the easy way to get into the bank is not an option. The top of the bank has a single slit large enough for a fifty-cent piece. It is always open. However, when the bank is turned upside down, iron bars appear across the opening, preventing coins from falling out. So, where is the weak spot in the bank's security system? The movable bars. I found a hairpin of Grandma's, straightened it out, and began pushing in bars as I held the bank upside down and slightly shaking it. After numerous tries, a nickel fell out. Voila! Success!

The following day, on my way home from school, I stopped at the gas station near the school. Days earlier I had "cased the joint" and spotted a coin-operated candy dispenser inside. I walked out of the station that day, chewing candy and walking tall, with the knowledge that I was a successful genius. I now had a source of unlimited wealth. I was thrilled. I felt no guilt because I had stolen from myself. I was my own victim, and that was fine with me. The fear factor that Grandma would find out was only strong enough to add spice and excitement to my doings.

One Saturday afternoon I was downtown with my Dad, and he was talking business to someone. I interrupted him to tell him that I was hungry and wanted to go home and eat. I was amazed and delighted to hear him say as he handed me a quarter: "Go over to Shulte's Drug Store and get a hamburger and coke." To this day that is the best hamburger and coke, I have ever eaten. I also learned that if I played the game just right, I could get repeats. Over the years Dad bought me a number of hamburgers and Cokes. That first time, I learned never to tell anyone about this way of eating for when I got home, Grandma found out that I wasn't hungry. Upon interrogation, she found out that I bought a hamburger and Coke. She scolded me for wasting money: "We have plenty to eat at home. Next time you put that money in your piggy bank." Even then, that hamburger was keeping me happy.

I learned that: what Grandma doesn't know hurts nobody. I was earning more money, so why shouldn't I be allowed to spend a little? Not much, just a little. Mowing a lawn, for example, brought 25 cents for sure, mostly 50 cents and occasionally 75. If

I put the money in my piggy bank immediately when I got home and entered the amount in the record book, who would know if a nickel stayed in my pocket? It was all my money. There might be something wrong with this, so I'll admit to having told a lie when I go to confession, but God won't care.

Once I got to the fourth grade, Grandpa began rounding up jobs for me for Saturdays so that I could earn some money, nearly all of which went into my piggy bank and from there to the post office where I bought savings stamps under Grandma's supervision. Economically, that was not a bad idea since by the time I finished the eighth grade I had nearly $1000 saved.

There were at least three occasions when I was allowed to spend my own money. One summer, three of my cousins, one at a time, spent a few days of vacation with their dad and us. It was stipulated that if there were a decent movie in town, he wanted his child to have the experience of seeing a movie. Grandma had little choice but to let me go too. I got 10 cents of my money, and the movie was nine cents. Most of the kids I knew who got a dime to go to the movies, got to spend the penny on popcorn. Grandma wouldn't go along with that idea. We had popcorn at home; that penny went into my piggyback. Yes, she was very determined and disciplined, at least where it came to my upbringing.

As I saw it, money was pouring in. I had lots of lawns to mow in the summer and more sidewalks to clear of snow in the winter than I could manage. Grandpa was my manager. He found the jobs, and I did the work and kept the money, nearly all of which went into my piggy bank. Grandpa also kept the old hand push lawn mower oiled, sharpened, and generally in good order. The only tools I needed in the wintertime were a shovel and a broom.

Some of my customers helped me find other work. A good example was Mac McCloud, the town barber. His shop was at the corner of Main and Vinegar Street. Vinegar was the nickname we had for the street that had all the town's taverns. Mac's shop was in the basement below the Hartington Bank and next to the furnace room. The first time I mowed Mac's lawn, he gave me tips on how to mow in straight lines and equal sized passes so when I finished, the lawn would have a nice design. He also increased my pay from 50 cents a cut to 75 cents. Sometime later he helped me set up a shoe shine business in his shop. That was a failure since most of his customers were not interested in getting their boots shined.

He introduced me to the bank's president and asked him if he had any work I could do. The president talked with the janitor, and they decided that I could wash the bank's windows, inside and outside, every Saturday morning. The janitor was happy to show me how to wash and dry the windows outside using long poles. An old man, he was glad he no longer had to do it.

As the cold weather set in, I got the job of stoking the fire in the coal-burning furnace late in the day and then banking it so that the next morning there would be live embers with which to get the fire going again. The thought occurred to me that if I played my cards right, I probably could get the janitor's job when the old man retired.

Doing the windows on the inside was fun. I got to go where all the bank employees worked. They were very nice and talked with me a little bit. Once, when I was alone in the office of one of the bank officers, washing the window, I noticed that there was a big pile of coins on his desk. A thought passed through the criminal side of my mind that I could put a hand full of coins in my pocket and no one would ever know. Wow! The religious side of my brain was scandalized. Had I really sunk so low? Here I am, considering robbing a real bank. I'd be right up there with Jesse James, John Dillinger, and that guy who was asked when he was caught, why he robbed banks. He had replied: "because that's where the money is." Hey! That is exactly what I was thinking the first time I stole from my piggy bank. I knew I was a thief and getting to be a liar. My conscience became so laden with guilt. that it frightened me and so I hurriedly finished the window and got out of there.

I was working hard one hot spring day, clearing a man's garden and getting it ready for planting. The garden had been overrun with weeds the previous year, so there was a lot of pulling and hauling. I was hot, sweaty, and tired when Uncle Florenz stopped by. Grandpa had told him where I was and that he had agreed for me to clean this man's garden for a dollar. Uncle Florenz got a glass of water for me and told me to sit in the shade and cool off. He then went over and talked with the old man. They seemed to argue, and Uncle Florenz was pretty mad.

I learned later that he told the man to pay me more than a dollar. He was working me way too hard so that I would finish the job in one day. The man told Florenz he couldn't afford to pay me more. At the end of the discussion, the man promised that he would take me fishing within the month as part of my pay. The man did just that. He and I took along a lunch and fished for several hours in a big creek he knew. We caught some good-sized bullheads. He took the fish home with him, including the ones I caught, which was OK with me. That was the first time I went fishing, and it was a lot of fun.

With the coming of World War II, everyone in the family was worried about the men folk being drafted. It turned out OK for everyone but Dad since they all got some kind of exemptions because farming was considered essential to the war effort. People talked a lot about the war and happenings overseas. They also talked about who was being drafted or enlisting in the army and navy. Every once in a while, they'd talk about someone's son or brother being killed. There seemed to be more funerals, and we did a lot more praying in church about the war.

Rationing of sugar, gas, and tires began. The most serious was sugar rationing since candy, cakes, pies, and other sweets became scarce or were changed. Grandma continued to make pies, for example, but now instead of apple, cherry or real chocolate; they were made of a yucky chocolate pudding or lemon pudding. It ruined my love for chocolate pie, and to this day I don't eat chocolate pie—even the old-fashioned, yummy kind

Almost everybody had a garden which was called a Victory Garden. At some farms, you could see the garden from the road, and it would have a big V in the middle of it made of one kind of plant. Grandma now spent even more time on her foot-powered sewing machine making clothes. Colorful flour sacks were an important source of materials. The darning of socks, the repair of clothes and the hand-me-downs prolonged the life of socks, pants, shirts, and coats. Uncle Clarence and I must have been about the same height because I got a lot of clothes from him which made Grandma happy because I didn't have many clothes and I was growing fast.

Men are built differently than boys. His shirts had the right sleeve length if I wore a sleeve band, but there was way too much shirt. I was embarrassed when I wore his pants because boys my age just didn't wear the kind of pants that men wore. Furthermore, while the waist was OK if I wore a belt, and Grandma could adjust the pant length, but the crotch of the pants came halfway to my knees.

Once I got an almost new pair of tan dress shoes from Uncle Clarence. They didn't look like anything boys wear, and they hurt my feet because they were too narrow. Never mind, they would be just fine, according to Grandma, and anyway, I only had to wear them for dress (i.e., going to church and the like). On another occasion, Dad bought me a nice pair of black shoes, and they fit perfectly. I was proud of those shoes until the first time I wore them to school on a rainy day. The shoes began to disintegrate. It turned out that they were not leather at all. They were made of a paper synthetic that did reasonably well until they got wet.

There had been times of plenty on the prairies of Nebraska during the 1920s, followed by drought and recession. It was a time of maturing as a culture, a time of nation-building, and yes, a time of sacrifice. It was made worthwhile by the euphoria that poured forth with the victorious end of the war in 1945.

My Dad was drafted. In the fall of 1942, he had an altercation with a union organizer on the docks of his trucking company. He ended up hitting the guy and throwing him off the dock. Unbeknownst to Dad, either the guy or a close friend of the guy sat on the draft board. A month after the altercation Dad, was called into the army at 37 years old. The policy then was that no one who was 38 or older would be drafted. Dad went through basic training and then was assigned to an air defense unit at Camp Callan near La Jolla, California. In July of 1943, when he turned 38, he was honorably discharged.

He was not fond of the army, was angered at the Red Cross for what they did or failed to do for some of his fellow soldiers, but loved southern California. I thought he might decide to live there, and I hoped that he would take me with him.

When Dad got home and back to his trucking business, he found that he was deeply in debt, and the whole business was in bad shape. He had the opportunity and, according to many, the justification to declare bankruptcy. Instead, he chose to honor the debts and spent many years eking out a living and paying off his debtors. I greatly pitied him during the last twelve years of his life.

We got to know each other as adults. His was not a happy life.

His family life was empty in many ways, although he truly loved his daughter Joan and son Tom by Mary Olive. His trucking business was close to failing., and he didn't have much to live for. He was a beaten, unhappy man. To make ends meet financially, he had a part-time second job working in the milk parlor of a bottling company. The cold, wet concrete floors aggravated phlebitis in his legs which was very painful most of the time. I first noted this one day when he was laying on the floor, playing a card game with Tom and me. Tom jumped up, tripped and fell on Dad's lower legs. The agonizing yell that followed attested to a man in great pain.

Grandma also had lower leg problems. I don't know if she had phlebitis, but I did hear "milk leg" mentioned many times. Her leg shins would become greatly ulcerated, and she kept them dressed and bound. When the pain got really bad, she saw the doctor, and part of the remedy always included staying off her legs as much as possible until the ulcerations healed. At such times, I felt a new emotion for Grandma—compassion. The doctor finally arranged for Grandma to go to the Mayo Clinic in Minnesota for treatment. Grandpa went with her, and I was left in the care of Grandma Daugherty.

I liked Grandma Daugherty very much. She was a lot like Grandma Wieseler. Often, when I was younger and feeling down, I would sneak to her house, and she would give me a cookie, and we would talk, but very briefly so I could get home before Grandma knew I was "out of control." Grandma told me not to bother Grandma Daugherty, so I wasn't supposed to visit her.

When Grandpa and Grandma were in Minnesota, I must have been about 11 years old. I could go to my house anytime I wanted, but I slept at Grandma Daugherty's. She didn't pay much attention to Grandma's rules about me not; "roaming about town, getting in with the wrong crowd, getting into trouble, or traipsing or gallivanting around." About the only rule was that I had to be in her house by 5 p.m. Freedom!

On the second day of this newly found freedom, I worked on my piggy bank again. This time I extracted forty cents. The following day, after school, I went to the grocery store, bought a bunch of grapes and a banana (two of my favorite fruits which were scarce as hen's teeth in my world), went to the bowling alley, sat in the bleachers and watched people bowl while I enjoyed the fruit. For a long time, I had wanted to watch bowling, but this place was emphatically "off limits" because of "the goings on there and the people it attracts." I did not understand why all of this was so bad and yet felt so good. It was the first time I began to wonder why I could not be like other boys and girls in town. Why is so much of the goings on in life "sinful" for me but not for them? For the first time in years, I felt like I was living life like everybody else. I wasn't bad. I was simply happy. Was that bad? I thought Grandma had the problem, not me. Well, I had a problem too—Grandma.

One day, Uncle Florenz stopped by. He said he wanted to see if everything was OK with me and the house. When we went into my house, Uncle Florenz stopped at the kitchen table and stared at a glass jar half filled with canned peaches topped by a glob of mold. He said, still looking at the jar, "I don't think I would eat that" I said: "I don't think I would either." And we both laughed. After we walked through the house to make sure everything was OK, he asked if I had any money. I told him I thought Grandpa left some with Grandma Daugherty. Uncle Florenz handed me two quarters while he said "Don't tell Grandma that I gave you this, and for heaven's sakes don't put it in your piggy bank. Sometimes a guy just feels like he's gotta have a candy bar or stick of gum." And he winked at me. We both smiled as I said: "Thank you."

The last thing he said to me as we walked out the back door was: "Be sure you always keep this door closed, so the varmints don't get in the house." After he left. I wondered: why couldn't everybody be like Uncle Florenz?

One summer I vacationed with Dad, Mary Olive, and Joanie in a park called Lake of the Ozarks in the Ozark Mountains in Missouri for a couple of days. I went along primarily to take care of Joanie so Dad and Mary Olive could have some fun together like going dancing in the evenings. The highlight of my trip was an airplane ride in a seaplane, the kind of airplane with floats instead of wheels so it can take off and land on water. Mary Olive went with me. She did not want to go because she was afraid, but Dad finally talked her into it. We were the only ones on the plane except for the pilot. I thought it was great fun. Mary Olive sat beside me, and she was hanging on tight, gasping with every little bump the plane made and was really scared. When we landed she told Dad that the plane was just an old bucket of bolts, the wings were flapping, ready to fall off anytime, and she thought the thing should be banned from flying. Dad and I laughed at her.

My model airplane hobby was going well. I built eight planes, most of which were US fighter aircraft. Grandpa helped me hang them with string from the bedroom ceiling. He was good at that. Each plane was hung differently; two were climbing, two were diving, two were turning, and two were flying level. I liked to show them off to my cousins when they came. I'd also tell them the name of each airplane and a little bit about it

I dreamed of getting an airplane like the Thielen boys had. They lived two houses down from us. They were much older than I, but always let me watch when they were flying their planes. They had sprayed their planes with paint, so the surface of the plane was hard and smooth, like a real airplane. Mine were OK but were covered with special tissue paper that came with the kit. Their planes also had real gas-powered engines, working propellers, and movable flaps and rudders. I hoped someday to have an airplane like theirs.

Any live aviation event boosted my love of airplanes. One day a long line of high flying bombers, passed over from northeast to southwest. I had never seen so many airplanes at one time, and it was an exciting thing to see.

One Saturday a plane flew low over Main Street and dropped a lot of leaflets. People expected this was going to happen. I guess it was advertised in our weekly paper, *The Cedar County News*. There were a lot of people in town, and Main Street was crowded. There was a slight breeze, so when the papers came out of the airplane, they scattered for blocks around. The leaflets were actually gift certificates from local businesses, and there were lots of them. People scampered after them all over town. It was great fun.

I was mowing a lawn near downtown one Saturday when a Lockheed P38 Lightning fighter aircraft flew over Main Street. People who saw or heard it stopped to watch. After a steep climb and turn, it flew low and slow for the length of Hartington. The pilot then gunned the engines, rose steeply, made a big turn around and then dove to a low level and as fast as all get out passed over Main Street, zoomed to the sky and was gone. For my buddies and me, and for much of the menfolk of the town, that was the center of conversation for weeks after that.

The fourth and best event was an airplane ride Grandpa got for me from a local farmer who kept his airplane at the small airport north of Hartington. The plane was an old biplane with tandem seats and no canopy. We flew for a long half hour. When the pilot saw a farmer he knew working in the field, we did several long dives towards him which were fun. But the g-forces on pulling up from the dive were scary. We did a lot of twists and turns and flew high and low. When we landed, and the guy gave us a ride home, I talked so excitedly and so much that Grandpa told me I should be quiet for a while.

Life was getting more exciting. I was in the 5th and 6th-grade room with a new teacher. Mother Dorothy had been transferred, and she was to be the last of her kind. Henceforth we had disciplinarians, and Mother Clemens was up to the task with her torture device—the ruler. If you committed an infraction, you were called to the front of the class, told to hold out your hands, palms down, and WACK! I am proud to say neither I nor any of my classmates were slow learners. The ruler ruled!

Beginning with fifth grade, Holy Trinity had a different order of nuns. The new teachers were more focused, stricter and made us do some serious studying and homework. Learning became more fun and interesting. Also, I became a compulsive reader. Grandma seemed to have backed off a bit.

One Christmas I got a bike. It was big, heavy and beautiful. I enjoyed riding it, and I enjoyed the freedom it gave me. It was the beginning of some "gallivanting and traipsing." I did not know what those words meant, but when I rode the bike, I could go anywhere, and no one would ever know. I could do it quickly and not get caught. That must be what Grandma was so determined that I not do.

The only downer was that I had to park the bike on the porch, in front of the big living room window so we could keep an eye on it. The part I didn't like was lugging it up the six steps leading to the porch because it was so big and heavy, and I sometimes fell when getting the bike down those steps.

I never rode the bike to school because Grandma was afraid it would be stolen, but the next summer, I rode it out of town to the swimming pool near the fairgrounds. Some of my aunts (I believe they were Gert, Louise and Mary Katherine) convinced Grandma to let me learn to swim. They assured her that they went swimming there from time to time, and it would be OK for me to go. I knew the way to the fairgrounds because Grandpa and I had walked to the fairgrounds for several summers to care for Holstein calves that were being kept temporarily in the pens and barns there.

Holsteins are excellent dairy cattle, and the local farmers wanted to improve their herds of milking cows and expand the dairy business in the county. Someone would bring in a couple of truckloads of calves from Wisconsin, and after Grandpa and I fed them for a couple of weeks, there would be a big auction by Ferddie Pietz to sell the calves to local farmers. I remembered how tired Grandpa got walking home from the fairgrounds in the evening after spending all day at the fairgrounds. It made me appreciate my bike even more.

Grandpa did not have a car. He said he didn't need one. I thought it was because we had to save money. The old telephone in the hallway was disconnected because Grandma said we didn't need one. One luxury that we did have, and Grandpa was proud of buying it for Grandma, was an electric refrigerator. Most people we knew had ice boxes. The iceman came by once or twice a week with a horse and wagon carrying a big block of ice. He would chip off the size of a chunk you wanted and put it in your wooden icebox. Grandma's refrigerator was a big enamel box on four legs with a big coil mechanism on top. It sat in our dining room.

Without a car, our travels were limited to Sundays. About once a month a relative would pick us up after Mass and take us to their house. We would have a great dinner, and then the adults played cards while we kids played outside. Late in the afternoon before they had to do chores, they took us home. I liked it best going to Uncle Art's or Uncle Florenz's farm. They had kids my age, and we played well together. I knew Uncle Art's kids best and got to stay with them sometimes when school was not in session.

On most Sundays, we walked the six blocks to church for 8 o'clock Mass, and then walked home and had breakfast. I went back to church for 10:30 Mass and then home for dinner. We had three meals a day, breakfast, dinner, and supper. After dinner, I helped Grandma clean up while Grandpa read the weekly newspaper. Then Grandpa took a long nap followed by working in the garden. Grandma sewed. I would do homework, read, or work on my model airplanes. For me to go to somebody's house to play was out of the question.

Sundays were usually very boring, but once every month or six weeks, Dad would come by for a couple of hours. Then the whole world was rosy. I tried hard to get him to pay attention to me, but mostly he talked with Grandpa and Grandma. He usually brought a big bottle or two of beer and shared it with Grandpa.

For me, the big break was joining the Boy Scouts. Why in the world Grandma ever let me do that I'll never know. I actually began to associate with "publicans." Our scoutmaster was a coach at Hartington High. He and his wife were really good people and took an interest in each of us boys. Their family name was Kowalski.

One of the first things I noted was that all the boys in the troop were older than I. The oldest was in high school. They were friendly and very helpful. I remember early on where I had to run a couple of laps around the track for a specific time. The purpose was to learn to measure a distance by timing oneself in running it. When I finished the run, the two senior scouts who timed me made a big deal about the fact that I had come very close to the exact time expected. Later I found that all their excitement was put on to boost my morale. Everyone in scouting seemed to be that way. They encouraged a guy, which was nice.

Jack Dendinger was in my patrol which had seven guys. He might have been my patrol leader; I don't remember. One weekend he, another guy in our patrol, and I went overnight camping alongside a creek a short distance out of town. The site we chose to pitch our tents was in a park-like spot, under a huge tree. We played a made-up game of catching leaves. It was fall and leaves were falling from the tree. As a leaf fell, its fall was very erratic, and further disturbed by the breeze. The challenge was to spot and call out a leaf high in the tree and follow its fall until you caught it. After playing this game for an hour or so, we put up our tents and prepared our sleeping arrangements. Each of us had a mattress cover. Nearby and across a barbed wire fence was a straw pile. We climbed the fence, walked to the straw pile and began filling our mattress cover. "Let's get out of here," hollered Jack. I looked up and saw a big bull running toward us. We hurriedly scampered to the fence and over. Except I didn't quite get all of me over. I got a 3-inch barb cut on my left leg. By the time we got to our tents, my pants were bloody. My buddies immediately applied first aid. Scouts, in general, take great pride in doing first aid. They told me I should go home because it was a big cut. I didn't want to do that since this campout, my first was really fun and anyway we were going home the next morning.

When I got home my leg hurt, and I was tired from lack of sleep, but I did my best to hide my problem from Grandma; knowing full well that if she saw it, that would be the end of my camping days, and maybe even Boy Scouts. She told me to take some clothes with me, go down in the basement and change clothes and put my dirty clothes on the wash pile, and then get ready for church.

I was putting my camping gear away and washing up a bit when Grandma called from the basement that I should come down there right away. When I got there, she held up one of my socks which was red with blood.

"What is this?" she asked.

"Oh, one of the boys got scratched, and we had to give him first aid," I replied.

"Pull up your pant leg!" she ordered, with a worried look on her face. She gasped when she took off the crude bandage. She cleaned and bandaged the wound and told me to go to bed and rest for a while. I thought to myself: Wow! That's a side of her I've never seen before. I like it.

The summer after sixth grade we Scouts went to a jamboree held at a campsite along the Platte River. A lot of Scouts were there. We had great lessons in the woods learning about animal habitats, about edible plants and berries, and how to build shelters with some branches and grasses. At night we sat around bonfires telling stories. Our favorite game was "capture the flag." These were the greatest fun days I had ever experienced.

We went home in a pick-up truck with a roof which broke down on the way, so we didn't get home until 5:30 Sunday morning. I was really tired and looked forward to going to bed. Grandma said: "No. Get ready for church." So, I probably slept in church instead of my bed.

There were a lot of neat boy scout things to buy, but we just didn't have the money. I did get the actual merit badge patch for each merit badge I earned. I wanted a merit badge sash so I could show off the ones I had earned, but we just could not afford it. I enjoyed earning merit badges. I was proud that I earned the rank of Star and was working to achieve the rank of Life when early in 1945 I had to quit Scouts. Between school and work at the bakery and a few other activities, I didn't have the time to keep up with scouting. I quit reluctantly because I wanted to become an Eagle Scout. That was not to be. "*Ora et Labora*" had seen to that.

I had a Dad the night of the "Scouts' and Dads' Bean Dinner."

We also had contests between the patrols that night, and my patrol got a prize. Dad actually came. I told all my friends that my Dad was there. The word euphoria aptly describes my feeling and that night I felt it. I was equal to every boy there. I too had a Dad, and he was sitting right over there. Oh, if my Dad had only known what this meant to me. That night and the day of my high school graduation are the only times I can remember when my Dad attended a public function in which I was involved.

The summer after seventh grade, Grandpa told me to see Adolph Heimes, the owner of Hartington Bakery. He might have a job for me. That sounded great! My first real job. Grandpa thought it would be a great opportunity.

Mr. Heimes said he needed someone to clean up after the day's baking was finished. My hours would be from 2 to 4 weekdays and 8 to 1 on Saturdays. He would pay me 35 cents an hour. He also said that he might teach me a few things about baking, and if things worked out, I might be able to continue the job after school started again. If I wanted the job, I could start the next day. Then he gave me a tour of the bakery and described what I had to clean and how. The front area where the baked goods were displayed and sold was not my concern. The girls who worked there took care of that. With subdued excitement, I told him I would like to have the job. He told me to be back the next day at one, and he would help me get started. I rushed to the creamery where Grandpa worked to tell him the good news.

The next day Mr. Heimes and I cleaned up the bakery in the sequence and manner he expected me to do it henceforth. We scraped and greased the stack of baking trays. The big mixers were scraped and greased. As we did this, he pointed out how dangerous the machines could be. I heard him, but apparently, the message didn't sink in a month or so later when I was cleaning the big dough mixer. I had cleaned the inside but needed to move the mixing arm a little to clean the space under it. To do that I had to give the start button a quick tap. It was, for safety reasons, a bit more than arm's length away from the mixer door. For balance, I placed my right hand against the inner wall of the mixer while stretching to tap the start button. The powerful mixing arm moved farther than I expected. It pinched the skin on the outside edge of my right hand and yanked my arm hard. Fortunately, the mixer then came to a sudden stop. If it had begun running … Well, you get the picture. The skin along the outer edge of my right hand hurt for a long time, and I had a hardened mass there for several years.

The big workbench had to be cleaned next, and everything on or around it had to be put back in their places. We scrub-washed the pots and tools. I cleaned dusted and then swept the floor. Mr. Heimes said that there was a lot of work, but if I paid attention to what I was doing, I should be able to get everything done in two hours every day.

The girls up front said they were happy to see that he was getting help. He did all the baking and deliveries every day. They knew he dreaded the last two hours of the day when he was tired but had to do the cleanup. It was worse on Saturdays when his day began at 3 a.m. This was because all the farmers came to town to shop on Saturdays, and more people ordered decorated cakes for the weekend. He decorated them himself, and each cake took time. One of the girls said, "And so Saturday is his crabby day."

Usually, the entire family came to town Saturday. Infants and smaller children were put in the care of relatives or friends; the older children got to tag along with their parents or visited with relatives and friends, while mothers and fathers socialized for a few hours. A staple for the men was a visit to the barbershop where the conversations and arguments were more important than the tonsorial services. The taverns also did a lot of business on Saturdays. The women gossiped and shopped, more of the former than the later. The families had some cash to spend from the sale of cream and eggs, which they sold at the local creamery. About 10 or 11 o'clock p.m., they would get serious about shopping for the staples they needed: sugar, salt, flour, hard candy, tobacco, maybe some tools, or utensils, some cloth and accouterments for sewing of clothes for the family, or shoes, or bib overalls. By one in the morning, customers left, and the storekeeper could close up and go home, grumbling that something had to be done about this long day every week. And in a couple of years, something was done. The businessmen of the town got together and agreed that all stores in the town should close by ten pm. No exceptions. The notice went out; the farmers' grumbling soon abated, and another small triumph for democracy was realized.

Before the summer ended I was coming in at 3:30 a.m. on Saturdays, and I loved it. Mr. Heimes taught me to do many simple things sift flour and put the trays in and out of the big, new oven with the Ferris-wheel-styled rotating shelves. He was proud of that oven which had been installed earlier that year. It looked like a big box, six feet wide and seven feet high and deep. It had controls for temperature and the moving shelves. I put trays and pans of things to be baked in and out of the steam box, and took the dough out of the mixers and placed it on the workbench. He, of course, kept an eye on me and decided when I did things. At the same time, he was very busy working with dough on the workbench. I also sliced loaves of bread on the slicing machine, slid loaves into paper sleeves, and wax-sealed them. Once in a while, I would deliver baked goods to the stores, but usually, he preferred to do that himself.

By December I was doing some actual baker's work. First, I learned to make doughnuts. Above a large tub of hot oil, was a bowl held by a flexible arm. The bowl contained liquid doughnut dough and narrowed down to a ring the size of a doughnut. The bowl had two handles, one for maneuvering the bowl over the hot oil; the other movable handle controlled the bottom ring of the bowl which released a ring of doughnut dough with each turn of the handle.

After enough doughnuts were in the hot oil, the bowl was put aside, and a pencil-shaped tool was used to flip each doughnut as it readied. Then a screen with handles was lifted up from the bottom of the oil to catch all the doughnuts, put them aside and begin the operation all over again. After I had made doughnuts a number of times under the close supervision of Mr. Heimes, he felt safe in letting me do the whole operation on my own.

The workbench was where the real action took place. Here was where we made breads, cakes, sweet rolls, and cookies. He worked on one side and I on the other, and where possible we would be doing the same thing so he could teach me.

My favorite was making sweet rolls, which I felt was creative work. Take a cut of sweet dough, roll it out in a ten-inch-wide strip in just the right thickness, take the cutter that is shaped like a wheel with extended axles and crosswise blades an inch apart. Roll it over the strip of dough thus cutting the dough into one inch by ten-inch strips. Roll a strip to an appropriate length. On a greased pan, hold the end of the rolled strip down with the forefinger of one hand and twirl the rest of the dough around and around the downed end. Pinch the end of the strip to the dough. Fill up a tray with these and put it on a tray rack. When we, together, had filled the desired number of trays, I would put them in the steam box. Mr. Heimes would tell me when to take them out of the steam box and put them in the oven. He decided when they were done. Then

I would take the trays out of the oven and place them on a tray rack to cool. Once cooled, I put the icing on them. A jelly would be selected, and I would take a handful, form a fist and begin squeezing so that the jelly would come out at the top of my fist. I Cut it off with the index finger of my other hand and drop the jelly into the middle of the sweet roll. The roll is ready to be sold.

These were fun, creative, and rewarding things to do that did not seem like work to me. Once I got the hang of it, baking was like music and dancing. When Mr. Heimes and I were at our peak performance, it was grand choreography. The girls said as much, and they were happy that the Saturday crabbiness had disappeared. Now we would usually finish baking in late morning. I would commence to clean up. Mr. Heimes would go home for the midday meal, take a leisurely nap and come back in the late afternoon to meet and greet family, friends and other customers.

On weekdays, I came in well before the bakery closed and began cleaning up. When I finished, and before I locked up for the night, I fixed myself an ice cream cone, the bonus Mr. Heimes said he gave me for work well done.

The academics of the eighth grade were in many ways a waste of time. The notorious (among her former students) Sister Alberta was not the best teacher. In fact, she was at the extreme end in the other direction. I was bored in class, and it was destroying whatever good study habits I had developed. One of my classmates' mother, who was religious, well-educated and respected, had several rows with Sister Alberta, and finally took her daughter out of Holy Trinity Elementary and put her in the public school. I never heard what the true story was, but students "just knew" that it must have been Sister Alberta's fault. The cause of my boredom was not all her fault. The subjects and the quality of the textbooks were the main culprits. For my part, I used the town library and read a lot. I would soon see that there was a sharp contrast between eighth grade at Holy Trinity elementary and ninth grade at Conception.

In the winter of 1945, when I was in the eighth grade, Father Maur stopped by for a visit. During his stay, Grandma got him to talk to me about going to high school at the seminary run by his monastery. Since I figured I was going to be a priest anyway, it sounded like a really good idea. Here was that escape that I had dreamed about for nearly nine years.

By the summer of 1946 life was looking up. Elementary school was finally a thing of the past. It had been a boring venture those last four years. I was making good money at 35 cents an hour working at the local bakery. I didn't seem to have much trouble getting up at three thirty on Saturday mornings to go to work at the bakery. Above all, at the end of the summer I would finally be leaving the Burbachs and beginning my quest to follow my heroes: Bing Crosby in *Going My Way* and *The Bells of Saint Marys*, Father Kaup, the assistant pastor at Holy Trinity, and Fathers Maur, Cyril and Bernard, sons of my Grandfathers' brother Uncle Matt. Over the years I had gotten to know all three of his sons. I had the honor of being a participant in the procession at the celebration of Father Maur's first mass following his ordination. These men were my heroes.

They were my idols whom I wanted to be like—a Catholic priest. In 1946, within my church and family culture, that was a most honorable goal for a young man.

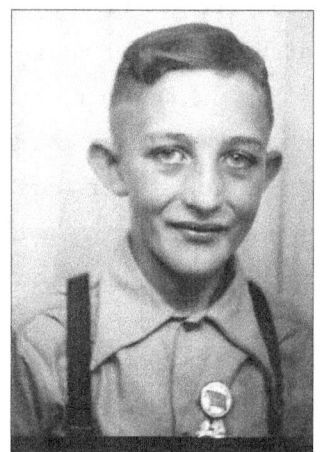

I join Boy Scouts.

Chapter 3
1946-1952 Boarding School

Finally, the day came to begin the trek to Conception, Missouri. Preparation for this undertaking had been in the works for weeks. In later life, I would travel to Australia or India, or other distant places with a lot less planning and preparation than went into this trip. My cousin Don and I were looking forward to starting high school and to living in a boarding school. Uncle Art was driving and looking forward to spending time with his favorite uncle and three cousins.

The Benedictine Monastery of the Immaculate Conception in rural Northwest Missouri was awe-inspiring at first sight (and at any other sight after that). The massive Basilica with its twin towers dominates. Attached to the basilica on the south side is the monastery, a two-story brick structure with an interior quadrangle. The hillside continues to the west where large buildings consisting of the seminary, the gymnasium and the power plant, Saint Maur Hall which contained the major seminary classrooms, and Dormitory Hall which housed the living quarters and study areas of the high school and first two years of college, and a low-lying building housing the music department and some offices. Down the hill to the south were the buildings and yards of the monastery's large farm. To the west, behind St. Maur Hall was a steep incline at the bottom of which was a flat athletic field beyond which was a small lake. To the north of these features was a nine-hole golf course. Except for the small village of Conception which lies to the east of the monastery, all one can see for miles around are rolling hills with fields of green. Between the monastery and the school was the infirmary, an imposing two-story stone structure that was under the care of Brother Paschal, an imposing, bulky monk with a heavy German accent who saw to it that we stayed healthy in body and spirit by his jolly good nature and boundless compassion. Early on we got to know Brother Paschal well because one of our first tasks was to go through a medical examination. The first stage was under his control, and he had the process well organized and efficient with the help of some senior students. Later in life, during my early years in the army when I would go through the annual, "mass produced" medical examination, I would remember Paschal and wonder if he had not learned his trade in some army. Under Paschals' method, we would go through each of about eight stations in groups of ten. The two stations that caused his nickname (known only to students and respectively so) was audio and visual. His nickname was Brother Tventy-Tventy (sic). In audio, he would hold his large pocket watch about three feet from the subject's ear, instruct him to hold his hand over his opposing ear and ask if he could hear the watch ticking. Then he would repeat the procedure on the other ear. If the subject answered in the affirmative, Brother Paschal would announce to his assistant with the subject's chart "tventy-tventy" (sic), and the chart would be so noted. Somewhat the same procedure was carried out for the eyes with the eye chart conveniently close to the subject, with the same "tventy-tventy" (sic) evaluations if the subject answered in the affirmative.

Saturday was dentist day. The bus took students to a dental office in a small town ten miles away for our dental examination. I flunked big time. Over the next several months I visited the dentist nearly every Saturday. He extracted my remaining eleven upper teeth and three of the bottom ones and fitted me with upper dentures. When I finally got a full set of teeth with which to smile, my classmates called me Mr. Hollywood for a while.

Because of the frequent visits to the dentist, I missed the doctor's exam which would complete our physical examination. But it did not matter. Every year, as the weather began to turn cold, a dreaded sick period would begin for me and last for several months and reappear for short spells throughout the winter. Sick meant having a very sore throat, high fever, and a just plain sick feeling. Each year it seemed to be worse than the previous year. I was determined this year just to ignore it.

By mid-November, my buddies began to see that I was very sick and one of them must have reported me to the Prefect, Fr. Joachim. One morning before class Father Joachim told me to see Brother Paschal immediately. Brother Paschal took one look at my throat, took my temperature and said I was very sick and would be in one of the beds in the infirmary until a doctor could examine me. The doctor came later that evening. He was not at all pleased with my condition. (At first, I thought he was angry with me, and that made me feel even worse.)

He told me that the little white spots on my tonsils were pus pockets. He asked me how many years had I had tonsillitis (after he explained to me what the symptoms are for tonsillitis). I told him: "I don't know, probably always at this time of the year." He said it must have been a long time because my tonsils looked like sponges, they had so many holes. He said I would have to stay in bed in the infirmary for a few days while they treated the infection and got me healthy again, and then he would remove my tonsils and adenoids and put an end to being sick every year.

That sounded both good and bad. The idea of an operation scared me, but the thought of not being sick each cold season trumped any fears I had. The doctor also said he would schedule the operation so I could go home for the holidays. And that is what happened. I had the operation a week before Christmas vacation began.

Art came to get Don and me and another boy. This time I got to sit in the front seat of the car where Don usually sat. Art was concerned about me. After several hours of driving, his concern turned to worry as my breathing got to be somewhat of a struggle. Later he told me that by then he had decided that he was going to stop at the next town and find a doctor. As luck would have it, relief came suddenly. I began to cough and gag when suddenly I coughed up a huge blood clot and began to breathe normally. What a relief! I apologized to Art for coughing blood on the window, dashboard, and floor. He seemed to be as relieved as I was and assured me that I need not be concerned. This tale ends happily except for an epilogue.

Several days after we were home, I walked downtown on an errand for Grandma. At the time, my weight was down to a little over one hundred and sixty pounds (I was about six feet three inches tall). I met Art on the street. He was not very happy to see me. He told me to get in his car, and he drove me home.

He walked into the house and confronted Grandma: "This boy has no business out of bed, much less walking around outside. For heaven sakes, he looks like death warmed over. What in the world were you thinking? Keep him home and warm, and feed him some of your chicken noodle soup." And with that, he stormed out of the house.

There were more than one hundred monks (priests and brothers) who belonged to the monastery at Conception, but I would get to know only a few of them since many of the priests were assigned to various activities throughout the Midwest and outside the United States.

Uncle Matt was the maintenance engineer at the school. I never knew his job title, or even if he had one. He had the demeanor of a monk—pleasant, compassionate, kind and gentle. He was well liked by everyone, especially the students. I was proud that he was my Uncle Matt.

Father Maur was the rector of the major seminary; he was very intelligent. Reportedly his high school academic record at Conception had not been surpassed by anyone. He was highly regarded by everyone although some of us found him reserved and somewhat difficult to know well.

Father Cyril was in charge of the farm operations. He had a drooping eyelid and was thin and frail. He told me that when he was young and would run fast or for long periods, his chest would hurt. He has assumed that the pain was normal and something everyone felt Only in later years did the doctors discover that a coronary artery, which should have been the size of a pencil, was actually the size of string. He was very open and easy to approach.

For those reasons Cyril was well liked but, given that academia has a level of snobbery, even in a seminary, he was considered to be a spiritual being of a high order but one whose intellect did not shine brightly. Keep in mind that I am reflecting the opinions of high school freshmen and sophomores. Then came Mother's Day 1947 and the priest to give the sermon at the high mass that day, not only to the monks and the student body but to a basilica filled to overflowing by people from the surrounding area and from afar, was no other than the saintly farmer.

As his sermon came to an end, I would not have been surprised if a host of heavenly angels and a chorus of mothers from times gone by, and the Virgin Mother Herself broke out in hymns of praise. I looked about and saw amazement on the faces of my friends and heard clearly two stage whisper "wow's." Later that day a group of us encountered Father Cyril pacing about, and we descended upon him with kudos for his brilliant sermon. Being a humble man, he was not affected by our praises and quickly turned the attention back to us by saying: "I can see that the sermon has reached you emotionally. But, tell me! What was the message?" We were nonplussed, and maybe a bit humbler. We did not know much about the "message." We just knew that the speech was superb.

The first time Don or I smoked a cigarette was in an abandoned chicken coop on the farm—an off-limits area. Smoking was against the rules for those under sixteen. I do not remember how Don got the cigarettes. We were smoking away (and doing a bit of coughing), feeling grown-up, naughty and safe when in walked Father Cyril. We were in serious trouble! Our fathers were dead set against us smoking, so serious punishment was in store for us. My Dad had made much ado about promising me a gold watch if I did not smoke before I was twenty-one. What was worse - hello Hartington and Grandma B; goodbye priesthood.?

Cyril looked at us for a long moment and then, in a very clear and calm voice, said; "You know that according to the rules which you should be living by, you should not be here. You also know that smoking is forbidden. You two are eligible for immediate expulsion." Then, after what seemed like a very long pause during which he stared at us he said: "I'll forget that any of this ever happened." He turned and walked out.

This incident was not brought up again until years later at a family gathering where he told the whole story with delight and with some embellishment. As everyone laughed and looked at me, I stared at Cyril and said in feigned disapproval: "Remember? You promised to forget that." His retort: "Fred, how does one remember to forget something?" Everyone laughed even more.

Over the years, Cyril and I stayed in touch by mail and saw each other occasionally. The last letter I received from him was shortly before his death. He knew he was about to die and told me how he felt about it. When I got the word that he had died, I cried. I loved him.

Father Bernard was present at Conception for a short time while I was there. He became prior at a priory (small monastery) in New Mexico. Its primary work was holding religious retreats. I visited him in New Mexico some twenty years later, a few months before his untimely death from a heart attack. I had noted that he did not look healthy, but was enthusiastic as ever about his work, and giving it his all.

Father Joachim was the prefect of the minor seminary for the five years I was at Conception. I had a lot of respect for him. He was serious but compassionate, very strict (he seemed to be very self-disciplined) and fair. Upon reflection, I would say he was the right man for the right job. He was an excellent role model for what it means to be a priest—a disciplined man of character and integrity.

Of the instructors, Father Lawrence was by far my favorite. He was known among the students as Gidley Dean. His family name was Gidley, but monks did not use family names, only the biblical or Christian name one chose upon becoming a monk. In Lawrence's case, the use of his family name plus the academic rank reflected the pomposity which he portrayed. He was an extrovert, melodramatic, fearless, in charge of our weekly entertainment session every Saturday evening, and a teacher of English Literature. On the platform, he was exciting, active, entertaining and very effective. He would recite a poem or a passage from Shakespeare, for example, "with feeling and understanding" and a bit of showmanship, and then explain in detail the message the author was intending. Even today, more than sixty years since sitting in his class, I am mindful of his instructions as I read a literary piece. I am of the belief that his class in English Literature was as good as any and better than most literature classes in any high school in America.

For English writing and composition, we had a diocesan priest who was every bit a match for Fr Lawrence but much more low-keyed and cerebral. Father Newton Thompson came to the monastery for two years from the diocese of St Louis. Some of us speculated that he must have gotten into trouble and this was his punishment. Later we learned that he was collaborating with a monk in writing a concordance to the Bible. The finished product was great in size and must have taken thousands of hours to prepare. Father Thompson earned his keep at the monastery by teaching; for which he was well qualified given the fact that he was an editor at the Herder Book Company in St Louis. He was a very demanding teacher with high standards. I was fortunate to study under him.

We wrote a composition every week, and he critiqued each one in depth. On one occasion, the assignment was to write a composition on instructing how to perform some act. I chose as my subject "shooting a basketball." I was quite proud of my paper and enjoyed writing it, in part because I enjoyed playing basketball and at the time thought I was quite good at the sport. Father Thompson's written critique of my work was both severe and encouraging. My ego was somewhat bruised, though, when I found that he knew more about the art of shooting a basketball than I did.

Father Thompson had a keen interest in students who had a high intelligent quotient and developed a faithful following of boys who welcomed intellectual challenge. He held court each weekday afternoon for an hour beginning at 3 p.m. If the weather allowed we would gather at a park bench; he would sit on the bench, and we would sit on the ground gathered around in front of him, much as I imagined the students of Socrates must have done a couple of thousand years earlier. He would postulate some axiom and then challenge us to confirm or deny its validity. We students looked forward to these sessions. At the time, they were very entertaining and taught us to look at both sides of an issue. Later in college, I was prepared for the Socratic method when I studied philosophy and law. Even today I find that Thompson's teaching serves me well.

If the weather kept us indoors, we usually spent the hour either testing our intelligent quotient or doing "stretching" exercises that would stretch our brain power. For example, he would recite a series of numbers and/or letters of the alphabet and then ask one of us to repeat the series backward. The "stretching" would be in starting with a series of six items and increasing the number of items to as many as we could recite accurately. An outgrowth of these informal sessions with Thompson was the formation, informally, of a debate club, which grew to be the most enjoyable academic exercise that I experienced at Conception.

Thompson, himself a man of great intellect, would lecture us on the power of the brain, how to strengthen that "muscle" and how to make it more agile. The most important lesson he taught was that brain power takes many forms, and no one form is superior to another. Some people have great creative powers but may not have a good memory; others may have near photographic memory but are weak in reasoning, etc. Fr. Thompson was another of those memorable contributors to my education.

Mathematics, zoology, and physics were courses I enjoyed. They seemed more substantive and real than the liberal arts courses. Languages were fun in a way, but I lacked both the interest and the discipline to master the subject. Reading prose and poetry in English and Latin was certainly entertaining, but did not stir my curiosity to the point of serious study. I was too lazy and bored to focus efforts on learning vocabulary and grammar.

Over the years I have often regretted that I had not taken the study of Latin more seriously. I saw its utility as confined to church matters. At that time, it was the official language of the Catholic Church. For six years I had Latin classes six times a week. Our weekly schedule included classes on Saturday mornings. Only years later did I come to realize that the language was important in any good education. Many scientific words have Latin or Greek as their root. The study of Latin is a great foundation for learning almost any Romantic language. The "learned man" has studied Latin. The part of studying Latin that I truly enjoyed and worked on was the history of the Roman Empire and its great writers.

History was interesting, but there were far too many facts, dates, and people to motivate me to try to remember it all. My usual method of study was to read and enjoy the story for the fun of it and, come test time, to cram like crazy to load my short-term memory with facts and after the test to let my short-term memory realign itself. As for religious study, my mind was saturated with indoctrination.

Choir practice and studying and engaging in rituals were routines. The study of the Catholic Church and its history was like any other history study. As for the study of the nature of God and religious truth, I have been having trouble with that all my life without satisfactory answers to a host of questions. Responses such as "it's a mystery," "it's a miracle," and "God has not revealed that to us" did not satisfy my question as to what is true. I much preferred responses to the question of truth that one got in the study of mathematics and science. And that seemed to relate better to the real world than the fanaticism of some or the blind acceptance by so many Catholics, of a body of alleged truth, without reasoning. The response we memorized from the Baltimore Catechism book to the question of "Why did God make you?' begins "God made me to know him...." As hard as I try, I do not "know" God.

What I am trying to say here is that I am not a good student. Never have been and probably never will be. Yes, I got satisfactory, good, and sometimes excellent grades, but they only reflected how closely my studying paralleled the teacher's expectations/assignments. I could spend hours, for example, studying something of real interest to me in history but end up going to class unprepared. Some would say that I am a very undisciplined student.

From a purely academic point of view, my high school and first two years of college afforded me the best education I could have wished. Each of the instructors had a doctorate or the equivalent thereof. Each of them had at least a master's degree in the subject he taught. Every one of the instructors was available for consultation, and each took a genuine interest in the student and his learning. These were truly honorable men.

As April came to a close each year, we all had a surge of excitement and anticipation for the events of May. In late May, it would mean the end of the academic year. That meant going home to family and friends for some if they were so lucky. For others of us, it meant at least a change in environment for several months, and the relief of being away from study, repetition, and isolation.

The second offering of May was a more immediate blessing - May Day - a day of fun and games. We never knew on which day it would fall, but it always came. The first inkling of its arrival was to wake up and realize that the wake-up alarm, in the form of the overhead lights being turned on, had not functioned. Soon music filled the air. In a short time, everyone was talking and cheering that it was May Day.

Excitedly, we did our usual morning toiletries, attended Mass and had a hearty breakfast in the refractory, which overflowed with exuberances instead of readings or silence. Throughout the day we engaged in various athletics, some for the fun of it, others for the first, second or third place trophies. I usually did well in the high jump and broad jump because of my long legs. I also could throw the baseball farther than anyone else, but had a terrible time keeping it in bounds.

In my freshman year, I used up all three attempts, but failing to keep the ball in bounds. On the first two tries, the ball curved to the right and out of bounds. On the third try I threw the ball towards the left, out-of-bounds markers only to have it go straight 'as a martin to its gourd' and land out of bounds to the left. In the mile run I was leading after the first quarter, in the pack at the second quarter, and dropping out exhausted after the third quarter. My good friend Gregorio won the class trophy that year, but I had given him a challenge.

Besides the individual competition, we also had the competition in softball, slow pitch for minor seminary and fastpitch for major seminary. Each game was the championship game of the season of that group with the best team vying against a team made up of "the best of the rest." Usually, I played first base (being tall and left-handed). The star fastball pitcher was fun to watch. He could throw the ball so fast underhanded that it would reach the catcher before he finished his follow-through. He could do crazy things with a softball. I would have liked to have faced him as a batter but never got the chance.

In the evening, we had a scrumptious meal of hot dogs, potato salad, beans and a soda. It was a fine feast followed by a big bonfire with songs and stories. The star of the occasion was always Father Lawrence. His performance came towards the end of the gathering when we would all chant for him to sing his signature song, Stormy Weather. No one could have sung it with more feeling and showmanship than he. Years later, as I was reminiscing with fellow alumni and monks, everyone remembered Gidley Dean's rendition of Stormy Weather as the singular event of May Day.

Supper nearly always included dessert. Most notable were cinnamon apple pie, chocolate cake, and ice cream. My favorite by far was the pie. But even ahead of that I liked an afternoon snack (candy bar, or coke, or candy bar and coke) at the snack bar in the recreation room. However, there was a problem. I did not have any spending money. Eventually, I found out that to some of my classmates, my dessert was worth a nickel, the price of a candy bar or coke. Problem solved. I wonder why I gave up supper desserts for Lent - but not candy bars or cokes.

In subsequent years I had a job as a busboy for which I got paid enough to do a little shopping from time to time at the snack bar. The snack bar divided the recreation room into two rooms. It had a counter on each side. It sold snacks and toiletry items. The two recreation rooms were identical. Each had two pool tables, a ping-pong table, some square tables with four chairs each, and a collection of board games and playing cards. One of the rooms was for freshman and sophomores, the other for those sixteen and above. They were allowed to smoke. I enjoyed both pool and ping pong, excelling in the later.

An amazing act of nature occurred one day, and some of us watched it with mixed emotions. A tornado touched down two miles away. We watched it devour a set of buildings. Although there were heavy clouds above, visibility below was very clear. I was fascinated by weather.

Conception had some hard and fast rules which got very little lip service, but we all knew them. For example, we students were confined to the area that encompassed the buildings and grounds of the monastery (excluding the farm) and the school. To leave that area without permission was grounds for immediate dismissal. And, as my good friend and classmate Dalton discovered, the rule was enforced.

Dalton was often homesick; he also was a trickster and a daredevil. He was fun to be around, but at the same time, he often got in trouble for infraction of rules. Sometimes I thought he broke a rule so that he could get caught. Today I can understand that he was in need of attention such as what he received from his mom and dad, and he found that breaking rules did that for him.

Dalton was from Kansas City. His parents were very staunch Catholics, very active in the church and generous supporters of the monastery. Dalton had one sibling, an older brother living in St Joseph, with whom he was very close. The family was very closely knit, as was evident from Dalton's severe case of homesickness. (Most of the guys had this affliction the first year but seemed to be more independent as the years passed.) I had a touch of it too, but mine was slightly different. I missed the familiarity of people, places, and things but was not in the least bit depressed by being away from family. In Dalton's case, his affliction became intolerable.

I found out about it when the Prefect awakened several of us late one Friday night and had us assemble in his office. He explained that Dalton was missing as was a pick-up truck from the farm. He asked if any of the three of us (we were Dalton's best friends) knew of Dalton's plans to leave and where he might have gone. We were of little help. Sometime the next day we heard that Dalton was home and would not be coming back. Several days later one of my friends heard from his mom, who lived in Kansas City and knew Dalton's family. Dalton could have gotten into some serious trouble for having stolen the pick-up truck. Fortunately for him, his dad was able to smooth the whole thing over, or at least most of it. The monastery officials stood firm on the question of whether Dalton might at some point be allowed to return to Conception. He would not!

A four-story red brick building, Saint Maur Hall, was my home for five years. For every day I spent at Conception, I spent about nineteen hours in that building, which could best be described as crowded, austere, and friendly. The entrance to the building was split level. To the right on the lowest floor was the recreation room. The left half of the lowest floor was the personal hygiene area: toilet room, large communal shower room, and a room with sinks lining the walls and a double row down the middle of the room. Keep in mind that we were all awakened at the same time each morning and had half an hour to be seated in the Basilica for morning prayers. So, pandemonium reigned each morning. It was our equivalent to the morning commuter traffic in the lives of the big city people back home in the "real world," with one exception: no talking before mass.

Individually assigned metal lockers lined the hallways in which we kept our meager belongings. Mine contained my toiletry kit, two cassocks which were the required garb at all times except during recreation or free periods, clothing (much of which was hand-me-downs) and the postal laundry box.

I sent my laundry to Grandma by postal service once every couple of weeks. She said that was much cheaper than the monastery's laundry service. The impetus that would get me to send laundry home was not that I was running out of clean clothes or that the dirty clothes were beginning to ferment. Grandma would always include some of her baked goods in the returning box, and she was noted for her baking preeminence. The first year was a test, by trial and error, of what could survive the shipment. The first chocolate cake was unrecognizable when it arrived—not that it mattered much to my buddies and me. We devoured the mess by the handful. By my second year at Conception, cookies were the prize in the returning laundry box, and then the only unknown was the type of cookie.

The next floor had classrooms, several offices including that of the Prefect, and a study hall that covered the entire width of the building on the south side, with windows on three sides.

The study hall had two columns of desk rows with each row having four desks joined together to form one piece of furniture. Each desk was sturdy, made of oak, had a sloping top with a hinged lid for the underlying box that housed one's books and school supplies. The desk and the metal locker downstairs were the only private spaces that a student had and contained all his possessions except for his pajamas which were tucked under his pillow each morning when he made his bed. At the front of the hall was a dais with a simple table and chair facing the hall. The moderator sat there. He was usually Father Joachim who, while very busy reading or writing, kept a close eye and ear for all goings-on. One command of "Silence!" from him and all was immediately silent. On the front wall was a crucifix. The study hall was functional with no clutter, no extraneous materials. It was a very good place to study.

The next floor had classrooms and the zoology and physics labs. Zoology fascinated my whole class, both because of the newness of the subject (most of us knew very little about the animal kingdom, dissecting, microscopes, invisible animals, etc.) and because of the instructor whom we theorized may have been a descendant of Charles Darwin, because he knew so many interesting things about evolution. The adjoining physics lab was even more exciting to me. Father Clement taught the course so well that I developed a lifetime inquisitiveness for the subject "*Scientific American*" and "*Discover*" magazines are two of my favorite monthly reads. My interest is in astrophysics, theoretic physics, and quantum mechanics. This is where I find God, that is to say, my interpretation of God, not the Superman/best buddy who is constantly at our beck and call that many religions have created and called God. My readings and understanding are limited for lack of the knowledge of calculus, so one of these days I may begin the study of differentials and integrals. If only there were such a thing as reincarnation. If there were, I would want to be a philosopher and an astrophysicist—make a living doing one, and have as a hobby the other. As it is, I do not qualify to be even remotely considered as either. Nevertheless, therein lies my interest and much pleasure.

I had a favorite classroom on this floor. The entire building had undergone extensive renovation. The high school which once occupied this building was relocated many years ago to Nebraska. Over my years at Conception, I had many courses in my favorite room, but the one memory that ties me to this room is the actions of the monk, whose name I do not recall. His first task as he entered the room was to go to the blackboard and print in bold letters: REPETITIO EST MATER STUDIORUM (repetition is the mother of study). And his last act of each class was to stand before the blackboard, read the words aloud, erase them, and then announce: "class dismissed." I do not know if educators today would agree with that bold statement but "it worked for me!"

Our daily routine was quite simple: arise at 5:30, attend mass in the basilica with the monks at 6. The mass was always a high mass which included much Gregorian chant on the part of the monks and the student body which formed a large choir. We had choir practice twice a week. A movie screen was used on which to project the music. The organist, Father Edmund, was reportedly an accomplished organist with a great reputation. He was master of the monstrous organ with tiers of keys and many buttons and pedals and a forest of pipes. Reportedly it was "one of the finest organs in America."

In those years the Catholic Church celebrated many religious feast days or days of special religious note, with colorful pageantry accompanied by organ music and choir. Father Edmond could make that organ speak with joy, or sorrow, or power, or reverence. His greatest production each year was the night before we left for Christmas holiday.

We would all gather in the basilica, and he would play for about 2½ hours. First, he played some religious and classical pieces, associated with the Christmas season. Then came Handel's *Messiah* and finally a medley of Christmas Carols which we, the choir, sang with great exuberance. Even this farm boy from Nebraska with near zero musical talent knew that what he heard from that organ was a maestro at work. As we left the basilica on one occasion, I overheard two upperclassmen talking about a classical piece played early on. One said to the other: "Did you hear that shy little mouse whisper a smile as it tiptoed across the keyboard early in the piece?" The other responded: " Yeah, and what did you think of the military precision with which that herd of angry elephants marched through the basilica?" Colorful complements.

After mass, we ate breakfast in the students' dining room, located just inside the monastery and across the hall from the monks' refectory. Fellow students served meals family style. Other fellow students cleaned up after the meal, all of whom received a small stipend. After breakfast, we had a few minutes to clean up, make our bed and get to study hall where we studied until we went to our first class of the day. We had lunch at noon and returned to class until 3 o'clock, followed by two hours of intramural sports or other activities of one's choice. Vespers followed this with the monks in the Basilica, supper and study hall from seven to nine. On Wednesday and Saturday, we had classes only in the morning. Beginning at 7 pm Saturday we had school-wide entertainment which many of the monks also attended. This could be anything including student recitals of famous speeches (memorized) or poetry (again, memorized) presented by students, often in a competition format, or music, a play directed by Gidley Dean, a movie, or a performance by some noteworthy group (for example, a personal performance by the von Trapp family).

On Sunday, we arose an hour later than usual, attended the midmorning high mass in a basilica filled with parishioners. After that, we were free until the late afternoon and evening study halls. One afternoon each semester Uncle Matt and Aunt Frances would invite Don and me, and later on Jerry (Don's brother), who was two grades behind us, to their house for Sunday dinner. Father Cyril and Father Maur would join us. The visits were enjoyable and very comforting—a touch of hominess. Also, it was always a refreshing experience. While I was not bothered by the restrictiveness of being confined to the school and monastery grounds and the constant grind of academics, nevertheless there was always an experience of euphoria when one got a break in the routine, especially if that included getting off campus.

Our daily routine was quite simple. We studied a lot, were pretty much cut off from the outside world and quite unaware of what was happening, except for the immediate world about us; and that was mostly made up of the religious events according to the liturgical calendar. I assume most all boarding school students look forward with great anticipation to going home for the holidays and summer. I did not. Escaping the rigors of study was inviting, but returning to the house of Grandma B, and for that matter, the association with most of my relatives, did not sit well with me in the least. The first Christmas vacation was not bad, but when I returned to Conception in January, I realized how good it felt to be back.

When summer vacation approached, I told Father Muer that I had heard that one of the upperclassmen who was from Boys Town outside of Omaha, had a job for the summer on the farm at the Convent about 5 miles away in Clyde, Missouri. Maur arranged for me to get an interview with the nun that was in charge of the farm operations. I got the job. The nun was noncommittal on salary; she said she would have to wait and see how I turned out.

The day school let out; I headed for the road along with a couple dozen other guys, most of whom were going into the direction opposite from mine. Hitchhiking was a common way of travel for young men without much money. I caught a ride with a local farmer who was going to Stansbury, ten miles away but was kind enough first to turn down the country road leading to the convent to drop me off.

I enjoyed my time at the convent. I had a semiprivate room in a small two-story block building used by the hired labor. The food was great. My roommate, the upperclassman from Conception, decided to leave after two weeks, giving me the room to myself. The workday was long. The weather was hot, and the work was continuous and very physical, but I enjoyed it. My job was to stand on a sled pulled by a bailer. As the bale came off the bailer, I put the bail on the trailing end of the sled. When I had six bales stacked, I took a metal rod and jammed it in the ground through a groove in the sled, causing the stack of bails to slide off the sled. Then I would hurry to the front of the sled, set aside the rod, all in time to grab the next bail coming off the bailer. All this was definitely a no-brainer, but I developed a rhythm in doing it so that it became almost melodious.

On the last day of the month, the nun in charge gave each of us an envelope containing our pay. I was downhearted when I found 50 dollars in mine. I contacted the nun and explained to her that I needed at least $100 a month so that I could pay next year's tuition at Conception. She was adamant that that was all she could pay me, assuring me that she was sure I could work out something at Conception. The next day I took to the highway once again.

Grandpa had told me back in April that he had talked with Adolph Heimes at the bakery who said he'd be glad to give me a job for the summer. It was a long day and late into the evening when I reached my grandparents' house. The next morning, I went to see Mr. Heimes. He was quite short with me. Yes, he had a job for me back in May and had even held it for a week even though he needed help. Since I did not show up, he hired someone else. I was disappointed and worried.

Briefly, I entertained the idea of going to Sioux City where I was sure I could find a job. But I did not think that Dad and Mary Olive would want me to live with them, and I did not have any money for food and rent to tide me over until my first paycheck. I did not want to live under the influence of Grandma B, even for the next two months - but then one cannot have everything he may want. When Grandma B. heard that I did not have a job, she was "beside herself" determined that I had to have a job so I could pay for next year's schooling.

It cost $500 a year to go to school at Conception, and the Diocese paid that. I learned years later that Grandpa had signed some papers with the Diocese that made me liable for reimbursing the Diocese. Another time I was told that I had a scholarship. Grandma had been taking care of my finances. For my freshman year, she took the money out of my savings. In subsequent summers she told me I had to make a hundred dollars a month for three months. Two hundred and fifty dollars for my half of the scholarship and fifty dollars for "clothing and whatnots." So, I understood Grandma's concern, and I was willing to work but did not quite know what to do next. And then Uncle Florenz walked in. He had a job for me at his farm. He and the family were coming to town on the Fourth to join in the festivities, and he would pick me up then. My introduction to the real world for adults was about to begin, and it began with women.

Nebraska farm women were good pioneer stock; not very attractive in their dresses made from printed flour sacks, no makeup, and burly physique but hard-working, creative, of sound character, moral and longsuffering. Usually, when a city girl or lady came to town, she looked to me like a movie star. But I doubted whether she would have been able to do the work, had the stamina, determination or loyalty that these women had.

Aunt Vernie, Florenz's wife, was exemplary of those daughters of pioneers. She would raise five sons and three daughters. Her kitchen was large with a wood-burning, stove with ovens and a large box alongside for wood. Electrical, (recently acquired) light bulbs hung from the ceiling. A long-handled dipper hung by a bucket of water. All water for the house had to be carried from the well a hundred feet removed. Variedly styled chairs surrounded a large table. Cabinets and counters lined one wall. A large, hand-operated separator and a 5-gallon cream can stood along another wall. It was used to separate the cream from the milk after the morning and evening milking. The cream would be sold to the creamery when the family went to town on Saturdays. The skimmed milk would be fed to the hogs. Near the separator was a wooden churn, used to make butter from some of the cream. The family would consume some of the buttermilk, and the rest would feed the hogs.

All the meals were prepared from farm produce. The lady of the house and children worked in the garden which was about an acre in size. It included many rows of vegetables, tomatoes, cabbage, root crops such as potatoes, beets and turnips, a melon patch of watermelons and cantaloupe (locally called muskmelon), and some berries and fruit trees. Near the house was a small stone building called the smokehouse which stored smoked meats. In the fall, the farmer, with the help of a neighbor or two, butchered a steer and a hog or two. Most of the meat was stored in the walk-in- freezer at the meat market in town, and in a freezer chest in the house. Some of the meat was canned, dried, or smoked.

Chickens were available at any time as they ran freely around the farmyards. The hens would have box-like nests lined with straw in the chicken coop where most of the hens laid their eggs, or at least those that could be found. Eggs were usually gathered by the children and used in baking and frying for breakfast for the family or saved up in an egg crate and taken to town and sold to the grocery store on Saturdays.

During the warm months, it was not unusual to see a hen appear followed by a few newly hatched chicks. The hen had found a secure place to lay eggs and then had sat on the nest as necessary for the eggs to hatch. Everyone, and especially the younger children enjoyed the baby animals, the chicks and piglets, the calves and colts, and above all the puppies that would brighten up life on the farm.

When a vegetable, fruit or berry was at its peak production, the mother and children would work together in canning, which included cleaning the food, preparing and placing it in glass jars (usually pint or quart size), loosely placing the rubber and metal lids on the jars, and putting them in a large metal canning tub that was on the stove. The food would be boiled until done, and shortly after that, the lids would be sealed tightly on the jars. As the jar cooled, it would cause the jar to be even more tightly sealed to ensure that the food did not spoil. There was also a way of preserving meats this way. Jams and jellies were prepared in somewhat the same way except those jars would be sealed with paraffin.

Once the jars had cooled, they would be placed on shelves in the cellar for use during the winter and spring, until the next year's garden began to produce. Canning continued throughout the summer and into the fall when many of the fruit trees would bear.

The kitchen was a hot place to be during the summer because of canning and cooking meals. It attracted lots of flies which would be killed with one of several fly swatters lying around or would be caught on the sticky fly paper that hung in long spirals from the ceiling.

Monday each week was laundry day. The gasoline-powered wash machine, with a long exhaust hose that was not totally effective, sat on the porch outside the kitchen. The menfolk carried pails of water and heated them on the kitchen stove. The clothes were washed using homemade lye soap. Clothes were rinsed in tubs of water and then run through a hand-cranked ringer consisting of two horizontal cylinders of heavy rubber about 16 inches in length and close together. The rinsed clothes were run through the ringer, one by one, the water was squeezed out, and the clothes were dropped in a basket, carried to the clotheslines outside, and hung up with wooden clothespins.

The next day was ironing day. At least it was according to tradition expressed in a nursery rhyme I remember from many years ago: "Wash on Monday, Iron on Tuesday, Mend on Wednesday, Churn on Thursday, Clean on Friday, Bake on Saturday, Rest on Sunday. Grandma Burbach was faithful to most of this schedule, especially the "Bake on Saturday." Saturday morning, she would fill the kitchen with baked bread, cinnamon rolls, cookies, pies (including apple strudel), cakes and rolls. She would fill the air with an aroma that would titillate the taste buds of boys and girls from age 2 to 92. The aromas alone were fit for a king. Imagine slathering some rich, home-made butter on a thick slice of just-out-of-the-oven homemade bread and top it with a generous layer of homemade jam, especially wild plum. There was a lot more to life than toil and talk.

When I began working for Uncle Florenz in the summer of 1947, I was surprised and somewhat put off by his treatment of tools as near-sacred objects. A hammer, a wrench, an ax, etc. were used and treasured. If pliers were left laying outside, or a wrench was rusty because of exposure, he rescued it and severely scolded the culprit responsible. I soon learned that some tools were almost impossible to buy because of short supplies in the manufacturing process. But most of the time it was because the farmer had very little cash. And that was what was needed to buy some tools and equipment. He could readily make a handle for his hammer or ax, and he could hone the blade of an ax or a knife, but many things he could not do or did not want to take the time to make. His workshop was a craftsman's delight. From wood, he could make about anything a man or a manufacturer could make: an ax handle, a piece of furniture, a building.

Making things from metal was much more difficult, but even then Florenz could do wonders. Once when he and I were cutting small grain, I drove the tractor because the fumes from the John Deere exhaust pipe bothered him. He rode the rough riding binder. I cut the corner too sharply and broke a wooden paddle blade on the binder. He hurried to his tool shop, made a blade from wood and a metal connector from scrap metal, hurried back and repaired the binder, and we continued to reap within the hour. There is a well-known maxim which soldiers repeat to proclaim their "can do" spirit: "The difficult. we do immediately; the impossible takes a bit longer." Judging by what I saw Uncle Florenz do the summers I worked for him, I believe it was a Nebraska farmer serving in the United States Army who inspired that maxim.

Florenz worked with an intensity found in few people. He was also generous to a fault, kind, pleasant and fun to be around unless he was working. Then it was all concentration and drive—for him and anyone around. In many ways, he and Father Cyril were alike. And I would like to think that I am like them.

On the subject of farm work, the economist John Kenneth Galbraith made a statement to the effect that "Once you have farmed, nothing else ever quite seems like work." By six am each day without exception, James, Florenz's oldest son who was my age, and Elaine, Florenz's oldest daughter two years younger than James, and I would be out doing the chores to include milking seven cows, feeding the horses and pigs, and carrying water, two five-gallon buckets at a time, and feed to the hogs located three hundred feet and across the road from the well and barnyard. After that, we ate a big breakfast, and then Florenz, James, and I would begin work in the fields. Florenz had two tractors and a team of horses. Guess who got to drive the horses. The first couple of weeks of the summer, I cultivated corn. I sat on the iron seat of a two-row cultivator and drove the horses up and down the rows. After the first summer's experience in the fields and occasional observations of storekeepers in town, I concluded that there are some very boring jobs in this world, and I wanted no part of them. To keep my mind at ease, I recited some of the poems or Shakespeare that I learned in school. In the evening after going to my room, I would refresh my memory by reading a literature textbook I kept with me. My favorite poem, favored because I could identify it with my lot in life at the moment, was "The Man With the Hoe" by Edwin Markham, inspired by a Jean Francois Millet painting of a French field hand leaning on his hoe.

Farming, like most other occupations, has its tedious, boring, or unpleasant aspects, but they do not constitute its entirety. One day, as old Dick and Dan plodded along pulling the cultivator and me, a United States Air Force plane flew low and loudly overhead. As it faded away, I looked at the South end of my Northbound team and imaged that the view for the guys up there was a lot more to my liking than this. I wished I could trade places with one of them.

The next fieldwork was harvesting the small grain (mainly oats, wheat, rye, and barley). Often James drove the tractor because the fumes from the exhaust bothered Florenz, even though the tractor was a much more comfortable ride than the steel wheeled binder it was pulling. The binder was fronted by a sharp-toothed blade that cut the stems while paddle blades above forced the stalks to fall neatly on a moving canvas platform that piled a group of cuttings and tied twine around it and dropped the bundle (or sheaf) on the ground. Over the next several days the bundles were gathered into shocks. Two bundles were set upright, leaning against each other, then four more upright bundles were leaned to the original two to form a shock. Over the next week or so the bundles would dry out thus facilitating the thrashing (separating the grain from the stalk).

One summer I shocked ninety acres. I was quite proud of the quality and the quantity of my work. The work was not hard, but all the bending was telling on the back. The field was exceptionally bright as the sun reflects off the shiny stubbles of the remains of the plants. At that time of year, the temperature was often in the high nineties, and the skies were clear—good weather for harvesting *a*nd good for getting a very dark tan. Work clothes included jeans, a white t-shirt, straw hat, and work boots. At this time of year, all farm workers had a two-toned head. The skin surface that was covered by the straw hat would be white (if you were Caucasian). I did not know anyone for miles around who was other than Caucasian. The skin that was below where the hat rim had been was darkly tanned giving the man or boy an odd, two-tone appearance.

The next step in the harvest was removing the grain from the stalk by the use of what was called a thrashing machine. Florenz had one and formed a thrashing Bee of six farmers. The machine was about the size of two elephants. It was powered by a belt, connected to a drive wheel on a tractor located about twelve feet in front of the thrashing machine. The front of the machine had an opening on top from which long arms chopped up and down very rapidly, cutting the twine and pulling the bundle into the machine. Inside the machine, the stalks would be strongly shaken and worked toward the rear where a huge fan would blow the remains, called straw, out a high, long pipe on a large pile called a straw stack. Meanwhile, the grain would be gathering and would be elevated out a much smaller, side spout and into a wagon pulled by a team of horses. Once the wagon was full, it held about fifty bushels. A waiting wagon would replace it. These wagons were usually driven by boys not old enough to handle bundles. The grain was hauled to the large round metal bins near the barn where an elevator, again powered by a long belt. from a tractor, would push the grain up a steep metal trough using paddles attached to moving chains on each side. The grain was unloaded from the wagon by hand by being pushed slowly out the back on to the reception part of the elevator. The wagon driver used a large grain scoop to push the grain out. He was also the guy that would stop by the house at mid-morning and midafternoon and pick up a large coffee pot filled with coffee and several large containers of homemade lemonade along with a large basket filled with sandwiches.

While Florenz did his thing running the thrasher; and the farmer at whose farm we were thrashing did his thing, the other four farmers and James and I each hauled bundles with a hay rack—a flatbed wagon which had a six-foot rack on the front and back and was pulled by a team of horses. Most teams were trained so that the horses would walk at a slow pace down the row of shocks while the man would neatly stack the bundles on the rack. It took me a while to learn how to make a rectangular load as high as I could reach with a pitchfork and with the butt ends of the shocks neatly aligned vertically and horizontally.

Midway through my first thrashing season I had the best load yet, and I was proud of it - high and neat. The forty-acre field was hilly, and I had to cross a small ravine to get to the thrashing machine. I did not know that, when loaded, the hay rack was very top heavy and would tip over easily. As the left front wheel went into the ravine, the wagon slowly tilted over to its side, and the bundles and I slid off. Men came running; first to quiet down the team and then to clean up the mess. I was quite embarrassed. I had been trying so hard to fit in, to hold up my end of the work like a man.

Three wagons would unload, one at a time, on each side of the machine. As soon as the wagon was unloaded, one had to head out immediately and get another load. The pressure was to get your load and be back at the thrasher while the third wagon is still half full so you could have time for a cup of coffee and a snack.

Harvesting was a family and group affair. While we were in the field, some of the other wives and daughters would help the lady of the house at the farm where we were thrashing, prepare the food. I sensed that the wives competed with each other to serve the best meal. These meals were some of the best I have ever eaten. The usual protocol: the men came in from the field, took their turn at the wash table, a small table set outside with a pail of water and dipper, a wash basin, soap, and towels. After washing, you would throw the dirty water away from the table, and all was ready for the next guy. Then one could go to a shade tree where there would be whiskey, beer, and soft drinks. The men thought that since we were doing a man's work, James and I should be able to drink like men. Florenz quickly qualified that to one beer. I had a beer the first few days. I guess to feel like I was a man but did not like the taste and drank soda after that. After a few minutes, the man of the house would announce that dinner was ready and the eight of us would go to the dining room. After the meal, we would sit around outside under the shade tree for a few minutes and then back to work. At the end of the day, I was tired and dreading the doing of chores. But after chores, we would have a good meal and then about nine, off to bed.

At the end of the threshing season, Florenz would have a fish fry for all the families in the Bee. He would contact a river rat (a man who lives by the Missouri River and makes a living fishing) and tell him what kind of fish he wanted and how many. I had never heard of spoonbill fish before, but that is what we had. Florenz went with the fishermen to make the catch. Florenz told us about how the river rats know the river well and know where the various types of fish are. They went down the river aways and began to fish, and in short order, they had 23 spoonbills and a couple of other types. The wives prepared the fish fry, and the men sat around playing Sheepshead.

The rest of the summer was busy with a variety of work from cleaning the barn to plowing. Florenz had a pasture in the hills about a mile away. One day I took Gip, a saddle horse, to the pasture to ride the fence line, making sure that the fences were all in good order. As we were trotting along on a steep hillside, Gip stepped in a hole and tumbled and rolled. I remember falling forward off the saddle and then quickly rolling away so he would not roll over me. I did not like riding horses. I had little experience doing so, and I guess I was afraid to ride.

The weather in Nebraska is often extreme—extremely cold, extremely hot, extremely dry, extremely windy. One day when I was cultivating a field about a half mile from the farm place, things got eerie. First, a quiet descended all around. Then the clouds began to blot out the sun. The clouds advanced across a straight front in the shape of three giant rollers, churning madly, and with various shades of color. I knew that a storm was brewing, so I hastily unhitched the horses from the cultivator and drove them at a fast pace to the road and headed for home. About then the storm hit: high wind, dust, torrential rain, hail, lightning, and thunder. I let the horses go and ran the half mile to the house in what I'm sure was record time. Everyone was in the house. Florenz asked about the horses. I'm sure he could see that I was frightened. I told him I had let them run free down the road. I was worried that he might tell me to get them now. What a relief when he said: "when this storm lets up, we'll go see if we can find them." We found them tangled up around a power line post about a hundred yards from the house. I was relieved to see that the horses and the harnesses were undamaged, but I felt embarrassed because I had lost control of the situation—not a very grown-up thing to do. That evening Florenz told me, in a kindly way, that there probably was a tornado in that storm. He said: " Anyone can be caught out in the open. When that happens, find the best shelter you can right where you are, don't try to run home. You need to protect yourself from the winds of a possible tornado and hail. I've seen hailstones as large as a baseball, and they can kill you just as likely as a tornado. In the case of a tornado, you want to get below ground level. Lay in a ditch or a furrow. In the case of hail, get under shelter. Today you could have gone to the bridge over the creek and laid down under it. It was only about a hundred yards from where you were. As for the horses, you did the right thing. Try to protect them, but if you can't do that, put your effort into protecting yourself." I felt a lot better after this talk. Maybe I did not do so badly after all.

I worked for Florenz two summers. The third summer Florenz arranged for me to work for Hans Bruning who was renting Art's farm which was adjacent to Florenz's. Hans had an operation on his back that spring and was not able to do much work. He and his wife Hildegard were great people and treated me well. They had three little children; the youngest was a one-year-old, stricken with some disease at birth, who was mentally and physically crippled and would die before he was six. The other two, a boy and a girl were great kids, and we got to be good friends. I had three reasons to be happy about this job: much more privacy, pride in knowing that I was doing a man's job and had the experience to do it well, and, very important, the electric milking machine.

Compare the twice-daily scenarios. At Florenz's, I would sit on a three-legged stool on the right side of the cow, in a manure strewn barnyard, wipe off her udders and begin to squeeze the milk when her tail, wet and smelly, slapped me across the face. Yuck! It happened only once, but even that was way too many times. At Hans's, I milked six cows inside the barn. There were three stalls. Once the cow was in the stall, I would wipe off the udders, attach the machine, and wait until her milk had been extracted (the machine would automatically disconnect), and on to the next cow.

Hans was a great fan of baseball and was an excellent player. The county had several farm leagues, made up of boys and men. Hans thought I had the makings of a pitcher and worked with me a lot that summer. I got on a team and did some pitching. I had a set of pitches but lacked control, much to Hans disappointment. In the evenings, we would play catch with intensity. He would get comfortable in a half-sit-half-kneel position, and I would pitch to him. Most Sundays the weather permitting, Hans and I would go to a ball game.

One Sunday we went to a try-out camp. Allegedly a scout from the St Louis Cardinals (Hans' and my favorite team) would be there. I got to throw a few pitches, but after watching some of the guys throw curves and sinkers with flawless accuracy, I knew that Hans was way overestimating my talent.

The next summer I worked for my Uncle Clarence Suing who had retired from farming and had established a furniture store in Hartington. Jolene and I were good friends from as far back as I can remember. She was an only child, and I was alone with my grandparents, so we had a sibling-like relationship. We both had nicknames. She called me "beetle-brain." Both she and Irene had a great sense of humor, and I was constantly on my guard for the next trick.

In late June of the year I was working in the furniture store, I received a letter from a scout from a movie company. The letter expressed great interest in me as an actor, given my "natural good looks, intelligence, and likeability." It stated that the movie company would contact me on the first of July to arrange for my flying to Hollywood for an audition and to sign a contract. For reasons that would be explained later, I was not to disclose any of this information to anyone. Needless to say, I was full of pride to the point of gloating. On the 1st of July, I received a postal card advising that I disregard all previous correspondence because the movie for which they had me in mind had been canceled. Shucks! But at least I could take solace in knowing that the scout had recognized my outstanding qualities. Even that evaporated when, over the coming weeks, it slowly became evident by their leading questions, offhand suggestive statements, and unguarded smirks, Irene and Jolene had pulled off another caper.

The final summer that I would spend in Cedar County, I worked for Ferdy Pietz who was having a dance hall built on the edge of Hartington. Ferdy was one of those guys that everybody knows and has an opinion about, but you never know whether he is well liked or just interesting and entertaining. I do not remember anyone stating simply that they liked or disliked him. The usual scenario was one man telling another something that Ferdy did or said, and the other responding: "Yeah, that's Ferdy alright!" Or, another might say: "Ferdy's not the most honest man in the county, but he did…" Ferdy was short in stature, muscular, barrel-chested and wide shouldered. He had a strong voice and spoke in fast, staccato bursts, much like a machine gun. He was very personable, tried hard to have people like him, and had a limitless reservoir of humorous tales. He was also the county's premier auctioneer.

He had a dance hall in the woods near the Missouri River, Homewood Park, which was very popular with the younger set. The first summer I worked for Florenz he allowed James and me to go along with a group going to the Saturday night dance. When we got there, I was dumbfounded. I had no idea that this kind of frolicking was happening on any and every weekend. I thought dancing and partying happened only on rare events during the year. My grandparents did not engage in this kind of wasted time together. Grandma allowed housework and an occasional conversation with someone, mostly within the family, to interrupt her all-out effort to save my immortal soul by praying and attending church and seeing to it that I did the same. And as far as I knew, the monastery condemned any hedonistic activity, which in my mind most certainly would include the goings-on I was witnessing. People were drinking lots of beer, dancing close together, music and songs that were great but must be sinful, and a couple of people were hugging and kissing. I had a lot to learn about life that was not coming through in the classroom.

The first year of college at Conception was no different than high school. I was bored, felt like I'd been isolated from the real world for too long, was convinced that I did not want to take up the life of a monk at Conception, and convinced myself that I needed a change in venue before deciding whether I would give up on the idea of being a priest or go for it. I remembered that Father Kaup had gone to St Lawrence in Wisconsin and had liked it. I talked with him about going there for my second year of college, and he helped me do the administrative things with the diocese and the school to make that possible.

So, in the fall of 1951, I arrived at the door of St Lawrence Seminary. It was a most joyous experience, not only those first few days but the entire year. The school consisted of four years of high school and two years of college. It was run by the Capuchin Friars, part of the greater Franciscan community. Franciscan and Dominican are mendicant orders of religious monks who combine monastic life with outside ("real world") religious activity. This is in contrast to monks of the Benedictine order whose motto of "*Ora et Labora*" (pray and work) was indelibly etched in my brain. Father Maur, highly educated and dean of the seminary represented one type of Benedictine work. His biological brother and my close friend, Father Cyril, as head of the monastery's farm operations, represented another. Both men were deeply religious. Generally, the Benedictines stress scholastics which is heavily influenced by their religious convictions; and liturgy which is exacting in following the rubrics.

Imagine Gregorian chant well-rehearsed, the Latin language

in pure and simple form, the huge basilica with spacious aisles for processions, Fr. Edmund on the huge organ with favorable acoustics, the fifty to seventy-five monks many of whom had exceptionally fine voices and much experience in the liturgy, the prose, and the chant, two hundred boys ages fourteen to mid-twenties with many fine voices and many hours of rehearsal in choir, ornate robes that gave regality to the ceremonies, the air filled with the aroma of incense, without any pressure of time, with little thought of the outside world or the problems of yesterday or tomorrow, only the unity of focus by all towards the greater honor and glory of God. These were the ingredients that forged the great ceremonies which took place year after year on the special holy days in the church calendar, and to a lesser extent, but still mighty powerful each morning as we all gathered for high mass. This is the rich memory that I have of my five years at Conception. I do not favor the undoing's of Vatican II that took away some of this, nor would I defend the validity or utility of much of this, but it has left me with memories of powerful experiences that enriched me greatly.

My years at Conception also left a yearning in my soul for being part of life outside the monastery walls, the real world, with real people, real problems and real successes, and failures. The *"ora et labora"* reduced life to the work ethic that glorified manual labor and a cult of religious extremism that characterized life with my grandparents. So, it was time for a change.

My classmates at St Lawrence were most gracious. They readily accepted me into their group. On occasions when we had time away from campus (holidays and occasional long weekends), I was always invited by several classmates to spend the time with one of them and their family which I did. I met the real world and lived in it and loved it. Young parents would talk with their sons (and me) about interesting things on many subjects. They would be light-hearted and friendly, and they would do things with us - take us to a professional ball game, a church bazaar. There would be fun and talk and not severely churchy.

The first invitation I received was from my first close friend in the class, Ralph Merkatoris. His family lived in a house by some locks on the Fox River. His Dad ran the locks. His family seemed to be living the ideal life, and they made me feel like I was one of the family. I visited with them several times during the year when they came to see their son.

The first time I went home with someone from Green Bay we were invited by his dad to meet him the next afternoon at his work. He worked in a brewery. When we arrived, we joined three other classmates. The four classmates had been together at St Lawrence since their freshman year in high school. They and their families were close friends. The dad at the brewery said this was a very special day because I was there, and then he told us to pick up a number ten can and fill it halfway with beer. We all sat around drinking beer and communicating for about two hours. The dad had warned us at the very beginning that there would be no refills because he didn't want to see anyone drink too much. We had great fun telling tales, often at the expense of someone present.

Jim Feeley invited me to go on an ice skating hike with him one cold winter morning. I told him I wasn't much of an ice skater, but he wouldn't have that. "Yeah, you might fall a few times until you get the hang of it, but soon you'll be paying more attention to what you see than to the skating. Trust me!" Well, I didn't exactly believe him, and I did fall a few times but all in all, it was a great experience, and I surprised myself in skating fairly well while enjoying nature's beauty. We skated up a creek, through some wild and wooded areas and saw some animals. It was great fun— as was the return to the warm dining room and a cup of hot chocolate.

The daily high mass we attended each morning was a new and gratifying experience. We seniors (i.e., in the sixth and final year of the school's curriculum) gathered in a small room off the side and open to the sanctuary and participated in voicing the refrains in unison with those in the sanctuary supporting the celebrant. It gave one the feeling that he was participating in something- not just being an observer. The busy participant was the master of ceremonies. Each of us, by this time in our life, had attended hundreds of high masses and knew every move and every response by heart, or thought we did. When faced with the task, for the first time, of actually being the master of ceremonies, I was a bit befuddled. In preparation, I had studied carefully every part of the high mass and wrote some notes on the palm of my hand. I did well for the first time, although on two occasions when I was slow in moving to my next position, I was aided by whispers from classmates.

Academics at St Lawrence were on par with Conception's. Father Roemer taught History of the Catholic Church in America. He was the author of our textbook, and he always lived up to our expectations. Most students like to get the lecturer off subject, and so he will just tell us some interesting stories. Father Roemer was a sucker for this. He fell for it more often than not until we realized that he was manipulating us. In covering a subject, he'd mention that "the creation of (something) was an interesting story of behind the scenes manipulation by some church official, but we didn't have time to digress." A bit later he would mention that "so and so" was a real conniver in getting done what he wanted to be done, "but. I'm getting off the subject." As if on key, someone would beg Father to tell us the juicy story he is trying to omit. He would look at his watch, sigh, lay aside his notes and in an air of submission to a student's demand he would tell us the whole story, and we would miss not a word of it. Eventually, we caught on. If he could get us to beg him to tell us what he was going to tell us in the first place, he would have our undivided attention. Even after we had figured out his scheme, we played up to him and begged him to tell us whatever he hinted. Now when that happened, he would give us a conniver's smile and comply. It's a good teaching technique, and I have used it with success in my days of teaching.

A marvelous old monk, whose name I regrettably have forgotten, taught Greek. I liked him very much—maybe because he treated me so well as his "newbie.[1]*" He taught two years of Greek. My classmates were in the second year. I, who had no previous Greek, joined the college freshman class.

He was an old man but with joy in his eyes and youth in his spirit. The first class each week was devoted to vocabulary and syntax. The rest of the week would be reading and analyzing material in our reader, which was the New Testament of the Bible in Greek and Latin. The left-hand page would be in Greek, and the facing, right-hand page in Latin. Students were called at random, asked to read a section first in Greek and then voice it in English. We were told beforehand which pages would be read that week and we were expected to come to class prepared. I didn't take that very seriously since I could always fall back on the Latin text and, anyway my senior classmates assured me that he was a kind old man with lots of patience.

The kindly old man called on the "newbie" to do the first reading and translating. It wouldn't have taken a genius to detect that I had not done much preparation for class. The kindly old man kindly decided that we would meet in his office at 2 o'clock Saturday afternoon and he'd give me some tips on learning Greek.

I wasn't keen on the idea of giving up some of the most precious time in the week when we would either be playing sports or going off campus for a hike or milkshake or whatever. But I guessed that a half hour might be worth getting some tips on learning a subject that interested me.

Two o'clock Saturday afternoon I met the teaching monk in his office. At four o'clock I was still grinding away, reading a passage in Greek, then in Latin, then again in Greek and then voicing it in English. At about 4:20 he decided that we had had a good session, he was sure that I would do well in my studying of Greek and bid me have a good afternoon "or whatever is left of it." Upon saying the later, he smiled and left.

When I entered our recreation room, various of my senior classmates taunted me with such questions as "How's Greek?" " "Been studying all afternoon?" "We had a great hike. Where've you been?" A small group had gathered when two smiling classmates walked in. One said, in a voice loud enough for all to hear: "That old monk is such a nice man!" To which the other chimed in with a loud voice: "And soooooo patient." Everyone laughed, and for the next few minutes, I heard tales of how some of them had had similar "tutoring'" from this kindly old monk. Someone observed that this old monk was a true genius. He could make a young man into a serious student of Greek in one afternoon. I'm proud to say I never needed tutoring by him again.

The year at St. Lawrence was one of the best of my life. It is incomprehensible that upon graduation with an AA degree, departing for Nebraska and a summer job, and bidding farewell to the faculty and staff of a fine school and a fantastic group of classmates, many of whom were close friends, I would not maintain contact with anyone, not one person. A half-century would pass before I again set foot on campus. It is not good for a person to be so focused on the present and the future that he loses all contact with the past. And yet that is the way I have lived most of my life. It is a case of "out of sight, out of mind." It is an oxymoron to have many friends yet be nearly friendless. One must always be alert when new friends become overly reassuring—and of "kind old teachers who have lots of patience."

Chapter 4
1952 - 1953
Creighton University

The time had come for me to make one of those big decisions in life. I had long ago realized that I would probably not be a priest, although I had not said as much to anyone. Now was the time to take that step. I had gone along with the idea of being a priest, which seemed to be my entire identity. I decided to enroll at Creighton University, a Jesuit institution, in Omaha, Nebraska. The University of Nebraska would have been cheaper and more appealing for many reasons, but that was unacceptable according to the standards I had been taught. It was not Catholic.

I informed Grandpa and Grandma that I would not be going to the seminary in the fall, that I was going to Omaha next week to enroll at Creighton. Grandpa did not seem to care one way or the other. Grandma got that smug, superior look on her face and said nothing. I asked Grandma to give me some of the money from my savings. She made arrangements for me to get the bare minimum I needed.

Since Don had a year's experience at Creighton (we both left Conception after our first year of college, he to Creighton, I to St. Lawrence), I had hoped he would drive me to Omaha, but he did not seem very keen on the idea. When he asked his Dad the answer was no, he had to work. He and Jerry had summer jobs working on the construction of a bridge north of Hartington. I had a summer job helping Ferdinand Pietz build a dance hall on the south end of Hartington.

I got a ride to Sioux City with one of Dad's truckers to tell Dad of my decision. He was somewhat upset at first, thinking that he may have had something to do with my decision not to be a priest. He was not a practicing Catholic. My assurances relieved him of any cause to feel guilty. Mary Olive expressed concern since they would not be able to help me financially. She said they had good friends in Omaha whom they had not seen for some time so they would be willing to take me to Creighton when school began.

As I rode the bus to Omaha, and for the next week or two, I gave a lot of thought to my lot in life. Once again that old feeling of isolation that I had felt so fiercely when I left home for Conception six years ago was coming back with a vengeance. Now as then I concluded that I had to face up to the fact that I was alone in this world. I had to rely on myself. I was not a family member. I was an occasional, tolerated guest at my grandparent's house and my Dad's house. I had long fantasized being a part of Art and Gert's family, but I was not.

Gert was my second most beloved adult relative after Grandma Wieseler. After about the age of seven, I had scarcely any contact with Wieselers, except for Grandma and LeAnn. Those contacts were on the rare occasions that I would get to go with Gert's family. Those were difficult visits: immense joy on seeing LeAnn and Grandma and getting a hug from her that seemed to satisfy for days; and a painful goodbye with the realization that I was not part of their life nor they of mine.

Gert took an interest in me. We were open and honest with each other and shared many private thoughts. I did not find Art as approachable. On several occasions when the three of us were together, sharing thoughts of life and the future, he would say that LeAnn and I were his second family and made suggestions that one could interpret that he would do things or give us things as might be expected from a father. At such times Gert would chime in: "Art, you shouldn't talk like that. Remember you have ten children."

Art was a great father figure for me, and I loved him for it. In many ways, he was very good to me, but I learned to avoid disappointments where he was concerned by not expecting much from him. I did receive two very valuable gifts: the example of what it means to be a father, and a compass for living. The compass for living is six words that take years to understand fully, and a lifetime to follow and make life full and worthwhile. The six words are: "Life is what YOU make it." For me, now was the time to bring that idea to fruition.

Enrollment at Creighton was uneventful. I enjoyed a good tour around campus. I found out that the dormitories were full. So, I had to find a place to sleep and a job in order to earn enough to pay for a room and food. Creighton had guidance on such matters.

Crosby & Kunold Mortuary had a living space for free in exchange for ushering several evenings a week. Blanche, the administrative assistant, showed me the sleeping room and the employees' lounge with television. Also, there was a washing machine and dryer available at no charge. All in all, it seemed like a good deal. The mortuary was about six blocks from Creighton, easy walking distance. I didn't have much luck with finding a job but figured that I could work on that when school started. I would have enough money to get me through the first couple of weeks.

The selection of courses was simple. I professed that my career field was premed; so, physics and chemistry, both with laboratories, were selected. Since a minor in philosophy was required as either the related or unrelated minor, I needed to get started on that. Two courses, Philosophy of being (Ontology) and Logic, were selected, as was a religious course, Dogmatic Theology. Attendance at Friday morning mass in the chapel was required.

At Conception, the guys in the third and fourth year of college studied philosophy, but I never found anyone who could explain what philosophy was all about in a way that I could understand. The Jesuit who taught Philosophy of Being was superb, and I immersed myself in the study. However, I was a bit skeptical that it was indoctrination as was the study of religion. The course in logic, also taught by a Jesuit, was probably the best course I had in college, and to this day I am amazed at the lack of logic in so much of public discourse.

Physics was a great course. It was a fun class, great fellow students, and an outstanding teacher. I had no idea how a physicist might make a living, except for teaching which I did not find to be an attractive profession, but I would like to be a physicist. The chemistry class was the worst of the courses I was taking. I did it to myself.

Lectures took place in a room with over a hundred students. In the second or third day of class, the professor talked about the three stages of matter. I am sitting up front in the second row. (I sat in the first or second row of all my classes because I was determined not to miss a thing.) For the life of me, I could not think of how water could be in a solid state, so I put up my hand. The professor appeared not to appreciate my interruption of his lecture but looked at me disapprovingly and said: "yes?" "What is the solid state of water?" I asked. He stared at me while snickers filled the quiet. Finally, he said, in a very cold way, "ice" and continued with his lecture. My ego never got over that embarrassment. After that, I felt uncomfortable in that class. As for the chemistry laboratory work, consisting mostly of individual experiments which proved predictable results (e.g., this chemical, when heated, has a green color) seemed like a waste of time, boring. I put in enough effort to make a grade of C, but with no interest in continuing the study of chemistry, much to my later regret.

Money was getting tight. I needed a job immediately. Bernie told me about his work as an insurance salesman for White Cross. We had been together at Conception. He had come to Creighton a year and a half ago and was now making enough money to live, pay his way through college, and save some on the side. He was a pre-med student but was thinking of giving up college and concentrating on selling insurance since it was such a lucrative field. He talked me into trying it. He put in a good word for me, and I was soon getting leads to follow in my quest to sell insurance. As with all new hires, or so I was told, I got leads for the poorest districts of Omaha. I had two problems: I was very shy, and I didn't believe the potential client could afford to buy what I was selling. I lasted a couple of weeks. By then I was desperate to find a job.

I talked with Blanche at the mortuary to see if there was any way I could get a part-time job with them. We had established a friendly relationship, and she was predisposed to help me. She said she sure could use some help in the office and wanted to know if I could type, knew filing, and could write well. She talked with Mr. Cosby and got an OK for me to work ten hours a week from 3 to 5, Monday through Friday. I would start the following Monday. I thought my problem was solved until Thursday morning when I found that I had thirty-five cents and wouldn't get paid until Friday afternoon.

I stopped at my favorite cafe and ordered pancakes. I told the gal behind the counter, with whom I had often talked how desperate I was. She brought the pancakes, but they were terrible. Nevertheless, I ate away since this was going to have to last me for a day and a half. She came by and noted that I didn't like the cakes much. She went in and talked with the cook. The cook admitted that he was trying to use up some old batter that seemed to have gone sour. As an apology from him and kindness from her, they said they were treating me to all the pancakes I could eat that morning for thirty-five cents. I accepted their generosity and ate. Friday evening finally came, and I ate well. I resolved to be very frugal after that. The absolute maximum per day for food would be one dollar. It didn't make for a great menu, but I had enough to eat each day.

Institutionalization is a word one seldom runs across. It used to be applied mostly to mental patients who were in institutions. The word has since been applied to people confined for a long period in an institution. There the basic needs of the individual are provided for, decision making on the part of the individual is severely restricted. If he lives under these conditions for a long time, it becomes for him the norm. If he is released from this lifestyle suddenly, without a transition period, the resultant shock may be debilitating from fear, confusion, and apathy. Unbeknownst to me at the time, I now believe that I experienced a huge dose of institutionalization the academic year I spent at Creighton in 1952/1953. The externality of life was grand, but the internality of being was sheer agony. My lifestyle from age 5 to age 20 set me up for what I experienced that year. Fortunately, I survived but with scars.

I was a twenty-year-old man with great book learning but a total stranger to the American culture of a free society. I was terribly lonesome but unable to talk and interact with guys I did not know, and certainly not with girls. In many ways, I was probably equivalent to a ten-year-old. I was obedient to obligations of going to class or church, but as soon as that was over, I had a strong compunction to go home (home being the mortuary) immediately rather than go to the library or student union or watch a sports event. Once back at the mortuary, if I was not working for Blanche, I found it hard to concentrate on studying so I would escape to the lounge and watch television late into the night, except for ushering duty. I never shirked from work, in fact, I found fulfillment in work. I began to oversleep often, miss the early morning class and the religious services at the chapel on Friday mornings.

I was called in to meet with a Jesuit priest who was a counselor. My brief talk with him is summed up in three words: kind, quick, gone. He observed that I was "living a life more restrictive than a Benedictine monk." I needed to get out and about. He gave me the name of a lady who had a large house two blocks away and took in student boarders. He said she'd probably have a vacancy next semester. "Tell her I sent you!" As he dismissed me he said no action would be taken on my absences up to now, but if I didn't stop the absences I could be expelled, and he certainly would not want that for me.

When the semester ended and the grades came out, I was relieved. I got a C in chemistry which was good news. All the rest were B's. I knew that if I had continued the semester with the enthusiasm I had at the beginning those should all be A's. Don told me I should give up wanting to be a doctor. His pre-med roommate said that it takes mostly A's to get into med school. So, I readjusted my status from being a pre-med student to a pre-law student.

I told Blanche that I was leaving, that I was moving closer to Creighton. She was sorry to lose me but said she understood. She gave me a sealed envelope and said she and Mr. Crosby had a Christmas present for me. It turned out to be a nice card and ten dollars (more than a week's pay).

My Jesuit counselor was good at his word. When I called on Mrs. Ryan, she told me she had been advised to expect me.

She showed me around her very large house with five bedrooms. Mine was a very comfortable room on the second floor with a bath down the hall. She explained the house rules which were few and reasonable. I paid her the first month's rent in advance with the money Grandma had recently sent me from my savings. According to her, my savings were now exhausted.

I got a good job working for the Book of Books Store. The store was a supplier of religious publications and associated materials to Protestant churches. My job was to package materials for mailing. I was paid a dollar an hour and could work evenings and Saturdays at my pleasure as long as there were orders to be mailed. I liked the work and became quite proficient at packaging. The store manager was an exceptionally nice employer. Two middle age women worked in the sales part of the store. Both were very friendly. One of them was a widow with two little boys. She enjoyed bringing baked goods to work to share with us. She knew I was struggling financially, and she often brought me sandwiches. Two very religious girls in their early twenties were sales clerks. We got to be friends and on occasion went out for coffee together. I was beginning to feel almost "normal.»

In February, I got to know a Marine recruiter. Our paths crossed at a Greek restaurant where I had become friends with the waitress, Darlene. She and I got to be friends and began spending time together. This was the first time a girl seemed to pay much attention to me, and it was great.

In the middle of all this, I was looking into becoming a Jesuit. School was a real drag. I couldn't buckle down and study as I should. But then, it really didn't matter because at the end of the semester I would be broke and had no way of continuing at Creighton. Furthermore, I still felt way out of sync with the rest of the people about me and their way of life. I had great respect for the Jesuits whom I had met and for the Jesuit order. The head of the physics department, who was my teacher both semesters, had just announced that at the end of the year he was leaving Creighton. He said he greatly enjoyed his role as a professor, but he had a wife and kids, and for their sake, he just could not, in clear conscious, turn down a research job offer that would nearly double his income. I liked the idea of becoming a Jesuit priest and a physicist and someday teach at Creighton.

When I received the packet on how to become a Jesuit and the application forms I got excited. I read everything several times. One requirement might turn out to be a stumbling block. I had to be debt free. However, the Diocese of Omaha records showed that I owed them $1,500 for six years of schooling. In talks with Grandpa, I learned, for the first time, that years ago he had signed some papers on my behalf to that effect. Once again, Florenz came to my rescue. He wrote a letter to the Diocese stating that if and when I was ordained a priest he would assume full responsibility to pay the $1,500. His letter was well received by both the Order and the Diocese.

The final requirement was to visit a psychiatrist of the Order's selection. Since I assumed I was one mixed up kid, I expected the visit with him would not go well. Just the opposite took place. We spent most of the visit talking about a paper he had just published. Two weeks later I received a letter from the Order giving me a specific date and place to report as an incoming novice.

It was June 1953. The semester had ended. I had completed the courses satisfactorily. I would not be able to continue at Creighton since I had no money. I needed to move from Mrs. Ryan's house since she rented only to Creighton students. As I saw it, I had only two options: join the Jesuits or join the military. I knew that I was one mixed up, depressed, immature, probably neurotic, and socially underdeveloped teenager at the age of twenty-one. Joining the Jesuits was tempting, but it also seemed "the easy way out" of my predicament without solving my personal need of getting a hold on life, of becoming a sane man. I needed a good dose of discipline and direction and, from what the Marine recruiter had told me about the military, it seemed that was the better choice for me. The date of reporting to the Jesuits came and went without any action on my part. Instead, I went to Sioux City to talk with my Dad. I planned to join the Air Force, become a pilot, serve the required years, save lots of money, and then return to Creighton law school. This plan gave me the hope and courage that I would break loose of whatever was keeping me down. I had found my place in life. All I needed now was to get on with it. Action.

The next day I went down to the Air Force recruiting station to sign up. I talked to a sergeant who had a lot of stripes on his sleeves. He gave me the bad news that at the height of six feet four inches I was too tall to be an Air Force pilot. Over the years since, I have known some Air Force Pilots who were as tall. Probably Sarge was having a bad day; or had his quota filled and did not want to bother with this kid. I knew I had a good plan, so I went to see what the Army had to say.

Chapter 5
1953-1954
Army Enlisted Time

There was a Greek restaurant at 24th and Farnam which I passed on my way to Creighton, and there I met and befriended a United States Marine Corps recruiting Non-Commissioned Officer (NCO) who always dressed in his uniform. I do not recall the Marine's name, but he was a fun guy and did not ply me with any recruiting talk (or did he?). It was he who told me about military service, the distinction between officer and enlisted and the GI Bill. The more I talked with him, the more I was convinced that the best thing for me to do was to join the Air Force, go to officer candidate school, become a pilot, serve three years, save lots of money, and then return to Creighton law school. Yeah! I had finally found my place in life. I knew I was unhappy, lonely, and confused, and this plan gave me hope and courage that I would break loose of whatever was keeping me down. I had found my place in life. Now, all I needed to do was do it–get moving!

My Dad neither encouraged nor discouraged me when I told him my plans. Today, upon reflection, what should he have said? Here was his son, in whom he had very little interest, who was so fickle that in the past few months was thoroughly convinced that he wanted to be: a medical doctor, a lawyer, a scientist, a philosopher, a Jesuit priest, and now a military officer. "Good luck, Fritz! I'll see you when you get back. Just don't ask me for money because I don't have any."

The next day I went down to the Air Force recruiting station to sign up. I talked to a sergeant who had a lot of stripes on his sleeves. He gave me the bad news that at the height of six feet four inches, I was too tall to be an air force pilot. (Over the years I have known some air force pilots who were as tall. Probably Sarge was having a bad day, or had his quota filled and did not want to bother with this kid.)

I knew I had a good plan so I would see what the Army had to say. In a few days, I was on a bus with six other guys headed for the Army induction center at Fort Riley, Kansas. After a few days of standing in line, or killing time, or being told about what a soldier is and is not, and being sworn into the Army, I again found myself on a bus headed this time for Fort Leonard Wood, Missouri for basic training.

There were two buses filled with recruits. I was placed in charge of the first bus (whatever being in charge meant) and the occupants were told that I was in charge. About two hours after leaving Fort Riley, one of the guys was having difficulty breathing. He identified it as an asthma attack. The bus driver, an older man, civilian, asked me what we should do. He reminded me that I was in charge. I asked the asthmatic what he usually did about this, and he knew the name of a medicine that would relieve his attack. So, I instructed the driver to stop at the drug store in the next town we reached, which he did. The asthmatic and I went in the store, and the druggist knew the medicine we asked for which cost $4.10. The asthmatic stated that he didn't have any money. I paid for the medicine, and we were on our way again without any further incident.

Over the next several months I went to his barracks; he was in a unit other than the one I was in and asked him to pay me back the $4.10 which he owed me. His answer was always the same (including once when it was after pay formation on payday), "I don't have any money." Once when I went to his barrack and asked one of the recruits if they knew where he was, the recruit turned and in a loud voice asked the others in the barrack: "Anybody know where jewboy is?" So! I had encountered my first Jew outside of Hartington. Were they a people to be only whispered about as Grandpa and Grandma did? Time would tell. And it did. The answer is an emphatic no! Who knows? Maybe I am of Jewish extraction. Ey vay! I should be so lucky, already!

The lifestyle of a soldier is learned quickly, seemingly instinctively. Don't volunteer for anything. Never seek the limelight. If given a task to do, do it quickly, and as quickly fade into the background. Never snitch, always support your peers. If there is a rotten apple among you, get rid of him. Never put your best effort forward if it will be used as competition with your peers. If the NCO pits you against a peer, the winning way is to tie. This is no reflection on the soldier you may know today or ever. This is the introduction to military life that most guys go through. It allows one to survive army life before you get to know the ropes of how to survive in a very different lifestyle than the one you knew.

The first impressions a young recruit has of the army leads to the conviction that it is a gigantic mess, much ado about not much, disorganized on the whole, and over-organized, over disciplined and over managed in its particulars. It overwhelms the recruit on the one hand yet gives the impression that all activity sums up to "hurry up and wait."

It's an uncompromising, dictatorial monster that overtakes all aspects of one's life, yet it gathers you to its bosom with care and concern for your welfare. It probably is more threatening to a draftee since he is in its claws unwillingly. For me, I was there because I chose to be, and in a way, I found familiar characteristics, or at least I thought I did, to life as I had experienced it for the past 15 years: rules, regulations, restrictions, single-mindedness, extremism, an abnormal culture, and control.

A popular song that played constantly and irritatingly on the radios night and day was a lamenting grind that began with the words "I don't want a ricochet romance." It encapsulated, in a bawdry way my rejection of the feeling of helplessness as I surrendered into the open arms of this vanquishing behemoth—the United States Army. The innocent recruit will find peace of mind once he understands and accepts the idea that there are three ways of doing things: the right way, the wrong way, and the army way. For him, the right way is the army way—it's the only way.

Marching is a mainstay of the army. It disciplines the mind and body. It awards with orderliness the unity of effort by the individuals, and it moves. It moves the recruits from the barracks to the farthest corners of the camp and back again—and again and again. Parades are tedious, but also, they can be uplifting and beguiling.

Basic training consisted of two, eight-week sessions. The first eight weeks were devoted to individual training in soldiering: physical conditioning, close order drill, marksmanship, personal hygiene, hand-to-hand combat, combat in cities, small unit tactics, discipline, the military justice system, military tradition, and whatever else the harassing NCO's saw fit to throw at us. All the NCO's were combat veterans of the Korean War. To them, a recruit was the lowest form of life, and their concern was to make life as miserable as possible for the fledgling soldier. Life was hectic and stressful. My fellow recruits came from all parts of the country and all walks of life. Most of them had been drafted, and many of them were extremely disgruntled with their lot in life at the moment. Three come to mind.

The guy in the bunk next to me got stoned every night. After "lights out" he would pull the sheet over his head and smoke some smelly substance. During the daytime, he seemed to be in a daze. One day he was acting weird; the MPs came and took him away. We never saw him again.

Sergeant (SGT) Jim was a super nice guy. He occupied the private room upstairs in the barrack. We never saw him during the day. He was easy to talk to, and even though he was an NCO, not a recruit, he was even more miserable than we. He had been caught cheating while a cadet at the United States Military Academy at West Point, New York, was thrown out of the Academy, but would have to serve in the army for several years to pay back for the several years of schooling he had received at army expense at West Point. One day he moved out, and we never saw or heard from him again.

Bull was a fellow recruit in my barracks. He was about six feet four inches tall, weighed about 260 pounds, muscular, immature, not very bright and mean. He delighted in pulling childish pranks on someone. Many days he would pick a fight with a lightweight and start to beat him to a pulp until he tired of it. Most of the guys were afraid of him. A tall, muscular farm boy from West Virginia approached me one day and suggested that the two of us, plus two of my friends, who also were big guys, form a pack. We would warn Bull that either he stops beating on little guys or we would take care of him. But we never had to execute our plan.

The last guy Bull beat up was a Puerto Rican. He had a bloody face and probably a broken nose. He was in the latrine cleaning up and surrounded by his buddies who were speaking rapidly in Spanish when I left the barracks to go to a briefing on the military exercise we would be doing the next day. The meeting lasted about an hour, after which we headed for our barrack. Several of us were held back and were given specific assignments for the next day. After that, we were returning to our barrack when we saw a group of guys surrounding a commotion. We started to go over there to see what was going on when a Puerto Rican guy stopped us and said: "you don't want to go there." Something in the way he said it convinced us to keep walking and mind our own business. Several in my group said they saw knives in the hands of some of the crowd. Back in the barrack and about an hour later we heard a siren stop nearby. We never saw Bull again.

Weeks into our training we were spending a lot of time marching to and from training sites. As we were beginning our 2-mile march back to the barracks one chilly afternoon, it began to sprinkle, and the darkening clouds suggested that a downpour was imminent. To our luck, a deuce-and-a-half (2 1/2-ton truck with covering) stopped and we all crammed into the already crowded truck. About a week later it was rumored that an article in a local newspaper stated that officials at Fort Hood had emphatically denied that trainees were being hauled around like animals, crammed into freight trucks. Our Sergeant called us together and announced with a smirk that if any one of his recruits would rather march in the rain than ride a crowded truck to let him know and he will personally see to it that that recruit never will be so inconvenienced again.

Our barracks was a two-story, wooden structure of World War II vintage, unfinished on the inside, airy, spacious and vacuous except for our bunks and footlockers. The latrine was devoid of any privacy. The entry area of the latrine, out of sight to any cadre entering the barracks, was often crowded with gamblers throwing dice. Real money was changing hands. I, as a pauper, avoided any involvement with that activity.

It can get cold in Missouri in October, and so the coal furnace in each barrack was fired up. That introduced to us the concept of duty roster. The night watchman was a safety and security guard and the furnace feeder. At the end of his two-hour watch, he was responsible for seeing to it that his replacement was up and about. Coal burning created fine black soot. As the sun rose in the morning stillness, a heavy black cloud of soot hung on the horizon, and soot covered everything about us including our faces. It was a health hazard, but not the only one.

Early one cold morning, as we began a three-mile march to the firing range, Sarge noticed that one of the guys in the rear did not wear a field jacket. Sarge brought us to a halt, announced that in the army uniformity is the order of the day. If one man doesn't wear a field jacket, no one wears a field jacket. So, we all removed our jackets, placed them in our backpacks, and continued down the road. Only now we were double timing (trotting) to keep warm. And the old "hurry up and wait" principle applied when we reached the firing range thirty minutes too early. So, we sat around in the grass shivering.

Over the next week many of us ended up going on sick call, and a few of us wound up in the hospital. Two guys were quite sick. They had their lungs pumped and were sent home on convalescent leave. The rest of us got well quickly. We were in the hospital for a week or ten days. After the first couple of days, the stay was a gift from heaven—warm, comfortable, no harassing sergeants, but lots of beautiful nurses.

Since I missed a lot of training while in the hospital, I was recycled to another training group which would be formed a week after I had spent a week confined to the barrack while recouping from pneumonia. During that time, I pulled duty in the orderly room. The sergeant in charge of administration and his clerk found that I had some usable skills, to wit, I could read, write, type, and file papers. Since neither of them had a yen to do those things or any other kind of work for that matter, my services were appreciated. But not so as I would notice.

Another job I found to my liking was KP (kitchen patrol) duty. It had three benefits. The work was in a warm building, lots of food was always available, and harassment by cadre was minimal. The only negative was the four o'clock morning wake up. Once the training cycle began, I spent about 20 percent of my days either working in the orderly room or pulling someone's KP duty instead of training. It beat the misery of going to the field and putting up with the "army ways."

Probably the strangest army way happened one Saturday morning about a quarter of a mile from our barracks. The training site was a baseball diamond. The training was a two-hour lecture on a soldier's field gear and equipment in general. It was a "make-up" class. It had been scheduled before last week's training since it was an introduction to that training, but it had been canceled for some reason. Since it was a part of the schedule of training, it had to be done, no matter that to do so now would be redundant.

The clouds overhead threw a few snowflakes at us, as the Lieutenant instructor busied himself with laying out the late-arriving equipment, which he was going to discuss. He was also tinkering with the public-address system which he didn't seem to be able to get working. We were seated in the bleachers, pressing together to keep warm. A little more snow was falling. Fifteen minutes into the first scheduled hour, the Lieutenant called for our attention. He stated he would talk loudly since the loudspeaker wasn't working.

As if on cue, the wind strengthened and the snowfall thickened. The Lieutenant continued his spiel, undaunted by the worsening weather conditions. As for us, we could barely see or hear the Lieutenant because of the falling snow and the howling wind. We huddled together and tried to sleep. After nearly an hour of this, a jeep stopped by, the Lieutenant announced that the training session was completed, and Sarge marched us, at "double time route step," back to the barracks. There is a lot to be said for "the army way," and we said it—in the best army lingo we had mastered to date.

Our training was interrupted briefly when some of us got a weekend pass to Kansas City. One of the sergeants had a vehicle, and so eight of us crowded into his six-passenger sedan and ended up in a bar in Kansas City drinking blackberry brandy. This was the first time I tasted brandy.

The NCO with us advised that there is nothing more effective when you are "cold to the bone" than "triple B." I was to find out later that in the mind of many military men the true medicine for "cold to the bone" was AAB (any alcoholic beverage), and that very few military men experienced prolonged suffering from "cold to the bone." When we returned to the barracks Sunday evening, I immediately checked the bulletin board to see who had KP on Monday and pleased the poor guy by volunteering to take his place.

Some weeks later we finished the first phase of basic training, and we were permitted to take leave for a week to ten days. I headed for Omaha where Darlene and I were married in the Creighton University Chapel. My sister, Della, and her husband, Al, were our sponsors. Several days earlier we had visited Dad in Sioux City. He explained that he wouldn't be able to come to our wedding, but he did want to give me a good wedding gift—$100. After a little discussion, he gave me the money right then so I could buy Darlene an engagement and wedding ring.

Grandma Burbach informed that she had invited uncles and aunts and my Dad and Mary Olive for a brief wedding reception for Darlene and me for Sunday evening. We went. It was an awkward and forced event. I felt that nearly everyone there would have preferred to be somewhere else, anywhere else. But on this occasion of being with some of my aunts, I experienced a different feeling towards most of them. I did not feel that cringe of subjugation, nor succumb to their inferences of superiority and disdain. Rather, I felt very relieved. Here was a fitting time to ponder a famous line by Clark Gable in the movie "Gone with the Wind:" "Frankly my dear I don't give a damn."

The gathering was short. Each couple had a special reason why they had to leave early. After everyone left, Darlene and I counted our newly gained wealth: a tablecloth with napkins and 95 dollars, fifty of which came from Florenz and Vernie. We thanked Grandpa and Grandma for their kindness in having the get-together and went to bed. The next morning as we ate breakfast in the kitchen, Grandma was very apologetic that they didn't have a real present for us, but she thought Darlene could maybe use some kitchen utensils and such since Grandma had more than she needed. Grandpa found a cardboard box in which to put the things. We gathered our things, bid Grandpa and Grandma good-bye and drove away.

I experienced that deep and complex set of feelings of joy and sadness at the same time; love and hate; the final ending of a part of my life and the beginning of another part. I was excited about the future and all that it promised, but I didn't know how to prepare for it. I felt that I was focusing too much on the here and now. Art's guiding advice came to mine: "life is what you make it." So how am I doing so far? I have no idea. The year at Creighton was sheer hell. I felt that I had a lot more control of my life this year than last. I could handle this army thing, and maybe a year from now I would be an officer. That should be something.

In mid-December, I reported for my last eight-week training

phase. Our barracks NCO was a black corporal. Why? Maybe that means he is inexperienced and will be a lot more lenient than a sergeant. The only corporal I knew to date was the company clerk in my previous unit. He was a real "softie." By the end of the first day, I knew that Corporal Washington was danger. He seemed to have a huge chip on his shoulder and hated people in general, and recruits in particular. He was an exemplary member of the cadre. He barked loudly and harshly. He whipped us into obedience immediately. We all tried to stay clear of him. And then things changed.

I had missed the event. One of the trainees had been hurt quite badly and was laying on the floor when I walked in. An occupied, upper bunk had fallen on him. Corporal Washington was kneeling beside him with a first aid kit by his side. Some guys had gathered around. The victim had a big gash on his forehead and some blood on his arm which was bent grotesquely. Washington was calming and softly talking to the victim. He was way out of character. He was showing sincere compassion. The ambulance arrived and took the victim to the emergency room. As the ambulance left Corporal Washington announced, in a calm voice, "lights out in ten minutes," and retreated to his room. Each barracks had one private room on the ground floor for the barracks NCO.

Over the next several days we found out, mostly from Sgt. Jim, that Washington grew up in a gang-ghetto community in a large southern city. He had avoided being a "bad boy" with the help of a loving but strict mother and two honorable men in the neighborhood. He had early on developed a "tough guy" persona as a protective shield, but inside he was a "softie," a kind and gentle guy. Sgt. Jim summed it all up in one sentence: "Corporal Washington is a standup guy, an outstanding soldier, who earned the bronze star for valor and the purple heart in Korea and plans on making the army his career." Corporal Washington had our respect.

This last phase of basic training included training in a military specialty. Upon completion of basic training, every soldier receives a military occupational specialty (MOS) and the number that denotes that qualification. His subsequent assignment ideally will be doing that work so that he builds proficiency in his MOS. For example, I received basic training in doing "engineer construction in a combat zone." My records showed, upon completion of basic training, private E2, MOS 1729, Combat Construction Specialist. All jobs in the army fall under this classification system.

One week we spent most of the time in the field, including three nights. It was a tough week. On the firing range, we fired for record with the rifle, the carbine, and the 45mm pistol. Each of us threw a live grenade. Each of us fired a bazooka. The target was an old vehicle. My round went right into the vehicle and exploded. Pure luck, but it makes you feel great, and everyone notices and cheers. We observed the firing and impact of mortars and artillery howitzers. There were demonstrations on how to survive in the wild, what the medic can do, how the communications systems are set up in combat and how they work. Our food was combat rations.

One day we spent mainly with the engineers and the heavy earth moving equipment. Several of my buddies were hoping to be heavy equipment operators. One was from Iowa. We had enlisted together. His dad drove a bulldozer and he was hoping to do the same during his time in the army. I was interested in the equipment because I had gotten the word that I would be going to Engineer Officer Candidate School in March or April. My order of preferences of branch schools was Engineer, Artillery, and Infantry. Naturally, I assumed I would get my first choice - Engineer.

The first night we spent in the field we slept in pup tents. Camping out army style is not nearly as much fun as camping out Boy Scout style, but it does have its rewards. Several of the cadres were spending the night with us, and they had shed their gruff and dictatorial demeanor and were engaging us in conversation. The main topics became the army lingo, both the profound and the obscene; and their personal experiences in combat in Korea.

The profound in army lingo is a method of stating the most with the least. Acronyms are a good example. Never say military occupational specialty; rather say letters MOS. Never say absent without leave, rather, say the letters, AWOL. A lot of the lingo was developed in World War II and is in common usage in conversations anywhere in the English-speaking world. The word snafu, for example, is defined in the Webster dictionary as "a state of complete confusion." To a soldier, snafu is an acronym for "situation normal all fouled up" in the profound but the f-word in the obscene army lingo.

Another acronym is GI which means soldier. It originates from the two words "government issue." Everything the army has is provided (or issued) to it by the United States government. The soldier feels that he is treated so impersonally that he is nothing more than one more commodity issued by the government to the army. Books have been written about army lingo profound. The army lingo obscene is best left to the army in the field.

The second night spent in the field was spent in foxholes in a simulated combat situation. The first four hours of darkness we had a lot of action, duties to perform, security challenges, and enemy operations to observe and report. The next five hours we were allowed to sleep. It was a very cold night. My partner had a solution. He took from his knapsack a bottle of clear fluid, took a few swigs and then passed it to me;

"Here, this will warm your bones." My initial thought was that what he was offering me was probably an alcoholic beverage which we are probably forbidden to have in our situation. If we get caught, it may mean a court-martial and years of internment at the military prison in Leavenworth, Kansas. My second thought was a conviction that if that stuff can fend off this cold, I want some. The gin was smooth and good for my cold bones.

The last night we spent in the field was very cold and windy. Fortunately, our NCO knew the area well. We were dropped off from the larger body of marching troops in a large and open field. Our NCO ordered: "Take five but hang on to your gear" as the larger body passed out of sight.

"Gather round!" he ordered as the cold wind howled and made it hard to hear him. "About 60 yards behind me is a wooded area. You are going to march, double time and in route step; which means you are going to walk fast, in single file, and close together; no gaps. Ok. Line up and follow me." About a hundred yards into the woods we came to an old barn. Inside was a lot of hay. It was a huge improvement over that campsite we had been assigned.

In the morning, we arose early enough to be at the campsite before the main body of troops arrived, but not early enough to beat the Lieutenant in charge. He had discovered that we had not camped in the assigned campsite, and he gave our NCO a long, verbal reprimand. Our NCO didn't seem very disturbed. It was as though he expected the reprimand and felt that what he did was a good thing.

The weather had greatly improved, the wind had died down, and the temperature jumped from very cold to cold, as we arrived at a wide-open grassland cut through by a deep gulley about fifty feet across. Some large, flatbed trucks loaded with metal frames were parked nearby. We stood together, and a Captain addressed us as follows: "Welcome to the Engineer Corps of the United States Army. Your exercise today is to build a Bailey Bridge, cross that bridge to the other side, the trucks as well, to make sure it is a solid bridge. Return to this side. Disassemble the bridge; load up the trucks, and march five miles to your barracks. You will be broken down into teams. The sooner we get started, the sooner you'll be back in your barracks. Good Luck!"

It was a busy day and impressive work. By noon we had put together a Bailey bridge across the ravine by working from only our bank of the ravine. The main features of the bridge are the prefabricated, rectangular ten-foot metal panels that make up each side of the bridge and connected crosswise with twelve-foot, metal girders. More panels and girders are added by joining — the panels with thick metal pins, as the structure is fed forward toward the far bank. Panels can also be added to the top and side of the primary structure to increase the bridge's capacity to hold heavy traffic.

We worked hard and fast, and by late morning we were really in the grove. I was holding a panel while a guy with a sledgehammer prepared to drive in a large connection pin. He missed the pin but got my big toe - straight on. I was sent back to the barrack with the mess (food) truck. I went to the orderly room to ask to go on sick call. I was sure my big toe was broken.

The First Sergeant looked at my foot. The big toe was swelling. He told me, yes, I could go on sick call, but I should think if it's the best thing to do. He explained that he had seen broken toes before and that there is little the medic can do but tell you to stay off your feet for a while. Also, the medic will classify me as unfit for duty. That means that I'll be recycled and sit around a barrack for a couple of weeks until the next cycle begins so it would be another ten or twelve weeks before I would finish training.

Right now, I am on course to go to leadership school after completing this cycle in less than two weeks, and then I'm off to OCS, probably in March or April. In other words, ten weeks from now I could be well into OCS. He told me that he would see to it that I spend the next two weeks on KP or orderly duty. He said he knew the "Top" at leadership school and he'd ask him to keep an eye on me.

"How about it?'

"But, Sarge, it really hurts."

"Yeah; but bite the bullet! That won't last long. A couple of aspirin and a cold soaking of your feet—come tomorrow and your toe won't hurt much."

"What if it does?"

"Look! If at any time you want to see the medic, you let me know and I'll see to it that you go right away. For now, go to the mess hall and tell Cookie that I told you to soak your feet in cold water."

I survived two weeks, mostly hanging around the orderly trying to look busy. My week and a half in leadership school was little more than a place to wait until my time came to report to OCS. I attended a few classes and worked some for the top NCO. I didn't go to the Engineer OCS at Fort Belvoir. It closed the month before I became available. Instead, I went to Artillery OCS at Fort Sill, Oklahoma.

Officer Candidate School (OCS)

"Easy Battery five minutes," I blared as I stood at attention on Easy Street forewarning my barracks comrades that in five minutes they would dash out of the barracks and assemble in formation in front of me. I then smartly snapped into a stance of parade rest. When I heard our two tac officers, whom we had nicknamed Able and Baker, in conversation as they approached me from behind, I quickly snapped to attention.

Able: "Candidate Burbach is standing tall today."

Baker: "Yes but notice that lanyard hanging from a rear pocket."

Able: "He deserves five demerits for such a gross uniform."

Baker: "Oh, I think his appearance is much worse than that. Notice that brass belt buckle! It has too high a sheen to it. Do you suppose he has borrowed some girlfriend's colorless fingernail polish to make it dazzle so?"

By now the two tac officers are standing within inches of me, one on each side, facing me.

Able: "Do you suppose Candidate Burbach uses a Brillo pad to shine his boots? I say. That is no ordinary spit shine he has there. Such a dull, uniformly bland-black."

This entire conversation was carried on in a quiet and almost consoling tone; making every effort to get me to smile, whereupon one of them would feign shock and dramatic disapproval of such loss of discipline (i.e., smiling when at attention) and shout in my face that I give him ten push-ups. If I did that, I would miss calling the barracks to "fall in" at exactly 0600 hours. That would cost me many, many demerits and maybe even threats of reassignment to Korea. So, since it was exactly 0600 hours I blared as loudly as I could: "Easy Battery fall in" and awaited their anger for having damaged their hearing. Instead, the tac officers moved on to attend to other candidates. And so, began another day, my 105th, at the Artillery Officer Candidate School in Fort Sill, Oklahoma.

The school opened in 1941 to help fulfill the need for officers for the conduct of World War II. It closed in 1946, having trained and commissioned over 26,000 second-lieutenants. It reopened in the early days of the Korean War and continued until 1973. The 22-week course of education and training, preceded by six months of soldier's basic training and leadership school, is intense, stressful and demanding. The purpose of the school is to produce highly qualified, motivated and thoroughly tested leaders. Allegedly, the founders of the school stipulated from the very beginning that the candidate be worked as hard as possible to weed out those who cannot take the pressure. When I attended the school, most of the cadre and instructors had recently returned from combat in Korea and did their very best to ensure that the founders' desires were fulfilled to the max.

We, candidates, were challenged continuously to uncover any weakness we might have; attitude, aptitude (especially gunnery and map reading), handling stress, sense of humor, team player, attention to detail even minutia, etc. If a weakness were detected, the cadre zeroed in with harassment until the candidate overcame the weakness, lost his cool, or gave up. Any candidate could voluntarily withdraw from the school at any time and would be assigned elsewhere in the army to complete his obligatory tour of duty, normally two or three years, in the rank and pay grade he held before entering the school. During his assignment to the school, he was confined to the school grounds except when in formation or with a pass (very unlikely) from the Battery commander.

The physical facilities of the school were simple. The buildings were World War II barracks and administrative structures. A wide, main street ran from the support facilities and exercise area on one side of the compound to the mess hall on the other side, a distance of about two hundred yards. Most of the foot traffic took place on this street. On one side of the street was the orderly room of each battery and across the main street from it was a row of four barracks for the unit's candidates. The barracks were uniformly aligned fronting on a street that fed into the main street and bore the alphabetized name of its battery. Mine was Easy Battery. A network of sidewalks connected all the buildings but was of no use to the candidate since he was forbidden to use it. Candidates used only the streets for movement, and that would be at double time (trotting) from place to place; walking was forbidden as was lingering outside.

A candidate would come to quick step (walking) when approaching an officer or Red Bird; salute, and when a counter salute acknowledged the salute, he would continue on his way double timing. However, chances were pretty good that the officer or Red Bird would approach the candidate, inspect his uniform or ask him questions of fact until the candidate did not give the correct answer, and then chastise him loudly and severely, and end with a demand for ten pushups. Red Birds were candidates in their final four weeks at OCS. They wore red tabs on their epaulets, and all other candidates were required to treat them as officers (salute, address as "sir," obey their orders). They walked. Imagine all the cadre of five batteries, plus approximately fifty Red Birds harassing (an art form in OCS) several hundred, very serious dedicated, and hapless candidates. Main Street was a beguiling and belittling valley of woes. The Red Birds were the most annoying. They had four weeks until they left this hellhole. They were quite sure of graduating and being commissioned, and they had a pent-up need for retribution.

The first few days at OCS was zero week—not part of the twenty-two-week schedule. Upon reporting, the new candidate was assigned an 8 foot by 10-foot area in a World War II wooden barracks, on the wall of which was a wooden shelf under which was a wooden rod for hanging and displaying uniforms. From the supply room, he was issued: a steel bunk, mattress, two sheets, "horse" blanket, pillow and pillowcase, footlocker, uniforms, 10-15 field manuals, bookends, cartridge belt with canteen and first aid kit, and rifle. He carried these to his barrack, made his bed, cleaned and oiled his rifle and placed it in the rifle rack in the middle of the barracks, arranged his footlocker display precisely as required by OCS regulations, sewed the OCS patch on his uniforms, changed uniform and turned in his personal items (with a few exceptions) for storage until he would leave the school. During these days, there was also a lot of physical training, close order drill, and indoctrination on rules and regulations.

Each of the issue items would eventually be a liability, a basis for harassment, and a lesson in "attention to detail." On the first day of the first week of the 22-week course, when I returned midafternoon from classes, I found my neatly made bunk in disarray. Sheets and pillow were strewn on the floor; the mattress was crosswise on the bunk. And my books were all over the place. And so also it was on the second and third day until we got the word from some fellow candidates in a class ahead of us.

One of the tac officers would inspect our barracks and individual areas daily. He would give the bunk a once over. If it looked correct, he would toss a quarter on the middle of the "horse" blanket. If the quarter bounced—OK. If not, he would tear up the bunk. The quarter would bounce if the blanket was very tightly tucked in at the sides. Hence, there was no more messed up bunk when I returned from classes; however, I had acquired a bundle of demerits, as did everyone else in the barracks. That would have to be "paid for" on the coming weekend by trekking up MB4.

Friday evening, at a scheduled time, one of the tac officers came to our barrack and explained what Saturday morning inspections included: personal appearance, each one's area and all contents including footlockers, the building, and the latrine. He ran a white glove over a window pane—dust, and over a far corner of the floor—dust. "This place is filthy; let me see what your latrine is like!" We were all standing at attention by our bunks. He was in the latrine for less than a minute. He came out very displeased and held up a white string (probably from a mop) for all to see. He referred to it as a lanyard, which we later learned is the rope used to pull the firing pin on artillery weapons. He ranted and raved about how "gross" our latrine was, and he gave us two hours to get it all cleaned up. Upon his return, he immediately concluded that we did not understand what OCS standards were. He lectured us on sanitation, germs, diseases, odors, and on and on. He warned us that it might take us all night to get the barracks ready for inspection. He warned that if we didn't pass the inspection Saturday, we should be ready to get down on our hands and knees and use our toothbrushes to clean up "this pigsty." And he stormed out of the barrack.

Two of the candidates had been fraternity brothers in college from which they had dropped out only to be drafted by Uncle Sam. Now they would transfer some fraternity humor to barrack humor. Not a good idea! They made a very large poster inscribed with 'In Honor of Those Two Great Greek Philosophers EUKISMAS and EUKISURONAS and tacked it up above the sinks in the latrine. Many of us objected to this, but one of them was the latrine orderly for the week and insisted that it stay, citing the fact that he'd get whatever blame came.

Saturday morning's inspection was a disaster. A tac officer and NCO came in. We were called to stand at attention. The inspectors checked first the latrine and then came down the line inspecting each of us and our individually assigned areas. Quietly they voiced a string of demerits the inspected was receiving for a host of infractions, and in some cases turned his area into a mess. All the while the candidate stood at attention facing the center of the room. As the inspectors left his area, the candidate stood at parade rest and remained so until the barrack was called to attention. With quiet but firm voice, the tac officer said: "It is obvious that you do not know how to stand for inspection. I gave you some tips last evening. There will be a reinspection this afternoon at eighteen hundred hours. It seems to me that some of you either don't understand the standards we maintain at OCS or you are not serious about being here. For some of you, this evening may be a good time to decide if you will continue as OCS candidates. And in honor of the Greek comedians in your midst, you are all invited to take a tour of some of the local sites Sunday afternoon. There will be a practice run this afternoon at fourteen hundred hours. Dress is fatigues with full field gear including rifle." He and the NCO walked out smartly.

We left the compound shortly after 2 p.m. in high spirits. We were in formation and singing military cadence when we halted at an open field and were told to put rocks in our backpack too, as the tac explained, "give our march some realism and purpose." From there we double-timed most of the one and a half miles to Medicine Bluff 4. a hill known well to every OCS candidate as MB4.

When we returned to the barrack exhausted; the tac informed us that this was only a preliminary. The main event was tomorrow, Sunday, when we would be making the trip twice. He also said that this would work off some of the demerits we have been accumulating and should convince us to take OCS seriously. After the tac left, one of the candidates said: "Hey, guys, let's keep our sense of humor—but a long way away from the cadre."

The 1800-hour inspection was long, detailed and filled with constructive criticism. Since we all were already overloaded with demerits, no demerits were doled out. As the tac said: "This is a learning experience." This was one of the very few times before I made Red Bird that a member of the cadre fulfilled the role of teacher instead of tormentor.

On Sunday morning, we were permitted to attend chapel. We would find it to be, throughout our stay at OCS, the saving grace that kept us going. The serene atmosphere, the kind and gentle chaplain, the tranquil attendees, the beautiful women, the happy-go-lucky children, and, above all else, the absence of all that was Army nourished our souls and reminded us that there was a beautiful world outside the compound of OCS.

Going into the second week of OCS, I still had the problem of aligning my books properly. The books were to be displayed in descending height from right to left. Early on I had discovered that my shelf was warped. The center was lower than the sides. Since day one I had been getting demerits for not having them in the proper order. Things were getting hectic, and I saw the book thing as petty, of no importance except for the demerits I was getting for it which would keep me going up MB4 every weekend. I had decided that I'd just forget about the problem of aligning books when I was told to report to the orderly room.

The cadre in "Easy Battery" totaled five: The Commanding Officer who was Captain Riordan; two 2nd Lieutenants whom we had nicknamed Able and Baker; and two NCO's whom we had labeled Heckle and Jeckle. The five were in charge of molding us into 2nd Lieutenants in all matters and manners except academics.

In that regard, they came down hard on us constantly and relentlessly, especially the first eight weeks.

Upon entering the orderly room, I was immediately shuttled into Captain Riordan's office. I saluted and immediately I was "read the riot act." There was no place for me in the officer ranks if I could not comply with simple directives. Lieutenant Able was there and spoke in the role of prosecuting attorney. Essentially, he said that I had been violating a directive every day since day one and had made no effort to comply. Captain Riordan obviously was in the role of judge in this kangaroo court which had me stressed to the max. I was given forty-eight hours to begin complying with the directive or I would be on my way out of OCS.

"Dismissed! " he stated.

I saluted smartly, did an about face, and marched out of the building. The books were never mentioned. It was my job to figure out which directive I was violating. Deduction was easy since I had tried everything humanly possible to get those books in descending order. It just wasn't possible. As I left the orderly room and ran across Main Street, Sgt. Heckle called out:

"Candidate Burbach! Front and Center!" meaning "get over here right now." I did just that, and in a loud voice, I said, as I snapped to attention in front of Sgt. Heckle: "Yes, Sergeant."

Early the previous week he had beckoned me the same way. In response, I had run to where he was, saluted smartly, and in a loud voice said: "Candidate Burbach reporting as ordered, Sir." He responded angrily: "Candidate, don't you ever, and I mean ever salute me again or call me sir! Do you hear me?"

"Yes, sir. err, ah, I mean yes sergeant." I muttered.

Again, he flew into a rage and blurted out: "Candidate. I'm going to tell you this just once and don't you ever forget it. There is a big difference between officers and NCO's. Do you know what that is and why you don't salute NCO's and call them sir?"

"No, Sergeant," I replied

"I can't hear you!" he stated in a loud voice.

"No, Sergeant," I yelled at the top of my voice.

Quietly and very emphatically he said: "NCO's work for a living. That's why."

I smiled.

"Candidate, do you find something funny about that? Give me 10" I dropped to the ground and began doing push-ups as he walked away.

Since then I had avoided Sergeant Heckle at all costs and successfully. He obviously had a low opinion of me. It would take me a couple of weeks to realize that none of the harassment is personal; it's all part of the game. For now, I assumed he knew of my predicament and was about to take pleasure in making me squirm. I hurried across the street to where he stood, snapped to attention and loudly stated: "Yes, Sergeant."

In a calm, quiet voice, he said: "Parade rest, Candidate. And keep your voice low, on a conversational level. You know you are in very serious trouble. What specifically is the problem as you see it"?

"Well, Sergeant, I continually get max demerits because I can't get my books aligned in descending order. The problem is that the shelf is warped."

"Candidate Burbach, I want you to hear me. Hear me really good! Never, ever say I can't about anything ever again!" He brought his face close to mine and with fire in his eyes, he said: "Look at me, Candidate! "Can't" not a word in the soldier's dictionary. In the army, we do the difficult immediately; the impossible takes us a bit longer. Do you think you can remember that?"

"Yes, ssss er ah, Yes, sergeant." I stuttered.

He stared at me for a long little while (a short time that seemed long} and then said: "Now tell me what options you have in solving this impossible problem of yours."

"Well, I think the best thing I can do is replace the boards of the shelf with straight boards. But I can't because, ah, ah, ah, that would be hard to do since I don't have access to boards and tools."

To which Sergeant Heckle responded: "That moaning and groaning about not having access to boards and tools is an excuse) and in the army, excuses rank right up there with can't. Don't give excuses, give solutions. As for replacing the boards, that would be against regulations, which forbid the unauthorized modification of a building. What other course of action could you take?"

"Well, I could saw a quarter of an inch off the bottom of a couple of books," I replied.

"BINGO! Now think carefully! When we in the army need something like a tool, or clothing or cartridge belt, where do we go? He asked.

"We go to the supply room," I answered.

Sergeant Heckle said: "Get your books, take them down to supply and tell Sergeant Wilson that I sent you and tell him what you have in mind. Dismissed!

I did as he said. Sergeant Wilson took the books and added them to the shelves where he had hundreds of field manuals. Then he dug in a box and selected two manuals of the subjects of the books I had given him. He handed them to me, and he said: "Here, try these."

They did the job, and my field manuals were untouched in every inspection after that. I stewed over this experience for a few days, especially about the fact that supply had several books that had been previously modified and fulfilled my needs exactly. I told the story to a couple of fellow candidates. John, who I thought was the smartest guy in our class, laughed and said: "It sounds like a put-up job, a great teaching format. Look. First, they got your attention." With a grin, he emphasized that fact with "I mean they really got your attention. Then they gave you a simple little problem. Remember that Lieutenant Colonel last week who was giving us a lecture on the ins and outs of being an officer? He said that the secret to success was not in making lots of big decisions. Rather, it was attention to detail. What Sergeant Heckle was telling you were pearls of wisdom. You, my friend, have just had a superb bit of training."

Integrity was an expected and assumed quality of every candidate. The lack thereof constituted immediate expulsion, as was demonstrated early in our academic studies. We were taking a final exam in one of the lesser sub-courses. The instructor had forewarned us that he accepted only two targets for our eyes: at the test paper or straight ahead. Looking anywhere else in the room during the timed exam would be assumed to be an attempt at cheating. Midway through the test, he stated in a loud voice: "Candidate 'name' report back to your battery," and the subject left the room. Later that day when we returned to the barracks, all that was left to remind us of him was the eerie sight of his area, which now contained only a steel cot with a rolled-up mattress. That was the second time that I could remember (Dalton at Conception was first) when I start the day with someone, and all at once he is gone, never to be seen by me again. It's a shock that I would experience a few more times in OCS and a few times in my life after that.

Sometime around my twelfth week I, along with several others on my floor, were called to the orderly room and told to have a seat in the adjoining room. I thought the others were tops and so I assumed this was going to be something good. Our tac walked in, told us to keep our seats and said that the Battery Commander would be in shortly. About five minutes later the tac called us to attention as the Battery Commander walked in. He left us at attention and looked carefully at each one of us. Then Captain Riordan said: "Gentlemen, this will be very short. Barracks inspection report this morning noted that there was rust on your rifle. I need not tell you that even for the most junior soldier in the army today, that is not acceptable. I'm letting the demerit system take corrective action this time. Be advised that if this happens again, you'll be out of OCS in a couple of hours. Return to your barracks.'

I was really down in the dumps as I trotted back to the barracks. I knew the importance of keeping the rifle at its operational peak; and also, the fanaticism which the army directs towards the care of weapons. In basic training, this would call for having that weapon on you day and night. At night, you slept with it. During the day, you either held it in your hands or slung it over your shoulder. Knowing all that, I had meticulously cleaned and oiled my rifle every day since it was issued to me. The minute I entered the barracks I got my rifle out of the rifle rack and examined it closely for a long time. Suddenly I noticed a tiny spot on the rear sight that looked like rust. I applied a little oil, and it disappeared. I still could not believe this was happening. I couldn't have done a better job of keeping that rifle flawless. This just could not be. Now I truly was fearful that at some point I was going to get kicked out of this place. I dreaded the thought since I had no material wealth, and I did have a wife and a son on the way. I was depressed. Little did I know that the worst was over. Over the next couple of weeks, everything seemed to improve. I was getting very few demerits; in fact, I got a four-hour pass the next Saturday. I wasn't required to make the Sunday afternoon trek to MB4. And the cadre pretty much left me alone as far as harassment. Was that rifle rusting a put-up job? Was that designed as my last test, other than academics? Was that the last kick-in-the-pants? Even today I still wonder if all that worry and woe I experienced was all for naught.

The academics at OCS were presented well. The general subjects which prepare one for military life (code of conduct, uniform code of military justice, customs and tradition, the role of the army, its command and organization structure, basic tactics and strategy, etc.) were essential to the making of an officer of any branch. The heart of the education and training was field artillery.

Field artillery is often referred to as the "King of Battle" because of its mass destruction capability over a broad part of the battlefield and deep into enemy territory. The artilleryman will tell you that his purpose is to "move, shoot, and communicate," hence that is the core of our training.

We spent time in the classroom and the motor pool studying the motorized vehicles, both track and wheeled and the towed cannons, caissons, etcetera. I found that I do not have an ear to detect a flaw in the purring of a truck's engine. The care and maintenance of equipment is a "big deal" to an artilleryman. I had the fun of driving a truck without lights at night in convoy. Also, we saw and analyzed a World War II movie of two convoys crossing each other. The vehicles keep moving by getting into a rhythm. We tried to talk our instructor into setting up such an exercise so we could try it but we never succeeded.

The study of the radio and telephone was short on theory but long on hands-on use. Included was "artillery-speak:" the codes and acronyms in use, the proper procedure in making calls such as a forward observer (FO) calling in a fire mission to the fire direction center (FDC), or from there to the gunner. We laid telephone wire and set up a telephone network in the field.

The FO, the FDC, and the guns are the necessary factors in getting an artillery shell on an enemy target. The FO has to position himself in the forward area of the battlefield where he can see the enemy territory. He receives a request from the unit to which he is attached. He locates the target as accurately as he can, using the geographic coordinate system. He calls the FDC and relays the location and description of the target in a standard format. When the first artillery round lands, he gives corrections to the FDC for each subsequent round until the target is destroyed.

At the FDC, a table is laid out with a plotting board and map. The exact location of the artillery pieces has been plotted as well as the exact direction the pieces are initially pointed and the altitude of each piece. When the FO sends a fire mission, the target is plotted, and then the FDC determines the settings to be put on the artillery piece so that the piece fires in the desired direction and the desired height (for distance). Those numbers are then relayed to the crew who set them on the weapon, the safety officer checks, and the weapon is fired. Each time corrections are made, a round is fired until a call for "fire for effect" is given at which time all the weapons fire at the target, using the latest corrections.

The FDC, knowing the coordinates where the guns are, computes the direction and angle of fire for the gun decides the type of shell and fuse to use and passes this to the gun crew. Also passed on is the number of guns that will fire and how many shells when the order: "fire for effect" is received. Only one gun is used during the adjustment phase. Once the gun has fired, the FO is advised: "on the way." If the projectile explodes within 50 meters of the target, the forward observer will relay to the fire direction center: "fire for effect." The FDC will pass this to the guns.

If the projectile bursts more than 50 meters from the target, the FO will commence with a series of firings until the shell burst within 100 meters of the target. For example, if the burst is between 50 and 100 meters to the left of the target but in line with the target (i.e., less than 50 meters over or under the distance to the target), the forward observer's order to the fire direction center would be: "right five zero, repeat range, fire for effect"

In combat, the artillery battery would use the data from the first mission of the day to compute a correction factor to the firing tables available for each type of gun. There are a lot of variables that can affect the reliability of firing tables, such as age and condition of the gun, quality and exact measurement of propellants, defects in the shell casings and the howitzer tube lining, weather, wind, temperature, air density, and curvature of the earth. Considering that the maximum range of the 105 mm Howitzer is seven miles and that the shell is in free fall from the time it leaves the tube until it impacts, and considering the time that elapses from firing to impact, it is evident that only in ideal conditions would the firing tables accurately predict the exact direction, distance and flight time to impact.

At Fort Sill, Oklahoma, the home of the "King of Battle" the artilleryman has the pleasure to engage in the greatest of target practice - the "King's Sport" the adjustment of fire. In due respect to the FO whom, I'm told, has the shortest life expectancy of any officer on the battlefield, the challenge of calling for correction adjustments the fewest times to get to "fire for effect" is very competitive among students.

For the practical exercises and fieldwork in the subject of field artillery, our section was broken up into three groups and performed all the functions: make up the crew at the guns; man the FDC and serve as FO. The small group of candidate FO's would arrive at the observation point carrying in their left hand their stool held by the crossbars. The sagging seat served as the carrying space for plotting equipment, map, and clipboard. A pair of binoculars hung from each one's neck.

We were all very familiar with the binoculars, having had a special class on how to hold the binoculars tightly to our face with cupped hands to steady the glasses and to cut out cross light between the binoculars and the face. I often marveled at how detailed our training was and how exacting the standards and the insistence on meeting all standards. Often the instructor would reinforce the need to "pay attention to detail" with his personal experiences in combat in Korea.

The firing ranges at Fort Sill are ideal for observation. One can see for miles since the terrain is reasonably flat but riveted with shallow ravines. Here and there are objects, most notably old automobile bodies, which serve as targets. Once we set up with our equipment on our lap, the instructor identifies an object several miles in the distance. He identifies it as, for example, "a stalled enemy tank in the open" and tells us we have five minutes to compute what data we will send to the FDC. At the end of that time, he calls out: "Candidate (name)! Your mission." We all listen intently as the candidate begins but then messes up, and the instructor calls out: "As you were! Candidate (new name), your mission." The newly named candidate has this mission all the way to "fire for effect," unless he makes a wrong adjustment (e.g. "left two hundred" when the correct adjustment should be "right two hundred.") If he does, he will hear those words that every artillery student hates to hear: a loud "Cease fire! Candidate (different name)! Your mission." I'm proud to say I never lost an Forward Observer mission at OCS.

We went to the field for a few days right after we made Red Bird. Harassing was almost absent and all the tac officers and NCO's, while being militarily correct, were far more friendly and supportive in the field than when we were back in the barracks. The challenge for the first day was camping near a creek where there were snakes. We saw several snakes that someone identified as cottonmouths. We pitched our tents on a sandbar. Each of us dug a shallow trench around his tent and poured a little gasoline in the trench. According to the instructor, this would keep the snakes away. Sleep did not come early that night.

The second day and night we practiced setting up camp and breaking camp and laying a howitzer in the daytime, and at night We also practiced moving in a convoy. The third night we had a night shoot, which is different than adjusting fire in the daylight. I liked being in the field. Learning seemed much more relevant than in a classroom.

Darlene came in June and found a pleasant lady who boarded several young wives. At first, we could only spend an hour or so together in the parking lot twice a week, and that was spent standing and talking since we did not have a vehicle. But once I made Red Bird, I was able also to get a pass each week from Saturday noon until Sunday evening. Our son, Michael Joseph, was born on the 24th of July. I was not with Darlene when she gave birth at the military hospital at Fort Sill. I got to visit her and Mike most evenings. Darlene had a hard time. First of all, she was in a large ward, and each mother had a crib by their bedside and cared for their newborn most of the day and night. Besides that, Darlene was exhausted from the delivery, had an infection, was constantly in pain and pretty much had to take care of herself as well as Mike. In one of my early visits, she said to me in a pleading voice: "Let's not do this again." I felt sorry for her and guilty because I couldn't do anything to comfort her or help take care of Mike.

On the other hand, she was very supportive. She recognized that what I was doing was in the best interests of the three of us.

We found a small, cozy apartment when she and Mike got

out of the hospital. I got to spend more time with them but still, most of my time was at OCS. We looked forward to the day when I would graduate, and we could go back to Nebraska and Iowa on leave. I don't remember how we did financially, but it must have been hard. Also, at this time, I bought a 1950 Nash car which Darlene named Inverted Bathtub because of its shape. With a very positive spirit and grand hopes for the future, we survived.

Making Red Bird was a real treat. We now were treated with respect by all. We could actually walk the streets and sidewalks of the OCS compound unmolested. However, the highest standards of decorum, dress and military custom were still stringently enforced. Several classmates did not make the transition to Red Bird completely enough and earned demerits to win the dubious honor of spending Sunday afternoon taking some junior candidates up MB4.

We Red Birds did our share to help "shape up" junior candidates. The first few days we enjoyed being on the other end of harassment, but some of us were mindful of a most unfortunate event that allegedly happened several months earlier. A soon-to-graduate Red Bird was severe in harassing candidates, almost to the point of being vicious. Many claimed that he had a Napoleon complex. One day a warrant officer was on Main Street and encountered this Red Bird. The warrant officer berated browbeat and belittled the Red Bird for about 15 minutes until a tac officer invited the warrant officer to accompany him to the orderly room. The harassment meted out by the warrant officer was heard by many candidates. Rumor had it that the Red Bird was "destroyed" by the experience. As for the warrant officer, rumor had it that the Commandant of OCS sent a blistering letter of complaint to the warrant officer's commanding officer even though the warrant officer had been a candidate at OCS and had quit because of the unrelenting, mean-spirited harassment he had received from this same Red Bird. My fellow candidates and I recognized that this whole story could very well be fiction. If it is, it probably came from a tac officer who was trying to get the message across to Red Birds that harassment has its place in the overall training and testing functions of the school but there is a limit, and meanspiritedness is definitely beyond the pale.

Several days before graduation I was at home with Darlene and Mike when an army sedan pulled up, and the driver informed me that the Battery Commander wanted to see me immediately. "Gulp!" "What now?"

Captain Riordan returned my salute and asked me to sit down. My thoughts: 'Oh, Oh. This has never happened before. Something big is going down, and it involves me. This cannot be good.

The Battery Commander began by talking about military life, both for the officer and for his family, and interspersed in his talk were questions about my plans for the future, possible interest in being a career officer, etc. Then he explained a little about the Regular Army and the advantages of being a Regular Army officer. Then he said that I had been nominated by the tac officers and NCOs and he will add his endorsement that I be a distinguished graduate. I could not repress a smile, nor could he. We stood, and he said: "Now my driver will return you to your family. Good luck!" I saluted smartly, said "thank you, Sir" and left.

As we drove back to my apartment, my thoughts went back over the past 22 weeks. In all of that time, I lived in constant stress that I was on edge, about to be kicked out. Lesson learned: try not to worry or get stressed out; just do your absolute best and accept the consequences gracefully.

On August 10th, 1954, I felt like I had never felt before: on top of the world. The yearlong training, indoctrination, and discipline were finally over, and I was somebody. I had an identity other than student. I was an officer in the United States Army. Also, I now had a life. I had a family, a job and a future. I was free! Tomorrow we would drive to Nebraska and spend a week, accountable to no one, visiting relatives, and friends. We would drive in my recently purchased car, my first, a 1951 Nash. I had a son, born the previous month, who I would get to know; and Darlene and I would begin living together. I wondered what my first assignment (17th Field Artillery group, Ft Sill Oklahoma according to my orders) would be like. I was six-foot-four, weighed 175 pounds and in excellent physical condition, healthy and mentally alert. "Burbach, Frederick Joseph, front and center! the adjutant repeated as my mind quickly came back to the "here and now—standing in formation for the last time at Officer Candidate School and being called forward to be pinned with the gold bars of a 2nd Lieutenant, United State Army.

Finally, I have a real family. Mike and Darlene

Chapter 6
1954-1956 Fort Sill

After ten splendid days of fun and freedom in Iowa and Nebraska, I reported to the 17th Field Artillery Group at Fort Sill, Oklahoma whose mission was to support the Artillery School and the Artillery Board. The school had two major courses, the Artillery officer basic course and Artillery officer advanced course. The former was to train newly commissioned officers to function effectively at the battery level, leading to full qualifications to be a battery commander. This included the Artillery Officer Candidate School as well as the Basic Officer Course for officers commissioned through Reserve Officer Training Corps or the military academies. The Artillery Officer Advanced Course (or Career Course) was for experienced Artillery career officers to prepare them to serve as battalion commanders or staff officers.

Darlene and I found a furnished apartment just off post. I was much too junior to get housing on Fort Sill. The rental complex had several two-story buildings; we were on the second floor. Many of the occupants were 2nd lieutenants, most had wives, and there were a few toddlers. We quickly made new friends. Many of the wives did not work outside the home, so Darlene had companionship and also transportation, important since she did not drive.

On the home front, the biggest shock to me was the budget. Even though I was 22 years old, I had never had much experience in handling money or paying bills. By October, our money was gone well before the end of the month. I borrowed $50 from a friend and paid him on payday. After doing this twice more, he told me I had to get a grip on my finances. He suggested that I see the retired artilleryman at the Fort Sill Bank. That turned out to be great advice. The gentleman was a retired senior artillery officer who knew well the financial challenges faced by a 2nd lieutenant with family. He was both understanding and helpful. He assisted me in securing a small loan with a little monthly payment. We worked out a budget with his advice. I opened a checking account, and he set up a small credit line. Somehow Darlene and I managed to support our family, but I believe it was a case of doing the impossible.

Several of the battalions of the 17th Field Artillery Group had the mission of supporting the Artillery School by following the directions from the teaching staff of the school. This entailed setting up and firing weapons on the East and West Ranges of Fort Sill with the support of instructors who would hold classes at observation points. The 548 Field Artillery Battalion was such a unit; and I reported to the battalion commander, Lieutenant Colonel Seeley, that day. After a brief chat, he assigned me to Charlie (C) Battery, one of the three firing batteries of the battalion. I met the Battery Commander who was polite but very brief since he was being reassigned out of the battalion in a few weeks. A week later the battalion held a briefing for us newly assigned officers.

Among other things, we learned that the headquarters (HDQRS) and barracks of the three firing batteries and service battery were housed in one of the very old, three-story, mortar and stone buildings common at Ft Sill. The HDQRS battery, the motor pool and the park area for the battalion trucks, trailers and artillery pieces were nearby. The Battalion HDQRS was contained in a one-story frame building. We also learned that the

Group as a whole was very short of officers above the grade of 2nd lieutenant. Hence we could expect assignments above those normally given to 2nd. Lieutenants.

The first two months were easy. I was the battery motor officer, a position for which I was eminently unqualified—knowing very little more than a week's training on the subject at OCS. Most of us 2nd lieutenants in the battalion spent most of our time on a firing position in either the East or West Range in the role of safety officer. The safety officer's function is to ensure that the artillery piece is properly and accurately "laid" on the firing position which years ago had been surveyed and properly marked. The artillery piece is "laid" with the use of a theodolite, mounted on a tripod, the directional sight on the weapon, and two aiming stakes. Also, the safety officer ensures by personal inspection that each time the weapon is fired, the propellant charge, and the direction and elevation settings on the weapon are such that the artillery round will land within the approved impact area. If the weapon is fired and the artillery shell lands outside the impact area, the safety officer is held responsible and liable. If it lands within the range but at great variance to the proper settings, he must reimburse the army for the price of the shell. A rumor was going around at this time that an Honest John training rocket (a non-explosive) had landed in a vacant lot in the nearby town of Lawton. The mayor of the town called the commanding general at Ft Sill and stated: "Ceasefire, we surrender."

First Lieutenant Ward had become our battery commander. He was a pleasant, quiet, early morning jogger who had his mind set on being a career officer. He had started but not finished the career course the past year. As time went on, I found him to be indecisive and not very bright. For now, he was trying to decide who would be the battery executive officer. Normally this is the second most senior officer. Usually, a battery has a captain as commanding officer and a 1st Lieutenant as executive officer. In this case, of the five assigned 2nd Lieutenants, the two senior ones, both ROTC graduates, respectfully declined the honor.

The Executive Officer (XO) is the unit's operations officer. It is he who prepares the weekly training schedule for the battery and who takes the firing units to the field. When I was asked by the two more senior 2nd Lieutenants to take the job which they did not want, they assured me that they had informed the commanding officer (CO) that they'd be willing to serve under me even though I was junior to them, so when the battery commander asked me to take the job of XO, I agreed. My thinking was that anything was better than the oppressively boring job of safety officer (which XO's did not have to do) and the XO job sounded challenging. Things went smoothly for me for the next couple of months, but my poor CO did not fare very well. On a good day (weather-wise and when within walking distance of one another), I could observe the functions at each site and gauge the efficiency with which we did our job. Most often the students are at the observation site, practicing the job of Forward Officer, (FO). In the non-hostile, non-killing environment of the ranges at Ft Sill, forward observing is the "king's sport," and I excelled at it

The working hours for an XO were quite demanding. I had to be at the office before six in the morning and remain on duty until 5:30 p.m. except on Saturdays when I usually left about two or three in the afternoon. About every other week we had a night shoot which meant that I didn't get home until about 10 p.m. I must say that I was doing the very best I could and felt that I was doing a good job. Lt. Ward and I got along well, but we spent little time together since I was usually in the field or involved with training.

After several months as XO, I talked with the battalion operations officer, Captain Walpole, about organizing a field exercise for the officers and senior NCOs of Charlie battery and battalion HDQRS. He liked the idea and got it approved. The field exercise would be a competition of teams in the performance of all activities at the gun site, the Fire Direction Center (FDC), and the Forward Observer (FO) post. Teams would be formed by lottery. Charlie Battery would provide the weapon (howitzer) and equipment. Referees would come from either the Artillery School or other battalions.

At the FO post, the Battalion Commander and I were pitted against each other. He, of course, had the advantage by virtue of his years of experience. I had an edge with my knowledge of the East Range impact area that had many deep ravines and narrow mesas. The contest was to go to "fire for effect" with the fewest corrections. The referee would choose the targets. It took the Battalion Commander three, and me two. His congratulatory remark was "every artilleryman deserves a lucky day once in a while."

I had the pleasure of serving with LTC Seeley for about a year in the 548th. We had a good relationship since we, along with our wives, attended a few social gatherings together, and he always made it a point to introduce me to the senior officers present. He thought I had great potential as an army officer, and he took an interest in my professional development. To my thinking, he was an ideal mentor. I was fortunate to have been under his command.

When a standard military unit is activated, it has a table of organization and equipment (TO&E) which describes its organization and lists precisely what equipment it is authorized. In the case of the 548th, the TO&E authorized four self-propelled track 155mm howitzers per firing battery. When the 548th joined the 17th Field Artillery Group in support of the Artillery School, its weapons were replaced with six 105mm howitzers per firing battery.

In 1955, shortly after I became the XO, Charlie battery received an additional issue of twelve 4.2-inch mortars (4 Deuce) and an additional mission of supporting the Artillery Board. This mission was especially interesting because I was about to see two branches of the army, (artillery and infantry,) compete for control of a weapon. Traditionally, the 4.2-inch mortar was an infantry weapon. It could be broken down into parts that were portable by soldiers, thus giving the infantry commander his own heavy firepower, especially in mountains and jungles where field artillery could not deploy. Also, the maximum range of the four-deuce was roughly 2 *miles*, which extended the battlefield in rough terrain and jungles. Its shell was roughly the size of the 105mm howitzer. And finally, it could be argued that the mortar was more in line with the capability of infantry rather than artillery. The later sought pinpoint accuracy in its weapons whereas the infantry sought more area coverage. In other words, the mortar had a much greater circular error probable (CEP) than artillery weapons. Nevertheless, the Artillery Board was tasked with the job of determining the feasibility of including the 4.2-inch mortar among the artillery weaponry.

Over a two-month period, we fired for the Artillery Board eight times. Each time we had two mortars in position and ready to fire. On the last day that we fired in support of the Board, we were told to have six mortars in position and ready to fire. The weapons were emplaced just behind a low ridge and behind and slightly left of the observation point which had a small bleacher. A small group of military and civilians had gathered on the bleacher. A member of the Board stood at the podium with a microphone for the benefit of the crowd as well as our unit which had both an FDC and weapons deployed to support the Board. The person at the podium would select a target, using the public-address system to inform the crowd and me. We had live microphones at the FDC and the gun emplacements so the crowd could follow each mission. The Board member at the podium functioned as an FO and would give corrections, each of which would be followed by a discussion in the crowd. Then a different member would take over as speaker/forward observer. I had no idea what they were discussing, but I could tell that acting the role of FO was a treat for everyone who did it.

We had been at this for several hours, and it was getting close to lunchtime when a Colonel, marching with determination, arrived at the podium, glared at the crowd and in an air of unquestionable authority stated:

"The four-point-two-inch mortar is an infantry weapon used for area coverage and not an artillery piece used for pinpoint accuracy!" Then he turned toward me and with microphone in hand commanded: "Lieutenant! all six mortars, four rounds each, repeat range, fire for effect!" The FDC quickly gave the settings to the mortars (mostly to ensure that each weapon had followed along on the previous adjustments). Rapidly each gunner raised his hand indicating his mortar was ready to fire.

I raised my hand high and brought it down shouting "Fire!" Probably no more than 15 seconds had elapsed from the time the Colonel had called for "fire for effect" until the shells were on the way. It is noteworthy that artillerymen of all ranks take great pride in tradition and professionalism. They see themselves as disciplined, precise and consistent. They acknowledge that artillery is the King of Battle, whereas the infantry is the Queen of Battle. As the King of Battle, artillery is the most lethal fighting force on the battlefield. To artillery officers, especially junior officers, they see the adjustment of fire as the greatest measurement of marksmanship and call it the King's Sport.

The Board members, with binoculars held tightly to their eyes, waited patiently as the first rounds completed their high angle trajectory and descended on the target area. Suddenly the pulverized target area gave rise to a churning cloud of dust, and again, and again, and again. Then silence. It was a sight to behold. The infantry Colonel at the podium spoke into his microphone: "Gentlemen, that is how you use the four-deuce!" And he strutted off to his vehicle and away.

The officer with whom I had dealt each time we supported the Board came over and said, with a smile; "Lieutenant, please pass on to your men the Board's thanks for their support. "Then, with a chuckle, he added, "I don't think you will be doing any mortar firing for the Board anytime soon."

The clipboard was the essential tool of the commanders and executive officers of the units in the 17th Field Artillery Group. In my case as the XO, I was in charge of unit training and the scheduling of battery support missions, so I needed to have that handy always. I made the 0600 formation each day except Sunday and ensured that everyone in the battery was accounted for. On the back of the clipboard, under a sheet of acetate, I had a variety of data and statistics including the names of those who were not present for battery duty and why: post detail, leave, pass, hospital, temporary duty, special duty, and AWOL (of which I had none all the time I was in '"Charlie" battery).

The cost of living on 2nd Lt's pay was almost too much. As the months went by, our budget was holding up, but it was a real strain. Every little bit helped or hurt. We got a little bit of a break when Darlene found a less expensive apartment that was about the same quality as the first. We had an unusual experience several days after the move. We came home in the evening to find an epileptic girl having a seizure in the hallway in front of our apartment. We tried to console her about the time her mother came out of their apartment and took care of the girl. We had some occasional chats with them after that.

A pleasant surprise came one day when Mary Olive called and said they would be visiting us in a couple of days. The highlight of the visit was my five-year-old brother's excitement when he got to see both a day and a night shoot. Tom was quite impressed with me, and I was enjoying the compliment. That two-day visit was one of the very few I would get from relatives over my career, so it is a special memory.

Battery Commander Lt. Ward's relationship with his superiors was not good. I don't know why. On one occasion, I heard the Battalion XO tell him: "just stay in your office and let Burbach take care of things." I did not like hearing that because I did not want a rift between us. After a few months, Lt. Ward was relieved of command of Charlie battery and assigned as CO of HDQRS battery. Consequently, he had to write a performance appraisal on me covering the time he had been in command. It was not a complimentary evaluation. In fact, it was the worst I would ever receive.

The new CO was Captain Walpole who had been the battalion operations officer. I had a lot of respect for him; we had worked very well together. I showed him the evaluation that Lt. Ward had given me and he agreed that it was totally unjustified. He suggested that I discuss it with the officer who would endorse the evaluation, the battalion XO Major Brown. Brown was nondescript in my view. He didn't seem to do much. I made an appointment to see him and later wished I hadn't. He told me he was surprised when he saw the report. Judging by the comments of others, he understood that I was doing a good job. And so, he had graded me a point higher on each one of the evaluation factors which is the greatest variance he ever does in an endorsement. As for talking to Lt. Ward, I would have to do that myself since he believed Lt. Ward was calling it as he saw it.

When Lt. Ward returned after a thirty-day leave I went to his office and talked with him about the evaluation. He showed me the evaluation he had received and noted that it was a lot worse than what he had given me. I was flabbergasted.

Then he said: "The evaluation of a CO is really an evaluation of his unit and so, as you can see, the unit is not very highly regarded. When I wrote your report, I was mindful of what a good job you are doing, but under the circumstances, I probably rated you higher than I should have." Since it was futile continuing with this, I bid him farewell, and our paths seldom crossed after that, although I felt no animosity toward him.

I thought to myself that it didn't matter in the long run since I had no desire to remain in the army beyond my three-year obligation. All in all, Lt. Ward was a fine person. I felt sorry for him and his family when a year later I heard that he had flunked out of the career course a second time and was now serving in the grade of sergeant.

Cpt. Walpole and I got along very well. I respected him a lot and learned a great deal from him, much of which was other than artillery. Probably the best lesson he taught me was always to seek to work for one who will teach you the most and to always seek jobs that challenge you the most. Easy jobs are the hardest. For the most part, the easiest jobs I've had in the Army were also the most boring, demoralizing, unproductive and unrewarding.

Walpole was a sly old fox who would get his point across in devious ways. We shared the same office but spent very little time in it together. At one time, he told me that he found it helpful to jot notes on his calendar about people or events. Soon I found myself checking his calendar once a week. I found notes that probably were about me. I guessed that to be one way of counseling. On one occasion, a soldier was accused of stealing another soldier's can of coins from his locker. He told me that they had been playing poker, and the accused lost what money he had and left the game but returned soon after with a pocket full of change. Later that evening the accuser found his can of coins missing. The next day I called the accused into the office. He came in, saluted, and remained at attention while I asked him questions, always getting back to the question "did you take the can of coins? After about 15 minutes of this he suddenly blurted out: "Yeah, I took his damn can of coins." I then referred him to CPT. Walpole who had been sitting at his desk across the room all the while appearing to be very engrossed in reading a report. Several days later I checked his calendar. For the date of the above incident was one word, "brusque." I must be a slow learner since that word would come up in my evaluations several times over the years.

In my junior year of high school, I developed a keen interest in boxing. Being tall and lanky, I wasn't the usual specimen of a boxer. As in basketball, so also in boxing, I have very quick hands. While in high school at Conception, I often watched Dave MacDonald of Boys Town and Gene Leahy of Omaha (who became an attorney and eventually mayor of Omaha) sparing, and it looked like fun. Both of these guys had been in boxing golden gloves for years. I had never been in the ring. I asked Leahy if I could get in the ring with him. He was very obliging. He taught me more than I ever wanted to experience again in boxing. I told that story to Cpt Walpole who laughed and talked me into sparing with him. He assured me he wouldn't "teach me a lesson."

It was fun, and he was good. How good? I learned later that in his weight division he had been the US Army champion in the European theater at one time. During our sparing encounter,

Walpole got a bloody nose from an elbow of mine. (This would be a better story if I could only *leave* out "from an elbow of mine.")

Cpt. Walpole received orders to attend the Career Course beginning in the fall of 1955, so I became the battery commander of a unit where morale was high, and discipline was good. Many of the one hundred and twenty-six soldiers in the battery were combat veterans of the Korean war or had recently returned from a tour of duty in Korea. These soldiers were easy to command either because they were careerists or had only a couple of months to serve before being discharged. As for the rest of the men, they were generally well behaved.

I learned the truth quickly in the saying that 90% of the personnel problems come from 2% of the labor force. (Many years later, in a conversation with my son Jeff who had recently completed a tour of duty in Alaska in command of an ordnance company, we agreed that at times this 2% group makes you feel like a glorified babysitter.) If you spend the first 14 years of your life in rural USA under the close scrutiny of a strict grandmother, and the next six years in a secluded monastic boarding school where your peer group is made up of boys thinking of becoming priests, you will find it challenging to deal with the plethora of problems faced from a cross-section of the teenagers of America.

A case in point was private Billy Bob Smothers, a tall, slightly overweight defiant who did everything in the slowest motion he could. He would remain motionless until told specifically what to do and how to do it. And then he would perform at a pace that would make a sloth appear to be a nervous Nellie. He could be depended upon to be as unproductive and irresponsible as is humanly possible without violating any rules or regulations.

Everyone around him knew what he was doing—trying to get a discharge based on his incompatibility with military life.

Supporting him in his efforts were members of his immediate family, especially his mother, who insisted that his place was at home, helping with the fall harvest. She sent several letters to me and made several phone calls. These were angry demands that Billy Bob be home now! "The government had no right putting him in the army!" Walpole had not warned me about him, but then maybe he didn't know the half of it since Billy Bob joined our unit the last month that Walpole was in command.

I discussed the problem with the Field First Sergeant who was confident that the kid would come around. We just needed to be patient and do our duty of training him to be a soldier. I discussed the problem with a couple of officers at HDQRS. They found humor in my predicament and merely commented that "this is a good test of your leadership abilities."

After three weeks, the Field First told me that Billy Bob had not changed a bit. Furthermore, this whole thing was having a bad influence on the rest of the troops. I told him to have an NCO bring Billy Bob into my office and have him clean and shine the brass hinges and door knobs on the two doors in my office. I wanted to see this guy in his act of defiance.

He was a class act in slow motion. Twice he turned to look at me sitting at my desk, each time with a slight smile and smirk on his face. This guy was making us look foolish. I needed to do something. And then lady luck smiled on me.

I got a call from HDQRS asking if I could give up a private immediately and not expect a replacement for several months. "YES!" I heard myself say. I found out that the 17th Group had a five-man quota for assignment to Korea within 30 days. So, several days later Billy Bob Smothers, with orders to Korea in hand, went home for a ten-day leave. What I did was not professional; one should solve problems rather than pass them on to someone else. The next time I would try harder to be truly professional.

Staff sergeant Martin Whitcomb returned from Korea and was assigned to my battery to complete his last three months of service before discharge. Most short timers keep a low profile, stay out of trouble, and look with anticipation and joy on the coming of the day when they leave the army and go back to being a civilian with a future. In the case of Whitcomb, he saw himself as a great comedian. He was a good soldier, did his duty very well and got along with most everyone. In his final days in the army though he set out to belittle the Second Lieutenant, or at least that's the way it appeared to me. Since the five officers in "Charlie" battery were second lieutenants, it would appear that this was going to be a great place for Whitcomb humor.

It was customary to either start a training session with a joke or ask for a volunteer to tell one. The first time Whitcomb was in one of my sessions he volunteered, and the theme of the joke was to show how the soldier is far smarter than the second lieutenant. His story, which was in itself poor taste ended with "When 2nd Lt. Burbach told me that in OCS he was taught to wash his hands after using the latrine, I pointed out to him that in basic training I was taught not to get my hands dirty when I used the latrine." Amidst a few snickers, the Field First said, with a disapproving look: "Alright, Sgt. Whitcomb that'll be enough of that." Several of the other officers had similar experiences with Whitcomb. It was quite clear we did not want this to go too far, or we'd lose the respect of the soldiers. I discussed the problem with the Field First who was already working on it.

He enlightened me on the status of the 2nd Lt. in the eyes of many soldiers. The 2nd Lt. is a greenhorn, full of himself, and endowed with far more authority than he can handle. In other words, to the soldier, a 2nd Lt. is a dangerous person to be around.

In Whitcomb's case, he probably felt superior because of his military experience and resented being in a unit where all the officers are 2nd Lts. The Field First said he would have another talk with Whitcomb and would keep an eye on him. He suggested that the officers in Charlie battery ignore Whitcomb's shenanigans and that he and I ought to make it a point to give Whitcomb the least desirable jobs until he straightened out.

I had a meeting with the other officers in the battery and explained what was going on and how it was to be handled. I learned that one of Whitcomb's antics was to call out a first name and wave at an imaginary friend in the distance while an officer by the same first name was within hearing distance. The consensus was that Whitcomb was a likable guy and did good work, and they weren't much upset by his attempts at humor, but they understood the need to harness it for the sake of military order and discipline.

Through selective details and assignments, and some minor events Whitcomb got the message that he was not going to put any of the officers on the spot or get an embarrassing reaction from any of them. All he was doing was making himself look bad and getting a lot of the less desirable duties around the unit. In effect, he found that being a team player was "where it was at." When his tour of duty was finally over, and he was being discharged, many of us were sorry to see him leave.

On the home front, Darlene gave the budget another boost. She found a two-bedroom duplex, spacious, partly furnished for a lot less than we were paying for a one-bedroom apartment. As we moved in, we realized that finally, we felt like we had a real home. We got some furniture and curtains from the thrift shop at Fort Sill. Later on, we splurged and bought a used television set. I built a stand for it out of 2x4s that was so bad that Darlene laughed about that stand for years.

A soldier and his wife lived next door. They invited us to join them in watching some special event on tv but warned that the screen was small. The screen was mighty small. It was about 6 inches by 8 inches and framed in a box about the size of a small refrigerator. He admitted that it was an old-fashioned one, "but it works!" He had enlisted in the army so that he could get some surgical work done. I don't remember what it was, but he said in civilian life it would cost him more than he could afford. I never heard of anyone doing such a thing before. Shortly after that, we got to know a newly assigned officer to the 548th FA Battalion and his wife and daughter. He had a misaligned jaw. His was the same story. He came in the army for surgical treatment that he could not afford in civilian life.

The army has many customs and traditions that go back hundreds of years. Some of these traditions are of a social nature. Darlene told me about the battalion commander's wife calling and arranging for a welcoming visit by her and several of the battalion wives. In the early morning hours of the day the visit was to take place, I was awakened by Mike. I went into his room and, as expected, his diaper needed changing. So, I changed his diaper, and in my sleep-deprived stupor I folded the diaper and contents and laying it on the floor by my bedside, I sought another hour of sleep. When the clock alarm went off, I jumped out of bed stepping on the diaper and said "Ah sh_t." Mike was standing in his crib, wide awake and listening. He repeated what I had said over and over again and with varying inflections. Darlene was beside herself. "How can I have these ladies over when Mike is constantly saying that?" I left for work as quickly as I could.

When I got home that evening, Darlene had to tell me the whole story. Mike had repeated his new expression a number of times that morning. Darlene was hoping that he would get tired of it before the women came. All went well as the visitors arrived.

Mike was very quiet and was amused by them. When everyone was seated, and things were relatively quiet, Mike said "it" over and over again, and as clearly as he had ever said it. Mrs. Seeley unwittingly (we hope) saved the day. "Oh, isn't that cute. He can say horsey, and so clearly." We were at some social gatherings with the Seeley's in the months after that, and Mike's vocabulary never came up, so I guess he may have been saying "horsey" all along.

'The chain of command is to be always used. To do otherwise is at your own peril. I did otherwise. We 2^{nt} Lieutenants had been bickering among ourselves that we should not have to join the Officers' Club. Most of us could not afford to pay the monthly dues, and even if we could, we would not choose to spend some of our paltry monthly pay on dues at the club. Also, we were convinced that legally we could not be forced to belong to the Officers' Club. However, all of us belonged because at orientation we were told that it is army custom for all officers to belong to the club. Furthermore, every officer would find that throughout the year there were functions that he was obliged to attend, yet he could not enter the club unless he was a member. Any officer who chose not to belong must personally seek the approval of the commanding general.

The wives joined in the bickering and proposed that we recommend to the commanding general that since our pay is so meager, 2nd Lieutenants should automatically be members and not be required to pay dues provided that they spend the equivalent of the present monthly dues each month in the club. Someone had done some research and found that there were more 2^{n} Lieutenants than any other rank at Ft Sill and that the dues rate for them was a higher percentage of their net disposable income than for any other rank.

No one wanted to be the one to approach the commanding

general with our suggestions. The word got around that the sacrificial lamb should be Lt. Burbach. The argument used to support that was that I was the only 2^n Lieutenant who was a commanding officer so that I might have more clout than any other 2nd Lt.

With faith in my cause and determination in my mind, I ascended the hill of power and authority. I walked to the desk of whom I thought was the General's secretary, caught myself almost saluting, and asked to see the General.

The lady looked at me with a twinkle in her eye and a near smile on her lips and said she had no record of my appointment and asked what the purpose of my visit was. I told her I could only speak about it to the General. She excused herself and went into a nearby office. Shortly a Major came out and told me that the General was out, but the Chief of Staff said he would see me. I followed him into a plush office.

I was amazed at the "high class" of everything I saw in this building. I had been in the army two and a half years and had never seen anything comparable to this. A colonel sat behind a highly polished wooden desk. The floor held a large, expensive looking rug. Large drapes adorned the high windows, and framed portraits and paintings hung on the wood-paneled walls.

I walked briskly to the Colonel's desk, saluted smartly and said: "Lieutenant Burbach requesting to speak with the General, Sir." The Colonel coolly and calmly returned my salute and said in a quiet but forceful way: "Lieutenant, the General is out and may be out for several days. He has a crisis on his hands. I am the Chief of Staff. I work very closely with the General. Tell me your reason for being here, and I will see to it that the General is informed." By now I felt the unfriendliness of the mood in this office and wished I were a long distance from it.

But I had the courage of my convictions, so I related to

the Colonel the little speech I had prepared for delivery to the General. When I finished, he said: "I'll relay your concerns and recommendations to the General." Thinking that I was being dismissed, I saluted the Colonel. He did not return this salute. Instead, he slowly arose from his chair and walked to the side of his desk. I held the salute but turned my head to follow him. I noticed the Major was standing nearby at parade rest, fully focused on the Colonel and with a blank look on his face.

At OCS I had been ridiculed, criticized, embarrassed and chewed out in loud voices and angry faces by the best of them. In the first few weeks, those harassments caused a guy to be bewitched, bothered and bewildered. Later on, chewing outs did not penetrate to my emotions. In my eye, the criticizer had a serious problem; and I mentally graded him on his effectiveness at being a jerk. This Colonel was in a class all by himself. Quietly, he began to spit out words that pertained to me personally and to my professionalism in a very negative light. He stayed at it for about ten minutes and then turned his back on me and left the room. The Major said: "Come on Lt! I'll get you out of here." As we walked to the front door, he said: "Lt. You better brush up on the chain of command. Also, it would be wise for you to brief your commanding officer on what happened here today. I'm sure he will be hearing from his boss." As I drove back to my unit, I reviewed what had happened. I was glad I did what I did.

En route to my unit, I stopped by the hospital to pay courtesy calls on two people. One was a soldier in my unit who had been hurt in a car accident the previous day. The other was a fellow 2nd Lieutenant who had had an appendectomy. When I returned to my unit, Master Sergeant Madden told me that battalion had called. The battalion commander wanted to see me the minute I got back.

As I walked into the battalion HDQRS, LTC Seeley was standing in the doorway of his office and said in a loud and stern voice: "Lt. Burbach, get in here, I want to talk to you." This was something new. I knew that the battalion commander respected my work and me. He had been an excellent mentor and had never found it necessary to raise his voice with me. I hurried to his office, gave him a smart salute and said: "Lieutenant Burbach reporting as ordered, sir."

He threw at me something resembling a salute and asked in an angry, loud voice: "Lieutenant, what the hell are you doing? Who the hell do you think you are?" I replied: "I know I made a mistake by going to the General without telling you about it, and I'm sorry." His reply: "Dammit Lieutenant, I don't want any of your 'I'm sorry' crap. I want to know what's going on." "Well, sir, the 2nd lieutenants on post are upset because we have to belong to the officers' club. After we pay the dues, many of us can ill afford to use the club. The rule is that anyone who does not wish to belong to the club has to get the permission of the commanding general. Yet, if any one person took that step, he would be ostracized. I was asked by a number of 2nd Lieutenants to bring up the issue with the commanding general and to make recommendations. We all believed that since I am a battery commander, I might have more clout than others." LTC Seely asked: "Why didn't you talk to me about it: And let me make one thing perfectly clear to you, Lieutenant. You don't tell me what you are about to do outside of this battalion. You get my permission to talk to or do anything army wise before you act. Do I make myself clear?" I noticed that the colonel had said that last somewhat less loud than the opening barrage. I knew how LTC Seeley reacted to bad news. First, he blows his stack, loudly and with some slang words. That is followed by a more controlled voice and cleaned up vocabulary. And finally, if all things are working out and the culprit is honest, listens, and shows sign of reform, he tells the culprit to sit down, and he has a heart-to-heart talk with him.

"Sit down, Fred, and tell me everything about this event? I got a call from the Chief of Staff at 17th FA Group asking me what kind of battalion I'm running here. He said he had been called by the Chief of Staff at HDQRS who had some choice words to say about this whole affair." After about twenty minutes of discussion, LTC Seely ended up with giving me three orders to get done within five days: 1) Within two days, submit a formal paper to him explaining the problem of the 2nd lieutenants with membership dues at the Officers' Club and recommendations of corrective actions to be taken. 2) Within five days, prepare a one-half hour presentation on all aspects of the chain of command and get with the operations officer to get that on the next week's training schedule for all officers in battalion headquarters, and get that presentation on next week's training schedule of each battery. And 3) that I personally give each presentation and that I take roll and ensure that every enlisted man and officer in the 548th Field Artillery Battalion, including him, attends a presentation.

After a year and a half in the 548th, I got bored with the assignment, and Darlene and I were anxious to move to somewhere more exciting. A little research brought us to consider Monterey California where the US Army had a language school (ALS). I had never seen an ocean, and to Midwesterners like us, living in California was a dream. Going to such a school would add another year of obligatory military service. But we were young and adventurous, so that did not sound bad. Anyway, the job market wasn't very good on the outside, and so far, we were able to eke out a living on military pay—admittedly, with sacrifice. Several officers who had been to ALS assured me that there were few duties associated with attending the school beyond six hours a day of classes, five days a week. That sure beat the 60 plus hours of duty time a week which I had been doing since graduating from OCS. So, at age 24, I was going west, beyond the sand hills of Nebraska, all the way to California and see the Pacific Ocean. I was excited.

The full-time study of a foreign language intrigued me. In my academic training, I had enjoyed the study of languages and even thought of making it my life's work, but I did not know if one could make a living doing that. I had a good foundation in the Germanic languages, (English and German), and in Latin, and I had some exposure to Greek. Adding a Slavic language seemed like a good idea, so I applied for a number of them and was selected to study Serbo-Croatian. The study of a language also entails the study of the land where it is spoken. Studying Yugoslavia, a communist country, somewhat independent of the Soviet Union, headed by Marshal Tito sounded like heady stuff. Once again, the future looked bright as I relinquished command of "Charlie" battery and began the process of clearing post.

My final duty at Fort Sill would be to clear post. It means that a person who is being permanently assigned outside of Ft Sill visits a number of organizations that need to know that he is leaving permanently so that he and they can resolve any unfinished business between them. Normally this includes but is not limited to the finance office, personnel, the Officers' Club, and the unit to which he was assigned. For commanders, it means that an audit is made of the supply records and a complete inventory of all materials is made and signed for by the relieving (in-coming) commander. Usually, the incoming commander does the inventory and brings to the attention of the departing commander any discrepancies as they arise. Over the four days of inventory, four discrepancies arose.

Early on the first day, a big snafu was uncovered. Fifty wall lockers were missing. I remembered that when I relieved Capt. Walpole, wall lockers were discussed, and it appeared that there were plenty of wall lockers, not only because the building had so many, but also it seemed impossible to identify where Baker Battery's ended, and Charlie Battery's began. He said that when he took over from his predecessor he just assumed that Battalion Service Battery would ultimately be the owner of all lockers. I decided to go along with that and never gave it another thought until now. Technically I was accountable for 50 wall lockers that did not exist. I wished I had done a more thorough job of inventorying. And immediately three words came to mind and would come to mind off and on throughout my military career; "attention to detail."

The battalion commander got word of my predicament and called me to his office. He remembered that about two years ago he remarked to the then commander of Charlie Battery that the wall lockers on the second floor of his battery were a disgrace and told him to get rid of them. He knew that Lieutenant Ward had been the battery XO at the time so he might recall what happened.

Lieutenant Ward remembered that the battery commander had instructed him to get rid of the wall lockers, so he loaded them up and hauled them off to the dump. I asked him what he had done about it when he took inventory when he relieved the then commander. He responded that the commander was in a hurry to get to his next assignment and had told him that everything was in order. All Lieutenant Ward had to do was sign for the property, and he would be the new commander and the old one could leave. And so that was what happened

I related all this to LTC Seeley. He called in the incoming commander and instructed him to write a memorandum for the record explaining the whole story and to note that he, LTC Seeley would see to it that the subject wall lockers would be duly accounted for. He added that he personally would endorse the memorandum. He told me not to worry about the lockers; I was off the hook. It will take some paperwork but resolving this issue would get done satisfactorily.

The next problem was the case of twelve flashlights. The ones in the supply room were inoperable. The supply clerk had tried to turn them in to salvage. Salvage noted that each flashlight had an imprint which is placed there when a flashlight is turned in for salvage. Normally, salvage would issue a credit slip which could be turned in to post supply for a new flashlight. These twelve had already been turned in once as the imprint indicated, hence they were worthless, and Charlie battery was short twelve flashlights. I told the Field First about this, and he said if I would go with him late in the afternoon we could get the problem solved.

As we drove off to "Problem Solution Center" he told me he was going to introduce me to the real world—how the army supply system really works. He cautioned that I'd have to keep this to myself or heads would roll. He said that we had some overages in our supply room. Things that had been "found-on-post" which should be turned in, but to survive in the real world we hang on to them, and when we have a shortage, we do some bartering.

We arrived in an old part of Ft Sill where there were some decaying World War II barracks. They looked like they might be condemned. A senior NCO let us in one of the buildings which had lots of 4x8 plywood tables covered with all kinds of military equipment. The Field First gave the NCO a couple of items, and in turn got twelve new flashlights and we were out of there. Problem solved. On the way back to the barracks, I asked the Field First: "If I were missing an army tank, could the "Problem Solution Center" help me?" He smiled and said: "Rumors have it."

The next day I was told that we were missing a trailer. All army trailers of a particular design look alike: same color and shape, and in prime condition. They only differ from one another by their inventory control number which is stenciled on the back. In fact, we had the number of trailers that were on our books, but we did not have one trailer that had the inventory control number that was on our books, but we had a trailer with an inventory control number that was not on our books. I talked with my supply sergeant, and he said he had checked with his counterparts in our neighboring units and had found the battery with the same inventory control number as ours. He said the supply clerk had told him that the trailer had been repaired and repainted several months ago. That was strange he said because ours looked like it was newly painted.

When I told the Field First about all this, he got a sheepish grin on his face and told me that about four weeks ago, when he and a firing crew were returning from the East Range, a newly assigned trooper was driving a three-quarter ton truck that was pulling this trailer. He turned that sharp curve on Range road which most of us who have spent any time on the East Range knew because it was deceptively sharp and had flipped the trailer. Nobody was hurt because everyone was in the back of the three-quarter ton. The troopers were able to upright the trailer and came back to the motor pool where he found out what had happened. He had taken it to the post-repair shop and a friend of his fixed the trailer like new. He must have had the other trailer in there at the same time and screwed up stenciling the inventory control number. He said he would have someone take it over to the shop and get the right number put on. Problem solved.

The in-coming commander didn't know about all these conversations. He was getting on my nerves. He let me know that the right way, in fact, the only proper way to handle this is to turn in the trailer with the unrecorded inventory control number as found-on-post and to accept the fact that I was missing a trailer. He seemed to gloat each time he found or thought he found a discrepancy, and he seemed to look down on this unit as some kind of out-of-control mess that he would have to "clean up and straighten out." I resented the later but knew in my heart that he would soon have plenty of problems of his own, so I kept my cool. What irked me most was that he was exceedingly slow, taking up the time of a number of people scurrying to satisfy his demands and putting in about five or six hours a day at this task while spending a lot of time taking care of his personal affairs. I was anxious to get out of there and be on the road to my next assignment.

On the morning of the fourth day, when I had cleared everywhere but Battalion, I faced up to the last problem. A wheel puller, costing fifteen dollars, was missing. The supply sergeant assured me he had searched the supply room thoroughly and it was not to be found. It was on the books, but he didn't remember ever having seen it. There was no record of anyone having signed for it. All I could think of was that for fifteen dollars I could walk out that door, get in my car and leave, headed for the Pacific Coast and a whole new adventure. "Sergeant, here is fifteen dollars. Give me a receipt and square the books." As he prepared the receipt, the in-coming commander came in the supply room and witnessed the exchange of money and receipt. He followed me out of the room and informed me that what I had just done was highly unethical and possibly illegal. I smiled and calmly told him: "If you really think so you must report this to LTC Seeley." I turned and left, feeling vindicated, especially if he actually does talk to the battalion commander about it. I knew with certainty what LTC Seeley's reaction would be.

In signing out at battalion HDQRS, I spent a couple of minutes with LTC Seeley. I was going to miss working with him, and I knew he felt the same way. I'm sorry to say our paths never crossed again.

In high spirits, I picked up Darlene and Mike, and we headed out the gate, not knowing that in three and a half long years we would return. It was a warm and sunny day in late February 1956. A few days earlier I had celebrated my 24th birthday. Darlene and I chatted away and Mike, sensing our enthusiasm and high spirits joined in with his special language.

En route to California, we made a brief visit to the folks in Nebraska and Iowa. Most memorable of that time is the day we departed from Sioux City and headed for California. It was late in the morning, and we stopped by the shipping dock where my Dad had his trucking business. We are standing by our car talking with my father who is holding our son Michael. Dad hands me a five-dollar bill as a farewell gift which was appreciated because money was very tight. I worried about my father. Ned Sadler, his friend, and foreman had told me that Dad's arteries were badly clogged, and he had had several seizures recently while working on the dock. I did not know then that this was to be the last time I would see my Dad alive. He died in November. A few days earlier we had visited my paternal grandparents; my grandfather had just learned that he had terminal cancer. He would die on his birthday in April. So, our euphoria was somewhat tempered as we headed west.

Chapter 7
1956-1958 Monterey & Fort Holabird

There is a rocky shoreline and point on the Pacific coast in the village of Pebble Beach that to me is one of the most beautiful spots in the world. And that is where I first saw the ocean. At the time, there was a motel sitting isolated in a sparsely wooded acre, only a stone's throw from the beach. That is where we lived our first month in California. From there we moved to a garden apartment up the hill from fisherman's wharf in Monterey. There is an old army saying: "There aren't any good or bad assignments, only good or bad housing." Military duty is about the same everywhere. The living accommodations, and hence the family satisfaction, is what makes an assignment good or bad. Monterey was a good assignment.

The Presidio of Monterey, a small, picturesque fortress up the hill from Monterey Bay was then the home of the Army Language School (ALS). Most of the buildings were frame, of World War II vintage or earlier, and painted white, contrasting with the extensive green shrubbery, giving the Presidio its rightful place among the renowned spots in Monterey Bay: Fisherman's Wharf, Cannery Row, The US Navy Postgraduate School, and nearby Carmel.

Six hours of classes plus homework is a lot of language study in one day, but it beats doing just about anything else, especially when one gets paid, meager as that may be. The first hour was a recitation of dialog, memorized the night before or morning. I found that memorizing is much easier and more lasting if done in the quiet of early morning. The second hour was devoted to grammar, and the third hour, conversation. In the afternoon, the first hour was laboratory. Through the use of voice recordings, one could listen to one's own voice (pronunciations and inflections) followed by the same phrases spoken by a native speaker. The second hour was conversation. The third hour of the afternoon was going over the dialog for the next day. Each dialog was built around a real-life situation. An example would be the conversation between a customer and a butcher. Each student was given a set of sketches of what might take place. I found that this is a very effective way of learning vocabulary and common phrases.

The teaching staff for Serbo-Croatian was superb. Three teachers were most memorable. The first was a young man who wore the thickest glasses I have ever seen. He was losing his eyesight but not his enthusiasm to teach his native tongue. All of the instructors at the school were native speakers. He was fun in class and had a way of inspiring us to want to learn. "The Colonel," an elderly gentleman, had been a colonel in the royal army in Serbia. During the war, he was with the forces of Draža Mihailović who were at odds with the forces of Marshal Tito. I, as a student of history, delighted in hearing of his experiences in the guerrilla war that tied down a number of German units and used the rugged terrain of their homeland to conduct successful operations far more than what their small and poorly supplied elements would normally be expected to achieve. The third teacher was a former judge in Bosnia which eventually became part of Yugoslavia. He was a kindly old man with many stories, some with historical significance. My favorite is about his friend Gavrilo Princip.

In June of 1914, he and his friend were attending law school

In Sarajevo, Bosnia. The word about town was that the pretender to the Austro-Hungarian throne, Archduke Franz Ferdinand and his wife Sophia, were going to visit Sarajevo the next day. Sentiments were high since many felt strongly that Bosnia should not be incorporated into the Austro-Hungarian Empire, and rumors were flying that a huge demonstration, or worse, would occur the next day.

Both boys were members of a politically active organization known as the Black Hand Gang that in the past had organized demonstrations, and a number of the members had been arrested on numerous occasions. Our teacher's mother was aware of this, and therefore the following day she forbade her son to leave the house. On that day, Gavrilo Princip (and some others of the Black Hand Gang) killed the Archduke and his wife. Historians aver that the assassination was the immediate cause of World War I.

Our class of twelve officers and enlisted men was a mixed bag. My favorite was Air Force Major Richardson. He was a very diplomatic gentleman, well-liked by everyone, exciting company and very positive about almost everything and everyone. Since he was a pilot, he had to get in a certain number of hours of flying time each quarter. A DC6 was brought down each month for use by the pilots at ALS to meet their quota of flying hours. Richardson would take several of us with him when he went flying. Usually, it was Ralph and I. Ralph was a draftee, a graduate of Harvard University and gay. At one time, he encouraged me to try the gay life, assuring me that once I tried it, I would never go back to being straight. I declined the offer, which was never repeated, but in spite of that Ralph and I were friends. We both had studied Latin, Roman history and the early philosophers. We had great conversations about the men and the society of ancient Rome.

Flying with Richardson was fun. We would usually fly up the

coast and around San Francisco and Oakland. I usually sat in the cockpit with him, and occasionally he would allow me to handle the controls. He taught me some of the basics of piloting. I was in third heaven. I remembered making model airplanes during the war, my ride in a biplane and a seaplane. In my boyish exuberance, I dreamed of being a fighter pilot flying off a carrier in the Pacific. Those dreams continue to this day; only now my dreams are embodied in writing fiction—a marine pilot flying combat missions from a carrier during the Korean War. Maybe someday I'll get it published.

Flying with Richardson brought back these remembrances and that burning desire to be a pilot. The highlight of our last flight together was a night flight. We were over San Francisco, and Richardson was in contact with the tower. We were going to do a touch and go on instruments only. He told me to shade my eyes and not look out the window, to watch only the instruments. After a few exchanges with the control tower, he told me to look up. We were centered on a runway and about twenty feet above it. Impressive!

Another classmate was Hal Bryson. He was from Los Angeles, was drafted and was willing to extend his military service to experience a year at ALS and to learn the language of his mother's people. His wife was a charming and beautiful young lady who had aspirations of being an actress. She claimed to be a friend of Gina Lollobrigida.

The four of us became good friends. They lived in a small house, called "The Shack," in the woods near the motel that we had stayed in our first month. They eventually moved to a "hovel" in Carmel, and we enjoyed visiting them and walking about Carmel, and also taking the famous 17-Mile Drive to and fro.

A few of the officers I had known at Ft Sill were also at ALS. John and Mary Randa and their daughter were frequent companions. Their daughter was the same age as Mike, two years old, and cute as a button. When she would visit, she would give Mike a big kiss, much to his chagrin. She also liked to hug Mike. Once she stood on the coffee table and with arms outstretched threw herself into Mike's arms. Both of them crashed to the floor and then cried loudly. Two-year-olds are fun to watch and need a lot of watching.

One Saturday morning a group of us went deep sea fishing. We boarded a commercial fishing vessel and went out about three-quarters of a mile for some bottom fishing. The swells were about twelve feet high, and I got seasick. I was so sick that I thought I was going to die and afraid I wouldn't. We had great success in catching grouper. There I was, leaning over the rail of the boat, heaving my guts out, and at the same time working my line with success. Finally, in the early afternoon, we were back on shore. The human spirit is indomitable when having fun. I heard myself saying to Darlene: "We must do this again some time." Fortunately, it was years before I again went deep-sea fishing. And then with a good dose of Dramamine.

Adjacent to Monterey to the south is the village of Pacific Grove. One of its attractions was Lovers' Point, a small protrusion of the coast that had a small sandy beach for swimmers and surfers and a dilapidated fast food diner. In 1956, it was a favorite hangout for young people.

Another attraction for which Pacific Grove is world famous is the Monarch Butterflies' migratory habitat on a couple of city blocks of parkland. Over a year's time, the Monarch butterfly migrates for thousands of miles on the North American continent with three such habitats. How is that possible since the lifespan of the Monarch is less than a year? We had the privilege of seeing the Monarchs when they were in Pacific Grove that year.

Walking on Fisherman's Wharf is a treat. There are a few shops with interesting things, but the most fun is dining at one of the excellent restaurants or sipping a drink while looking out over the water to the long, manmade breakers, which are inhabited by lots of seals. And of course, there are lots of seabirds flying and swimming around. One can also walk the short distance to Cannery Row and see the sights made famous by John Steinbeck in his novels. For years after this tour of duty, I remembered Monterey Bay as the place I wanted to live when it was time to retire.

The coastline along much of this area of California is rugged and rocky. A favorite exercise among us less worrisome (or is it less astute) was to run on the rocks. It looks very dangerous but I never fell nor did I encounter anyone who had. You might ask: "what is the point in doing it?" To that, I would answer as the mountain climbers do: "because it's there." Running at a fast clip on the rocks, with no idea where to put the next step until you must, stirs up the adrenaline.

About midway through my year at the ALS, I began working on my next assignment. I had no idea what the army had planned for me. I did not see how my studying a language fit into my assignments at my junior grade so I probably would get an overseas assignment with the artillery. That did not stir up much enthusiasm, given the stagnant routine at the 548th. I did not cherish the thought of continuing training for military operations for the next few years.

Granted, if I had to go into combat, field artillery was for me. But peacetime had to have more to offer than what I could then see. So, I began to research what other schooling might be available, and I found a beauty - nuclear physics effects. The army had a program under which it would send several officers to graduate training for two years to study nuclear physics effects, leading to a Master's Degree in Science. I met all but two of the prerequisites for applying for the program. I did not have college-level calculus, and I did not have a college degree. Being an eternal optimist, I decided to work on satisfying those two requirements over the next two years and then apply. What strengthened my resolve even more, was to read that the course was at the Naval Postgraduate School in Monterey. I had toured the institution several months earlier and was envious of those fortunate enough to be there. As fate would have it, my concerns about my future in the army were about to be answered.

 The Colonel informed me before class one day that I was to report immediately to HDQRS to meet with the Staff Intelligence Officer (S2). It sounded mighty serious. I assumed I must have done something bad but had no idea what it was. When I got to the office of the S2, a clerk asked to see my ID card, and after determining that I was who I was, she escorted me to a nearby office and informed that the two men therein wanted to interview me, and she left. I walked into the office and was immediately greeted in a friendly manner by each who identified himself and flashed an official-looking badge. They began by asking me a few simple questions about myself, my family and my studies. They threw in a few compliments now and then, informing me that they had done a background check. Finally, they got down to the nitty-gritty, and it was truly spooky. As I understood it, they wanted me to go someplace, to study something, and then to serve in some capacity, all of which was classified at a higher level than for what I had been cleared. They wanted me to volunteer for that assignment which would commence as soon as I had finished language school. They appeared to be intelligent men, and so I assumed that all this must make sense, but it surely did not make sense to me. I probably would embarrass myself by appearing downright dense if I asked for a more thorough explanation, or

I could just tell them I'm not interested and let it go at that. But for some reason, I was interested. So, I told them I was interested, but I must have a lot more understanding of what I was getting into than what they had told me so far. That seemed to have satisfied them somewhat, so over the next few minutes they explained that if the background investigation of me was satisfactory, and if I am acceptable to the intelligence corps of the Army, I will be going to the intelligence school at Fort Holabird, Maryland for training in an intelligence specialty. My fate for the next assignment or two had been sealed, and it all sounded great to me.

Major Fielding Greaves had been the Executive Officer (XO) of the 548th after Major Brown retired. I had high respect for him. He was a West Pointer, intelligent and dedicated. The Greaves were now living in Monterey. The Major studied in the romance language department which was on the other side of the Presidio from where I studied, so we seldom saw each other. We babysat for them several times at Monterey and had been at several receptions together. At one of those receptions, I told him about the interview and that I was headed for the intelligence school after ALS. He did not seem to share my enthusiasm, but nothing more was said on the subject. Two weeks later I received a call from him Thursday evening inviting me to join him at the club for happy hour after Friday's last class.

When I met Major Greaves (we were good friends but too far apart in rank to be on a first name basis in a military setting) he seemed preoccupied, and I could tell that something was up. We got a cocktail, and he suggested we move down to the end of the bar where it would be "more private and quiet." I was about to learn firsthand what the phrase "advice from a Dutch uncle" meant. After a bit of small talk, he told me he wanted to give me a bit of career counseling. He thought I had great potential for success in or out of the Army, and he would like to see me be a great success. Further, he and his wife were fond of Darlene and me and wished only the best for us. And then came the bomb! He advised that I get out of the army as soon as I possibly could and get on with a civilian career. Getting tainted with an intelligence assignment was anathema to any meaningful career. Intelligence was not a career field for regular army officers. Hence I did not have much chance developing a progressive career leading to high rank. For the most part, high ranking positions in intelligence within the army were held by combat arms officers who had had successful career progression within their career branch and had not had that progression tainted previously by intelligence assignments. My career branch in the regular army was artillery, but hereafter I would not get assignments such as command of an artillery unit or a key staff position. Those would go to artillery officers who showed promise for advancement in rank and increased responsibility. And those assignments are essential to have on your record when your name goes before a promotion board. Rather, I would be getting any old assignment in intelligence which artillery personnel had to fill to meet their quota of non-branch assignments. In the long run, someone in my situation would be lucky to complete twenty years of commissioned service and retire as a major. If I demonstrated that I had general officer type potential, I might make lieutenant colonel but nothing more. And as he sees me, I can certainly do a lot better than that in the civilian world.

I appreciated his frankness and his taking such an interest in my welfare, and I told him so. Furthermore, I explained that his assessment of my career interests might be a little off. I might come across as gung-ho but that is just my way of doing a job, and I try to learn well whatever I'm doing. However, I am not very motivated to follow a military career, in fact just the opposite. I hope someday to go to law school, but for the present, I will serve the army the best I can and will take every advantage the army offers. I told him about nuclear physics effects. He knew nothing about the program.

Our few encounters after that were pleasant, but we never broached this subject again. I am sorry to say I never saw Major Greaves again after I left ALS. For the rest of my career in the Army I often thought of this conversation, and over time saw how right Major Greaves had been about times past. Neither he nor I could see the future wherein I was able, a couple of years after this meeting, to join the newly formed Intelligence Branch of the Regular Army and over the years to serve as an intelligence officer in senior command and staff assignments; in other words, to have a fruitful career in the army doing intelligence work.

The biggest reward personally from this assignment was having some time of my own. And I put some of that time to good use by spending time with my son Mike who became three years old midway through this tour, and by developing a hobby I had long wanted to get involved in - woodworking. As for the later, my biggest accomplishment was building a coffee table. Most people would not think that to be much, but to me, it was a big deal. Over the years I have done a lot of carpentry work and thoroughly enjoyed it.

My son and I grew to be great friends; although I often worried (and still do sometimes) that I was too strict with him because he was so good. I clearly remember a time when we were in church, and I was returning to our pew, having read the epistle from the lectern. I saw Mike sitting there beside his mother, and he looked very serious and proper. Behind them sat a couple with a son about Mike's age and he was carrying on like a cornered Tasmanian Devil. Did I see the results of two extremes of parenting? Why don't I know instinctively how to be a proper parent?

Years later I was touring the wilds of Denali in Alaska with a busload of tourists. On one occasion, we saw firsthand an animal's instinctive knowledge of parenting. First, just the facts, without interpretation. A wolf and her pup were on the bank of a ravine by a creek. The pup was sitting alertly watching his mother descend to the creek. Shortly the pup turned its back to its mother and was looking around. The mother reached the stream and turned to look at the pup. She came up the bank to her pup, which had turned around by now and was looking directly at his mother. The mother tarried a bit and then went back down to the stream. This time the pup sat perfectly still and watched his mother who jumped into the stream and tangled with some prey in a flurry of splashes., She lost whatever it was she had caught, came up to the pup and they walked away. We tourists delighted in analyzing what we saw. The consensus was that the mother had chastised the pup for not paying attention to her lesson on how to get food. The pup responded by giving his mother his undivided attention. Can we be good parents by merely following our instincts? For the most part, that is how I raised six children. I am proud of the way all six turned out, and especially the firstborn who set the example for his siblings, all of whom have stories to tell of the times Mike came through as the exemplary big brother.

Late one afternoon Darlene and I discovered that Mike was missing. After looking everywhere around the garden apartment, with the help of several of the residents, we decided that we had best call the police. The desk sergeant informed me that my son was sitting on his desk eating a cookie, and I had better come down and pick him up. The station was two blocks down the hill alongside the four-lane avenue down which my son had trotted. When I walked into the station, there sat Mike on the desk sergeant's desk eating the cookie. He appeared to have a stern look on his face as if to ask: "what took you so long?" Or was it a mask for fear: "what's my punishment going to be?" I will never know, but to this day I can see that expression clearly in my mind.

The desk sergeant told me that an elderly gentleman had dropped him off at the station. He said that Mike was walking down the middle of the avenue and saying he was going to the store to buy bread. The police officer admonished me, pointing out that we needed to do a better job of keeping an eye on him. And that was that! But it did not end there.

Things got more serious. Several weeks later, as I came walking down the hill from school, Darlene met me, and she was truly beside herself. Mike was missing, and the little girl from the next apartment, who was about Mike's age and his daily playmate, was also missing. The two mothers and several others from the apartment complex had been looking for some time with no success. Reluctantly I called the police and told him our problem, and he immediately dispatched an officer to our place. Darlene and I identified ourselves to the officer when he arrived and then we three went to the apartment of the little girl. The poor mother was sitting in a chair crying and fearful. As we entered the apartment, a closet door slowly opened and out stepped the little girl and Mike. They had been playing in the closet for the past two hours.

The mothers each picked up their child and smothered it with hugs and love. The police officer was relieved but informed me that he would have to file a report. I thought nothing of that until the next Monday. When I got home that afternoon Darlene told me that she had been visited that morning by a state or county official who warned us that if they get a third report about the care of our child, there would have to be an investigation to determine if we were fit parents, and Mike might be taken from us and put in a safe environment until a determination was made. There never was a third report!

On a Thursday afternoon in November, I got a call from Darlene. She said that Mary Olive had called to inform us that my Dad had died that morning. I was able to get emergency leave, and we were on our way. We spent the night at a motel and then drove continuously until we got to Sioux City. A big scare happened about four hours before we reached Sioux City. I fell asleep at the wheel. The car was halfway off the roadbed when the bumpy ride woke me. That is a scary experience. I had no problem staying awake for the rest of the drive.

All the while we were driving I had a difficult time accepting that my father was dead. I just could not bear it. Years later I got some insight into why. When my family disintegrated when I was two I was devastated and, given the life I lived after that, especially the fact that my father was alive but not making me part of his life, I developed a subconscious hope or expectation that he would eventually put the family back together again, minus my mother. With that hope or expectation, I could tolerate life the way I found it. The promise, or at least my understanding of a promise from Mary Olive and my Dad when I was in the third or fourth grade that "next year you may come to live with us" helped to solidify the expectation that Dad would bring back the family. By then I must have believed that family really meant living with my Dad. Whoever else is "in the family" doesn't matter. With my father's death, this nearly lifelong crutch disintegrated, so I could not or would not accept his death until I saw physical proof.

We arrived at Dad's house the day before the funeral. A lot of relatives were there, and for the most part, I wished they were not. I saw them as a bunch of hypocrites. My brother Tom came over to greet me and immediately said: "Let's go see Dad." I was so glad that Tom was there. So together we went up to see Dad lying in his coffin, and I lost control and cried intensely. I have never experienced such agony as I did then, seeing my father dead. I don't remember the funeral, but I do remember the long procession from the church to the graveyard, and the police escorts. It was good that while he was not loved much within the family, there were many people out there who loved him.

I had several conversations the next day with Mary Olive before we returned to California. My first concern was for her and Tom and Tom's sister, Joan but she assured me I need not bother. I asked if I might have Dad's watch or onyx ring, but she was going to give them to Tom and Joan. I asked for a couple of other things, but it was obvious she was not going to let me have anything of note. I found that strange because she had criticized the Burbach family for the mementos of Grandpa's they had passed out to family members—one of Grandpa's handkerchiefs. And yet she would give me nothing of Dad's things. I took care of that on my own. Before we left, I went into the garage to the workbench that Dad had and found a stainless-steel wrench that I remembered once when we did something together, and he used that. I kept that wrench for many years; and each time we moved, it would surface. Finally, I gave it to Goodwill. I realized that I kept it, not as a memento of Dad but a memento of a spiteful act.

In the last conversation, I had with Mary Olive before we departed she let me know how angry and filled with hate she was toward the Catholic Church for not allowing Dad to be buried in the nearby St Boniface cemetery. That was the first I had heard of it. I was aware of the animosity she had felt for years toward the Catholic Church and now was not the time to get into that subject. Furthermore, I did not care, but I did not tell her that.

When I returned to ALS, I was out of phase with the rest of

the class and finished the course on a somewhat different schedule. The Colonel gave my final oral exam, and he passed me with acceptable marks, although I thought I did very poorly.

Fort Holabird

Fort Holabird was crowded in among the industrial sites of East Baltimore. The ticky tack houses (a term from a post-World War II song) and row houses sheltered the mostly unionized laborers of the nearby industrial plants and mills. The cultural setting reminded me of Omaha where people grouped by national origin, were proud of their heritage and very defensive of it but lived in harmony with their neighbors. As neutral outsiders, we military were reasonably well received by whichever neighborhood we lived in and yet could roam the other ones freely. During the year and a half we lived there, we participated in several cultural events.

The Greek wedding and the celebration that followed was as Greek as if it took place in Athens. Although we knew only a few of the people there, we were included wholeheartedly in the festivities as though we were one of them in every way. The same can be said for an Italian affair we attended. I learned that for these people, and probably for people most anywhere, the joie de vivre is de rigueur. That had not been true in my life. I remember when I lived with Grandma Wieseler that she and her extended family enjoyed life in many ways, but for the fifteen years I lived with Grandpa and Grandma Burbach, they and their extended family were strictly dedicated to a life of prayer and work.

Attending a Jewish wedding was an education. Some of the ceremonials and symbolism were known to us, having read about them or been told, but witnessing them for the first time was enlightening. I felt a deep reverence for the entire affair, including the frivolities. The Jews have a unique role in Western Civilization, and it behooves all of us to know, understand and appreciate their traditions.

Bill Exley introduced me to another side of life in East Baltimore, the neighborhood bar. It is usually in a house where the entire downstairs is the tavern. These establishments, along with their colorful clientele, frequently have been the source for television serials (e.g., Cheers). Bill's favorite was one such place, called The Bavarian Pub. The bartender was an older man, jovial or serious depending on the conversation at the moment. His name was Dolphy. The one time I went there with Bill, an event took place which I assumed was not an unusual happening. We had just come off duty from Ft Holabird and therefore were in uniform. An elderly gentleman at the bar spotted us and began a conversation about the conflict between the "Rooskis" and "we Yanks." He was about "three sheets to the wind" (local slang for drunk,) and the more he talked, the louder and more agitated he became. Finally, he stood up and began taking off his clothes shouting "we ought to nuke them sons-a-bitches! Nuke them sons-a-bitches!" The barkeep came from behind the bar saying: "Mike, you've had enough now, it's time to go home." And he helped the old man put on his clothes and headed him out the door. The barkeep explained that Mike lived just down the street and was a good guy, he just couldn't hold his liquor.

We had a place to live immediately upon arriving in Baltimore. A couple we had befriended at ALS preceded us and invited us to stay with them in their row house while we looked for a place to live. When they made the offer, they may not have envisioned that it would take us three weeks to find a house, but all in all, they did not seem to mind, and we continued a friendly relationship all the while we were at Holabird. She was from Ketchikan,

Alaska, which intrigued me. She told us interesting tales of the people (especially the Native Americans) and life in Ketchikan. Some years later I was in Ketchikan and thought of her, I found the town very much as she had described it, and even more inviting than I had expected.

The row house was a new kind of dwelling to me. It is a series of two or three-story houses connected by common side walls. In many cities in the Eastern United States, they are called townhouses. I thought they were a great structure for other people to live in, I prefer a free-standing house. We found one to our liking in Dundalk. A couple had just divorced and needed to rent or sell the house quickly. It was a two-story bungalow, about 800 square feet downstairs. An open staircase led to the finished attic. The basement had concrete walls and floor and contained an oil burning furnace. The lot was small, probably 50 x 75 feet, and the backyard had about a 12-foot-wide shore on the water that was part of the Chesapeake Bay. The sale price was $9,995, which I could not touch; besides, I expected to be moving on in eight months when the course I was taking ended. The rent price, $75 a month, I could handle quite nicely, so we were living in our first house, and it was a delight. Our neighbor to the west, an elderly couple, had a remarkable resemblance to the main character family in the television show Archie Bunker. He was a dyed-in-the-wool union man, had been on strike for over a year and, according to him, running out of money. He loved to fish and showed me his "bait probe," a metal stake attached to an electrical extension cord. He would hose down an area of his yard, drive the stake into the wet earth and go into the kitchen, a safe distance away, and throw the juice to the earthworms which would come to the surface by the tens. He had very strong opinions and shared them with all who would listen. His wife was a grandmotherly type who baked a lot of cookies and loved everybody. To the East of us was a younger couple with ten-year-old twin boys. The parents reminded me of Dennis the Menace's parents in a popular comic strip in local newspapers. The father spent the evenings and weekends digging out from beneath his house so he could have a basement. He worked at a local mill, showed me several certificates of appreciation he had received in recent years, along with monetary rewards, for suggestions he had made at work. These were ideal neighbors, never demanding or bothersome but always willing to visit or help out. Across the street was a family I never got to know, except for their four-year-old son who played a lot with Mike. He was a good kid but strange. The only two people with whom he would hold a conversation were his mother and Mike. Most days, when I walked home from the bus stop, Mike would be at his house, but when he saw me, he would come running and give me a big hug, as he had always done since he began to walk. Later on, my other children did the same as do many of my grandchildren and I love it! One day, as Mike was playing with "The Quiet One" and I walked up, he said "Hi, Dad!" without looking up, and continued to play. Hey! That hurt!

Early on we acquired a puppy, a nondescript black bundle of happiness. His name, Piddle, was in recognition of what he did best. We had Piddle for some months until he was sideswiped by a car. I did not think he was badly hurt, but the next day he was dead. I buried Piddle in the backyard, crying all the while. Piddle had been only the second dog I ever had owned, and the first that meant something. I must have been about ten when grandpa brought home an old sheepdog. Grandpa thought that every boy should have a dog. Unfortunately, ole Shep was long past anything worthwhile, and I never "took" to him. After a month or so Grandpa got rid of Shep, but I think Grandpa thought that by rights he should get rid of me; any boy should want a dog. Piddle was everything ole Shep was not, and I loved him. I also felt very guilty that I had not taken him to a vet the night before.

Part of the excitement of moving into one's first house is to paint the rooms and fill them with furniture. We went in for color. We painted our tiny living room coral and received a lot of comments, not compliments, just comments about it. I painted the bedroom, and it was a disaster. I did not know that paints differed in any way but color. I learned that mixing a flat, light blue with a gloss, dark blue comes out strange. Our furniture ensemble was also strange. It consisted of some pieces left by the previous occupants; some purchased at the thrift shop at Ft Holabird, a couple of pieces donated by friends and some bought for a song from some friends who had bought out a whole household of Italian furniture at auction. Our friends and neighbors may have thought of our house as odd, weird, certainly unique. But it was our house, our home, and we enjoyed it.

The first ten weeks at the intelligence school were all classroom, all academic. The subject was foreign intelligence, whatever that means. The instructors, all with field experience, were excellent teachers but had to follow the written lesson plan closely. A copy of the lesson plan was at a visitor's table at the back of the classroom. The class was often monitored by a member of the school staff. Since I sat behind most of my classmates, I was obvious to any visitor. One day I slid my chair back a little to cross my legs and lo and behold my uniform included a pair of argyle socks. Naturally, I quickly put my feet on the floor and slid up tightly to my desk—to no avail. When the visitor got up to leave, he tapped me on the shoulder and in a whisper said: "it's against regulations to mix civilian clothing with the uniform." Often, I failed to get my uniform on properly. I would forget my belt, or forget some part of my brass, or wear the wrong tie to an affair.

One of the essential qualities of a good officer is "attention to detail." Well, maybe I was not a good officer in all respects, but then I was not a good civilian either because my taste in color, style, and matching of clothing was abominable.

The most enlightening subcourse in these first ten weeks was on the subject of dialectic, historical materialism, or, as more commonly titled, Soviet Communism. The first day was devoted to a very negative view of the development of western civilization, culminating in the state of affairs in the free world, and especially the United States. Everything was free game: religion, capitalism, democracy, equality between the haves and the have-nots, the empowered and the weak, and on and on. Facts upon facts, statistics upon statistics, projections upon projections asserting that everything about our society was bad and all the bad was true, and that message was forced upon us. It was downright sickening and demoralizing. By the end of the first day, most of us were pretty fed up with the whole exercise. It was depressing, especially by the fact that we were unable to refute much of what was said, nor did we have the opportunity to try since this was a one-sided diatribe.

The second day was an indoctrination of a whole new way of looking at the history of man: dialectics, a new philosophy, materialism, the ultimate freeing of man from the evils, and the limiting powers of authoritarians of whatever ilk. The third day was combining the past two days' ideas with an open dialog with the class but in a very controlled manner that kept any exchange focused on a specific topic and limited to the materials previously presented. This day was devoted to brainwashing, pure and simple. And it was gruesome. People hollered, several people cried, several stormed out of the classroom on occasion. These were all very intelligent people. One would think they could sit back, relax, and employ both ears, one for info input and one for info exit. Days later, after we had recovered from the preceding, we were amazed at the power and success of brainwashing. The fourth day was devoted to a worldview of communism and its expansion, to the futility of arguing realism, the free world as it is with all its pluses and minuses, with idealism, noting that Soviet communism is only an idea. It is not practiced in any communist country. The governments of all communist countries are all ruthless dictatorships bent on world domination-and only then can the withering away of the state, and all the other utopian factors of communism become a reality.

Several hours of the fifth day were devoted to a summation of this subcourse, and an evaluation of it. For me, it was the most intense, engaging and enlightening four days of study I had ever encountered. I came away with a deep understanding of Soviet communism and a conviction that any person is vulnerable to brainwashing.

The latter part of the course allowed the student to choose a subspecialty. I chose electronics and enjoyed it very much. It was a tough course. I was also able to take a three-week computer course: one week of science, one week of hardware and one week of software. Little did I (or the members of the faculty) envision that the electronics we have today would come about in only fifty years.

As we neared the end of the course, I was getting anxious because I did not have orders for my next assignment. Faculty members gave me reason to believe that I was probably headed for Europe. But where? Finally, a few days before the end of the course, I got my orders: 45th Military Intelligence Company, Ft Holabird, Maryland. Why me? I had been a good student; I was a good soldier, far more military-minded than many of the officers on post. In fact, if the 548th was an example of the military, many of the officers on the post were more civilian than military. One of my "close encounters of the wrong kind" had happened on that very subject. It happened at a roundtable discussion and drink-fest at the officers' club. A captain (CPT.) of more years than normal proclaimed that "the corps" (he was a member of the counterintelligence corps, a division of intelligence) was really the FBI of the United States Army. "We are not really soldiers." I walked out and went home. In my way of thinking, if you are in the army, you are first and foremost a soldier. You should acknowledge that and be proud of it. Too many officers at Fort Holabird were like the outspoken captain. They imagined themselves as above the lowly soldier. Anyway, why am I staying at Fort Holabird, in a unit that is hardly more than a holding company? For an answer to that question, I went to see the top man in charge of personnel assignments: Brigadier General Orlando Epp.

I still had this proclivity to start at the top to resolve things, which is not the army way. The time I went to see the Commanding General at Fort Sill and came away encountering the Chief of Staff instead, with the realization that he was a lot more upset by the whole ordeal than I was, and I had accomplished what I had set out to do. Late in my career, I was a party to similar happenings but from the other end of the chain. While following the chain of command is the proper way to resolve an issue, it is always a pleasure to have junior officers who have the spunk to go all out to right a wrong. The junior officer always got a curt lecture on the use of the chain of command, but his complaint was also attended to, usually without his knowledge. Also, unknown to him were the laughs and jesting that reverberated up and down the chain for the next few days.

"General Epp is not currently in the office, but the chief of assignments will be glad to talk with you." said the General's secretary when I arrived at the personnel office. Apparently, the purpose of my visit was obvious. A Lieutenant Colonel explained that over the past several months, the European command had received what was called an M allocation of officers over and above normal replacements. He pointed out that a RIF (reduction in force) was about to be instituted. A board had just completed its work and the officers to be involuntarily released from active duty would be notified shortly. To ensure continuity of operations in this instance, an M allocation, meaning more assignees than presently needed had been allotted. It would be several months before all this could be straightened out. I would probably go to Europe, but not for a couple of months. In the meantime, he suggested that I make the most of my time in the 45th and at the school.

There is an adage in the army, 'if you don't want to be "volunteered" for something, keep a low profile. Another way of saying it is that if you draw attention to yourself, someone will find something for you to do. Several weeks after the above visit with the assignments officer, I was told by the company's Executive Officer, an older major, that I had been selected to "represent Ft Holabird in the selection of a junior aide for the incoming Commanding General of First Army, Headquarters (HDQRS) at Ft Meade, Maryland, Lieutenant General Reed." The Major informed me that this was, of course, a volunteer assignment but he was sure that for a regular army officer it was a golden opportunity for me. (I had a few choice words in my mind to say to the Major, but I held my tongue.)

At 8 o'clock on the morning of the appointed day, I reported to the commander of the 45th for his and some of his staff's inspection of my appearance. I had a fresh haircut, spit-shined shoes, starched Khaki uniform, and glistening brass belt buckle and insignia. With a few words of advice on the fineries of military comportment from the Commanding Officer (CO), I was dispatched to the Chief of Staff's office where I was once again scrutinized and counseled. Then an Army sedan with driver carried me to Ft Meade and First Army HQ. Here, the level of luxury and military decorum was in stark contrast to the environment at Ft Holabird. I found it very appealing. I was escorted to an office where I met the General's senior aide. He informed that I had been duly honored by being selected to represent Fort Holabird. He stated that each post in First Army had been invited to send their best junior officer. (I recognized the patronizing but given the surroundings, it did my heart good.) He then noted that the general was to retire in a year and had decided to keep his present junior aide, but in gratitude for my coming, he would like to meet with me. A few minutes later I was escorted into the General's office. The General was most gracious, and we chatted for a few minutes after which I was dismissed and returned to Ft Holabird to report on the day's events. I was greatly relieved. I would probably have taken the assignment if it had been offered, but I did not want to be a general's aide, too much attention to detail, servitude, and exposure.

Life in the 45th was easy, too easy. There was not much to do. Several of us "techies" came up with the idea of establishing a laboratory consisting of electronics, security devices, and photography. We put together a plan, presented it to the CO and got his ok. We had to scrounge a lot of materials and equipment but in general were successful in constructing an impressive looking lab in part of a vacant barrack. A major was put in charge, and we had a going concern, in part providing orientations to visitors on what a typical intelligence lab looks like and can do, and in part by actually doing some tech work. Two years later, when I returned to the 45th for a visit, I was given a tour of the lab of which the unit was proud. Little did my escort know how the lab got started, and I was not about to tell him.

The army is one huge educational system, and I decided to

take advantage of that fact. I enrolled in an informal course in German, being taught an hour a day by an officer in the unit. I began taking a series of college correspondence courses at the Army education extension center on campus, and I enrolled in college algebra at the University of Maryland extension center. The later was the first step in what I hoped would be completion of the math requirements for application in the nuclear physics effects program. I also was trying to find some way of completing the requirements for a college degree. There was ample opportunity to expand my knowledge of the Army. A good example was an orientation course at Fort Bragg, North Carolina to learn about the Special Forces. It was emergence training where one participates in various training that Special Forces personnel go through. Yes, I ate bugs and snake—it tastes like chicken.

And then there were special assignments. General Prather, the Commanding General at Fort Holabird, loved parades; so, every Friday we had a parade, band and all. In a way, it was nice and patriotic; but it was also a pain. Since I was a combat arms officer, (I was still an officer of Artillery) and a regular army officer (which many interpreted as "career motivated") many of my "not-really-soldiers" intelligence compatriots were of the mindset that I "really ate up this military stuff." It also meant that when there was a purely military job to do, it was mine to do.

When the annual inspection of the 45th came around, guess who was put in charge of preparing for it. The same was true when an army-in-the-field display of pup tents, field gear, weapons, etc. was needed for an open house day on November 11. When an honor guard was needed for burial details, it was my privilege to take care of it. On the occasion that an urn containing the ashes of some city dignitary was being placed in a niche of a new structure in Baltimore, Ft Holabird was asked to provide a military escort and to fire a salute. Again, the regular army, combat arms Lieutenant was given the job;

and rewarded by appearing on the televised evening news, much to the pleasure of both the firing squad and the Post staff.

On December 29, 1957, our second son was born. He was premature and needed some minor surgery. It was heart rendering seeing the little guy lying in an incubator, unable to hold him and cuddle him, but he gained weight quickly and was soon in our arms. The day his surgery took place was another emotional event. There he laid on the gurney so very very tiny and shivering. As they wheeled him off to the OR, Darlene and I experienced a very deep sense of parental love and caring. All turned out well, and in a few days, he went home with us. He was christened Mark Kipling. We liked the works of Rudyard who many years earlier had been a patient in the hospital in which our son was born. We called our son Kip, and the nickname stuck. At about the same time Kip was being christened, my sister, Della and her husband, Al's second son was being christened Mark Kimberly, yet names had not been discussed previously among the four of us. Mike was okay with Kip being in our home, but his interests laid more in playing with "The Silent One."

Now that I had so many relying on me it seemed prudent to buy some life insurance. At the time, it was a big decision. With some trepidation and distrust, I bought a $10,000 whole life policy from New York Life. The elderly salesman was very considerate and understanding. Throughout my life, I had had very little experience with money, and it was a very scarce commodity now. I made out an allotment which meant that the monthly payment was automatically taken out of my salary and the purchase was timed to correspond with an annual cost of living increase, so our budget never changed.

On a Saturday morning in early October of 1957, as I entered the barber shop on Post, there was a lively discussion going on about Sputnik. The Soviet Union had launched an artificial earth satellite on October the fourth. The news media were repeating the same sparse stories then available. Few of us knew much about the space research going on, even in our own country. In the next few days, we learned that the launch had been a big surprise to our government, and it meant that the Soviet Union must be way ahead of us in space research. It also became clear that the military significance of that was alarming. Since this was at the height of the Cold War, it caused heightened concern at all levels of the United States armed forces.

I was becoming quite bored with duty at Fort Holabird, and nothing was happening about an assignment to Europe. But I could not do much about it, and I was committed to serving two or three more years because of all the schooling. I was about ready to volunteer for most any assignment that would take me out of Holabird. I had periodically made my anxieties known to the personnel people. My day finally came. I was issued temporary duty (TDY) orders for travel to and from the Pentagon for an interview at the office of the Assistant Chief of Staff, Intelligence (ACSI), Department of Army. I had been to the Pentagon on two previous occasions and thought that working there must be a great experience. Upon arriving, I was met by Cpt. Moreno (an alias) who informed that I was to be interviewed for his job, but first I would be talking to some other people about some entirely different work. He said that those interviews were hush-hush and I was not to speak of them neither before nor after they took place. So, I will continue herein not to speak of them except to say they were exciting sounding jobs and I declined both of them.

Colonel Ben Davis was a disarming gentleman who got right to the point. He needed an administrative officer: he was not pleased with the one he had, who would be transferred to other duties as soon as a replacement was found. The Colonel had a small private office situated to the back of a much bigger office, with an additional large office on the side. All this was windowless, below ground in the Pentagon. The entry to the office complex consisted of two, thick steel doors. I was to learn that all this was a highly secured vault. The more the Colonel talked, the more I was convinced that this was exactly what I wanted, and more. The interview ended with my agreeing to the assignment and his noncommittal assurance that I would know in a few days if I were selected for the job.

I discussed the situation with Darlene when I returned home. We both had some real misgivings about the living conditions and the costs. At present, we were able to live within our budget, but barely, and we were comfortable in our cozy little cottage. We were young and adventurous.

My dad, Joe, Joan, and Tom and Stepmom Mary Olive

Chapter 8
1958-1960 The Pentagon

A week before I reported for duty; Darlene, the boys and I drove to Northern Virginia to find housing. Someone told me about the Frederick Apartments on Columbia Pike, about three miles from the Pentagon. The complex sat on a hill, back from the road, with lots of trees around. A bus that served the Pentagon was just below the complex. A strip mall and a Safeway grocery were on the other side of Columbia Pike. Darlene did not drive, so the arrangements seemed the best possible. Since the apartment was furnished, we could dispose of our furniture. We gave most of it to the thrift shop at Holabird. Near the apartment, we found a small, idyllic Italian restaurant with red checkerboard tablecloths, candles, and classical Italian music. We celebrated the day by having lunch there. It became our favorite place for an occasional outing.

I was assigned to the staff of the Assistant Chief of Staff, Intelligence, Department of Army (ACSI, DA) and further assigned to the Operations Branch of Collection Division of Foreign Intelligence. When I reported for duty, Captain Moreno was a great help. Even though he hated his job, he spared me the details and hoped that I would have a better experience there. He had a form outlining the various military offices we would visit so he could introduce me to my counterparts and necessary contacts. He also gave me a copy of the form for future reference which proved to be helpful. When we went to the security office for my ID tags and to check on the status of my security clearance, I was surprised to learn that my clearance had been granted. Apparently, the background investigation on me had begun before I was interviewed.

The Pentagon is huge; messengers ride three-wheel bikes down the corridors, making their deliveries. We found the nearest eating places, visited the mezzanine with its stores which included Brentano Books, Brooks Brothers haberdasher shop, and the Pentagon Federal Credit Union, all of which I would frequent in the coming months. We stopped by the military medical clinic to turn in my medical records, and on and on. The orientation and in-processing took the better part of the day and was worth every minute of it.

The next morning, we nine officers, newly assigned to ACSI, met in the ante-room of the ACSI, a major general, and lined up according to rank (two colonels, three lieutenant colonels, three majors and me). The ACSI came in, said a few words of welcome and encouragement and then proceeded to shake hands and chat with each officer beginning with the senior colonel. When he reached me, he said with feigned surprise: "Well, Well, Lieutenant! What are you doing here.?" I was dumbfounded and mumbled something about having orders to be there; all the while everyone in the room was laughing. Only later did I learn what the joke was. I was the only Lieutenant assigned to ACSI staff, and one of two Lieutenants assigned to the Army staff. In simple words: rank wise I was way out of my league.

As with all military organizations, ACSI has a precise organization, and each element had its own title. Our office was Operations Branch of Collection Division. The offices that I would be working with were Foreign Affairs, Security, Document Control and Intelligence Library. Within the big room of our office were two sections, one on the left side of the room, the other on the right.

The administrative staff consisted of three secretaries, a senior noncommissioned officer, several junior enlisted personnel and myself. The left branch consisted of three retired senior army officers and two career civilians. One of the retirees was of Serbian extraction, spoke fluid Serbo-Croatian and had served in Yugoslavia during World War II. We had many chats together. As a retiree with twenty years of active military service, he was drawing a pension and drawing the pay of a GS 14. Maybe I should consider a military career. The seeds of an idea had been sown!

The right-hand branch had a retired senior officer, a lady on special assignment, and two active duty officers, Major Cliff Decker and Captain-soon-to-be-promoted Bill Exley. Both of these officers were very popular and highly respected in and outside of the office. And both of them became my friends. They obviously had mutually agreed to take care of this naive and lowly junior officer. They knew from the beginning that this assignment was going to be a serious strain on my finances, and so Decker helped me get my name on the waiting list for substandard quarters on South Post, Ft Myers which abutted the Pentagon. After a couple of months, I was offered quarters, but I pointed out to Decker that I had signed a year's lease for the apartment and I could not afford to pay the consequences of breaking the lease. He showed me that there was a military release clause in my contract which would be satisfied with military orders to occupy the quarters, and so that was done and our financial situation improved. He also put me in touch with a warrant officer who worked nights and weekends at an industrial engineering company printing blueprints. I was able to get in a few hours from time to time there, which also bolstered our finances.

Living on post was an advantage in many ways. I could walk to work, saving both time and money. The military exchange and the commissary were close by where we could shop at significant savings. We were on the second floor of a converted World War II wooden barracks which would not have won an award in House Beautiful but was more spacious than the apartment and far friendlier since all the heads of households in our immediate area were junior commissioned officers or warrant officers. Many had children, so our sons had play-mates and a playground. Also, there was a spirit of belonging, cooperation, and mutual support, especially among the mothers.

Our best friends in the housing area were a warrant officer, his wife, and two children. His wife was delightful but a bit squirrelly. Late one evening she came to our door with a shoe box in hand. She was sad because their colorful, singing bird had died. She opened the shoe box, and sure enough there he lay on his back with his claws together and near his chest. In a pleading voice, she begged me to turn the bird over on its stomach. I did, and with gratitude, she returned to her quarters. The family held a ceremonial funeral for the bird in the shoe box the next evening and buried him among the shrubbery near our building. My family and I, with fake remorse, attended.

Service in the Pentagon is a learning experience in many ways. One day, when I was walking the corridors of the Pentagon, escaping the duties of the office for a while, I met Bill. He seemed in a hurry, but he stopped and chatted for a little while. When I got back to the office, Bill suggested that he, Decker and I have lunch together at the snack bar in the Pentagon gym. This was a first for me; in fact, I did not know that the Pentagon had a gym. (Later I joined the Pentagon Athletic Club and often played pickup basketball at lunchtime.)

The purpose of the luncheon date I soon found out, was to teach this junior officer a lesson on how to properly loaf in the Pentagon, which was what I was doing earlier when I encountered Bill.

Cliff started the conversation: "Everyone loafs some. The long hours we put in are the Secretary of Defense's idea. He believes that true professionals devote the bulk of their time to their profession. The military officer in the Pentagon should be at work before seven in the morning and should not leave until six, preferably 7 or 8 at night. There is not much the Sec Def can do about the civilians because of unions, regulations, overtime pay and many other factors." We all laughed at that part of the scenario. The word is: "don't ever get caught in the exits at 5 p.m. or the hordes of civilians going home will trample you to hamburger."

To fill up these long days, which far exceed the time it takes a good officer to do his work, he is forced, for sanity sake if for no other, to do a fair amount of loafing. But it would look very unprofessional to be seen loafing. That could get one in serious trouble. So, the solution is as follows: once you decide to loaf, put some papers in your hand, any old papers that look official will do, walk down the corridors in a medium to fast pace, and a frown, on your face. The next day I followed Decker and Exley's advice and guess what, 90% of the people I encountered were seemingly loafing.

Working for Col. Davis was a pleasure. While he had high standards and expected a lot, he was also tolerant and understanding. His first demand on me was to do something about the one-foot high intelligence reports and analysis that appeared on his desk early each morning. According to the Colonel, my predecessor would not take the responsibility of deciding what the Colonel should read in the alleged fear that he might miss something. Office rumor was that about six months ago, the admin officer got a severe talking to by the Colonel because some notice in a piece of paper was missed. His revenge was to put everything on the Colonel's desk, even low-level administrative memos which the Colonel had no need or reason to see. From that time on the relationship between the two had deteriorated quickly and finally, the Colonel had fired the admin officer and was giving him a very low evaluation, which would mean that the officer would be on his way out of the army in short order. I heard all this from the senior NCO, which I appreciated to know but we never spoke of it again; nor did any of the people in the office ever bring it up. A true mark of professionalism is to avoid involving oneself in rumor mongering

Every morning I would place on the Colonel's desk the daily intelligence summary from several intelligence agencies that he wanted to read first thing. For the next two hours, I would scan all the incoming distribution and select what I thought he needed to see and place it on his desk. If he needed to be out of the office those first two hours I would also have a brief printed summary prepared covering the major issues of the day. The total accumulation on his desk would be about an inch instead of twelve to fifteen inches. I know he appreciated my efforts which also had a selfish bent. Now he spent a lot more time out of the office instead of so much reading and being cranky about it. He also would let me go home about five o'clock instead of seven since he no longer needed to stay and catch up on all the reading. A real win-win situation.

The military staff wore civilian clothes, suits, coat, and tie, on all work days but Wednesday, when wearing the uniform was required. I heard that the one day of uniform was to remind each of us that we were soldiers. Rumors had it that we avoided wearing the uniform on the other days to avoid the appearance that our nation's capital was overrun by, and maybe run by, the military. I have always been amazed that we maintain so many military personnel and units in and around the District of Columbia. If they were distributed among the other military installations around the country much land and facilities in the area could be released for other purposes, and the population congestion could be greatly reduced.

The two suits I owned became almost like uniforms since I wore them so regularly because money was tight. The lady in the left section created a stir some years earlier. She was the first woman in our area of the building to wear a pants-suit to work. Soon after that many of the ladies began wearing pants-suits to work, all without much ado. The lady's name was Audrey, and she began working in the Pentagon sometime after World War II. Also, the widow of a West Point officer began about the same time. Her name was Dorothy, and over the years, as the peers of her late husband rose in rank to colonel and general officer status, she developed a reputation as a person of influence and one with whom you did not want to be at odds. Some years ago, she had surpassed Audrey in the quest for ever higher rank and now was the deputy chief of the Counterintelligence Division and in the pay grade of GS 14. Stan Hayes, a section chief, had given me some papers to take to Counterintelligence Division for coordination and immediately return with them in hand. He had been interrupted by Colonel Davis, who overheard the orders given to me. He said, "Stan, I've told you before, I don't want anyone dealing with that woman except chiefs!"

Some weeks later Col. Hayes got a rebuff from the boss when he decided to make me liaison officer between our office and that of a counterpart at the Central Intelligence Agency.

Mankowitz told me about this. His desk was just outside the side door of the boss' office, so he heard most everything that went on in there except when the doors were closed. Col. Davis looked at Col. Hayes for a long moment and then said "no way!" Mankowitz explained that the job was not much more than a courier, a messenger boy, but the title sounded impressive and Hayes thought it would give me another job title, one with prestige. A few days later Col. Davis announced that our liaison officer to the agency would be Mankowitz.

Mr. Howard of the left section was an unexciting, middle-aged plodder who didn't seem to be held in high regard by Col. Davis. A case in point. One morning Davis returned a letter to Mr. Howard who had prepared it and was submitting it for signature. Davis told him in a stern voice to correct the mistake in the letter. Howard fretted all morning, trying desperately to find the error. He asked the help of Audrey, who found none. Finally, he asked his chief, Hayes, to ask the boss to identify the error. In the body of the letter was "a historical document" which, according to Col. Davis, should read "an historical document." Petty things happen, even in high places.

By far the best writer in the office was Bill Exley. He was often asked to help out in other parts of ACSI when an important document was prepared. Bill told me that he had had an excellent teacher of English in high school, and he enjoyed creative writing. About this time, his brother Frederick came out with a book titled "A Fan's Note" which achieved national acclaim.

Sometime during this year Bill Exley and I went to a promotion party for a mutual friend on a Friday night at the Officers' Club at Ft. Holabird. The party was a blast. It was great seeing a lot of people I had known or met. Very late into the night Bill and I decided to go home. Since he was in worse shape than I, it was decided that I would drive his car.

Several times we stopped to relieve our stomachs of excess liquid. After going through the Baltimore tunnel and over the bridge, we should have followed the road as it turned right and on to either the Parkway or I-95 South. Instead, I ended up going into Glen Burney. Realizing my mistake, I tried to get turned around and go back the way we came. But I got lost. Luckily there was an all-night station a couple of blocks ahead, and I pulled in there. The attendant came out, and I told him my problem, and he gave me directions on how to get on the road I should be on. He assured me that in less than a mile, after a couple of right and left turns; I'd be on my way.

Well, he must have given me some bum advice because I did not end up where I wanted to be. I drove around for a few minutes and again found an all-night service station. When the attendant came out, I explained to him our predicament. He gave a little chuckle and said: "Fella, you must really be in bad shape. I just gave you directions a few minutes ago." This time I paid real close attention to everything he said, and this time he got it right because we found the road we needed.

In the spring of 1959, Col. Davis was assigned overseas, and his replacement was Colonel Stewart McKenny, a West Pointer, militarily correct in all manners, demanding, and out of the office much more than Davis. At the time he came to Operational Branch, his good friend Col. Doug Halten became chief of Security Division. Several weeks after they arrived, I was given the task of helping them arrange an orientation trip that would take them around the world. After two weeks of planning and busy work, I had everything prepared, including orders, reservations, tickets, everything. The long legs of the journey were aboard commercial aircraft. Col. McKenney noted that these flights were aboard propeller driven aircraft which were slow. He wanted jet aircraft. Jet powered aircraft were just beginning to come into the inventory of the major airlines at that time. Special approval was required for military personnel to use those aircraft because the cost was significantly more. Col. McKenney looked at me and in a stern voice said: "Burbach, I don't care how you do it, but you get us on jet aircraft." I gave him the proper response: "Yes, sir." I left the meeting, wondering how in the world I was going to do that. And then I remembered Sarah.

Sarah was an elderly, kind, grandmotherly type who worked in the travel office and with whom I had had many previous dealings, getting transportation for all kinds of people for all kinds of reasons with all kinds of caveats. I believe she saw in me a naive young man over his head in this environment who was trying so hard to do everything right, and she was my fairy godmother, making all things right. At any rate, I went to see her, with feigned panic. After I explained to her what I needed and why it was so important that I do as my new boss commanded, she smiled and said: "Let me see what I can do. Come back early tomorrow afternoon."

I didn't have time to fret about all this over the next twenty-four hours because I was way behind in my normal work. Trip planning had taken up many hours of my time. The next afternoon I went to see her. She was with a client, but she saw me. She picked up an envelope from her desk and walked across the office to hand it to me. She looked up into my eyes as I looked in the envelope and found tickets for two booked on the jet aircraft flights. She had a big, triumphant grin on her face. I said thanks with a sigh of relief. I felt like kissing her but did not. Now I wish I had. It probably would have made her day. I had dealings with her several times over the next two months. The last one was to thank her for everything and goodbye, as I was being reassigned. She got up out of her chair and kissed me on the check. With a big grin, she said: "I like you." I never saw her again.

During Col. McKenney's absence on the long trip, an evaluation throughout ACSI had taken place and determined that a housecleaning was in order in regards to all the classified documents that were in ACSI. A directive came down stating all classified documents, secret and above, except working paper's, would be reviewed and either destroyed or be placed in the intelligence library. It was noted that the library now has a special security section where very sensitive documents or those that are accessible only to specific people by name could be safely stored. I could see that this was going to be a big job and a fight. The fight would come from Audrey who had an emerging empire in the corner of the left section.

I would find out later on that a government employee has two ways to move up the salary scale, i.e., the GS rating scale. One way is to find a vacancy somewhere and apply for it. The other is to build up your present job to the point where it is reevaluated, hopefully justifying a higher pay grade. This can be either by increasing the importance of the job by the nature of the work done, or by the grade levels of the people with whom you normally work; or by expanding the amount of work done by increasing the physical space the operation occupies and filling that space with more file cabinets, desks, and assistants. I had a sneaking suspicion that this later was how both Audrey and Dorothy had risen from their origin grade level of GS 3 or 4 to their present level of 12 and 14 respectively.

In fact, Audrey was making progress along those lines. Besides her one four-drawer file cabinet, she had recently acquired two more. She also had a six-foot-tall, old fashion, freestanding iron and steel bank safe with two heavy steel doors with built-in dial locks; the kind of safe one often sees in old cowboy movies. She claimed that there were files in there that went back to OSS days and could never be downgraded or destroyed, and only she would see to it that they get the security protection they required. She also had the full-time assistance of one of the two enlisted men, and recently I was told that I would be working for her on a part-time basis. Stan Hays had explained: "It would be good for you to get some experience as an action officer on the Army staff."

She was really sly! I showed her the directive, hoping that if she was going to experience apoplexy, she could get it over with before the boss returned. She read the directive and then said very calmly that she was going on vacation for two weeks beginning the very next week. Then in a firm and stern voice, she said, looking at me with fire in her eyes, "Don't you let anybody, and I mean anybody, touch one piece of paper of mine. Do you hear me?"

When Colonel McKenney returned, I gave him an up-to-date briefing which included information on the classified documents directive and its impact on our office. He passed it off as of little import and said he would talk with Col. Halten about it. Two days later Halten visited McKenney, and I was called in to brief the two of them on the nature of the problem we had with the classified documents directive. They clearly did not like what I had to say. Basically, if everyone could devote a couple of hours a week reviewing documents, and if we could get one additional experienced staff officer to work full time on this, we should be able to complete compliance with the directive in about one year. That included Audrey's holdings provided we had her cooperation. I was dismissed. The bit about Audrey seemed to upset both Colonels. I assumed Col. McKenney did not like one of his employees dictating to him, and both were aware of the alleged power of some civilians. They certainly did not want to jeopardize their careers and future promotions over some administrative fiasco. Markovitz told me he thought the boss was going to try to replace me with a warrant officer who was a specialist in administration. For the next couple of months, everyone except Audrey made some feeble attempts at reviewing documents, but progress was slow.

It was a pleasure and an honor to be working in the Pentagon, but I was worn out. I found that a staff officer has one job and one boss, generally speaking. The admin officer has many jobs, and everyone in the office in some way is his boss. I did not know how to say no to anyone giving me work to do or asking for assistance. In fact, I don't think I even knew that I was ever allowed to say no. That's how naive I was about working in that job. My family life was practically nonexistent since I was at the office all the time. Of late, because of the directive on reviewing classified documents, I had worked every day of the week for the past two and a half months. I had no life, and I needed to squeeze in working a few hours each week at my part-time job because of the insufficiency of money.

Cliff was a good friend. He gave me some good advice from time to time, and he was prepared to help me in any way he could. At first, we discussed flight school. He checked with a contact in army personnel assignments and found out that I could get on the waiting list, but it would be about nine months before I would go to flight school.

Cliff knew that I did not have a college degree. He gave me some materials to read about the army Bootstrap program. It applied to any officer who did not have a college degree, but who could complete the requirements for one within a nine-month period. Such officer may apply, and if accepted would go to the accepting college en route to a new assignment. Cliff told me that my first priority in assignments should be to get a college degree. It was too late for me to apply for the coming year because the program quota was filled. However, Cliff said he was working on a way around that. I filled out an application and attached the necessary documents including a letter of acceptance from Creighton, which also contained a list of courses that I could complete in a semester and a summer session and which would satisfy the coursework requirements for a Bachelor of Arts degree. I placed the whole packet on Col. McKenny's desk.

Col. McKenny knew that I wanted to leave, and he told me that he would help me do so but only if I would leave the Army staff. He thought well of me and was very satisfied with my work, but he felt that the army staff is no place for a junior artillery officer. He felt strongly that I should be in the field with the troops. McKenny was also artillery, and at one time he told me he had asked some people at Sill about me, and that I enjoyed a fine reputation. But, if he approved my application for Bootstrap, he had to acknowledge in writing that if he lost me, a replacement for me would not be available for some time.

A week later it was still on his desk, and so I asked him if he was going to sign it. He said something to the effect that he may or may not sign it, and when he decides I'll be the first to know. The next day he signed it, and I started it up the chain. Several days later I heard that there was talk in ACSI personnel that I must be some of loser—McKenny was willing to give me up right now, even if he did not get a replacement. Some criticisms are very unfair, but often it is best to ignore them.

An earlier experience came to mind. When I first came to Ops Branch the Colonel's secretary was very pleasant, and we worked well together. She was new to the Pentagon and had visions of starting a new career with the government. Her husband was a recently retired lieutenant colonel and had not yet found employment. For Martha to move up to professional status, GS 9, (she was currently an administrative GS5), she needed to pass an entrance examination which included a segment on math, mostly algebra. She studied some at the office (during her lunch break or when things were slow) and would ask me to explain things from time to time. Since I had just finished college algebra at Holabird, the subject was fresh in my mind.

As time went on, I began to tutor her, and the last two weeks before the exam we spent the last hour of each day, with Col. Davis' consent, working on algebra. Some weeks later her disposition toward me changed. She was cold and very patronizing. Everyone in the office but me was aware of her intense dislike for me, even to the point of sheer hatred. At this time, she terminated her employment, and the people in the office told me about her attitude. I also learned that she had failed the math part of the examination.

Cliff was not yet finished with helping me get into Bootstrap. In late November, he asked me if I could be ready to go to Creighton if I were notified as late as the week before registration. The answer, of course, was yes with a capital Y. Then he explained that every year one or more people drop out at the last minute because of some crisis or emergency. His contact at personnel assured him that if that happens, he would slip my name into the vacant slot, and I'd be on my way.

On average Cliff Decker, Bill Exley and I had a "training session" lunch together once a month. All of the sessions were very instructive, with a due amount of joshing. I had noted that there was a constant amount of structural changes to offices and office complexes going on throughout the Pentagon, yet most of them seemed to be changed in the size and shape of offices rather than repairs or renovations. This is the plausible explanation they related to me.

All career officers in the US armed forces want to continue service and want the next promotion. In fact, if you fail to get the next promotion in a specified period, you are out of the service. Promotions bring more prestige, better jobs, and privileges and more money. The higher you go in rank, the more important it is that you demonstrate in your new job that you have made a noticeable and significant, positive impact. That is especially true in staff jobs, hence very true for officers assigned to the Pentagon.

Staff officers in the Pentagon work in organizations made up of cells that work with other cells to form a whole, which in turn works towards a common goal. These cells per force must interrelate with one another providing a free flow of essentials between them and contribute to their individual as well as the overall goals. Since these organizations are humanmade they are imperfect, having flaws and weaknesses; Most of them have many strengths and also some facets which are neither good nor bad, they are just there.

It is the goal of every new chief when he takes over, to highlight the weaknesses known to exist in the organizational structure and to blame whatever shortcomings the organization demonstrated previously on these weaknesses. He may find them in people, their moral, motivation, and preparedness for doing the job at hand. This is the least desirable way to go. Or he may find fault with existing regulations and systemic procedures. This is often a hard way to go. And since the chief will not have direct control over these, they are hard to change as well as dangerous; he may step on some toes or get into fights with other chiefs and end up spinning his wheels, getting nothing changed and looking bad. Changing the organizational chart is one acceptable method. Here one would split up cells where the components lack commonality, especially in the area that has been identified as the greatest weakness and put together components that working closely together will most likely improve on the major weakness. Keep in mind that this will be at the expense of other functions that are presently very strong. Each element normally has many facets, some strong, some weak, and some neither.

The most demonstrative and effective change the chief can make is to physically rearrange the office, putting people and equipment in an ideal setting and grouping that will do the most to improve the identified weakness. The method draws a lot of attention to the change and brings about the greatest reward if successful, making the new chief look like a genius. Now the best thing for the new chief to do is milk this for all its worth and get it noted on his annual performance appraisal and then skedaddle. In a while, the strengths of the latest system will show deterioration and some new chief with repeat this whole cycle. Hence the constant construction or changes to existing structures. Whether any of this is true is up to the reader to decide. As for me, I enjoyed the training session and lunch.

Some unfortunate officer was on a motorcycle, had an accident, and would be in the hospital for some time. I was notified on Thursday that orders were being cut assigning me to Ft Sill, Oklahoma to attend the Artillery Officer Career Course with temporary duty en route at Creighton University, and I would have them the next day. The last day of registration at Creighton was the following Wednesday. Going through the clearing process to be released from the army staff, the Pentagon, and Ft Myer was a (or is that an) hectic but joyous experience. We did not have time to arrange for shipping our household goods nor to clearing quarters. Our neighbor next door volunteered to do it for us, so we gave her a limited power of attorney and some expense money. In my mind, she was still squirrelly, but also a real sweetheart.

Chapter 9
1960 Creighton University

It was a joyous Saturday morning that we headed West away from the stresses of a tour in the Pentagon. Mike, now five years old, and Kip, two, were tucked away in blankets and pillows and would sleep for a couple of hours more. This was a pattern we would often repeat in the coming years. When traveling: leave at 5 a.m. and get a good start for the day, maybe cover a hundred miles before the "I'm hungry," or "I'm thirsty," or "I've got to go to the bathroom," or that most often repeated question: "Are we there yet?" would result in a rest stop. Imagine making the mistake of leaving at 7 in the morning with a carload of active, excited children who, before they settled down for a day's drive made constant demands for attention because of the boredom with being cooped up in a car with no outlet for their excitement. On such mornings, we would be lucky to cover a hundred miles during the first three hours on the road. For someone whose sole goal when he sits in the driver's seat for a long drive is to get to the destination as quickly as possible, I found that any delaying interruption of aiming that car down the highway was aggravating.

While driving, I was easily irritated by any repeated annoyance. In later years, Kip was my worthy nemesis in that regard. He usually sat behind me. He would put his feet under my seat and raise them up. I could feel the movement, and it annoyed me. I would scold him for doing it but to no avail. An hour later he would be doing it again until he got my grouchy attention. This went on for many years.

In fact, it even goes on to this day. When a number of us in the family are driving somewhere, and I am the driver, Kip will maneuver to sit behind me. After a few minutes, he'll do the foot thing, and I will do the scolding thing, and we will all laugh, and silently recall the good times of old—and explain the laughter to grandchildren or in-laws who are aboard.

On that first night of our trip to the Midwest, I was so bent on driving as far as we could, ignoring Darlene's pleadings, that it got dark and we went for miles without seeing a motel. Finally, we reached the village of Salt Lick, Kentucky where we spotted a vacancy sign. The motel was shabby, but we were too tired to care. An old hag, missing a few teeth, unlocked the office door and gave me the once-over. It was clear that she mistrusted me and my intentions. Once she got the message that we were looking for a room for one night, and after she saw our two boys asleep in the back seat, she demanded to see identifications of both Darlene and me. Once we got in our room, Darlene and I had a good laugh. It took the stress of a long day's ride "right out of my hair"—words from a popular song at the time.

On Sunday evening, we arrived at Darlene's mother's house in Hawarden, Iowa where Darlene and the boys would stay until I got a place for us to live in Omaha. The next day I drove to Omaha, rented a room for two weeks, and went to the Creighton campus. I felt compelled to report to someone.

Since I was majoring in history, I decided to call on Dr. Arthur G. Umscheid, head of the history department, and let him know that I was back and my status. He received me warmly, although I was nonplussed when he admitted he did not remember me from seven years earlier. Later, in my days of teaching college, I found that while students easily remember the few professors they have, the professors have a difficult time remembering and recognizing the hundred or so students they may have that semester, much less the thousands that preceded them.

Umscheid and I talked a good while about the world situation, and he encouraged me to enroll in his class on international relations. He said it would be a plus to have someone in the class who has some firsthand knowledge and involvement with U.S. current affairs. He introduced me to a young history professor who was relatively new to Creighton. Umscheid encouraged me to take a new course about the history of the South that was being offered by the new professor.

From here I visited the library and the bookstore and strolled around campus which was not much different from seven years earlier. It felt good being at an institute of learning. Oh, how I would like to be a college professor at some small university such as Creighton. But that was not to be, at least not at present; so, the next best thing to do was to enjoy what I had, seven or eight months of college life. I stopped by the Chapel, said a prayer of thanks, and sat and meditated on my good fortunes compared to my trials and tribulations the last time I was a student at Creighton.

The following day I registered for the spring term. My first required stop was at the counselor's table. To complete the coursework needed for my degree, I needed to take 12 hours of history. I followed Umscheid's advice and enrolled in International Relations and History of the South. That would mean I would need to take two history courses summer session. I signed up for two philosophy courses, leaving a need for one additional philosophy course in the summer. By taking these courses, I would satisfy the requirements for a major in history and the minor in philosophy. I also needed to have a second minor, and for that, I needed the advice of a counselor.

Based on my acquisition of credits I could manage to complete a minor in either English or Latin. If I chose English, I would need 12 more hours (four more 3-hour courses) which would give me a very heavy load both for this semester and for the summer term. If I chose Latin, I would need six more hours which I should be able to satisfy this semester, leaving a manageable nine hours of coursework for the summer session. My immediate response was that I must take English because I would have a very difficult time with Latin because I had been away from the subject for years. The counselor insisted that I at least visit the classical languages table first and talk with the department head, Dr. Jacks who was "not only a very nice person but a very dedicated professor and helpful."

I introduced myself to Dr. Jacks and told him my dilemma. He decided that we would chat a while before we got down to business. He was interested in my military service and delighted that I was an officer of artillery. He told me a little about himself and his serving in the artillery during World War I. He had kept a detailed diary during the war, and upon discharge, he wrote a book entitled *The Artilleryman*. Thus began the first of some interesting and enjoyable conversations I would have with him. When we got back to the question of my taking two courses in Latin, he seemed to assume that our camaraderie was enough for me to decide that I would take two Latin courses. I said to him: "But Dr. Jacks, you don't understand, I'm not very good at Latin, and it has been a long time since I studied it." He stared at me for a long moment with a disdainful look. Then a smile appeared on his face, and he said: "But Lieutenant, you don't understand! I teach both of those courses." We exchanged knowing smiles. "Nuff said." One of the two courses, which was taught using the English language, was Roman Social and Political History. Each of us had a working knowledge of the tactics and strategy of Roman legions. What a fun class this might be! And so, it was.

On the second weekend, I drove to Hawarden, Iowa to gather up the members of my family and move them to Omaha. I had found a two-bedroom, prefabricated bungalow in a "respectable" but "financially strapped" community several miles from Creighton and had acquired the necessities of occupancy. Over the next two weeks, we were able to furnish the house, even including a television set, through the generosity of relatives and friends, a used furniture mart, and some garage sales. It was astonishing what begging, generosity, and $150 could acquire.

We were fortunate that Art, Gert, and family had taken up residence in Omaha. Gert was generous to a point. She gave us some things for our house which included a table, four chairs, curtains, and kitchen utensils. The point was reached when I asked if I could have/borrow/rent/buy the small television set off to the side in the dining room. I assumed it was not being used much. "No. Dick watches that when he comes home from school." I still remember my unspoken thought at that moment: "patronage ends where motherhood begins."

It was a real treat going to Art and Gert's house for a meal, or to play bridge, or to be part of a gathering of family members. Jerry was ordained that year, and so we got to participate in his first mass and a big reception in his honor. Over the seven and a half months we were in Omaha, we got to spend more time with Art and Gert's kids than had been the norm up until then. I wished we could have continued doing that but as things worked out we would move nine times over the next ten years and the nearest I would be assigned to Omaha was a five-month assignment near Kansas City, Kansas.

All in all, our social life was limited but good. There was time to renew old friendships and be brought up to date on things. We bonded with a neighbor family with two boys who were about the same age as Mike and Kip. Both parents had served recently in the armed forces, so we had that in common. It was a pleasant reprieve to work forty hours a week rather than sixty plus.

Academics were an enjoyment. International Relations with Umscheid was challenging and enlightening. Of the eighteen students in the class, two graduate students and I seemed to dominate the participatory part of each session. He was a worthy opponent in a debate of almost any issue of the day in foreign affairs. On national matters, he was vocal in expounding on the strengths and weaknesses of men like the Kennedys, Lyndon Johnson, and FDR. My favorite president at the time was Truman, a man for whom he had the least compliments and challenged me to defend Truman's actions, or lack thereof, on some issues. Dr. Umscheid was unrelenting in his demand for unbiased reasoning in analyzing situations abroad, in using logic in all arguments, and in employing "creative thinking" in one's search for solutions. Those were the main ideas that I took away from his class, and years later, when I taught International Relations for Florida State extension in the Panama Canal Zone and Seminole State College in Florida, I emphasized the same points in my classes.

The two philosophy courses, Philosophy of Morality and Philosophy of God, were easy Cs. I never really got interested in the subjects. I also felt that they were limited to Catholic thought and indoctrination. The second course in Latin which I was taking with Dr. Jacks was entitled The Confessions of St. Augustine. I made an effort to stay up with the class even though I also found the subject Catholic moralizing and indoctrinating. Grade wise I did very well in this course; far better than I thought I deserved.

These months at Creighton were some of my happiest. I loved the process of learning and still do. But I refuse to be constrained by the academic requirements of tests and grades. In that light, I am a very poor student. For me, there is a contradiction in subjugating creative thinking and an intense curiosity to academic discipline. But generally, I do what I must to keep the "D" and "F" wolves at bay. A case in point was my experience in the course, History of the South. I scanned the textbook and then began reading what my curiosities dictated. When the first exam took place, I was unprepared. I could answer maybe a fourth of the questions. I sought help from the instructor who was observing the class taking the test. He had zero sympathy for me, explaining that all the questions were straight out of the textbook. Since I had not bothered to read the assigned material in the textbook, my ignorance was inexcusable. I hung my head and walked out of the room.

I went back to the old grind of buckling down and memorizing the salient features in the textbook in preparation for the next exam. Included in the new section was a somewhat lengthy discussion of President Woodrow Wilson's Fourteen Points. I was quite sure that there would be something on the exam about that subject, so I memorized all fourteen points. If his exam was formatted as the last one, there would be an essay question that would be worth at least half of the percentage points. Whatever the question, I would try to connect it to the Fourteen Points and "blow away" the professor. As luck would have it, the question was basically "tell what you know about the Fourteen Points." When the exams were returned, a nun, who sat behind me and who was the star student in the class based on her ready answer to any questions the professor threw out during class, whispered: "An A, Wow! The best I have gotten from him so far is an A-minus." And so, with this test plus a respectable research paper, I salvaged a C as a final grade. But true to myself, I still let my curiosities dictate much of what I read.

I don't know who enjoyed Roman Social and Political History more, Dr. Jacks or me. I am quite sure that anyone who took this course previously, never examined the tactics, strategy and military history of the Roman legions as much as we did that semester. That was not at the expense of the social and political aspects of Roman history. I spent more time preparing for each class than for any course that I can remember. Early on I was concerned that some of my classmates might begrudge my involvement in discussions with the professor. Then I learned that I was looked upon as the professor's assistant and many of my classmates were enjoying being spectators. While I felt that I did a lot of learning in the class, I was aware that all written material (research essays and tests) never had a critical or constructive comment as the papers of others had. Mine only had an A on each one.

In the summer, as I left Creighton for my next assignment, Dr. Jacks and I had coffee together as friends. As we parted, I said: "Oh, by the way, I was surprised when I got my grades last semester.

He chuckled, and as he walked away, he said: "I thought you would be" and after a couple of steps he turned, and with a twinkle in his eye he added: "And you should have been." He was one of those many men and women who stepped into my life, contributed to my life, and faded away never to be heard from again. How can anyone claim to be a "self-made man?" We are "made" in large part by others. If we are lucky, they are people like Dr. Jacks.

As I drove West, away from the early sunrise, headed for US Highway 81 which would take us South to within twenty miles of Fort Sill, Oklahoma, I settled into a comfortable position for the long day's ride. The boys were asleep in the back seat, and Darlene was preparing to do the same in the front seat. I was alone with my thoughts. It was satisfying to deal with familiar places and things. US Highway 81 to the North ran within a couple of miles of Hartington and on across the bridge over the Missouri River to Yankton, South Dakota where my mother had died in a hospital, where Uncle Mark lived, and where, as a little boy, I had gone shopping with LeAnn and Grandma Wieseler and Uncle Fritz. The city of Norfolk, Nebraska is on US Highway 81 about thirty-five miles South of Hartington where I had gone shopping with Gert and Art and kids in late summer before school began when I lived with Grandpa and Grandma Burbach. US Highway 81 was the first leg of the twenty-one trips that Don, Jerry and I made via Omaha to school in Conception, Missouri. It has been a privilege to be back in the Midwest for a while; and now to Oklahoma again for a year. My preferred place to live, though, was California, and more specifically, Monterrey, California. Maybe, if I am lucky, I can retire there someday.

Retire? From what? Being away from the soldiers' army since leaving Fort Holabird in 1958, I found that I missed it. I seem to have put together six good years since OCS: lots of education, command of an artillery battery, and a Pentagon assignment. In fact, it was almost six years to the day since I was commissioned. Five locations in six years was a lot of moving, yet Darlene and I had certainly enjoyed it. In that time, we lived in Nebraska, Missouri, Oklahoma California, Maryland, and Virginia. The only downer had been the shortage of money. That should improve as we get away from the Coasts and the big cities. Furthermore, I was on the promotion list to Captain which would mean a pay raise.

By attending the upcoming Artillery Officers' Advance

Course, I would be obligated to remain on active duty for an additional year. I seemed to be good at being an Army officer. Neither Darlene nor I had any commitments which would preclude us from continuing this nomadic life. It was obvious to both Darlene and me that the longer we were in the military, the more attractive it became as a way of life and career. So, I decided I would stick around for a while. Twenty years seemed like too long a commitment, but I did not have to commit to that now. We would just commit to a couple of years more, whatever my obligatory years were. For now, I would enjoy learning about becoming a career artillery officer.

"Daddy, are we there yet?"

"No, but I am hungry. Are you?"

"Yeah, can I have some Wheaties with marshmallows?"

"Sure."

"What are you going to have, Daddy?"

I was thinking of creamed corn and mashed potatoes.

Chapter 10
1960-1961 Fort Sill - Fort Bliss

We stopped at a roadside Café, and I had just been seated when a man came out of the kitchen wiping his hands on his white apron and walked to our table. "Lt. Burbach! Do you remember me?" And so, began a friendly conversation with a man who had served in my battery five years earlier. He reminded me that he had convinced me to transfer him from battery to the mess hall (dining facility) since he intended to be a cook once his term of service was completed with the army. He was proud to show me his successes: The Cafe was his as was a Cadillac that was parked outside. After a fine lunch, we drove away feeling very comfortable about being back in Oklahoma.

We rented a house in Lawton near the main gate of Fort Sill as did most of my classmates. The first few days were busy with getting the family settled and the orientation process at the artillery school. At orientation, we received an armful of Army manuals to study and met old friends from previous assignments. We were also advised that on Monday (the first day of class) there would be a test on map reading that seemed like a waste of time since all of us had extensive training in map reading in our pre-commissioning training, and most of us would have worked with maps in our assignments. Military maps are not as simplistic as the roadmaps one buys at a gas station. They are much more comprehensive; however, a lot of the symbols and data on military maps are seldom used by artillerymen. Confident then that I knew map-reading well enough that I need not spend the weekend cramming for the test, I did not prepare for the test (and neither did most of my classmates.) On Monday morning, the test was given in the first hour and was a shocker. I answered many of the multiple-choice questions with guesses. The officer in charge of the next class started his lecture with delight, telling us that we would be surprised when we got the results of our map-reading test and for that matter, any tests we might take from now on if we relied solely on what we already knew. "Keep in mind that if you fail to pass a seven-course test, you will be reassigned from the school and will probably not receive another promotion and will soon be out of the army. Later in the week, we received our grades. Most of us failed the exam. Admittedly, the test was tough, getting into some of the least used aspects of the subject. The test served its purpose well. We all got the message that this course was not going to be a ho-hum cake-walk.

Sixty-four was an embarrassment which I did not experience again throughout the course, although I did not do well in several subcourses, especially in supply and maintenance. I found supply a painfully boring subject. Maintenance was mainly about the care and repair of vehicles and weaponry. I never had much interest in working on the family car and had no ear for detecting problems based on the sound of a running motor. I was not very mechanically inclined. But a strange thing happened to me one day as I was leaving the building. A lady in distress asked me if I could see if I could get her car started. I agreed to try although I knew I would end up giving her a ride to the gas station to get professional help. Anyway, I checked to make sure that the car had gas and a charged battery. Then I looked under the hood. I tapped on the carburetor, the distributor, and jiggled a few wires and then told her to start the engine. It started! I closed the hood, gave her a smile and wave and walked off with an inflated ego.

As I recall, there were 200 in our class, further broken down into four groups and these into 25 student sections. I was impressed with my section. Some were West Point graduates; many were ROTC graduates, several from Ivy League schools, and several had received their commission other ways. Some had graduate degrees, and most were married. Most had had a tour of duty in Korea or Europe, and some were married to European girls with melodious names (e.g., Vicky Lykke, Greta Germine, and Helga Houser). I was especially pleased that I now had a college degree.

The instructors, mostly captains, and majors were bright, knowledgeable and enthusiastic. They followed strict military courtesy in the classroom. Every officer was addressed by his rank and surname. A student officer could ask or be asked a question at any time during most classes, and he would be treated with respect and courtesy. Nearly every class began with a joke. Towards the end of the school year many of us opined that if we had collected all the jokes we had heard during the year into a book, we would have a best seller for sure.

Classrooms were spacious, spotless and simple. Desks were long tables, fit to accommodate the use of charts and maps, and for students facing the dais. The auditorium, which could accommodate the full class of 200 or more, was used for lectures. Two of the more demonstrative presentations in the auditorium come to mind. The instructor, a lieutenant colonel, had just begun his introduction of a few lectures on combat service support branches of the army (e.g., quartermaster, ordnance, medical) when the house lights dimmed, and a colored spotlight focused on a voluptuous young lady in a scant waitress outfit, holding a tray containing what appeared to be a martini. She sashayed to the lecturer and stated: "excuse me, sir, it is 10:10. May I serve you your morning's pick me up?" He took the martini, and all lights went out for about 10 seconds. In the meantime, the audience went wild. A firecracker goes off, and the lights come on which momentarily silences the audience. The instructor raises his pseudo-martini as in a toast and says in a loud voice: "Gentlemen, there is nothing finer than good support for the combat services. Here is to the combat service support branches of the United States Army." The applause was loud and long.

Another memory begins with a major lecturing about the armor branch, one of the three combat arms branches of the army (the other two are infantry and artillery). The major was dressed in combat boots, leather jacket, A pair of goggles hanging from his neck, and leather gloves. He is about 10 minutes into his lecture which so far has covered a brief history of tank warfare and an exclamation of the effectiveness of General Patton's third army in World War II which penetrated deep into the enemy territory with great speed avoiding enemy strongholds. He just repeated the idea of speed and avoiding enemy resistance when a loud commotion in the back of the room turned out to be an officer wearing a black jacket with the stars of a General, combat boots, large goggles, leather gloves, two silver pistols, and, holding a swagger stick in one hand, on a motorbike which he rode down and up a ramp to the stage. He dismounted and walked quickly to the microphone, gently pushing aside the major as he gruffly grunted: "excuse me, son." George C Scott, who played Gen. Patton in the 1970 movie by that name to the applause of the entertainment world for his stellar performance is an exact copy of the Patton who is now staring at us. Everyone in the room is quietly awaiting his words. After about a 10 second stare, he says, in a loud, gruff voice: "gentleman what you need to remember about armor is its call sign: *Haul ass and bypass*. Carry on!" He saluted with his riding crop and smartly marched off the stage. Loud applause followed. A powerful act of teaching which stays with me to this day.

During 1960–1961, when I was taking The Artillery Officer career course, the field artillery subjects were taught at Fort Sill, but the air defense artillery subjects were taught at Fort Bliss. So, for several months of the career course, one of the four divides of our class would be at Fort Bliss. Most of us took our families with us and lived in El Paso in one of two motels that offered to the artillery officers a special deal.

Those of us who had booked reservations at the same hotel traveled together in convoy mindful of the speed trap along the route about which others with experience had warned us. One officer of our hotel group did not join the convoy but instead ferried an L 19 airplane to Fort Bliss. Many of us envied him, for the trip but pitied him once we got together again at Fort Bliss when he told us of the long flight, something about headwinds and 5 to 10 miles an hour ground speeds.

These three months in a motel were rewarding in the sense that all the officers and their families socialized with one another and formed some lasting friendships. My three sons each had a great time. Mike who was in elementary school and who rode the bus to school with his many new friends, made me very proud and too often exclaim: "yep, that's my boy." Four-year-old Kip and his friend Woody Merritt who lived next door to us would spend many hours each day exploring some groundwork that had recently been undertaken in our backyards. We often noted that the two boys played together for about five hours each day. They were definitely "homebodies" and spent much of their time in the backyard dirt. The first thing in the morning, one of them was at the door of the other, ready to play outside until the day came when they were gone. Four of us started out in four different directions. I looked for them, heading down the street in the direction of the small grocery store two blocks away. Then they came up the street, dirty face and all, and each eating a candy bar. One of them told me matter-of-factly, "Man at the store gave us a candy bar and told us to go home."

One-year-old Jeff who had been born at Fort Sill would take a nap in his crib each day in his bedroom which was a few steps from the swimming pool. By late afternoon a crowd would be noisily enjoying the pool, and Jeff would wake up and let out a long mock cry, wanting to join the fun. His mother or I would go in the house, and his cry would stop immediately upon hearing the screen door close. As one appeared in the doorway, he would put on a big grin and extended his arms to be picked up. If we stepped out of his sight, he would start the mock cry again. What a voice!

The weather was hot and dry. Mounted in the ceiling of the living room of our motel was an air conditioning unit which was relatively small but very efficient bringing in the cool air by evaporating water. I had never seen such a device before. The weather was monotonous as each day was the same except for the day a huge sandstorm came. I had never seen anything like it. We watched as a very high dark wall of dust and sand was approaching. When it reached us, it was a blizzard of wind and sand. In its own way, it was a copy of the blizzards of cold wind and snow back in Nebraska. When it finally passed, we noted that the interior of our house with all windows and doors closed was covered everywhere with dust and sand.

The highlight of the air defense artillery phase of our course was not organization, tactics, or operations but the hands-on and study of all aspects of a missile system. We worked and studied in a small laboratory with excellent teachers, mostly warrant officer technicians. When I first saw the missile laying out on the table without its skin, it reminded me of the time during the second year of college when a class field trip took us to the medical school at Marquette University. Our guide pointer in hand lectured on the various parts of the glassed-in-case cadaver with a scanned section. At the missiles school, a number of my colleagues and I spent some overtime hours examining the missile wishing that field artillery, our specialty, had missiles along with our howitzers and guns.

My favorite course at Fort Sill was several weeks concentrated solely on the study of nuclear weapons employment. The course had three phases: lectures in mathematics, the tactics and strategy of the use of nuclear weapons and last but most important, the computation of the intensity of heat, blast, and radiation from a nuclear explosion at various distances from the explosion site using various computation devices. The most difficult part of the course was computing in timed exercises while trying to avoid errors in simple arithmetic (e.g., adding 2 and 2 and getting five.

Upon successfully completing this course, the officer's primary military operational specialty (MOS) number was given a prefix of five, indicating that the officer was qualified in the field of nuclear weapons employment.

As we approached the end of our year-long artillery officer career course, we were given our orders to move on to our next assignment which for me was to join the troops in Korea for 13 months. My heart was heavy imagining being away from my family for such a long time. Those among us who had already served a tour in Korea were quick to volunteer that the time goes fast and that the Korean tour is the best-kept secret in the army regarding overall professional development

Chapter 11
1962 Korea

The trip to Travis Air Force Base, California from where I would fly to Seoul, Korea, was long, sad, and uneventful. For a young father to leave three sons for more than a year seemed insane. I wondered if they would miss me as I had missed my Dad throughout my boyhood years. And he was only 60 miles away, not halfway around the world. My Dad visited me for an hour or two every couple of months; I wouldn't see my sons for at least thirteen months. Well, I'd better get used to it because this was one of the hard facts of life for us.

Arriving at Travis brought me out of morbidity as I met up with fellow officers from Ft Sill who also were en route to Korea. For us, it would be a defining experience in our life and career, filled with a variety of experiences and culminating in a host of lessons learned.

We boarded a super constellation (four engine, propeller-driven, commercial airliner) contracted by the armed services, which included a civilian crew and hot meals. Ben, my seatmate, was a casual acquaintance from Ft Sill. We hit it off well together and enjoyed the camaraderie and the flight—he a bit more than I since one of the flight attendants took a special interest in him. By the time we reached Tokyo, he and she had arranged for four of us (including another stewardess) to attend a Kabuki performance in Tokyo during our five-hour layover en route to Seoul.

I knew next to nothing about Japanese culture, so Ben and the two girls, who were seated in the back seat of our tiny taxi, engaged in heady conversation, attempting to outdo one another on their knowledge of the subject. I missed most of the conversation. Imagine, if you will, sitting in the front seat of a tiny taxi; going down alley-like streets half filled with carts, vehicles, and people; at full throttle. It is something like a maniac rushing to a fire through a combat zone. Surprisingly we made it back to the airport unscathed, and with time to spare.

Upon arriving at Kimpo Airport in Seoul, I left Ben to board a bus that would take me to my unit. As I passed the sergeant who was monitoring the loading of the bus, a body odor of the first order (read horrible stench) engulfed him. Once aboard, I mentioned this to my seatmate, a captain returning to Korea from emergency leave. He looked at me and said: "New, huh? Sgt. Hern has gone native." Thus, began the orientation to Korean life and culture. Sarge was shacking up with a local girl and immersing himself completely in local ways, including the consumption of great quantities of kimchi, a spicy pickled cabbage with great amounts of garlic. Don't be fooled by the American version of kimchi which is super mild by comparison.

Two of us exited the bus at the Yong Dong Po compound, home of the future 502nd Military Intelligence Battalion. Hank (Henry Wilson Hogan from Texas) was also from the class at Sill, but we had not met. We briefly exchanged pleasantries but did not bemoan the dismal state of affairs in which we found ourselves. The part of Yong Dong Po we saw through the rain appeared to be a run-down slum; the compound was not much more than a few drab Quonset huts, and the GI who showed us to our quarters was about as enthusiastic as a wet dishrag. All in all, this was a demoralizing dump. Weeks later Hank and I laughed about all this, and each of us admitted that he had resolved that the Korean tour was not going to be like this.

Hank was a happy-go-lucky guy of Irish descent from a small town in Texas. He was always pleasant, easy to like, fun to be with, enthusiastic, industrious, untiring and professional. We became great friends and spent much time together. To some extent, we were a version of Hawkeye and BJ in the TV series about a Korean War medical unit entitled MASH. Hank, of course, was Hawkeye. Both of us were artillery officers who had served a tour in intelligence; Hank in counterintelligence and I in field operations intelligence. Upon being assigned to Korea, each of us had hoped and expected to command an artillery battery, but ten days before reporting for Korean duty we received assignment orders to the 502nd Military Intelligence Battalion.

We had arrived in time to participate in the formation of a new battalion. The HDQRS and the HDQRS company of the battalion had just been formed. Selected US Army intelligence detachments operating within 8th Army were to be reformed as intelligence companies and incorporated into the battalion. This restructuring of intelligence units was going on throughout the Army. Recently, intelligence had become a branch of the Regular Army (previously it existed only in the Reserve component of the Army) and had become a career field for active duty officers. Heretofore, officers from the combat arms branches (Artillery, Infantry, and Armor) had commanded intelligence units. Hereafter, career intelligence officers would do so. In my mind, this was a long time coming, and deservedly so. The "spooks," as intelligence officers were referred to by officers of other branches of the army, were looked upon as narrow-minded specialists, not equipped with the machismo needed to lead and command soldiers. That attitude was not wholly undeserved.

One evening ten or twelve of the officers from the HDQRS element and from the counterintelligence unit with which we were collocated were having a few drinks by the fireplace in our hut. A semi-inebriated, mousy guy began a tirade of criticisms about the pending reorganization. He had been in the army twelve years; the past ten years he'd been in civilian clothes as a counterintelligence investigator. "This attempt to make soldiers out of counterintelligence people is foolhardy and stupid" he shouted. "We're not soldiers; we're the FBI for the army." I wanted so badly to punch his lights out. I left the room. As I calmed down, I realized how dedicated I was to the military way.

Throughout recent military history, the mission of the intelligence component was to support military operations with data on the enemy, the weather, and the terrain.

To accomplish that, a certain amount of secrecy is necessary to deny the enemy knowledge of our sources and methods of collecting intelligence so that he cannot or will not take actions to counteract our efforts. As a result, during wartime very little is broadcast back home about intelligence successes. Rather, the news is about the gallantry of our soldiers and the trustworthiness and competence of their commanders. And that is fine. But if you study the great battles and the great successes of World War II, for example, you may be surprised to find that the key ingredient to success in most cases was good intelligence.

The source of good intelligence is not solely the intelligence units. Combat troops primarily acquire combat intelligence (Artillery, Infantry, and Armor). Also, military intelligence is not an empowerment for the people who work in it. In our private lives, information is often used as power. "I know something you don't know" conveys the idea that I am better than you, especially among gossips. But that is not true in professional intelligence work. The "need to know" policy applies in all cases: if you have an official need to know some piece of intelligence, it is made known to you forthwith. And if you don't have an official need to know, you are denied access to the information.

My first two months in Korea were spent on the formation of the battalion. The greatest part of the work for Hank and me was at the detachment level. Most of those units were organized with a TDA (Temporary Duty Authorizations) which meant that the unit was equipped and organized without any standard but based solely on perceived needs. Most army units (companies and battalions of a given branch of the army) are organized with a standard TO&E (Table of Organization and Equipment). Working with us was Captain Casey, the battalion supply officer (S4). (Headquarters staffs are organized according to functions with each function having a numeric identifier. The most common functions are (1) personnel, (2) intelligence, (3) operations, and (4) supply and maintenance.) Casey was a very senior captain, a bit crusty and brusque, but with a heart of gold and reputation for "getting things done right now unless it's impossible which takes a bit longer." We saw Casey at his finest one day at a detachment which had a lot of electrical and electronic gear. The electrical wiring in the Quonset that housed most of the operational equipment was obviously inadequate. There were extension cords all over the place. The adjacent Quonset had stores of fuels and munitions. The detachment commander told us that he had been trying for months to get the engineers to rewire the place but to no avail. "This is a job for your friendly S4. Where's the phone?" asked Casey. As he dialed the engineers, a transformation came over him. He began to speak in a high state of anxiety, loud, hurried, and with a stutter. "You people need to get over here right away. The fire department should be on its way by now. We're evacuating people from this area. The wiring in a Quonset has gone bad. Sparks are flying all over the place. High tech equipment will probably be destroyed, and I'm most nervous about the adjacent building which is filled with explosives and fuel. I understand these people have been trying to get you people over here for months because of the hazards so it might be to your advantage to be here if something happens". Casey hung up the phone and smiled as he said: "They'll be here in a jiffy. We'll get this done today."

In no time flat here came the engineers—two service trucks, crew, and a jeep with an engineer captain who walked up to Casey with a smile and said: "You're something else, Casey." Casey smiled. The crew spent the better part of the day doing what had to be done.

Casey's last comment of the afternoon: "If you want to get something done right now, don't get mad, get busy." Were Casey and the Engineer captain messing with us? Who knows? Bottom line: the detachment got their problem solved.

After two months of preparations, the battalion was finally activated and operational. The CO, a lieutenant colonel, proved to be an excellent commander and an all-around good guy. He was a personal friend of the G2, (the head of the intelligence staff at 8th Army HDQARS.) who saw to it that there was a good working relationship between his staff and the battalion. Our operations officer (S2/S3) was Dominic Riley, a bear of a man, of Irish ancestry who was a good man to work for, but from time to time he'd get some way-out ideas. Hank and I worked for him: I as assistant S2 for intelligence, Hank was assistant S2 for counterintelligence. My staff consisted of one non-commissioned officer, SSgt. Sisson, as fine an intelligence NCO as the Army had. The S4, Captain Jerry (who replaced Casey in October), was a very capable officer but a loner. We socialized with him on occasion, but he never seemed to come out of that quiet shell in which he was living. We guessed that he was truly sick—homesick. The S1, Tim Clark was a young, athletic officer and gentleman of the first order—but most of us paid little attention to him. Rather, we focused on his wife, a tall, well endowed, brunette with a winning personality, an infectious laugh, a charming and, above all else, she was head-over-heels in love with her husband. She epitomized all that femininity we had left stateside and missed so much—wife, or girlfriend, sister, mom, the feminine side of our humanity. So, it was safe and okay to fall in love with her—just a little bit.

By army standards, Tim would have gotten in deep trouble if the powers to be found out about her being in the country. Yes, dear reader, you are right. We live in a democratic society and enjoy individual freedoms. Tim, however, does not live in a fully democratic society; he lives in a military society and is bound to obey its rules, regulations, and customs. In this case, we are on an unaccompanied tour; our dependents, who enjoy certain privileges (not rights) within the armed services (e.g., shopping at the exchange and commissary, and health care) are not subject to military control, but their sponsor (in this case Tim) is responsible for their actions if he wishes for them to retain privileges. Be that as it may, Tim and his wife enjoyed a great year together in Korea.

Captain Bob, the communications officer, was a royal pain. He was a by-the-book officer who tried to ingratiate himself with senior officers to an embarrassing extent and seemed to see every one of equal or inferior rank as a threat. As a result, he was treated at arm's length by most of us. Big D was our intelligence analyst. I don't remember his first name; his last name was Davis. He was a warrant officer, very knowledgeable and professional. He was older than I by at least ten years, and this was his third tour in Korea. One of his children needed continuing medical care so whenever it was time for him to have an overseas tour, he chose to serve an unaccompanied tour while his family remained in Maryland. Big D was all-in-all a great guy and a good friend. He was always ready for a friendly chat but seldom left the compound. He spent much of his free time reading or writing. These were the guys within the battalion HDQRS that I had the most contact with.

When activated, the battalion HQ was moved from the dismal Yong Dong Po area to a small post adjacent to 8th Army HDQRS. It was a welcome improvement in location and facilities, and our morale went up noticeably. Hank and I were part of the "advance party" for the move. Among other actions, we laid claim to a former Japanese army building as our living quarters (our "hootch"). The building was about 30 by 30 feet.

In each corner was a bedroom; the center of the building was a sitting room. It had a communal bathroom and a front and back entrance. We invited Big D and Jerry to occupy the other two bedrooms. A Korean woman came in nearly every day to provide maid and laundry service. Thirty feet away was the battalion dining facility and recreation center. Hank and I shared the use of a jeep. All things considered, life in Korea was good.

Mail was flowing nicely. Darlene was keeping me informed of the goings on stateside. She had gotten a part-time job in the same store she had worked in when she was in high school. Mike had fallen from a tree and broken his arm. Kip was worried about and attentive to the stray dog that now had a litter of puppies living in the basement. Jeff was afraid of the tiger in the picture that hung in the bedroom. My sons!

Outside of our little Shangri La, life was not so good. The Korean war devastated much of South Korea. The scars of war were evident everywhere even though combat had been over for more than eight years. The agrarian countryside appeared much like prewar times. Papasan was still out in the field with his black stovepipe hat and his long whip scaring off locusts. But severe poverty lurked just below the surface. Rivers and creeks were plentiful and beautiful but without fish. Using explosives to harvest fish is not wise. Vivid in my memory are the emaciated bodies of a woman and a child lying dead underneath a bridge. Poverty was more evident in the city, in the dilapidated buildings, the scarcity of things, the pall of doom, the faces, the expressionless, emaciated hollow faces. This was the age of the "slicky boys," boys and men who became remarkably proficient at stealing, especially at US military compounds. Their loot consisted mostly of materials that could easily be disposed of in the black market (e.g., wire, radio, and telephone equipment, machinery, and spare parts). A friend from Ft. Sill who was commanding a battery in a remote area of northern South Korea, got in much trouble when the press learned that he had declared his unit as not being combat ready because it had lost so much essential communication equipment to slicky boys. Assumedly his action had a serious adverse effect on United States/South Korean relations. Abject poverty is often accompanied by a severe lack of sanitation which then breeds diseases. The case in point here was the Han River, a large river flowing through Seoul. It was, in fact, an open sewer with a worthy odor. For us foreigners, it meant chlorinated water which tasted more like chloride slightly diluted with water. In the second half of the twentieth century South Korea made great strides in economic progress, and by the beginning of the twenty-first century, she had one of the best economic success stories in East Asia.

May 16, 1961 there had been a military coup in South Korea, and the General Officer in command (G2) was caught unaware as was his staff and the joint (army, navy, marine) higher level intelligence (J2). Any intelligence office abhors that kind of situation. It would seem that he has failed in his job, embarrassed his staff and himself, and left his boss (the Commander of 8th Army) in a terrible spot. The normal follow on then is to conduct an investigation to determine who is at fault—who dropped the ball. This is one of those times when you don't want to be in the line of fire. This thing has the magnitude of a career buster. The question came down from G2 to investigate and report why subordinate units of the battalion had not acquired information sufficient for analysts to conclude that a coup was eminent in this foreign country in which we were living and in which we were closely aligned with their military. The last landed on my lap—my first staff action as Assistant S2.

Onion skin copies of all spot reports (unevaluated bits of information), regardless of subject matter, which had been sent to G2 between January one and May fifteen by subordinate units of the battalion were gathered together. It amounted to a stack six inches high. Next, copies of reports which in any way indicated, directly or indirectly, that a coup was possible were selected from the stack and amounted to about a half inch high of onion skin pieces of paper. Copies of these, along with a brief so written as to show that the units did, in fact, report a lot of raw data that pointed to a coup. Shortly a meeting was called by the deputy G2. Of the six attendees, two G2 analysts and I were on the hot seat. As to be expected, it was argued that the half inch of reports I had selected to make my case were lost among the remaining 5 ½ inches of reports, some of which clearly denied any possibility of a coup. My counter-argument was that the industriousness of the battalion units is self-evident, but also that the job of the analyst at times is next to impossible. I don't know how the investigation ended. The battalion did not receive any further tasking on the subject. The two analysts and I had a great time the evening following the meeting discussing various aspects of intelligence and what each of our jobs entailed.

Inherent in the profession of the intelligence officer is an awareness of world affairs and an insight into their potential impact on our country, the army, our unit, and ourselves. In August, 1961, construction of the Berlin wall began, and the wall remained for 28 years. In October a standoff between American and Soviet tanks in Berlin heightened Cold War tensions. Also, that month the USSR set off the largest man-made explosion, a 58 megaton hydrogen bomb. On November 18, President Kennedy sent 18,000 US military advisors to South Vietnam. At about the same time, the unaccompanied tour for US service personnel in Korea was extended from 13 to 15 months. For those who were within a hundred days of completing their tour in Korea the extension was a real downer. For the rest of us, we who had not yet constructed our double-digit fidget calendars, it was meaningless. (A double-digit fidget calendar is a pyramid chart of 99 squares, the top square being 1 – days remaining in country. Each day, a day is ceremoniously crossed out. These people are known as short-timers with double-digit fidgets because they get more anxious as the last day nears. The two months extension was known to most of us longer timers as the JFK. It was gradually phased out. My tour in Korea was about 14 months. In late November, Hank and I each received a letter from Army personnel center offering us the opportunity to immediately return stateside for 30 days leave, and then be assigned to Vietnam for twelve months. We declined the offer. On December 11th the Vietnam War officially began as the first US helicopters arrived in Saigon along with 400 US military personnel. Hank predicted that a tour in Vietnam was in our future. It came for both of us in 1968.

One day the CO called me into his office to tell me that he had just volunteered me to do a project for G2. The Command of US Forces in the Pacific area, with HDQRS in Hawaii, had tasked 8th Army G2 to do an intelligence summary of the eight largest cities in North Korea for use by the planning staff who do contingency plans to be used for all types of emergencies from natural disasters to open hostilities. The G2 staff needed help because they were presently understaffed and overworked. Staff Sergeant Sisson and I completed the summaries over the following two months and received kudos from both 8th Army and Hawaii. We were informed that our names were on the credit line of each summary. The best reward was a few years later when I was serving in Vietnam. A senior officer with whom I had served in the Pentagon told me that when Pacific Command HDQRS first learned of the seizure of the US Navy Ship Pueblo by the North Koreans who took it to the harbor in Wonsan, the first document the staff pulled out of the contingency plans was an intelligence summary on Wonsan compiled by Burbach and Sisson of the 502nd Battalion in Seoul, Korea. How about that!

We worked only half days in Korea – 7 am to 7 pm. Saturday was the best day since we usually got off duty by one, and had the rest of the day plus Sunday to do as we wished. (Actually, we usually ended up working a few hours in the afternoon/evening of Sunday.) I spent a weekend or two a month working in the 8th Army hobby shop. I had come up with a design of Danish living room furniture and had just started cutting out the arms and legs of a chair when Darlene wrote that she had just purchased a Danish living room set. With the help of a Korean who worked at the hobby shop, I began building a sizeable set of box speakers for a hi-fi set. By the time I had completed them towards the end of my tour, I realized that they were too large for my home. An NCO convinced me to donate them to our recreation room, which I did.

I got to know Seoul by driving to various parts and walking

through the shops. I took a liking to one warehouse-sized building with lots of booths selling various things, mostly clothing. It reminded me of a flea market stateside. The booths were operated by women. When I walked by, the ladies would make a hacking noise with their voice which drew the attention of the nearby booths. As a result, it was like a ceremony for me to walk through the long warehouse to the rear door outside where there were a few booths and a group of five urchins who followed me wherever I roamed. I called them "my gang." The apparent leader was 8 or 9 years old (the age of my oldest son Mike) who followed me very attentively like a little puppy. I also befriended one of the booth ladies. She seemed especially chipper, and from time to time tried to communicate with me with her hands (not unlike our game of charades). I always bought something from her and gave it to my gang along with pocket change. About the third or fourth time I visited, I took off my captain insignia and pinned it on the leader's shirt. He beamed. He also had a cold. The last time I saw him his cough had worsened, and he looked pale. The rags he was wearing were too little for the chilly weather, which soon would turn cold. The friendly booth lady helped me cloth him in a new pair of jeans and a quilted coat. That would be the last time I would see my little buddy. The rest of the gang was not there that day.

Six weeks passed before I got back to the "warehouse mall." When I arrived at the rear door, the friendly booth lady beckoned me to hers. All the surrounding booth ladies and a few customers were staring our way. My gang was there minus their leader. The friendly booth lady reached under the counter and brought forth my captain insignia and a plastic bag containing several handsful of cigarette butts which she handed to me. She had already explained in her charades-like communication that my little buddy had died, probably of pneumonia and had left me his prized worldly goods. (Street boys gathered cigarette butts and extracted the tobacco which they sold to smokers.) There I stood for all to behold. A tall American officer in his clean and starched khaki uniform, spit-shined shoes, and shiny brass all choked up with tears streaming down his cheeks. To me, this gang of five had been a surrogate for that gang of three stateside that I missed so much.

Hank and I visited the officers' clubs at the military compounds in town and found the Engineer's club to be the most active. There was always activity there, and often acquaintances from units outside of Seoul were there. It may have been the most popular officers' club in Korea for junior officers – the poshest was 8th Army HDQRS officers' club, but its mood was far too "serious" for the likes of us. Next door was the Scandinavian hospital. During the Korean War, the Scandinavians (Danes, Norwegians, and Swedes) had contributed a hospital ship to the war effort. After the war, they built the complex next door and agreed to staff it for five years, a transition period for the Koreans to take over the operations of the facility. That eventuality was still far into the future. Behind the three-story hospital, well supplied and staffed by Scandinavians, was a military post, an elongated grassy area, similar to a parade field. Along on sides were 14 houses for married residents. On the opposite side of the field were two two-story dormitories for single residents. At the end of the field was a large building that contained a recreation hall, a dining facility for residents and guests, and offices. Hank and I made friends with a number of the residents and spent much of our free time with them. It gave us a reprieve from Army life and from Korean life.

The smorgasbord each week in the dining room was an adventure in itself. There were open-faced sandwiches, specialty meats, seafood of many types, rich desserts, all flown in each week from

Denmark. There were interesting guests at times: a Soviet army colonel whose trip to South Korea was allegedly secret, several world-famous scientists from Sweden, a couple of Nobel prize winners, a musician very popular in Europe, etcetera. We also went on a number of outings with the Scandinavians; outings which were set up by us or we provided facilities or transportation. Several times we bussed to a large country parkland where we went on long hikes. On one of these, the wife of one of the doctors suffered a stroke. We hastily constructed a litter from tree limbs and clothing and carried her several miles back to the bus. After emergency attention locally, she was flown back to Sweden. She survived but suffered permanent damage. Neither she nor her husband returned to Korea. On another outing, we acquired a large fishing boat and went swimming in Inchon harbor where the tide is one of the world's highest. The tide was going out when we were there. Much to the surprise of us all, a swimmer who dove deeply surfaced some distance away from the ship and had to swim hard to overcome the tide and return to the ship. For most of us, after one dive we enjoyed the rest of the trip on deck.

It was about a twenty-minute drive from our compound to the Engineer Club. Part of the route is through a heavily populated area where people crowd the street looking for a chance to cross. I was driving about twenty miles an hour when a guy stepped in front of the jeep—a sickening thud and he went down. (Later I'm told that I went from sitting behind the steering wheel to standing over the guy without my feet touching the ground. That fast. And I repeated several times: "Don't die you son-of-a-bitch, don't die." The Korean police were there almost immediately. The guy was OK as far as I could tell. He was up and walking, but the police took him into custody. The MPs arrived on scene and told me that we all needed to go to the Korean police station. As we sat in the waiting room, we could hear what sounded like someone being beaten. After a bit, a Korean policeman came out and was very apologetic. He said the man was trying to commit suicide by jumping in front of my jeep.

The MPs told me:" We're through here, sir. Now you need to accompany us to the MP station to file an accident report," which I did with great care. I had had a few beers, and I was trying to be as sober as I could.

After that, I returned to my unit, informed the duty officer what had happened and then to my quarters where I stayed for the rest of the weekend. Monday morning Dom told me the CO had seen the MP blotter, and I had nothing to worry about but added: "don't make a habit of this." A few weeks later I got the CO's attention again.

US Armed Forces curfew in Seoul was from 10 p.m. until 6 a.m. Of late, Hank and I had been missing curfew quite often by fifteen or twenty minutes. We enjoyed playing a cat and mouse game with the MPs who would be cruising the roads, especially around 8th Army HQS compound, looking for violators. Several times we had been spotted by them just as we entered our compound which had tight security including roaming guards and a guard at the gate. Ours was a restricted area, and no one, including MPs, was authorized to enter without first obtaining clearance. Such is the nature of intelligence operations. Also, by the nature of our work, people may come and go at any time day or night. The night finally came when the MPs, with red lights flashing and sirens blaring, were approaching us from behind at a high rate of speed. We were about a block from our compound. Hank gunned it. As we approached the gate at high speed, the guard flung it open, and as we passed through, he slammed it shut. That was a close one. The next day the CO passed the word through Dom that he wanted to talk over a couple ideas with us that evening at 7:30 in his office.

Dom was in the CO's office when we arrived. After 10 minutes of friendly chit-chat, the CO said that the unit had been on the MP blotter again that morning. The MPs had been keeping an eye on our unit for the past several weeks because of frequent curfew violations. Last evening, they had chased an apparent violator who refused to obey the MPs order to stop but had sped away in a dangerously high rate of speed and into the compound before the MPs could apprehend the culprit. The CO said that he was quite sure that none of the professional intelligence personnel on post would do such a thing, due to the nature, importance, and sensitivity of our operations, so he assumed it may be one or two of the small group of young administrative people working for us. "This is serious gentlemen, and I want to nip it in the bud in such a way that it ceases immediately. Captain Burbach, I want you to prepare a hard-hitting thirty-minute class to be given to those non-intelligence people we have working on base. Without getting into any classified matters, tell them how important and sensitive our work is, why it is important that we do not draw attention to ourselves, but instead, we keep a low profile and obey the rules. You can mention what the repercussions might be, including court-martial, etc. but don't dwell on that. I want them to understand what is expected of them and for them to decide for themselves to do the right thing – rather than be forced to conform because of fear of reprisal. Captain Hogan, I want you to do a little investigating. But let me say up front, I'm not after names, I don't want this to turn into a witch hunt. Read the MP blotter, the duty officer log and our unit security regulation as well as 8th Army's policies on curfew and G2's advisories on the security of intelligence operations. Talk with the guard at the gate last night and to the duty officer and get their reactions. Let's get back together tomorrow evening at this time and go over what you've come up with. Also, please put all your findings and recommendation in a written memo. One last bit of advice. Please do not go looking for the culprit or culprits because if I know who is doing this, I'll be compelled to take disciplinary action against him or them." The next evening, with written reports in hand we appeared at the CO's office. Dom was waiting for us and invited us into his office. "The CO had to be elsewhere tonight," said Dom.

He stared at us for a couple of moments and then said:" The ole man is a wise old bird. He can also be a tough old bird. I'll see that he gets these reports." Hank and I never missed another curfew. The following week I was given an additional assignment: the unit's summary court-martial officer (comparable in civilian life to a justice of the peace).

Rumors were flying in February that someone would be going stateside in a month or two to conduct business on the East Coast. I knew about several of the matters to be discussed so I made a pitch to Dom that I should be the one to go. Several weeks later I was told that I would spend a week on business on the East Coast followed by a week's leave to spend with my family, including Easter Sunday. Wow! Cream corn and mashed potatoes! The waiting came and went, and finally, I got through a very long week on the East Coast and was home. Nothing compares to being home after a long absence. I remember a friend of Darlene's expressing pity for my boys because their daddy was gone so far away and for so long. My gang of five Korean urchins flashed through my mind, but I refrained from telling her how lucky my sons were. We spent Easter weekend in Fergus Falls, Minnesota where Al Bruns and Della and sons lived. We had a great time. On the way back to Hawarden on Easter Sunday morning our car threw a rod and gave up the ghost. I walked to a nearby farmhouse. The farmer knew a car salesman at the Chevrolet dealership in the next town who, when called, agreed to come out and take the whole family to the car lot. We ended up buying a hard-top Oldsmobile sports car with lots of whistles and bells. It had a lot of miles on it, but it looked good, seemed to run well, and the price was right. Anyway, I didn't have much choice. We had very little money, and we needed transportation now. As it turned out everything went well. Darlene had a car, although I don't believe she ever drove it outside of Hawarden. She and I agreed that when I got reassigned stateside, the car would be replaced pronto. I remembered my uncle Mark, "Fritz, things are never as bad as they seem." That certainly was true in this case.

Money was tight for us. I needed to get back to Travis AFB, California to catch a flight to Korea. A flight out of Sioux City would cost a lot, so I was told, that I should put an ad in the paper offering to share expenses with someone driving out there. It worked. In a day I had arranged a ride with a guy who claimed to be working for one of the leading race car drivers. We headed west and got as far as middle Nebraska when he ran out of gas. It was 8 o'clock at night. The countryside was flat, treeless and devoid of any evidence of mankind. I offered to walk to the next town, about 5 miles away, and get a can of gas. That was just the beginning of fiascoes. The guy turned out to be a first-class duffus, but somehow we made it to my destination, but too late to catch the flight I was scheduled to take. It would have been my first jet ride–and a lot faster than the 29 hours it took by super Connie.

The remainder of my tour in Korea was OK. The trip home at Easter had been a great morale booster, and I could see the end of the rainbow when I had returned to Korea. My duties were challenging and rewarding, I had a great circle of friends, and my next assignment was what I had hoped for. Life was good. At this point in my career as an artillery officer, I was up to speed: I had battery level experience, commanded a battery, had battalion staff experience, completed the artillery officer career course and had good ratings on my efficient reports. For the career officer, this is the time to get a graduate degree and pick up a specialty rating. After considerable research and thought I applied for the Foreign Area Officer Program. I had hoped to get Mexico. I was selected for the program but was offered either Brazil or the southern cone (Argentina, Chile, Uruguay, and Paraguay) as my area of concentration within the overall area of Latin America. I received orders to study Spanish at the Army Language School (now the Defense Language School) at the Presidio of Monterey in California and was told that, once there, I would be informed of what education, training, and utilization assignments were in store for me. Yes. Life was good.

On a beautiful day in October, Hank and I climbed the stairs to a "Super Connie." At the top of the steps, we turned around and gave Korea a smart salute. I have not been back since. When Hank and I arrived at Travis, we bid each other farewell for the time being. Although we have talked on the phone a few times since, I have not seen him. For that, I am truly sorry. Hank was a good friend.

Chapter 12
1962-1966 Foreign Area Officer Training

I met Major Smith who had recently finished an assignment in Army Personnel where his work entailed proposing the next assignment of junior officers based on the needs of the army, the quality of service recorded in the junior officer's official file and the junior officer's desire (in that order). I had not seriously considered a career in the military. I always assumed I would get out of the army soon, but opportunities in civilian life didn't seem very good at present. The responsibility of supporting a family rested heavily on me. During the nine years, I had been in the service; I had a great variety of educational experiences, assignments, responsibilities, and achievements. I was quite sure I would never be happy with a life that would be routine, repetitive or restrictive. I realized that I got a lot of satisfaction out of what I had been doing the past nine years. Major Smith and I worked in the intelligence branch and often worked on projects together and talked about our careers.

The army has 23 career fields called branches. To reach the grade of colonel, one serves approximately 25 years, through five ranks, much education, and many types of tasks and responsibilities. The Major pointed out that completing the Korean tour would be the ideal time for me to apply for a non-branch tour of duty that would include getting a master's degree. That sounded like pretty heady stuff to me since I was still enjoying the fact that I had finally gotten a college degree. With the guidance and counsel of the Major, I began the search through the army regulations for a program that would include graduate school.

I had not yet decided to stay in the army, but at least I was open to the idea. At the age of 30, I was looking for a career which would require completing graduate school and a utilization tour that would have some staying power, something I could specialize in and have a lifetime career. The first program I considered was Nuclear Physics Effects, but I soon laid that aside. It would take years of part-time study to complete the science and math courses that were prerequisites to apply for the program. Another program that peaked my interest was law school. I found a regulation covering a program which sent officers to law school leading to a degree in law. I had been classified as a pre-law student while at Creighton and dreamed of going to law school there if I could find the financial means to do so. I traced down the program only to discover that while it was kept on the books, it was not being funded and had not been for some years, nor was it foreseen to be activated anytime in the near future. At last, I found a field of study and a career program that seemed to fulfill all for which I was searching. It was the Foreign Area Officer Program (FAO).

In the aftermath of World War II, many studies were done on the conduct of operations in the various theaters of the war. Of interest were the ideas emanating from research on the China-Burma-India theater. General Stilwell, the commanding general in that theater, and his staff had found that operations were often adversely affected by the lack of officers with knowledge of the region; not only of the weather and terrain, but also of the people, their language, culture, customs, etc., and strongly recommended that the army equip some officers with thorough knowledge of selected regions of the world. During the 1950's a very successful and highly regarded program was developed to train a few officers to become experts on the Soviet Union. The program soon was expanded to include other areas of the world and was formalized as the Foreign Area Officer Training Program. In the 1960's a career field was established so that the Foreign Area Officer (FAO) would receive alternating tours of duty in his specialty, all the while performing alternating tours of duty within his branch (in my case artillery, and later, in military intelligence,) necessary to maintain branch qualifications for career development and promotions.

The training phase of the program spanned from three to five years. The first step was language training. For most trainees, this would mean six to twelve months study at the Defense Language Institute, Presidio of Monterey, California. Next would be a year of graduate study at a university with an approved area studies program. In the last step, the officer would spend twelve to eighteen months immersing himself in customs, culture, and language to develop an overall understanding of the area and its people. After completing the training, the FAO would be assigned to a position in his foreign area. By the 1960's the program had been expanded to include areas in Asia, Africa, and Latin America. I wrote a letter to Army Personnel requesting assignment to the foreign area officer program in southern South America. Much to my surprise, I received a call two weeks later from the colonel who was in charge of the program. He was very positive about the program and my credentials. He said I would begin the program as soon I fulfilled my tour of duty in South Korea and received orders to attend the army language school in Monterey California. Meanwhile, he would draw up a proposed schedule for my approval after which Army orders would be issued that would cover my entire training in the Foreign Area Officer Training Program.

1962-1963 Defense Language Institute

It was early October 1962, and I was with my family after serving 14 months in South Korea. Our spirits were high as I guided the aging Oldsmobile sports sedan off of highway 101, through a suburb and to a hilltop with a stunning scenic view. We sat for some time in awe and reverent silence. Mike was old enough to appreciate the scene, whereas Kip and Jeff seemed to sense the solemnity of the moment. Before us was Monterey Bay with the enchanting Fisherman's Warf. To the left was Cannery Row which John Steinbeck introduced to the world in his writings and to the right was the Navy's Postgraduate School. Below us was the United States Army's Presidio of Monterey, a monument to the history of Spanish America, and now the home of the Defense Language Institute. All this was framed by the colorful villages that housed memories from our residence here six years earlier. Filled with joy and excitement with the thought that we would be spending the next nine months living in Monterey, we retreated to the sand hills of Fort Ord where we would spend our first few days in the guest house.

The following day I expected to hear the same song I heard everywhere else I had been assigned: "there are no quarters on post available so you will receive a housing allowance to live off post." This time was different, and it was good news and bad news: "You will be assigned a brand new one-story four-bedroom duplex on Fort Ord" The good news meant that our financial struggle was coming to an end, or at least becoming more manageable. The bad news, of course, was that we would not be living in Monterey.

Commuting from Fort Ord to the Presidio turned out to be a pleasure since we four FAOs were on the same fixed schedule. My Oldsmobile was exchanged at a dealership near the school for a better used-car. So far in my life, I had purchased used cars, and I felt that I had done far better financially than my peers who had purchased new cars with what seemed to be enormous monthly car payments. As things turned out, I never bought a new car during my military career and never made a bad buy.

The study of a romance language is a lot easier than studying a Slavic one which I did several years earlier. And the motivation factor of knowing that one would be using what we had learned immediately after completing the course and for the rest of one's career added to the probability of studying much harder. Or at least one would think so. In my case, the pleasure of being back in the states and the delightful distractions in the Monterey area, and because some of us are not as disciplined as students as we should be, I made learning Spanish a tedious task. Fortunately, subsequent assignments would necessitate using the language, so one is immersed in learning without choosing to be. Eventually, I became somewhat proficient in speaking and thinking in Spanish as long as I used it frequently.

There were ten other Latin American FAO trainees at the school, all equally excited about the program. We soon had our own social group, including wives and children. This social grouping would expand over the years as we met others in the Latin American program and would engender a special bond between us.

The system of study in the Spanish Department was the same as that in the Slavic Departments with at least one exception. One class day no instructor showed up, so I conducted the class. I thought I was doing a noble act. The next day the department chairman took me to task. He was embarrassed and fearful that his position as chairman could be in jeopardy. He pleaded that if this should happen again notify his office. I agreed to do just that. Privately, I chuckled.

1963-1964 University of Oklahoma

Everyone was in positive spirits as we headed southeast from Monterey on our way to Norman, Oklahoma. Even Hansel, seemed content, curled up on his pad behind my seat. I was anxious to see how the window air conditioner would work. We had been forewarned that crossing the desert can be dangerous for travelers in August because of the heat. The air conditioner worked on the same principle as those that were in our apartment in El Paso (and worked efficiently); a dry air blowing through a wet filter. When the test came, the car window device proved to be totally useless.

We had spent some time planning the route we would take, to include a view of the Grand Canyon. I was determined to complete the 1800-mile trip in four days but to do so, we'd have to drive about ten hours each day. On the first day, we had an early start, and the boys went back to sleep for a while so by noon we had made good progress, and we stopped for lunch. I noted that the cool temperature at Monterey had changed to the 90's and we had not yet reached the desert. I was concerned. The crisis came about an hour later. We had seen only two cars in the past fifteen minutes, and the next town was thirty miles away. Darlene, who was in the third trimester of pregnancy was very uncomfortable. She told me she just couldn't take the heat and that we had to stop. Mike and Kip complained about being hot, and Jeff was crying. The dog was panting as fast as he could. The temperature was well over a hundred. I promised them that without fail we would stop at the next town and find a motel. All the while I was thinking: what if the car breaks down; what do we do? What if the next town does not have a motel?

The next town had a motel with rooms that were humid and warm but were a great relief from the car and the desert. The rest of the trip was enjoyable and uneventful. We arrived at Norman safely and eventually rented a house and got our household goods.

There were eight FAOs attending the University. Many of us attended the same classes together, especially those subjects that applied to all of Latin America. Socially, our families spent much time together. It was a most enjoyable year and very fruitful in that each of us supported one another in our quest for knowledge of Latin America.

The University of Oklahoma did not have a Department of Area Studies at that time, but it offered a graduate degree in area studies. A good geographer would tell you (and the University had some good geographers) that Area Studies is one of the divisions of the study of geography. A student seeking a degree in area studies would take courses in many departments; and in this case, be taught by the top professor(s) in each.

Dr. John W. Morris was a renowned geographer throughout Oklahoma and neighboring states. He published a number of texts on geography. He took us on several trips to define the word site. I was most appreciative of the assignment he gave in which two FAOs paired together to do a thorough site study of a nearby square mile and prepare for publication the research including photographs and sketches.

My faculty advisor was Dr. Harry E. Hoy from the geography department. Early on we established a good rapport, each of us identifying himself as a farm boy from Nebraska. He had a son working in Latin America whom I later met in Argentina. Dr. Hoy was very supportive of the FAOs and helpful in many ways.

Dr. Biddel of the Anthropology Department was the most demanding. To get three hours of credit for research in ethnology he required: successful completion of the undergraduate course in Anthropology of the South American Indians; passing the final exam in the basic course in Anthropology, and writing a critical review of each of three books of his selection. I thanked him for what I learned in a lot of hard study.

Our professor from the History Department was most popular. His specialty was Hispanic American history. He took a great interest in FAOs, was truly challenged by us (much to his liking), and took great effort in preparing every lecture in those classes which were made up mostly of FAOs and doctoral students. In true academic spirit, he socialized with us often over a brew or two as we gathered around him in some pub or café as he told of the things he had learned about Latin America and some of his personal experiences therein. A great teacher!

The Dean of the Graduate School, Dr. Arthur H. Doerr, probably played a big part in getting the army's foreign area officers program to use his school as one of its training sites. He was very familiar with all aspects of our program and most interested in knowing about our opinions and experiences at his university. He, a geographer, offered several graduate students and us a seminar in geography, in which we would cover a variety of subjects. It proved to be the seminal course in our program. I had been disappointed a year ago when I was told that I would do graduate studies at the University of Oklahoma. Assuming assignments to or near the Pentagon in future years, I intended to continue graduate studies leading to a Ph.D. I talked with Dean Doerr about this. He thought something could be worked out at the University of Oklahoma if I could get a leave of absence for one year. He said I had a good start on a dissertation with the paper I had written on the physical geography of the Gran Chaco. If I could do some field work while living in Argentina and work with a faculty advisor in the geography department, I should be able to satisfy most of the requirement of a dissertation. I was encouraged by his optimism but never found the time in the years that followed to do much about it.

When I told this story to a friend who was a retired non-commissioned officer in the US Air Force nearing the completion of the requirements for his Ph.D. in history, he overwhelmed me with arguments on why I should work toward the Ph.D. and begin tomorrow. He used his own experiences to prove his point. He had spent the past four years in intense study. He and his family lived in what was described as converted chicken coops – "cheap, cozy, and convenient–on campus property. He made enough money by researching for whoever would pay. And he showed me a letter he had received from an Air Force unit offering him a sizeable sum of money after he graduated to write the history of their unit. He was very convincing, but at the moment I had too many things on my platter to consider following his example.

The event most etched in my memory that year was the assassination of President John F Kennedy. I remember distinctly being in the library, researching the archives when someone announced it to the room. Over the years innumerable people have mentioned how they have clear recall of where they were and what they were doing when they heard the word. When I arrived home, Darlene met me at the door with a saddened face and asked if I had heard. We talked about what this might mean. This was a time of great danger during the cold war. The Cuban Missile Crisis of the past year had brought us to the brink of war. Was this an act of war? Will we be under a nuclear attack anytime soon? We learned that fear came to most everyone upon hearing that the President had been shot and died. Shortly thereafter, the assassin Lee Harvey Oswald was captured and had ties to the Soviet Union, the leading country of the communist world and our arch enemy. Soon, Oswald was killed by Jack Ruby. Was that further evidence of a plot to kill the assassin before he could reveal who was behind the killing of the President?

Command and General Staff College

The Command and General Staff College at Ft Leavenworth, Kansas is one of the best professional education institutes in the Army. For the officer selected to attend it means that he has demonstrated the potential for command of battalion-sized units and the ability to work on high-level staffs to include those at the Pentagon. The curriculum is broader and more academic than prior military training.

Money was scarce, and we expected some extraordinary expenses going to Argentina, so we agreed to get by as cheaply as we could in housing for the next five months. We ended up renting an old house, which was furnished but had two major drawbacks. The landlord, a ninety-six years old gentleman would continue to live in one room of the house and have the right to use an adjoining bathroom. Secondly, the laundry was in the basement, which could be reached by opening the trap door in the dining room and descending a rickety set of stairs to a dank, earthen cellar. After two weeks of occupancy, we realized that we had gone a bit too far on the cheap but made do for the five months at Leavenworth.

When I reported for duty at the school I met an Argentine lieutenant colonel who would be attending the same course as I. We became good friends, were table-mates in the classroom, and he and his large family were at our house frequently. They felt very much at home there since the furnishings were very old-fashioned. Heavy, dark, European furniture seemed to be the favored furnishings in the homes of most of the Argentine military families that we visited once we lived in Argentina.

Fifteen Months in Argentina

The message we had received from my sponsor, the senior FAO in Argentina, was explicit, "if you get delayed, do not message the Embassy; call us direct." If someone else did what I did, I would call him a real dufus. On Friday, I wired the embassy to inform my sponsor that we would be a day late—Sunday, not Saturday. En route to Miami, we had car trouble and a dog bite, which involved the police, veterinarian, quarantine, and communication lines from them to me in case the dog was rabid.

While the car was being worked on, the family and I, with Hänsel our Dachshund in tow, decided to enjoy this beautiful, colorful, warm and sunny semi-tropical clime by walking down the middle of the street in an upscale residential neighborhood, talking about the Midwest weather and how lucky we were to be here. Suddenly a baleful, barking terrier came tearing from behind a house and headed for our Hänsel who, being a Dachshund, is stretched close to the ground, which means he has to look up to most other dogs, hence his Napoleonic personality. He was stubborn, obstinate, pigheaded, and aggressive. I hurriedly gathered Hänsel in my arms as the terrier arrived and with open jaws chomped hard on my stomach. The befuddled owner of the terrier arrived shortly. He was a gentleman of the first order, and several weeks later informed me through the Embassy that the veterinarian had released the dog from quarantine. It was not rabid.

We had driven our car from Kansas to the port in New Orleans for onward shipment to Argentina. A rental car carried us to Miami, where we boarded a flight for Buenos Aires. It was a long flight and for me a "white knuckles" flight. I had never been fearful of flying, but having my family aboard aroused my sense of responsibility for their safety while feeling unable to protect them—hence stress!

When we arrived at Ezeiza International Airport in Buenos Aires, no one was there to meet us. I called my sponsor (which is no small feat when one first arrives in an unfamiliar foreign country) and received an aloof response that he would come out to pick us up as soon as he could get there—" an hour at least." When he arrived, I apologized for our late arrival, "but I had wired." He reminded me that he had emphatically stated in his welcoming letter that if I was delayed, I must contact him directly. The embassy communication center does not read FAO messages but is kind enough to pass any communications directed to the military attaché office. Monday morning the attaché will learn and pass on to my sponsor the fact that I will not be arriving yesterday. He went on to say that the arrival of a new FAO and family is big news to the five FAOs in the country. They all had gathered at the airport on Saturday to give us a grand welcoming, and he and his wife had a reception party set up for that evening. In telling me all this, he seemed to gain some therapeutic benefit for he began to be friendly and less distant. We arrived at our destination, a three bedroom, fully furnished house in an upscale neighborhood of Buenos Aires. He had made arrangements with some New Zealand friends who had gone home for a month's holiday to let us use their place until we found one of our own. He said he would be back in two hours to take us to his place where his wife was organizing a gathering to welcome us properly. There was the perfect host, the finest example of what a sponsor should do; and here was the dolt. That evening at the reception, which was a gala affair, we were well received, and all was forgiven, even to the point that "this was all part of an FAO's learning" which was followed by tales of goofs by those present.

After a couple of days getting settled and meeting people, my sponsor escorted me via the subway to the embassy where I met the warrant officer who would help me extract my automobile from customs and get it licensed and registered for use in Argentina. I prepared as he had instructed: two cartons of cigarettes and twenty-peso notes. With papers in hand, we made six stops. At each stop, our papers were endorsed, and we left cigarettes or pesos on the desk.

A realtor helped us find a house in two days. The two-story house was located in a quiet neighborhood of middle-class government employees. The backyard was enclosed by a 6-foot wall. We all got a laugh when we were examining behind the house, and Hansel walked to a long stairway leading to a 3rd-floor attic. He slowly looked up the steps to the top, gave a gruff noise and slowly walked away. In the middle of the backyard was a shipping crate which we had asked the shippers of our household goods to leave. The empty container became a Playhouse much to the joy of the children.

Early one morning while we were still in bed, Hänsel gave a few barks. I went to the front window and saw below two men loading our tv set in their truck and driving away. That morning everyone in the family was disturbed by the intruders, but we all took satisfaction in knowing that the tv set was broken and not worth fixing.

One day as I arrived home from school, Kip ran up to me and said that Jeff had been hit by a car. I was shocked with fear whereupon Jeff came walking around the corner of the house and greeted me. Mike told me the whole story of how a car had screeched to a halt just as Jeff stepped off the curb and was knocked down but not hurt. All three boys learned a lesson.

There came a day when Jeff decided he did not want to go to school (kindergarten). His mother told him he could stay home if that was what he wanted to do. Darlene told me that Jeff would soon find that staying home would be too boring for him. Three days later he readied himself with his brothers and went to school with them then and after that without comment.

A big surprise for Darlene and me the first month we lived in Argentina was our financial status. In a bank near the US Embassy was an exchange where the US dollar was worth more in pesos then elsewhere. Also, our rent cost less if we paid in dollars. We were surprised that we could go to a luxury restaurant on Corrientes Street in downtown Buenos Aires and have a scrumptious dinner of steak and fine wine for only $3. For the first time in our married life, we did not have to struggle each month to make ends meet.

The FAO officer requires a lot of travel and exploration to learn the culture and customs of the people of his area. I found that family members on occasion could go with me and have fun while I did my thing and not be disturbed. Places that we frequented were Buenos Aires, Bariloche, Cordoba, and Rosario. Darlene and I explored Uruguay and the Argentina Providences of Corrientes and Entre Rios without the children, and we both learned a lot about local customs

Paul Coughlin, a fellow FAO and I put together a long itinerary from Puerto Montt in Chile, through Valparaiso and Santiago to the city of Mendoza in Argentina. We hired a taxi to see some of the city which is world famous for its wine industry. As luck would have it, the taxi driver was a son of the family of one of the largest wineries in Mendoza. Once he found out that we were from the United States doing some studying his country, he insisted that we go home with him to meet his family and have lunch. The father and mother took a liking to us and arranged for his son to spend the day showing us the features of their winery and some interesting parts of Mendoza. From Mendosa, we went north to Iquique and on to Bolivia and Peru for a few days of exploration and then back to Buenos Aires filled with much new knowledge. Meanwhile, two other FAOs explored deep into dry and sparsely inhabited Patagonia en route to Tierra del Fuego. After several hours their car broke down, they ran out of water, and they had no means of communication. They were stranded for almost 5 hours of worry when along came a rancher in a pickup with several cans of gas and the know-how to get their car operating again.

Another FAO had decided to fly to Tierra del Fuego and spent several days exploring. On the day he chose to fly back to Buenos Aires the sky was cloudy. They took off up a deep, straight valley and into the clouds when the plane's engine started to sputter. The pilot made a 180degree change in direction and the plane dove with a screeching sound. Suddenly they were out of the clouds and headed straight down the valley to the airport with a smooth landing. Our friend said that he did some real praying that day. None of us challenged the tales, but each of us agreed that there are both lucky and unlucky explorers.

When I found out that my next assignment would be in Panama, I caught a space-available flight on the military aircraft that served US embassies. After two days of discussions with fellow officers at United States Army Southern Command and Southern Command HQ, I flew to Colombia to join several FAOs to explore from Bogota to Cali where I might get a flight to Ecuador. No flights were available, so I accepted an offer from a businessman who needed to get to Ecuador that night that we would share the cost of a taxi. An hour later we were well into the mountains where the road was very narrow, and the cliffs were very steep. Suddenly the lights of the car went out, and the driver continued to drive. I called the driver to stop. The lights went on, so I was quiet. A few minutes later the lights went out again, and this time I demanded that we stop. It was then that I saw that the driver was holding two electric wires together, and apparently, the driver let the wires separate when they got too hot. He told me that keeping the lights on all the time was very expensive. I told him the amount I would add to our fare if he left the lights on until we arrived in Quito. He agreed and was good to his word. When we arrived in Quito, the businessman insisted that they would drop me off first at my hotel and I bid them farewell. Early the next morning the businessman came to my room and asked if he could talk a little business. I saw no reason not to invite him in. He knew from our talks the previous night that I lived in Buenos Aires. He readily admitted to me that he was a jewelry smuggler and threw four bags of jewelry on my bed. He said that he joins a traveler such as I whenever he would leave Colombia to avoid suspicion by law enforcers. He offered me a piece of valuable jewelry for free. This sounded to me like it could be a setup, so I didn't touch any of the jewels. I told him I had a good job which I intended to keep and I had an appointment coming up very soon, and I escorted him to the door. My appointment was to buy a ticket on the train that goes from Quito at an altitude of 2850 meters to sea level at Guayaquil while passing through five climate zones. Most any geographer knows of this place and yearns to make that trip. The next day I returned to Buenos Aires.

The year I spent at the Escuela Superior de Guerra (Superior School of War) was a grand experience. The classes were taught in Spanish, and so I struggled in class at first, but as time went on, I could communicate in Spanish fairly well. My classmates were professional, well-educated and congenial, as was our instructor, an Argentine lieutenant colonel. The nature of our studies was very similar to that of the United States Army except that

Argentine military officers, in their training studied social, political, and economic subjects and the military history of their country. I found that while the military in the United States are apart from their country's society and spend their time in training and other military activities, the Argentine army is part of society and often serves their country in other labor. The same can be said of neighboring countries. I am indebted to my classmates for the many hours we spent together in travels and at activities that helped me become an FAO. And to answer your often-asked question – I do not know why we are called FAOs ('fey oh' means ugly in Spanish).

Chapter 13
1966 - 1967
Panama Canal Zone

The children looked forward with excitement to living on the military post where they could make a lot of new friends. They could watch television programs in English, although it would be the Armed Forces Radio and Television Service (AFRTS), broadcasting reruns of stateside programs a few hours a day. They had not shown much sign of suffering cultural shock when we first lived in Argentina, but then one never knows what goes on in the minds of children. I do know that they heartily accepted the culture of the Canal Zone, even though initially school was a disappointment for Mike and Kip. I enrolled them in the Catholic school in Balboa feeling obligated to do so as a Catholic and believing that they would get a better education and more discipline there. By the summer, we found that the Canal Zone public school system was far superior by almost any comparison and after that, not only in the Canal Zone but everywhere else we lived, my children attended public schools.

I looked forward to getting back into the United States Army system and for the family to be back into the United States way of life. The Argentine experience, both professionally and personally, was rewarding, but there is nothing better than living and working in one's own culture.

Our first residence was temporary, furnished, without air conditioning, and old quarters in Cocoli, across the bridge and several miles from Fort Amador. Cocoli was a residential community of more than 500 various-sized apartments, built in 1940 and acquired by the United States Army in 1964 to meet their rising housing needs. We lived there for a few weeks until the completion of duplexes at Fort Amador, home of the USARSO Headquarters. We learned two things quickly when we moved into one of the furnished apartments with maid service. When we moved in, we rearranged the furniture to our liking. The next day when we returned to the apartment after the maid had left, we found that the furniture had been put back in the exact arrangement that existed when we first came. Darlene was furious, especially about our dresser and the living room. Darlene spoke a little Spanish, and the maids spoke only Spanish (or so we believed). Darlene, standing by the dresser slapped the top of the dresser and said: "Este!" The maid was standing four feet from the dresser and giving Darlene her undivided attention. "Aqui!" said Darlene while pointing to the floor. She then repeated the two-word conversation with emphasis and then asked: "Comprende?" The maid, with eyes wide open, responded: "Si, Senora." A similar scenario was carried out in front of the living room couch. After that, we could rely on the fact that furniture would remain as we wished it. However, several days later we read in the "Welcome" packet in our room the following: "please do not rearrange the furniture if your occupancy is temporary." The other thing we learned was that Cocoli had a clubhouse, as did most of the other residential areas in the Canal Zone. The clubhouse was a gathering place for all ages and extensively used by all of us. The day finally came when we moved into our duplex near the 16th hole of the golf course, our household goods arrived, and we were finally settled in our new home.

Socially, we had from day one a close circle of friends from FAO training over the past three and a half years. When our daughter Amy was born, she had an "RH" factor conflict, so a blood transfusion was necessary. As I sat in the observation room awaiting the procedure, Maj. Pete Britnall, an FAO friend, walked in and took a seat. We chatted a bit, and then I asked Pete what brought him to the hospital. He said that there was an emergency call on AFRTS for someone of his blood type to report immediately to the hospital. With a smile, he said: "When I found out it was for your Amy, I came immediately." In the days that followed, Amy became popular among our friends, and it was frequently stated that she had Britnall blood. At one point, it was even suggested (humorously of course) that we should give Amy to the Britnalls since we had four older children and they had none. We feigned shock at the suggestion. We all rejoiced when they became the parents of a beautiful daughter of their own.

The Canal Zone in Panama, the location of the United States Southern Command Headquarters, had much of the stateside culture. The Southern Command (SOUTHCOM), is one of the area-commands of United States military worldwide. It contains the United States Armed Forces in Latin America. Its HDQRS staff is made up of personnel from each of the armed services and is referred to as a joint command. Subordinate to the joint command are commands of each of the armed services (Army, Navy, Marine and Air Force). The United States Army Southern Command (USARSO) Headquarters was located at Fort Amador, a small post on a small peninsula bordering the entrance to the Panama Canal on the Pacific side. In March of 1966, I was assigned there. Family life at Fort Amador was ideal. There were less than 100 families, most of which included children. Everyone knew everyone else, and most parents extended their paternal care to all the kids on the peninsula. It was a living example of "It takes a village to raise a child."

I regret that I didn't spend more time with my children, especially when they were young. My son, Mike, and Jim Lear's son were good friends and played golf after school most days. Mike invited me sometimes to join them. I declined since I was too busy, and they played during duty hours. I could have just as easily convinced my boss to allow me two hours off Wednesdays and make up the time as needed. The tee off to the first hole was a stone's throw from my office. It should be noted that Mike was gaining popularity among the golfers for his rapid development as a remarkably good golfer without having had any formal training.

The Headquarters of the 470th Military Intelligence Group was a five-minute walk from my office. I had the pleasure of working with some of the officers and NCOs in that organization. Darlene and I were frequently invited to social gatherings at the organization. We were especially fond of Polly and Jim Bosch and Mary and Henry Richarde of the 470th. I often thought that if I ever reached the rank of colonel, commanding the 470th would be my goal. Which reminds me of another big want I developed.

I was temporarily assigned to the annual worldwide command-and-control exercise, testing the Army's readiness. I would be an action officer on USARSO's ad hoc committee and would be briefing the commanding general and his staff twice a day. This turned out to be an absorbing exercise but USARSO, given its size, had a very small role to play. I thought how thrilling it must be to participate in this exercise at the Army command center in the Pentagon.

In March of 1966, I was assigned to the G2 (intelligence) staff, headed by Colonel John O Woods. When I reported in, he informed me that I had originally been assigned to the 470th military intelligence group, but they had an overage of officers of my grade (Major), so I was assigned to G2 (intelligence staff).

Although there was no vacancy there, the officer in charge of the Security Division would be leaving in about two months, and I would get a permanent position then.

What a disappointment! I visited the intelligence (J2) staff at Southcom HDQRTS the next week to see if I could be assigned a position there. Several of my colleagues (foreign area officers) with whom I had served previously might put in a good word for me. No luck. All the slots for foreign area specialists were filled. Over the next three weeks, while holding a meaningless "make work" job in Security Division, I made an exerted effort to find an assignment in which I could use my newly gained expertise on Latin America. It appeared that I was not going to get a utilization tour out of this assignment since all the Army officer positions designated to be filled by foreign area specialists were in fact filled. I had just finished nearly four years of study, and I was determined to use it. Also, the Army is under pressure to justify the cost of university study by assigning the officer, as soon as possible after the study, to a position designated by the Department of Army as requiring the subject education. It is also to the officer's best interest to serve that utilization tour as soon as possible so that he is available after that for other career-enhancement assignments.

The search for a challenging assignment was successful, or so I thought when I was contacted by a Colonel who had been told by several of my colleagues that I was just the type of officer he was looking for. He was working for a Washington DC-based special studies group entitled Interoceanic Sea Level Canal Study Group. Since the Panama Canal (opened in 1914) was too small to accommodate the largest military and civilian ships (aircraft carriers, tankers, and container ships), a commission was set up to study the feasibility of building a large, sea-level canal. The

Colonel was looking for an officer in the grade of major to be his assistant for the time being and ultimately to be in charge of establishing a support base at one of the five proposed canal sites for the scientists and experts who would be evaluating the site. After a lengthy conversation and lunch, the Colonel decided that I was well suited for the job. He talked to the commanding general of USARSO the next week to see if I could be reassigned to his organization. I was excited about the prospect of being part of such a noteworthy project and envisioned that this could lead to a lifelong career. It was not to be. Two weeks later Colonel Woods called me into his office and with a grin told me that I was not going anywhere. He assigned me Chief of the Security Division in G2. In my view, it was the best job in G2, but unfortunately, it was not a "utilization" tour.

As for the sea level canal project, I learned later that five sites, from Mexico to Colombia, were considered for construction of an Atlantic-Pacific sea-level canal. The United States Atomic Energy Commission (AEC), which later became the Department of Energy, had become very interested in the idea of building a canal in Mexico. AEC had established the Plowshare Program in 1958 to explore the possible use of nuclear explosives for industrial applications. A canal between the oceans in Mexico would be by far their biggest and most challenging use of "nukes" to date. AEC was fully involved with the Atlantic–Pacific inter-oceanic canal study commission since its inception in 1965. AEC conducted some nuclear tests in Nevada in the 1960s using nuclear devices as small as 0.5 kilograms. But early in the 1970s, the commission recommended that a sea-level canal at that time was not economically justified, environmentally unsafe and local governments and peoples of the region would not accept the risk of radiation fallout and the highly unpopular idea of nuclear explosions in their world. And so, I took solace in the knowledge that my dream of being part of building a sea-level canal between the oceans was not to be, even if I had been released by USARSO.

As Chief of Security Division, I had my first experience in supervising civil servants, which turned out to be very instructive for me, and destructive (in their minds at least) for them. In retrospect, it was obvious that some people were not prepared for my style of supervision. Years earlier, when I was working in the Pentagon, I noted that some of the senior officers had a disdainful attitude toward some civilians, holding that they were far less dedicated than military officers and therefore less productive and consequently less worthy. There were four civilians on my staff: a retired Army major, a somewhat nondescript career security specialist, Ted, a very capable counterintelligence expert with extensive World War II experience as a German employed by the Allied forces, and Margaret, a mature, delightful and capable secretary/administrator.

The retired Army major conducted himself as though his US Army retiree status took priority over his US Army employee status. Generally, an employee is not free to run errands and come and go as he wishes, and certainly not when a growing backlog of his work is taking place. His job description sounded substantial and appropriate, but his actual work was, by his own design, far less productive than I thought it should be. The job entailed assembling and summarizing investigative files that would be submitted for adjudication. I prepared several files myself to see how long it should take. I found that even though I had little experience in this work, I could prepare a file in two or three hours whereas the retired major would spend a day or more preparing a file. A backlog had built up to the point where I either had to convince the man to buckle down and do his job, or I would have to approach Colonel Woods with a request for one or two additional analysts to take care of the buildup. After a month of close supervision on my part, mostly trying to keep the retired major at his desk and working, he decided to quit his job and go back to the states. Before he left, he called me outside for a private chat, whereupon he gave me his idea of what kind of boss and person I was and assured me that someday he would even the score with me.

The nondescript analyst was a pleasant and likable person but very methodical, lacking in imagination, attention to detail and enthusiasm. He was a perfect example of what many criticizing citizens believe the typical government worker is like. When it came time for his annual evaluation, I showed him what I had written. He did not indicate in any way that he was fazed by low evaluations. A week after I had submitted the report a staff member in the civilian personnel office arranged a meeting with me. She pointed out that I could not give him such a low rating without first having gone through a lengthy process of consultation, which had to be duly documented. At the time of this conversation, I knew that I would be leaving for duty in Vietnam in a few months. Colonel Woods and his deputy, Lieutenant Colonel Jim Lear were fully aware of what I was doing and were not opposed to it. So, I began this sequence of actions that were required by the civilian personnel office. By the time I departed the Canal Zone, the subject was on his way out provided that the process I had set up, with the advice and assistance of the civilian personnel office, was being followed. If they did, the subject would be gone in about 30 days. Even as I left Panama he did not seem bothered by all this, nor did he seem resentful toward me. I was truly sorry for his family, although I knew he had other income.

While I was on leave in Albuquerque, I was contacted by Jim Lear of the USARSO G2 office. They were going ahead with removing the subject but wanted to take a different course than the one I had set up. To do that they needed some written information and some forms prepared by me. I responded that, as I had explained before I left, if they followed up on what I had outlined, the subject would be gone in less than 30 days. Since they are changing procedures, and since I was no longer in their command, they would have to do without my involvement. Several years later I was in the Canal Zone and was told that the subject was still employed in the security division of G2, USARSO. I was happy for him. I assumed that he proved to be a worthy employee.

There are two ways for a government employee to get promoted: 1) get transferred to a position calling for a higher pay grade, or 2) expand his present job so that upon evaluation, it merits a higher pay grade. Ted's efforts were truly a class act. I cannot say enough good about the competence, dedication, and productivity of Ted. Also, he and I had an excellent working relationship, except for the fact that he was very patronizing. Ted handled the classified counterintelligence staff work for the command. He had previously been promoted once or twice in his present job. The office space he had for his section was obviously inadequate for his needs. Recently he had acquired an enlisted man, to relieve him of some of the filing work that continued to grow. His assistant, Margaret, had been the secretary for the division until a year or two ago when her job description was changed to that of assistant section chief with additional duties of secretarial work for both the section and the division. In keeping with the increased work and responsibility, she was promoted. I assumed Ted had a part to play in all that. Margaret was a model employee: dedicated, capable, pleasant, and industrious. She also was an excellent baker, evidenced by the goodies she frequently brought to the office for all of us to share. She was to retire within a year and was a real loss when the day came. And, finally, beginning with the second month that I was chief, Ted hinted to me that he was badly in need of more file cabinets and space. I had noticed, when I first came to the division, that Ted seemed to have far more work and responsibility than anyone else, and yet he had little if any more space than others.

After working with Ted for several months, I saw what he was doing–something known as "empire building"' in bureaucratic lingo. I knew that his pay grade was without a doubt as high as the job would support. Also, the section next to Ted's was badly in need of more space. The whole of G2 staff as well as the rest of the USARSO HDQRS were the sole occupants of the building, which was very crowded. I decided to beat Ted to the punch before he could give me a long, well-documented argument of why he must have more space. That, of course, would be the first step in constructing a case of why his job should be evaluated up to the point where a promotion for him would be justified. By now I had observed that Ted was a pack rat and that some of the file cabinets were filled to the brim with needless documents. I told Ted that, regrettably, several of his file cabinets would have to be vacated because I needed the cabinets and space for the neighboring section. Ted made some attempts to discuss the matter, so I finally told him that it was not negotiable. He countered with the fact that much of what was in the files were classified and practically all the files were either needed, or he is required by Army regulations or policy to keep on file. At this point, I gave him an ultimatum; if he can't do it, I along with Major Dyson of our division, who had the necessary security clearances and knowledge of applicable regulations and policies, would do it for him. Either way, all the extraneous documents would be destroyed, and the emptied file cabinets would be transferred to the adjoining section within 30 days.

Ted was sullen and pouted for several weeks. To make matters worse, he found out that Margaret was retiring and returning stateside in a couple of months; furthermore, his enlisted man was being reassigned, and no replacement was available for months. His world was crumbling, his dream of promotion was squashed, and there was nothing he could do about it. For the eight months that I remained in the division, Ted was professional in every respect, but I could see that his heart was not in his work as before. Also, our relationship while reasonably good was never as it once was, and the patronizing had ceased. But things were not all negative, and I did manage to ingratiate myself with Ted and his wife by designing and developing a way of framing molas. The mola is an art form consisting of multiple layers of colored cloths using a reverse appliqué technique wherein designs are formed by cutting out shapes using various depths of the layers. The designs in the mola were originated in the ancient body painting of the Kuna Indians of the San Blas islands of Panama. The finely sewn molas are handmade by the Kuna women and are very popular tourist purchases. Ted's wife operated a souvenir shop in Panama City and was having much success in selling framed molas, or so I was told.

In December 1967, I received orders of assignment to Vietnam effective eight February 1968 to seven February 1969. The day we left Panama a few friends gathered to bid farewell. They chuckled when they saw that Transportation had sent a bus (for most families it would be a sedan) to haul the seven Burbachs and their luggage to the airport. The children were excited to be going stateside. Darlene had chosen Albuquerque to be home for the next year because we liked the city and its location. Many military families lived there; it had a large military base, military hospital, commissary, and PX. I took several weeks leave to help get the family settled. We were fortunate to find a desirable house in a friendly neighborhood. The children could walk to school. The neighbors next door had a large family and quickly became friends. Some neighbors assured me that they would take good care of the Burbachs while I was away.

On the Beach at Fort Amador. "Help a person,"
Amy, 4, is in front of me.

Chapter 14
1968 - 1969 Vietnam

The flight from San Francisco to Saigon in early 1968 began with a reluctance, endured with boredom and foreboding, and ended with a thrill. Landing in a hot combat zone is different from the norm. To avoid possible enemy ground fire, the plane's final approach is high, then a quick drop to the edge of the runway, and heavy braking after touch down. At the far end of the runway, there was fighting. A jolly green giant (C130 military transport aircraft with machine gun blazing from the open side door) was doing battle with a force on the ground.

At the terminal, we quickly transferred to waiting buses and under a heavily armed escort reached our destination, a barracks compound where we spent the night. A discomforting factor was lack of personal weapons in what seemed to be a "hot zone."

The following morning, again under heavily armed escort, we were transported to Koelper Compound for in-processing and onward movement to our assigned units. By nightfall, we were informed that because the Viet Cong (VC) had infiltrated the area of our planned route, we would spend the night at Koelper. Five days later the route had been cleared, and our convoy could proceed. During those days our supply line had been severed, so our eating facility got out the powdered eggs, powdered milk, spam and stale crackers. The field rations (K, C, and others) were, for the first time for many of us, preferred over the chow hall servings. Not exactly a "war is hell" experience but certainly a "welcome to Vietnam" jolt of the real world about us.

The day finally came when we left Koelper for our assigned unit. Mine was Headquarters Military Assistance Command Vietnam (MACV). During the past few days, I had been mulling over preferred assignments. Being a cog in the wheel of a large staff does not sound like justification for being separated from family for a year and living in a war zone. I resolved to find a job where I could put to use my years of training and experience, preferably command of an intelligence unit or the intelligence officer on a division staff. As soon as I got out of Koelper I would start making some calls, find out what is available and how to go about getting what I wanted. Surely, I knew enough people in positions to help me. But first I would have to report to MACV.

"Gentlemen, welcome to Vietnam! And welcome to MACV! And a special welcome to the MACV staff where you will be for the next 12 months! Each of you was specifically selected for duty on the staff. I tell you this up front to warn you that most of us on the staff prefer to be someplace else, but we are not. We, as a group, are unsympathetic to anyone trying to get out of this assignment since we were not able to do so for ourselves. Furthermore, if you try, expect to fail. Late in your tour, you will be given ample opportunity to seek employment elsewhere in the command and be given the opportunity to extend your stay to take up a new assignment. Now that we understand each other let's get on with the orientation briefing. WELCOME TO VIETNAM!" As the briefing officer droned on, I accepted my fate and tried to give him my undivided attention.

Later that day I was informed that in a day or two I would be interviewed for assignment to the briefing team. If I were not selected for that, I would be an intelligence analyst, staying abreast of intelligence in one of the four combat zones in Vietnam. And then Jim Bosch called me. Jim and I had worked together in the Canal Zone. He was with the 470th when I was in G2 USARSO. Jim was anxious to talk about assignments. He was nearing the end of his tour and had lined up his next assignment, but it had one glitch, he needed to be there several weeks before his tour ended in Nam. His boss had assured him that he would sign off on a request for early release if Jim could find a suitable replacement. His boss was Bill Exley (from my Pentagon days). Bill was chief of Field Activities Branch, Intelligence Operations Division of J2 MACV. This was a win-win situation all the way around. Jim got his early release, Bill got an acceptable replacement for Jim, and I got a challenging job.

The quality and dedication of the people in my section were commendable. The core of the staff consisted of three officers. The Army officer was the most junior, in excellent physical condition, good-natured, industrious, gutsy, and had a lot of intelligence operations experience of which he spoke little. The Air Force officer was the most senior. He was mature, calm, cool, very intelligent and an excellent conversationalist. He also was very closed mouth about his previous assignments. The Naval officer, of the naval reserve, was a senior civil servant with the US Agency for International Development (USAID) in Thailand and had volunteered for active duty for one year of military service in Vietnam. His appearance and name suggested that he was of Irish descent. He was a graduate of Harvard University and struck me as an idealist rather than a realist. He and I had a somewhat slow-developing friendship because he had confided in me that after this assignment he intended to volunteer his services to the IRA in Ireland. Over the next few weeks, after frequent discussions about the situation in Northern Ireland, cultural proclivities and

England's presence in Ireland, it finally dawned on me that this was a guy who really loved the Socratic method of discourse and was no more likely to join the IRA than I was. In subsequent weeks, we enjoyed many debates on subjects from classical Latin writers, to philosophy, to the social geography of the world. Early on I knew that the year in Vietnam was going to have some redeeming values, that is, working with these three. The function of my section was to develop and supervise unconventional intelligence collection methods and means. It was purely a staff job, with some travel to outlying combat units.

Everyone highly regarded Colonel Exley and we worked well together. He was a very professional intelligence officer and a good friend. His superior was our division chief who took a great interest in the activities of Field Activities Branch. We privately dubbed him Uncle Lloyd in a fond but humorous way. He had the demeanor of a Dutch uncle while coming up with a series of ideas for our consideration. Admittedly, some of his ideas were sane and sound, but most were really off the wall. He suffered from a lack of knowledge of intelligence operations but with a huge appreciation of the value of good intelligence. His deputy was a Marine Colonel who was very supportive in every way and had a great grasp of all aspects of both military and intelligence operations. He also was a great morale builder. From time to time he invited several of us to dine with him at a first-class French restaurant in Saigon. He had a pleasant personality, and he was always "up" (happy and active) even though he had had a great disappointment en route to Vietnam. He was notified that his orders were changed, from getting a command slot (which could likely lead to promotion to brigadier general) to MACV staff (which would lead to nowhere). On our last dinner with him, before he rotated stateside, he commented on how much the French restaurant and our association meant to him. He tried to get a copy of the restaurant's menu as a souvenir, but management refused to part with one.

When the Marine Colonel arrived home, he found in his mail the menu he sought. We perpetrators of the crime of theft had agreed that we are ultimate "conflict resolvers" bringing people together through common interests. In this case, we brought together a restaurateur and a connoisseur using a menu. We had a final dinner at the French restaurant, surreptitiously acquired a menu, and elected the most junior officer among us as the "couth" officer. His task was to place in the hands of the restaurant manager after the rest of us had left the building, an envelope containing a monetary sum believed to be more than enough to cover the cost of printing a menu and explained that our friend the Marine colonel had absconded with a menu. The Saigon environment as a combat zone had to be experienced to be understood. Stress needs divergence.

The economics of war is baffling! About once a month several officers from the finance and accounting office and I had dinner together in a dining room in a two-story hotel that was leased by the United States Army to house military personnel. According to my dinner mates, the lease would be sufficient for the owner to pay off the mortgage on the hotel within five years. Furthermore, the military had made it possible for him to get the financing to build this building since he was leasing to the US another hotel near the headquarters, which he had been able to buy with the lease payments over the previous couple of years. One might say that he was a very shrewd and successful businessman, but that may not be true for him after the communist government of North Vietnam took over in 1975.

The MACV HDQRS was housed in a one story, prefab building. It was clean, air-conditioned, quiet, and spacious. It was not designed to withstand much of anything. The only time I recall that the building was attacked was when an incoming rocket-propelled grenade lodged in the ceiling. Fortunately, it was a dude. The only time other ammunition hit our building was when a 45-mm round was fired into the ceiling accidentally by a Major, who was cleaning his weapon at his desk. The damage to the building was minimal. The Major had to pay for the repairs and suffer some embarrassment.

Within the enclosed areas around the building were several bunkers, which were walk-in structures with walls of sandbags and a reinforced roof. One evening when I was hurrying to a bunker, which was about 100 yards away, in response to an attack alarm, a shell exploded some distance away. In a few seconds, a second shell exploded, and it was a bit louder than the first one. Two more spaced explosions followed, and each was louder than the preceding one. I thought I heard some zingers with the last explosion so I jumped into a deep, muddy ditch and waited. Nothing happened for a minute or two, so I made a mad dash for the bunker. A laughing group in the bunker welcomed me in. Reportedly, I was "as white as a sheet."

The Tet Offensive was the largest military operation of the Vietnam War. It began January 30, 1968 when the Viet Cong (a communist-led guerrilla force in South Vietnam that fought its government and was supported by North Vietnam) and the North Vietnamese Army (NVA) surprised the South Vietnamese Army (ARVN) and United States Forces and their allies, with an all-out attack throughout South Vietnam. Neither MACV nor the folks in Washington could anticipate the political and psychological effect that the offensive would have on the leadership and the population of the United States. The leaders in North Vietnam and the Viet Cong saw that the people in the United States were shocked, convinced that they had been misled by our leaders who had assured them that we were winning this expensive war. It was obvious that the South Vietnamese Army and the United States had been caught by surprise by a very strong enemy. The North Vietnam leaders began to propagandize a proclaimed victory with much success, even though their forces had been devastated. The South Vietnam Army, as well as the US military assistance command forces and allies, were taken by surprise, due in large part to lack of good intelligence. Most of the 100 attacks on key sites and cities throughout South Vietnam were contained within hours. Two key targets were the national radio station, from which the communists hoped to win over the South Vietnamese people but never reached the microphone; and the United States Embassy where the attack began at 3 am and was over at 9 am. That was not the way the outside world received it. For the first-time live television brought the gruesome mess of war into the living rooms, bars, and theaters of millions of Americans. At that time, I was still with my family in Albuquerque, and I watched some of the bloody events on tv but did not share it with my children.

It is estimated that approximately 40,000 communist soldiers were killed and many more were wounded in this first phase (January 30 to April 8) of the Tet Offensive. The attackers had underestimated the strategic mobility of our forces. The communists' battle plans were too complex and difficult to execute. They violated a fundamental principle of war by dividing their forces, thus reducing the ratio of attack forces to defenders, and not having a meaningful backup plan.

Tet is the most important Vietnamese holiday and is celebrated the first day of the year on a traditional lunar calendar. Both North and South Vietnam had announced on national radio that there would be a three-day cease-fire in honor of Tet. The communist's deception attacking on Tet surprised our forces but did not find them unready.

I was quartered in the Lucky hotel, one of three adjoining hotels that served as officer quarters in Cholon. The first floor of the center hotel contained the dining room, lounge and recreation room. Each morning I would walk up one flight of stairs to the outside deck of the Lucky, take a few steps to the deck of the Center Hotel, walk down one flight of steps to the elevator and take it down six floors to the dining room. My small, barren room had two single beds and a small closet where I kept my personal items. Roommates came and went every few weeks either to civilian quarters they had found for themselves or military quarters in less dangerous locations. This area of Saigon was considered heavily infested with Viet Cong. A military bus transported MACV assigned personnel the 2 miles to and from our headquarters each day with a strong military escort. Small arms shooting was frequently heard in Cholon. One day I was flat on the deck of the Lucky and face down before I realized I had heard a burst of automatic small arms fire over my head, I resolved to find a better place to live. Lucky for me, when I told my story to Bill Exley, who was living in colonel's quarters near MACV Headquarter. He smiled and told me that his roommate had returned stateside a few days earlier. I moved in that very day.

The weakness of the enemy in South Vietnam and the overall superiority of the Allied forces were not clear to people outside of Vietnam. By and large, people of the United States were angry because they firmly believed that our politicians and military had misled them. A lot of our blood and wealth had been poured into this war, and we were being told that we had the war in hand. Yet the television clearly showed that surprise had caught our forces and South Vietnam was one big battleground. The United States should get out of the war NOW!

On 18 February 1968 MACV posted the highest casualty figures for a single week during the entire war–543 killed, 2547 wounded. On 23 February United States selective service system announced a new draft which called for 48,000 recruits, the second highest of the war. On 2/8/1968 Robert S McNamara, The Secretary of Defense who had overseen the earlier escalation of the war and had eventually turned against, stepped down from office. In mid-March the My Lai Massacre took place. A small unit of US soldiers went berserk and slaughtered the majority of Vietnamese civilians in a village. By March 21 protests began to grow on US college campuses against the politicians for their mishandling of all aspects of the Vietnam War. On March 31, President Johnson announced that he would not seek reelection. A huge abyss was forming between the citizenry and the politicians and military of the United States. We in Vietnam were beginning to seriously doubt the validity of continuing the war even though we knew that the enemy had suffered huge, unsustainable losses in February. We also were concerned about alarming events in the States: Martin Luther King Junior's assassination, riots, Bobby Kennedy's assassination, other events associated with the Chicago Democratic convention.

In Saigon, there were rocket-propelled grenades coming in from time to time, especially at night. Automatic small arms fire might pop up on occasion, but all in all, Saigon didn't seem much like a combat zone. All of that changed in May with the Mini-Tet offensive. In late April our intelligence warned that a second all-out attack was about to take place. It would include a large number of North Vietnamese forces. The Viet Cong had suffered heavy casualties, and therefore received approximately 50,000 men from North Vietnam who infiltrated into South Vietnam. In order to ensure close coordination between MACV and the embassy, a

MACV liaison officer (which was I) was posted in the embassy throughout the expected upcoming attack which announced itself in the early morning of May 1 by detonating a rocket-grenade 200 feet from the third floor of the embassy where I spritely hopped out of my cot and called MACV Intelligence with the news, but to no avail since they also were wide awake, and had identified Mini-Tet. I then ran up to the top of the embassy where the well-armed Marine detachment was at the ready. We could see a vast amount of Saigon and heard and saw much activity. The enemy did not have the embassy on their list this time.

The Paris Peace Accord was signed in January 1973. The United States withdrew their ground forces leaving South Vietnam to continue the war against the Communists. The North Vietnam Army captured Saigon in 1975. The war ended with the unification of North and South Vietnam. In the United States, strong discontent about all aspects of the United States involvement in the Vietnam War lasted for years after the war.

In early February 1969, my tour of duty was completed, and I joined my happy family in Albuquerque, New Mexico.

Chapter 15
1969 - 1971
Defense Intelligence Agency

What a joy it is to come home after a year's absence and be greeted with open arms by five great kids. But after that heavenly first day, there is a temporary awkward relationship when each of them is not sure how he or she should act or feel. And finally, as the week develops there is an abandonment of any doubt, especially by the younger ones, and a cascade of conversation ensues. We spent several weeks close together as we moved from Albuquerque to northern Virginia and got settled in as a family once more.

Navy Captain Ralph Traubel was Chief of the Latin American Directorate of the Defense Intelligence Agency when I reported for duty in March 1969. As I got to know him, I found him to be a tough old bird, somewhat rough around the edges, highly disciplined, a straight talker, fair and supportive, and someone who establishes and enforces high standards. He explained to me that all the key slots were filled for the time being, but in a couple of months, there would be a reshuffling as several division chiefs would be leaving. He said he would assign me to the Cuba branch in the interim, and I would have some time to look around and see what area in which I would prefer to work.

The few weeks I spent in the Cuba branch were interesting and well spent. The chief of the branch, Norm Duncan, and I had gone to language school together, and our paths had crossed in Nam. It was a pleasure working with him. Bill Hord was chief of the Latin American Environment Division located at Arlington Hall, a small post located a couple of miles from the Pentagon. But it was a long way from the hustle and bustle, stress and strain, and long hours at the Pentagon. It often was referred to by some in a disparaging way by some, as "Sleepy Hollow" because of the perceived nonchalance of the minions of government civilians who worked there. At the time, among many of the military officers with whom I came in contact, there was a negative attitude toward the work ethics of these civilian employees. It was a time of war, and many military officers looked upon themselves as highly disciplined, highly motivated, long-suffering professionals who willingly worked long hours each day as opposed to the lackadaisical, "8 to 5" civilians.

As for me, I liked the ambiance of Arlington Hall, and the geographer in me had a great interest in what Hord's people were working on, the physical geography of Latin America. His staff of fifty were made up of cartographers, sociologists, and the earth scientists doing studies and analysis of the topography of the American regions, including terrain, climate and physical constructs, and interfacing with other government entities. I visited Bill at his division often during the weeks I was assigned to the Cuba branch. With Bill's endorsement and my expressed desire to replace him, Captain Traubel assigned me to this the most desirable dream job I could imagine. So, for six months I had a great opportunity doing work I loved and being a highly professional 8 to 5er. This love fest lasted until one Friday in late summer when Captain Traubel called me in the mid-afternoon and told me to come to the Pentagon to his office. When I walked into his office, he said: "Fred, I need you in Current Intelligence starting

Monday morning. The job? "It is permanent." Then with a smile, he added," It's about time you do some real work around here."

Current intelligence is about the "here and now" of world affairs. The staff was a small group of highly trained and experienced analysts, both military and civilian, who contributed to the morning briefing of the Director of the Defense Intelligence Agency, contributed to the printed daily and weekly intelligent summaries, conducted desk-side briefings for senior officials, served on various standing and ad hoc committees, and continuously researched significant events or trends in their area of responsibility–usually a few contiguous countries of Latin America. It was busy work, interesting and at times stressful but always gratifying. The "brilliant one" among the analysts was young Jay Kingham. Conversations with him were always enlightening. An occasional weekday lunch in the District with him and a few other analysts was "an event." Regrettably, Jay was killed in the Lockerbie disaster of December 21, 1988, when a terrorist bomb destroyed Pan Am 103 in flight over Scotland.

The senior civilian in Current Intelligence was Margaret Mead, an exemplary intelligence analyst, and a remarkable lady. In truth, she, not I, ran the day-to-day operations of the Latin American Current Intelligence Branch. She was also very kind and was both liked and respected by many throughout DIA. She and I got along splendidly. On one occasion she told me I should buy her opera tickets to the *Barber of Seville* Opera and treat my wife to a weekend in New York City. While money was tight, Darlene and I splurged and took the three boys with us. We made reservations at an inexpensive hotel near Times Square. We had two rooms across from each other. The boys slept in one room and we in the other. On the night of the Opera, we fed the boys and then left them with strict instructions not to leave their room until we returned from the opera. Both of us were quite apprehensive about them being alone. We had trust that they would stay put until we got back. When we returned from the opera, we found the boys' room locked and received no response from rapping on their door or calling their names. I was beginning to worry that the boys' curiosity overcame their good judgment and that they were now lost on the streets of New York or worse. I contacted security at the hotel, and someone came up to unlock the door. To our surprise and relief, there were the three boys all tucked in bed and sound asleep. We told the boys the next day what had transpired and how worried we were. By then we thought the whole episode was humorous. Mike did not agree. He was miffed that we didn't have more faith in his good judgment. He was right!

New York City was a wonder to each of us since it was the first time any of us had been in the Big Apple. One of the big surprises was how expensive everything was. I had been told by friends to be sure and eat at Mama Leone's—reportedly the best spaghetti anywhere. So, we went there. We were seated at the table and given the menu. When I saw the prices, I told Darlene we just couldn't afford to eat there, and so we left. That seemed to be the story of our lives—for me, it was the story throughout my life. Spending was something other people did. Reflecting on life up to that time I appreciated how fortunate I was that on so many occasions we had done without rather than accumulate a huge credit card debt.

After I had been in DIA for a year I submitted my "dream sheet" to Army Personnel. In it, I requested that my next assignment would be a command or an ROTC unit in a western State, preferably at Oregon State University. My thoughts were that if I was to be truly competitive in gaining another promotion I needed a command assignment on my record. If I were not promoted, I would prefer an assignment where I could prepare for retirement and continued residence in the geographical area where I was stationed. In due time my assignments officer called and told me to forget about ROTC. He said I had a fine record and should be thinking of command, attending war college, and promotion to colonel. He said he would be working on future career developments for me. He left this conversation with his assurance that he was going to find a command for me. Two weeks later he called me and said he had a great command for me, which was in line with both of my specialties (military intelligence and foreign area specialist). When he identified which command he had in mind, I told him I was well aware of the command, and it would be a fine job, but I didn't see how it could be very career enhancing. I would prefer not to command that unit. He responded with," Well, what kind of command would you be willing to accept?" His question surprised me. I was not used to such deferential treatment, and I thought maybe this was just a lot of hype. So, I figured I would shoot for the moon. My response was: "How about the 470th Military Intelligence Group?" His response was: "Let me see what I can do. I'll get back to you".

The assignments officer called me a few weeks later: "Here's the deal. A colonel is being nominated to the Army Headquarters in Panama for command of the 470th. If he does not accept or is not accepted, the HDQRS is being informed that the next nominee will be in grade 05 (lieutenant colonel). As it looks now, you will be that 05. I'll keep you informed."

That weekend I discussed with my family our possible move to the Canal Zone. For those who could remember, the Canal Zone had been a good place to live—many fond memories. My big concern was Mike. He would be a senior in high school the next fall. He was attending an excellent school. Thomas Jefferson was the 11th school he had attended in as many years. Mike and I talked about the move to Panama and what it meant to each of us. I felt very guilty in placing such a big decision on his back. He chose to stay with the family and going to the Canal Zone.

My stay in Current Intelligence was much shorter than expected or desired. When Army Personnel informed me that I was being nominated for command of the 470th Intelligence Group in Southcom, I informed Captain Traubel. He assured me he would support my release from DIA, knowing how important a command position is in an officer's career, but regretting the fact of having the problem of finding a replacement for my position so soon. About a month later he informed me that he could replace me immediately with a well-qualified officer newly assigned to DIA if I would accept an in-house transfer to the DIA Alert Center where that officer was scheduled to be assigned. And so that is what took place.

The missions of the Alert Center are carried out primarily by four analysts, each of whom has responsibility for a geographical part of the world. He peruses incoming messages, reports, articles, et cetera in search of information of an emergency or highly significant nature and notifies the DIA area desk officer and others as appropriate. He is also watchful for multiple developments that may have a common cause. For an experienced analyst, the duties of this small center are simple and quite easy to carry out, although he usually is very busy during his eight-hour shift. His is one of five shifts, which rotate every five days. The biggest payoff is the fact that he usually goes home at the end of his shift (no overtime) and he is free from any continuing responsibilities. Once I got the hang of this job the thought occurred to me. Life would be a lot easier if I just kept this job and not try to "be all that one can be" (an Army recruiting slogan).

Things changed after a few weeks when my shift and one other were put on two weeks of special duty to participate along with the National Military Command Center (NMCC), in a worldwide command post exercise known as High Heels 74. For the first week, we put in 12-hour shifts performing our normal duties but using simulations and exercise data sent to us. The basic scenario was that world tensions between countries built up to the point where war was imminent.

The NMCC team to which I was attached was selected to participate in the second week of the exercise. That scenario began with war breaking out all over the world and ended with a cessation of hostilities and a reconstruction of our Armed Forces throughout the world and an assessment of their combat readiness. For this week we were relocated to an alternate command post in Maryland. Here I was the only intelligence officer, preparing morning and evening briefings and staying in touch with exercise counterparts in the major commands stateside and overseas. I got about eight hours of sleep total in those five days. The exercise ended Saturday morning with briefings.

I gave the intelligence briefing that morning in a daze that I had been harboring for three days. Midway through my briefing, a cartoon appeared on the television flat screen embedded in the podium. (The support staff, located in another room, can use this television flat screen to send facts and figures to a briefer so as to update an ongoing briefing or answer questions.) In this case, it was a cartoon depicting Roman soldiers being overcome by a civilian hoard. The underlying title read, "Christians one, Romans zero." When I left the podium and entered the support staff room, all eyes were on me. While I was practically brain-dead from want to sleep, I went along with the gag with feigned anger: "who was the so-and-so who did that?" All eyes turned to the man sitting at a desk in the far corner of the room with a big grin on his face. It was none other than our illustrious leader, a Brigadier General. Days later I received a letter of commendation from him and these kind words: "I have never known a cooler man under pressure than you."

In the spring of 1971 Army personnel informed me that they were about to cut orders assigning me to the 470th effective 1 July as had been decided previously, when they received a request from the Army command that I arrive there in May. I talked it over with Darlene, and we agreed that she and the kids would stay put until July when I would get leave and come back and help them move. It would allow the children to complete the school year, and it would make the move less hectic. It would also give me the opportunity to pay full attention to getting to know the 470th and my job. So, that is the way things went.

The family was sorry to leave our home on Charlottesville road in Edsall Park. We had been living the good life in an American suburb for two years. It was the only time we would do so with all six children at home.

Mike was attending Jefferson high school, an excellent institution, which today is a magnet school. He was doing very well academically and in sports. Although a junior he was on the varsity baseball and football teams. He made the All-Star team in his football division. His coach offered to let him live with the coach's family if he would stay the following year. If he had done so, I have no doubt that he would have received scholarships (academic and athletic) to any number of outstanding colleges. In the Canal Zone, there was little chance that he would be noticed by the same institutions. Mike's presence in the family was a joy to his parents and siblings. He was the consummate big brother, and even today his siblings tell of the time when they were kids, and Mike came to their rescue.

In Edsall Park, he had a large delivery route of the *Washington Post*. He got up early six days a week to deliver in all kinds of weather and to all kinds of personalities. On Sunday, his brothers and I delivered while he slept. For us, it was somewhat of an ordeal about which we still joke. Kip was our leader. He was the first to get up, was chipper, ready, willing and able to deliver papers. He and I put the sections of the papers together and loaded them into the station wagon. All the while I was repeatedly going to Jeff's room to get him up and going. Jeff used every excuse he could think of: it was too cold, he did not feel well, etc. Even when delivering, he preferred to let Kip carry the paper to a house. His attitude changed remarkably when we were back home, and in the warm kitchen where I prepared pancakes each Sunday. In fairness to Jeff, it should be noted that the above was not true most of the time, and he was only nine years old. But when I get around my children, and we tell tales of times gone by, fairness and excuses are not very noteworthy when teasing.

Kip was the sensitive and kindhearted one. It was quite sad the day his goldfish, Gilbert, died. We all chipped in to console him. Gilbert was placed in an eyeglass case and buried ceremoniously in a grave among the flowers in the backyard. We also made a grave marker (we called it a tombstone) of wood inscribed with GILBERT and the current date. It seemed to please Kip.

Jeff was at a fickle stage in his development. He was very active, popular and had a great sense of humor. He eventually became a fine baseball player, but at this time I had little hope that he would ever develop a love for the game or proficiency in it. T-ball was his level of play. He chased many a butterfly in left field, bored and oblivious to what was going on in the infield.

The boys and I shared a lot of time together during the spring of 1970 and 71. Saturday mornings and early afternoon were spent on the baseball fields. Since each of them was at a different level and therefore scattered to three different fields, sometimes miles apart, keeping up with the schedules and getting each to his field on time and picked up on time was work. Also, I did a little assistant coaching and umpiring, but mostly cheered them on. All three sons were great boys and were a joy to watch as they developed.

Daughters are so different from sons in a most enchanting way, at least in the eyes of their father. They have to work at getting their father's attention when there are three older brothers in the house. Shelly brought that to my attention one summer. The boys and I had gone camping and fishing in southern Virginia several times. The last time Mike could not go so Shelly, who had been saddened when she was not included, finally got to go. We four sat around our campfire until late in the evening. Kip and Jeff went to bed, and I was about to when Shelly said to me: "Talk me, Daddy, Talk me." A wave of compassion and guilt passed over me. The boys and I had been talking about camping and wildlife and had not paid much attention to Shelly, who wanted so much to be involved. So, for the next hour, she enjoyed having the undivided attention of her Daddy until she just could not stay awake any longer.

Amy was a cute little girl and very lovable. I had missed the first year of her life, but it took us no time at all to become close. She, her mother and I made a number of trips to doctors to see what could be done about her eyesight, damaged by toxoplasmosis which her mother contacted when she was pregnant. Eventually, we ended up at Walter Reed military hospital. It is a teaching hospital. During one visit, after the doctor whom we came to see had examined Amy's eyes, he had nine other doctors, one at a time, come in and look hard and long at Amy's eyes with instruments. He explained to us that Amy's condition was especially unusual and therefore valuable for student ophthalmologists to witness. We worried about Amy's condition and did all we could to get her the best medical attention possible. But at home, I made an extra effort to ensure that she was not looked upon as handicapped or different, neither by her peers nor by herself.

Susan was born at the Army Hospital at Fort Belvoir on May 2, 1970. Darlene's Rh blood type is negative, and mine is positive; mother-fetus incompatibility occurred. The risk increases with each pregnancy. Almost immediately after Amy was born, she had to be treated with a serum/blood injection. Darlene grew more and more apprehensive as childbirth approached, worrying what might be wrong with the newborn and whether it would survive. Susan arrived and endeared herself to each member of the family. I had my doubts about her acceptability on the part of Mike and Kip. Earlier, when they learned that their mother was pregnant, they responded with "Are you going to have ANOTHER baby?"

The family filled our small, framed house. I had been disappointed when we first came to Northern Virginia in 1969 to be told that, because of the size of our family along with the size of my income, we did not qualify for a mortgage to buy a house in Kings Park West where many of our friends were living. We were happy with the house we bought, but it was very small. It had two small bedrooms and a small nursery room. The house had a full, unfinished basement. I started immediately to finish the basement, two bedrooms for the boys, a workshop, a laundry room and a game room. Darlene bought a used pool table with a removable ping pong table top. The boys and I got a lot of pleasure playing pool and ping pong on that table.

Looking back, I wish I had involved the boys more in finishing the basement. Here was a chance to share quality time with each of them. Without the experience of growing up with a father, I found the role of father becoming more and more difficult as my children matured. I noted that at times I was too curt and domineering in dealing with Mike. Once Mike told me very directly that he was going to get a motorcycle. I looked at him, thought for a moment and then asked: "Where are you going to live?" I knew that he knew that I did not approve of motorcycles in general and definitely not for young people. Mike did not comment and never brought up the issue again. Wouldn't a discussion have been more parental?

I often think of those times when I flunked parenting in a big way, and I regret so terribly that I did not engage more in the lives of my children as they grew up. I guess I don't feel guilty as much as a longing for those days and those opportunities. As grandparents, we are the experts in child rearing, and some of us wish we could do it all over again and this time do it right. Well, that "wish we could do it all over again" may be a bit extreme!

Chapter 16
1971 – 1974 470th Military Intelligence Group

In late May 1971 Major General George Mabry, in a short but memorable ceremony, with most of the members of the headquarters in attendance, presented me the colors of the 470th and I officially assumed command.

I had arrived in the Canal Zone a week earlier, which gave me some time with the outgoing commander and the opportunity to meet some of the principles with whom I would be interacting. In the evening of the second day, the commander called an emergency meeting which brought together representatives from the Embassy, SOUTHCOM, USARSO, and the Canal Zone Government. I was impressed by the role of the commander among these people, but I thought the meeting was much about nothing much. Maybe it was for my benefit, to see the role I was to play with them. If that were the case, it was wasted, because I pretty much charted my course as a commander.

A week after the former commander left I was approached by one of the officers who headed up a section in Operations. He started out by telling me that he had been chosen by the Junior Officer Council to present to me their concerns about 12 matters and he gave me a list. I thanked him for bringing them to my attention, assured him that I would carefully study the list, and dismissed him. I could tell that it took a considerable amount of courage for him to come in to see me about these matters. He probably expected me to challenge or at least interrogate him. There were some serious matters on the list, most of which pertained to the misconduct of individuals. Fortunately, there were a couple of seasoned professionals in the organization whom I had known from previous assignments and whom I could trust to be discreet and thorough in investigating the twelve complaints. By the time I was ready to go back to the states and move my family to Panama, I had taken care of the 12 items. As might have been expected, several were petty gripes, several were cases of misunderstanding or misjudgment of an individual's actions, and three were downright serious which I handled with a firmer hand than I would have liked, given the short time I had been in the unit. As I learned later, it was that very firmness that some of the junior officers were looking for since they thought the previous commander had been too lenient in some matters. I never discussed any of this with the junior officers, nor did I have the opinion that the previous commander was wanting in any way. I also called a meeting of the Junior Officers' Council and announced that the Council no longer existed. Every officer was encouraged to follow the chain of command to air any grievances. If for any reason he deemed that inappropriate or ineffective, my office was always open to every officer under my command and he could expect discretion and privacy. Over the next several months I had every reason to believe that I had gained their loyalty and confidence.

The next items to be resolved were the Group's organization and mission, and the filling of key personnel positions. A Group (now called Brigade) has the essential command, control, and staff elements but no organic subordinate units; battalions, companies, and detachments can be added or detached as a situation warrants. In the case of the 470th, the subordinate units were appropriate for the missions assigned except for one over which the 470th had operational control but not administrative control. Within the framework of the mission, it seemed to me that the controls were opposite to what they should be, and I discussed the matter with Colonel John Sadler the Deputy Commander of USARSO. He had been the commander of the Special Operations Group (SOG) in Vietnam, so he was very knowledgeable of my type of organization. He concurred with my findings, and so we had it changed. Other than that, the 470th seemed to be soundly organized and running smoothly.

The mission of the 470th was boilerplate military and strategic intelligence, along with certain intelligence support features. Tasking authority was vested in SOUTHCOM and USARSO. A limited amount of formal and informal support was provided to selected United States entities and agencies, and formal liaison was maintained with the Panama National Guard.

The key personnel positions with which I was most concerned were: deputy commander, senior civilian, and command sergeant major. The Deputy Commander's position had recently been filled by Lieutenant Colonel Edward MacConnell (aka Mac) who was on special assignment for several months. Mac turned out to be an ideal deputy, and our families became close friends. Fifteen years later when Mac died, I was privileged to deliver a brief eulogy at his funeral.

When I was back in the States in July, Darlene and I attended a party at Polly and Jim Bosch's house. Our good friends Mary and Henry Richarde were there. Henry Richarde was the embodiment of characteristics to which most young men aspire: integrity, self-confidence, gregariousness, affability, and intelligence. At the age of 60, he still stood tall at 5 foot 10 with the physique of a football lineman, which he had been many years earlier at the University of Florida. Most people in Army intelligence knew him from the time he was the Secretary at the Army Intelligence School. I knew him from my previous assignment in Panama when he was the senior civilian at the 470th. He told us he had been alerted for reassignment to the intelligence center in Hawaii later that summer, and Mary had her heart set on enjoying a few years there before retirement. The six of us reminisced about the good times we had in the previous assignment in Panama. When Henry commented that they would be just as happy to be going to Panama as Hawaii, and Mary added that she had many close friends in the 470th and would enjoy spending the next few years with them, I seized the opportunity and asked Henry, "If you were offered a choice between Hawaii and Panama would you pick Panama?" His affirmative reply was: "Does a goat stink?" — One of his favorite ways to affirm the obvious. I responded: "Let me see what I can do."

The office of management of intelligence personnel was collocated with the intelligence school at Fort Holabird, Maryland, all under the command of Brigadier General Orlando Epp. Since I had zero success talking with the personnel managers, I went to see General Epp. After about a twenty-minute discussion, I left with the General's comment, "Let me see what Richarde says."

Next stop: the 902nd Military Intelligence Group. Over the previous two months, I had asked around among the old-timers, mostly Department of Army civilians in the intelligence corps, for a recommendation for the top NCO for the 470th. Nichols' name kept coming up. I found out that he had recently been assigned to that 902nd and that the unit had an overage in senior NCOs. The Group Commander was very cooperative, spoke highly of Nickols and acknowledged that he could be released for assignment if he so requested. He gave me the OK to talk with Nichols. Over a two-hour lunch with Nichols, we mutually agreed that he was the man for the job and several months later Mr. Richarde and Command Sergeant Major Nichols were on duty in the 470th MIG.

Our family residence for three years at Fort Amador was a two-story four-bedroom two bath compact (small) duplex into which we squeezed our family of eight plus a dog. The charm of our residence was its location. To the front of the duplex was a small yard beyond which was a paved road on a narrow mile-long causeway that ended on a small island which contained an abandoned old military fort and an arched beach front which was shielded from the sea by shark screens. At the center of this enclosed swimming area was a floating platform. A snack bar completed the scene. Nearby was a parking lot and a theatre house where the residents of Fort Amador presented performances several times a year. The causeway, about 20 feet above high tide, paralleled the path of ships headed for the locks. Imagine sitting on the front porch on a quiet evening watching a well-lighted ocean liner with romantic music playing, slowly pass before your eyes.

The backyard extended approximately 100 feet to the barren edge of the Bay of Panama; across which were the lights and sounds from the docks and streets of Panama City. Our serene site was on the very fringe of Ft. Amador. It was an easy walk from our duplex to the 470th HDQRS, and an easy walk from there, along the edge of our 18-hole golf course, to USARSO HDQRS.

The three years we spent in Panama in the 1970s were an exciting time for everyone in the family. Each of us has many memories, some good, some not so good, of aspects of our lives there. The following tales relate the experience of family members.

One Saturday morning Jeff and some fellow scouts were

climbing on the slope of the causeway when a large boulder rolled down and mashed Jeff's leg just above the knee. Minutes later Darlene and I were sitting in the waiting room of the Gorgas hospital while the doctor worked on Jeff's leg. Several hours later the doctor came out and explained that there had been a lot of grass and dirt in the wound, so he had to do a detailed cleaning of the wound. He said it would be a couple of days before he would know the extent of the damage. Several days later the report was good, but when I asked the doctor if Jeff would ever be able to play football, he declined to answer.

Jeff was in the hospital for nearly a month. I was able to spend the noontime hour every day with Jeff. I never missed a visit thanks to Mac whose response to everyone who called to speak with me or come to my office was that I wasn't available until 1:30 pm because I was at a previously scheduled important meeting.

Visiting Jeff was usually a joy. He would see me coming in, and his face would light up. It reminded me of that little boy years earlier in El Paso who wanted to get out of his crib and join the folks at the pool. I knew that he was lonesome and not happy about being cooped up in a hospital room. Several times when I was greeted with a happy face, I could tell that he had been crying.

At each of the visits, we had a great time playing gin rummy. After a few visits, he began to win too often. Then I noted that he was sometimes cheating. So, I began cheating also. Only I wasn't as smooth about it as he was. He caught my deviousness the second time I tried. I brushed it all with "an honest mistake." Henceforth, when either of us was caught cheating, it was brushed off as "an honest mistake." To this day when we get together we may work into our conversation a dubious tale to which is added either," and if it didn't happen exactly that way, it should have" or "maybe that was just an honest mistake."

After Jeff was out of the hospital, he and some friends were wrestling around when the broken leg cracked. What a disappointment for him! He ended up with a body cast for a while and became ultra-careful of physical activity after that. Ultimately all healed, and, yes, he played high school football.

One morning the kids came running into the house and excitedly said: "Come outside and see all the baby turtles." From a hole in a mound in our backyard crawled about sixty tiny turtles. They formed a single file, headed for the water and away. It was a sight to behold and a unique thrill for the children to see such a natural wonder.

Kip went to a three-day scouting camp, which he had been looking forward to for weeks, but stayed only a couple of hours and was brought home with his thumb in a splint. According to the doctor, the cut was close to a tendon, and so a splint was put on his thumb, and he was sent home lest he would sever the tendon completely and thereby permanently lose the use of his thumb. He was angry as he told me, "All I did was cut my thumb a little bit, and everybody went crazy about it."

Amy's teacher called Darlene one day and said:" a beautiful thing happened in class today. Amy, as you know is well liked by all her classmates. Today we were studying words and their meanings. The word "heaven" came up, so I asked, "what does it mean to be happy in heaven?" One of Amy's friends put up her hand and said, "heaven is like living in the Burbach family with lots of boys and girls." "I thought you'd like to hear that."

We all went to the theater one evening to watch Shelly audition for a play. Darlene often referred to Michelle as her Sarah Bernhardt (a famous actress of long ago). I referred to her as my Great Pretender. Her performance that night was impressive, except for her singing a song which obviously she did not care to do. Even though Shelly was not selected to play the part for which she auditioned, she was very happy with all the attention and applause she received because of her stellar performance.

After the auditions, many of us stayed for a while conversing. When we got in the car to leave, we could not find Amy. Many helped to look for her to no avail. We decided to drive home to see if she might have received a ride with some friends. When asked how she got home, she replied that she had walked home because she assumed that we had left the theater without her. That was so typical of Amy. She was always calm and resourceful. A case in point was the time she tried to swim from the beach to the floating platform. Halfway there she began treading water and called out in a calm, loud voice: "Help a person! Helper a person!" Kip and Jeff came to her rescue. To this day she is teased about the calm appeal for help.

Our duplex had three small bedrooms plus the master bedroom. We put Michelle and Amy in one, Kip and Jeff in another, and Susan (with crib) with Mike in the third one. Our thought was that after school began in the fall, Mike would have a full schedule. So, he probably would leave in the morning before Susan woke up and he would come home in the evening well pass the time she would go to sleep. All went well until school began. One Saturday morning we were awakened by an especially loud racked consisting of heavy jumping in a crib and happy, loud chatter by Susan. We went to see what the matter was. Outside our door in the hallway was joyful Susan jumping up and down in her crib. We rolled the crib and Susan into the girls' bedroom where it stayed for the rest of the three years. We went back to bed. A few minutes later Shelly and Amy came into our bedroom and said: "I can't sleep if she's going to stay in there." I told them that henceforth that was the girls' bedroom and they would just have to learn to get along together. They did not like it, but they returned to their bedroom and began to get dressed as did we all. Neither Darlene nor I said anything to Mike. And of course, he never brought the subject up. One day I told Mike that I thought he had handled the plan to get a private room most graciously. He smiled and said something to the effect that the only time he could sleep was Saturday and Sunday. Apparently, those were the days Susan had physical exercise and intense conversations with herself. He didn't think it was fair to have to listen to that. Case closed!

One evening when I came home from work, Darlene was upset and was anxious to tell me about what happened. She had not stopped at the guard gate when she was coming home from the commissary, and the three kids with her had been acting up for some time. She was anxious to get home, and so she slowed down going through the gate but hadn't stopped and waited until the guard at the gate entry waved her through, which was the proper thing to do. Before she got home the MPs, with sirens blaring, stopped her, made her go back through the gate and return making a complete stop and waiting until the guard waved on. I consoled her with the assurance that I agreed she had been mistreated and I would do something about it. The next morning happened to be the day the staff meeting was held with the commanding general. I forewarned the Provost Marshal that given what had happened I was going to discuss it with the commanding general. The Provost Marshal said he was sorry, but the MPs were only doing their job. I told him I thought the commanding general would agree with me that the MPs do not have the authority to punish housewives in distress. He admitted that his men had gone a bit too far. He promised to send them to our house to apologize to Darlene. He hoped I wouldn't have to bring it up to the commanding general. I didn't. When I got home, Darlene told me about the MP visit with their apology. She had put the whole thing behind her, and the subject was never brought up again.

After a year as commander of the 470th, I spent a few days in the hospital. My blood pressure was high, and I was a bit stressed out. One thing I knew for sure, but I wasn't admitting yet to anyone, was that I had been drinking too much alcohol. No, I was not getting inebriated, but I was drinking too much. In one of the buildings of my group was a posh lounge for meeting distinguished visitors. Col. Noriega, then chief of intelligence for the Panama National Guard, paid a visit one evening during which we drank some scotch and conversed until late in the evening. When he left with his usual bodyguards, two of the officers from our liaison section who had been with me all evening offered me a ride home. I told them thanks but I needed to clear my brain, and the cool outside air would be just what I needed. I usually did not drink hard liquor, such as scotch. When the night air hit me, and I had walked a fair piece, I began getting drowsy. I had some ways to go yet before I reached home, so I laid down in the grass at the side of the causeway road for a rest.

Darlene was waking me from a stupor to tell me that the commanding general's office had called. The CG wanted me to be in his office at 10 AM. I looked at my watch. It was 9 AM. I hurriedly got up and asked Darlene why in the world she hadn't awakened me two hours ago. I should be in my office. Then I realized I should not have said that because she was upset. She responded: "After the MPs brought you home in the state you were in and hauled you upstairs to bed, I figured you had best sleep off your condition."

In 20 minutes I was in my office, and Mac joined me. "Tell me all you know quickly. I have to be in the CG's office in 40 minutes," I said. He had received the detailed report on the MP blotter: a military police patrol had found me sleeping by the road. When they woke me I repeatedly claimed that I was Capt. Burbach. They put me in their vehicle where I threw up all over the backseat. They took me to my quarters and assisted me upstairs to my bedroom. Wow! I knew I had really messed up a good career. The CG will relieve me of my command and court-martial me for "conduct unbecoming" and more. If I'm lucky, I won't be kicked out of the army, but even so, my career is no more. So, with fear and sorrow, I appeared before the CG who sat behind his desk glaring at me.

" Have you seen the MP blotter Report this morning?" He asked me. I told him I was aware what it said. "Is it true?" He asked. I answered in the affirmative. His stern voice softened a bit as he said: "Col. Burbach, tell me what happened." I told him the whole story beginning with a detailed account of my conversations with Col. Noriega. The CG's voice was now down to ordinary conversation tone. He gave me a friendly lecture on what my responsibilities were as a commander, as an officer, and as a parent. His final words were something to the effect of "let this be a lesson for you, put it behind you and continue the fine work you have been doing" He stood up, shook my hand, patted me on the back, and opened the door for my exit. Believe me! I learned my lesson and repented by striving to do my best in all things.

Some weeks later I learned in a roundabout way that I was still "in the loop." The Commander in Chief (CINC) of SOUTHCOM, in person, called me on the red phone that rested on my desk. The red phone network was for senior commanders and selected staff officers. The CINC let me know by the tone of his voice that he was very angry. He had just read a classified report prepared by my unit, which, to him, seemed to contain criticisms of him and his actions. He was misreading the report, but at the time it was pointless for me to try to tell him so. I calmly rested my feet on my desk and relaxed, waiting for the inevitable, my removal from my command and his command. Instead, his last words were: "Colonel I want this corrected, and I mean immediately" and he hung up. Minutes later the red phone rang again. It was my Commanding General (CG). "Fred, I just got off the phone with the CINC. He said he wanted to let me know that he found it necessary to straighten out one of my officers. Thought you should know. Keep up the good work" and hung up.

In general, the senior commissioned and noncommissioned officers and the Department of Army civilians in the command were well trained, highly proficient, industrious and cooperative. One of the most respected DA civilians was Ed Davila who came down with stomach cancer but chose to stay on his job in spite of his affliction. Eventually, he accepted rotation to his home in Texas where he died a few weeks later. He and his family were truly missed.

One of the most respected military officers in the 470th was informed, sometime after I had left the command, that he was to receive the Medal of Honor for heroic action in combat years earlier when he was an enlisted corpsman in Vietnam. The Medal of Honor is the highest decoration a soldier (regardless of rank) can receive.

The well-trained but inexperienced young enlisted men were a credit to the 470th. A soldier who was not meeting expectations most often was a draftee who was in need of an attitude readjustment. If that failed, he was on his way to a new location and a new type of work.

The small crowd that gathered to send us on our way to the airport en route to Stateside chuckled when they saw that the Transportation Corps had sent a small bus to carry the Burbachs to the airport. This three-year tour had been rewarding in many ways for each of us. We looked forward to the next duty station with great expectations and the past with tinges of sadness for its passing.

Manuel Noriega and I discuss American Panamanian Relations

Chapter 17
1974-1975
St Bonaventure University

Several months before we left Panama, I submitted my assignment preference form to the Army Officer Personnel Center. At the time, I was disappointed by not being selected for attendance at one of the war colleges which I thought would be a natural assignment following three years of command. I applied for the Army War College extension course but was turned down. I thought it best to prepare for retirement by getting an assignment in an area the family would like and in which I could make a few contacts that would lead to a job after I retired. On the preference form, I asked for an assignment in the western United States. My first choice was ROTC at Oregon State University in Eugene Oregon. In reply, I received notice that a letter had been sent to the ROTC regional Headquarters at Fort Bragg, North Carolina nominating me for assignment in the southern region. I called my assignments officer to argue my case for the western USA but to no avail, other than his repeated assurance that my career progression was not at an end.

Sometime later I heard from the folks at Fort Bragg that my assignment would be Appalachian State University in Boone, North Carolina. Shortly after that, I was stateside on temporary duty, so I visited the campus and the ROTC unit. The Professor of Military Science (PMS) there was a highly decorated, military correct, alert, and intense infantry special forces officer. The uniformed personnel in the detachment had great morale and were proud of their program. There was a strong emphasis on outdoor activities (skiing, hiking, camping, and white-water rafting) and on physical training, marching, and discipline. The academic side of the program was, in my opinion, perfunctory and supplemental. I was concerned! Two weeks after I had visited the campus I got a letter from the ROTC regional HDQRS canceling my being considered for PMS at Appalachian State and suggesting that the Army needed the more intellectual officers to serve at certain institutions and gave me the option to choose St. Bonaventure, Seton Hall, or Mercer University. I chose St. Bonaventure University in Olean in western New York state. I put an ad in the local paper inquiring about houses for sale with acreage. I received a very interesting letter from an elderly couple who wished to sell their 56-acre farm with buildings, flower and vegetable gardens, acres of Christmas trees, many hardwood trees and a view overlooking the Allegheny Valley where Saint Bonaventure University was located, for a price of $32,000. It all sounded too good to be true.

When my family and I arrived at the school one of the officers in the ROTC unit escorted us to a guest house on the golf course complex nearby and informed us that arrangements had been made that we could stay in the house for 30 days while we got settled in our residence. The very next day we took a look at the 56-acre farm, and I was impressed. It was even more spacious, more attractive and more desirable than the kids and I had expected. There was only one glitch. Darlene had her mind set on getting a nice house in either Allegheny or Olean. After house hunting for several days, she came to our way of thinking.

The block constructed farmhouse was large. After camp, Jeff

and I did away with the upstairs rental apartment and the exterior staircase. The House had six bedrooms on the second floor from which there was an open, winding staircase to the living room and a closed-in stairway to the large kitchen and dinette room. The first floor also had a formal dining room, a small den off the living room, and spacious porches front and back. The large basement contained a food storage room, the heating system for the house and lots of space. Outside there were several buildings interconnected, a large two car garage and an attached low roof shed from which we would eventually give flying lessons to the three Mallard ducks we would acquire. They enjoyed swimming on the small pond we dug in the creek that flowed behind the buildings. A lengthy, old-fashioned, decrepit wooden fence with rambling rose emplacements ran along the creek. Several large lilac bushes grew alongside one of the buildings, and when the purple flowers blossomed, the entire farmstead was alive with the aroma. The gardens were extensive with great varieties of flowers and vegetables. The delicious apple and Bosc pear trees were very productive, as were current bushes that the children despised because I had them pick the fruit with which Darlene made jelly. Behind the buildings were acres of young trees intended for Christmas trees. A large field rose up to the ridge which had hardwood trees which continued to the end of the farm in a hollow that besides the trees had a large scattering of rocks that had the imprint of various sea life. Another intriguing feature of the farm was a non-operating oil well on the property. The oil rights belonged to a local church. Neighbors told me about an operating oil well located 50 feet from our property which had only recently been reactivated. Also, to our delight was the fact that several deer made their home among the trees.

With the first fall of snow, the children insisted that we had to have a snowmobile. It was an excellent investment, and during the many days when the land was covered with snow, the snowmobile was in use. Christmas week immediately comes to mind. My sister Della, her husband Al Bruns and three of their four boys (Chuck, Mark, and Tom) spent Christmas Eve and Christmas day with us. We had so much fun together that we got them to extend their stay to a full week. Della had called me earlier to say that they would open their presents at home before they came to visit us. Darlene and our daughters decided that everybody had to get presents, even if some were small, so before Della and family arrived, Darlene and the girls went shopping. This was a case of quantity before quality.

On Christmas Eve, as we drove to the chapel to attend the traditional midnight mass, we experienced the ultimate Christmas spirit. The slow and silent fall of wet snow, happy people, excited children, and beautiful melodies of Christmas Carols flowing from the chapel filled each of us with love and joy.

The opening of presents on Christmas day was a long drawn out event interrupted midway by breakfast. In our family, opening Christmas presents was a very formal process. The youngest child who was capable, in this case, Susan, would randomly pick up a present from under the Christmas tree, have Mom or Dad read the name on the present and then would give the present to that person, who would open the gift and hold it high for everyone to see. Everyone would join in saying "Oooh Aah, Ooh Aah" followed by "Pass around. Pass around!" The gift would be passed around for scrutiny while the young one would pick up another present and so it would go until halftime (breakfast).

At some point during this long series of events, Kip pointed to the front window and exclaimed: "Look!" A few feet beyond the front porch were two large fir trees. Their limbs were large and green topped with four inches of snow. On one of those limbs perched a red cardinal. It was the very image that appears on many Christmas cards.

Mike transferred from the United States Military Academy to St. Bonaventure University and enrolled in ROTC. He rented a small apartment off-campus, bought a guitar, and entered the world of journalism by writing for the Olean *Time Herald*. We were proud of him. I gained many bragging rights from the articles in the newspaper that bore his name. And most important, he always had time for family members and family events.

It was this year on the farm that Kip took a special interest in weather and climate. To this day he is looked upon as the family weatherman. Also, I learned that he is very compassionate toward man and beast. The day we went searching for varmints around the farmstead Kip shot a rat. When he saw the dead animal up close, he was really upset in realizing that he had killed a living being. At school, Kip went out for football and did well in academics with one exception. His math teacher warned him that he might fail the subject, and if he did, he would not progress to the 12th grade. That got his attention. He solved the problem immediately with higher grades.

Jeff was always the happy guy. He made friends easily and was a true leader with a great imagination and lots of get up and go. He also matured a lot that year. He developed a serious side which was every bit as solid as his jovial side. He survived a long bout of mononucleosis, succeeded in convincing his mother and me that he did not have anything to do with the burning down of a red barn on adjoining property where he and his buddies explored at times and was relentless in teasing his sisters.

July 1974 to July 1975 was the year that I got to know well each of my children. Michelle was the apple of my eye when she was born. After three sons, I finally had a daughter, and she was beautiful. My nickname for her was Oogie, which was the sound that she vocalized over and over as she made her first attempts to talk. For the first couple years of her life we were very close, but then two more daughters joined the family, and my professional job became more demanding, so she received less attention from her father. This year Michelle was ten years old, and we were able to spend a lot more bonding time together, and we enjoyed it.

Being Amy's father was an easy task. She was quiet, attentive, pleasant, and bright. This year she received her first communion, which is a major event for Catholic children. To my surprise, a priest and a nun brought the Blessed Sacrament to our house, so we had a very private and moving ceremony. I worried about her poor eyesight, but she didn't seem to be bothered by it, so we relied on her ophthalmologist to do his best in her regard.

Susan was an easy child to raise. She was a leader, made friends easily, and had very good judgment for someone her age. During the academic year Susan and I went to St. Bonaventure campus together each morning, she to preschool and I to ROTC. On the way, I would sing "Oh What a Beautiful Morning" with gusto so she would respond with that beautiful laugh that daughters have for their father's shenanigans. Even today when I speak with a daughter, I try to find a way to hear a giggle.

By the time the youngest child comes along, parents have the experience to recognize what is important and what is not. For example, Susan and I were on our way to school one day, and she was sitting beside me writing some homework. She dropped her pencil. She bent down to pick it up and said very softly in a slow and clear manner: "Oh dammit." I ignored her and began to sing, in a soft voice, "Oh What a Beautiful Morning." Years later at Susan's wedding, the organist at my request hurriedly played some of the music from "Oh What a Beautiful Morning" before the usual "Mendelson's Wedding March" as the newlyweds marched up the aisle.

Our terrific life on the farm in New York State began the second week we were in Allegheny and attended a state fair. I told the children about the role a fair played in a kid's life back in Nebraska. With that in mind they played all the attractions, and in no time, we had spent $100 which was a lot of money for us in those days. A little more money carried us through the rest of the time at the fair. It was a great beginning of the year. That year we all had a go at skiing at a small resort nearby, at playing golf, at fishing for bass, bluegill and rainbow trout (and catching some) at a state park. The first time we went fishing, I was fined for fishing without a license. I thought that the ticket we bought to enter the park permitted fishing. All in all, the year was outstanding for the family and each one in it.

My work as a professor of military science (PMS) at St. Bonaventure was surprisingly easy. The officers and enlisted men were enthusiastic and very good at their work. It soon became clear to me that the ROTC program was in fine shape and did not need me to improve it in any way. I was especially impressed by Maj. Tom Kelly, Captains Montana and Sheridan, and Master Sgt. Lewis. A second mission of PMSs at that time was to find ways to increase the number and the quality of second lieutenants that the program was producing. I made it my job to scan western New York state to find other colleges and universities that would welcome ROTC into their curriculum. I found what I was looking for in Fredonia State College in Chautauqua County southwest of Buffalo, New York. I met an assistant dean who had recently finished a tour of duty with the United States Army. He knew several students who had applied for entrance to West Point but were not admitted, and other students who might be interested in joining Army ROTC. Within a year we had a program established in Fredonia. In discussion with several faculty members, and administrative people at Fredonia I learned that the enrollment of students in the State University System of New York (SUNY) numbered about half a million and to the best of their knowledge none of the 50 SUNY campuses had their own Army ROTC unit on campus. Maj. Kelly and I put together a concept paper on how to form an ROTC master unit to cover all of SUNY. When the ROTC area commander paid his quarterly visit to Saint Bonaventure, we discussed the concept paper with him. He was impressed. Several weeks later he sent an army aircraft to take me to ROTC region HDQRS at Fort Bragg to present the concept paper as one of the briefings to the visiting Lieutenant-General commanding the First Army. The general stated that he knew the New York state adjutant general and offered to help us if we needed his help.

While at Fort Bragg I discussed with the ROTC region commander the actual implementation of the concept paper, Including the initial funding. We had an enthusiastic debate which ended when I realized he probably had already broached the plan with higher headquarters, and it had been turned down. His statement to me was: "I simply do not have the funds that you would need to get this project started." As I walked to the door, he patted me on the shoulder and said: "Fred, I'm sorry." I walked from his office to the adjoining office which contained his staff of five people. All of the people looked at me with awe and disdain. A major interrupted the silence with: "No one has ever talked to our general like that." I smiled and quietly left the building wondering if I was leaving a bunch of yes-men. At the Transportation Office, I asked for a flight back to St Bonaventure. The answer was that all Army aircraft were grounded because of severe weather (heavy snow storm). The only way I could return home was by train. The train ride was comfortable but slow. At one point the train was traveling at 20 miles an hour. The train conductor explained that the tracks were in such poor conditions that a slow speed there was necessary. After a long ride, Master Sgt. Lewis picked me up at the Buffalo station, and we maneuvered through the snow storm for several hours before reaching home.

The trip had been less than successful. Obviously, nothing would be done this year about a consolidated ROTC program for SUNY. I resolved that we would try again next year. When I got the word that my name was on the war college selection board for next year, I put in a request for a one-year delay so I could work on my pet project. A short time later I received a message from my assignments officer at Army Personnel Center that the PMS slot at St Bonaventure was being downgraded to lieutenant colonel, along with a lot of other PMS slots around the country. There was no way for me to stay at St Bonaventure another year. He added that career-wise I was in good shape.

As one leaves for a new assignment, it is customary to analyze one's performance in the previous assignment. Did I leave anything undone? Did I look after the welfare of my subordinates? After I was satisfied that I could move onto the next assignment with a clear conscience, I reflected on my status. The ROTC program at St. Bonaventure was in excellent condition thanks to my subordinates, not because of me. On the other hand, I did not do anything bad or stupid, so I guessed I got some credit for that.

At the first quarterly conference of PMSs that year I was awarded the Legion of merit for my three years as commander of the 470th Military Intelligence Group. At the second quarterly conference of PMSs, I was among the few PMSs in attendance who were notified of being on the list of officers to be promoted to the rank of colonel. At the third quarterly conference of PMSs, I was one of three PMSs in attendance who were selected to attend a war college the following year. At the end of the year, I received a copy of my evaluation report written by the commander of ROTC Area II. In the narrative part of the report which is always lengthy, it began with, "Col Burbach is the outstanding PMS of the 18 Professors of Military Science I command" and ended with: "He will make a great general officer." Dear reader, if you are not familiar with US Army officer evaluation reports let me explain that the last bit of information is nothing more than the comment made famous by Marlon Brando in the movie *On the Waterfront*, "I coulda been a contender." I was still a contender. A year earlier I thought my career was at an end. My worries were pointless.

The house and farm we wished we could take with us.

1974-1975 St Bonaventure University

My family is complete. Michelle (Shelly), Jeff, Mike, Kip, Darlene, Susan, and Amy. Real Wealth.

Susan, Amy, Shellie, Jeff, Kip, Mike

Chapter 18
1975 - 1976 InterAmerican Defense College

Fort McNair is a small army installation in Washington DC and is the site of three of the war college-level institutions of the United States Armed Forces: National War College, Industrial College of the Armed Forces, and Inter-American Defense College. The latter School is open to senior military officers and government civilians from the Americas. It was at this institution that I spent an academic year of study. It was the culmination of my military education as well as that of my Foreign Area Specialization (Latin America). My class had 40 students from 12 countries (five students from the United States).

The daily routine was simple yet fulfilling. The first hour was a review and discussion of current events followed by several hours of lecture and discourse proffered by a guest lecturer. In general, the lecturer, an expert in his field, who recently had published to critics' acclaim, or a public figure who was popular at the time, or a professor of note from a prestigious university spoke. In the afternoon a seminar of several hours was devoted to the subject discussed by the morning's lecturer. These seminars were small in size (10 to 12 students) and brought out both the facts and the feelings of the students on the subject at hand. Occasionally someone would take offense if he thought a statement had reflected negatively on him or his homeland. This happened less often as the year progressed. We all learned to be diplomatic in expressing our views and to try to avoid being overly sensitive. In one of the seminars, two officers argued vigorously over an issue under discussion, but calmly and with aplomb, while back home their respective governments had recently broken diplomatic relations with each another.

On another occasion, an officer from Brazil made a lengthy position statement in heavily accented English and then looked at me to respond. I began with: "I will need a little help on this because I don't speak Portuguese." The room exploded with laughter. I looked at my friend, gave him a big grin, and then continued with, "I think there is a lot of misunderstanding on this issue both in Brazil and in the United States." The room quieted, and we continued the discussion as the moderator summarized the Brazilian's position and I presented a response. In truth, I had thought the Brazilian had spoken in Portuguese since I could not understand him very well and caught only a few of his ideas. When the laughter rose, I knew I had committed a faux pas. I hoped that my comrades would see this as an attempt at humor, which they did.

Colonel Bill Harris, a friend, and fellow foreign area specialist was a member of the faculty and had been a student here the previous year. He clued me in on some of the quirks of the school, not the least of which was where I stood among my colleagues. A student from a Latin American country may criticize, almost without limits, three countries: his own, Cuba, and the United States. The United States officers might criticize the United States (with encouragement from many, especially if it is in-line with their opinions), but not any Latin American country with the possible exception of Cuba, and then only if the criticism was clearly limited to the communist regime in Cuba. Colonel Harris and I also discussed what I had noted while I was attending the Argentine Superior School of War. In the minds of many Latin Americans, the United States belongs to all America and its greatness is an achievement of all Americans. Its shortcomings and mistakes are the faults of those in power in the United States government. Its successes are mostly derived from its luck in having extensive natural resources, quality immigrants, and its extension from sea to sea.

An important requirement in the curriculum was that each student must write and defend a dissertation. The defense would be carried out by formal oral presentation of the contents of one's work before the faculty, staff, and attendees at the school, followed by questions and critique. Col. Harris warned me ahead of time that each year after the Mexican officer has defended his publication, he will read a letter prepared at the Mexican embassy lamenting the fact that Mexico could not sell unrestricted amounts of tomatoes in the United States. Harris told me that as senior United States student I would be expected by the audience to defend the United States whenever it was criticized in one of these dissertations. The best thing to do is calmly withhold comment or to be complimentary of some part of the dissertation presented. I soon got the swing of things when a Venezuelan officer defended his publication. It appeared that his paper was divided into two parts. Part one was a diatribe of criticisms against the United States and a plea that the United States get out of Venezuela and its business. The second part was a series of demands that the United States do much more in and for Venezuela. The officer came across as angry and demanding. Given the situation, I felt obliged to respond. I did so with a few words to the effect that the writer certainly gave the audience a broad survey of the defense and offense of United States/Venezuela affairs and had produced a very significant paper worthy of further study.

For the most part, language was not a problem at the college. There were in-house interpreters proficient in Spanish Portuguese French or English. Headsets were available at each seat so one could listen to a presentation in any of the four languages. Obviously, it made it possible for the presenter to speak in his native tongue if it was of the four mentioned. If not, a translator would be made available from the vast number of polyglots in Washington DC.

Each guest speaker was invited by the school to stay for lunch. The lunch was informal, and it usually included the speaker and five students, one of whom would act as host. The purpose, of course, was to give the speaker a chance to get to know some of the students and to receive some feedback on the morning's work. For the students, it was a treat during which they could engage in a person-to-person conversation on the subject of the day. I had the privilege of being the host the day Gov. Averill Harriman, former ambassador at large during the Vietnam war, was our speaker. I was surprised by some of his statements. During the Vietnam war, there was a major disagreement between the State Department and the Department of Defense over the conduct of the war and the reports that came out of Vietnam. At lunch, he was quite outspoken in his defense of the State Department and critical of General William Westmoreland and the military assistance command in Vietnam, notably for the year 1969. I had spent most of that year on the intelligence staff at Military Assistance Command Vietnam Headquarters and knew well that there was a good bit that could be said of the military side of the argument, but this was neither the time nor the place to resurface old debates.

Almost any student at any school will tell you that it is great to get out of the classroom and into the real world where the goings-on you are studying can be experienced firsthand. Such was the case here. Our first trip was a short visit to New York City and especially to the World Trade Center. It was an enlightening venture. I remember well, being on the top floor where construction had not yet been completed. I presented a plaque to our guide on behalf of the college in memory and appreciation of our visit. I remembered the scene vividly on 9/11 the day that that floor, that building ceased to be. We made two extensive trips during the year. The first one was within the United States, the other was in western South America.

The United States trip was awesome. Keep in mind that the purpose of both trips was to see and experience first-hand the economic, social, political, and cultural customs of the places that we visited. Our first stop was Omaha, Nebraska and its environment. The economics stressed was agriculture. We visited several huge stockyards and of course, saw the extensive fields of corn and other grains. A day exploring the city of Omaha and assessing its culture and customs was interesting especially to the foreign students. The visit to Offutt Air Force Base and the United States Strategic Air Command (SAC) brought many excited comments on the part of both American and foreign officers.

Overall, our visit to the middle of the United States was a big success. Then we went on through Colorado to Seattle and the northwest. A visit to the Boeing aircraft factory was enlightening. One evening we had a boat ride across Puget Sound to a small island where we were treated to a Buffalo barbecue and entertained by native Americans in tribal robes, performing native dances. A day in Seattle brought out the similarities and differences between the agricultural Midwest and the coastal Northwest. After a brief visit to Fort Lewis, Washington, we proceeded down the coast to San Diego to the delight of some officers who had never been to California. In the San Diego area, we visited several military installations: an air base, a US Marine base, and two US Navy facilities. We also toured some of the commercial port systems. Then on to New Orleans. For me, this was the most intriguing part of the trip, and I say that because it was all new to me. We were introduced to the mighty Mississippi, and its role as the Gateway to the interior of the United States, the busy business of international trade, of port authorities, and we had someone describe and explain the management and government of all this. No less an experience was to partake in the customs and culture of the city. All of us students, foreign and domestic, were impressed with the extent and depth of the informative tour of the United States. We looked forward with high expectations to making a trip through South America.

Our trip to South America included the countries of Ecuador, Peru, Bolivia, and Chile. I had hoped that Brazil would be included since I had never been there and because it differed in many ways from the countries above, but it was not to be. Our tour began in Ecuador with a very formal introduction of each of us to each of the three members of the junta that had recently formed the government of Ecuador. After a short stay, we moved on to Peru where we were well received by the head of the military government, General Francisco Morales Bermudez. The first day we attended a horse race followed by a delicious seafood lunch. We toured several military installations. At one, a military museum, there were a large number of flags in a display case. The United States of America flag was there, but it was upside down. I brought that to the attention of our guide, a senior officer, and he made much to do getting some soldiers there immediately and having it corrected. I had told him that to an American soldier an American flag flown upside down is a signal of distress. He was very apologetic about the upside-down display and assured all of us that there was no distress signal intended; some recruit had made a mistake. As we passed near an airstrip, I whispered to my companions; "No airplanes!"

They smiled, and one of them whispered back, "They don't want you to see their Russian MIGs."

Arriving in Bolivia, we were welcomed by General Hugo Banzer Suarez. Included in our visit here was a day on the altiplano (high plane) at 12,000 feet above sea level where we were treated to a great social gathering that included a brief dance with young hostesses. The last stop on our tour was chilly where the event was enlivened by having General Augusto Pinochet in our midst. At the time we met him, he had already become a man of international attention. He was thought to have been instrumental in the slaying of the Chile President, socialist Salvador Allende. Gen. Pinochet was a member of a junta who, with the support of the military, seized control of the government and served as its dictator. He became president in 1980, was indicted by Chile for human rights violations in 1998, and charged with some crimes. He was arrested and confined until his death in 2006 without being convicted of any crime.

Overall, the Latin American trip was a disappointment. The culture and customs in each country were much to my liking, but we did not learn much about the economies. It seems that we concentrated mostly on political and social factors. There was not enough learning of the unique characteristics of each country and how and why they differ from one another. On the other hand, we seemed to have made the maximum use of our time judging by how tired we were each evening. In summation, it was a worthwhile tour even though it did not fulfill my expectations.

As a Foreign Area Officer for Latin America, I was interested in the goings-on in Nicaragua. In December 1972, a powerful earthquake struck Nicaragua. Much of the millions of U.S. dollars of international aid was provided to Nicaragua, but much of the money was absconded by the dictatorial Somosa Family.

Over the previous 20 years, guerrilla groups had been forming and conducting minor operations. In December 1974, a guerrilla group seized a large number of government employees and took them hostage including some Somoza relatives. Guerrilla groups continued to grow in numbers and size, and eventually, a group called the Sandinistas became the leaders of most of the guerrillas. By 1980 the Sandinistas were in control in Nicaragua, but a conflict developed between the Sandinistas and the non-Sandinistas. The former was showing signs of planning to establish a communist system of government and was developing ties with Cuba. The latter group was dedicated to forming a democratic system and allying themselves with the United States. They soon would be labeled Contras.

Ronald Reagan who became President of the United States in January 1981, accused the Sandinistas of bringing Cuban style socialism to Nicaragua and aiding leftist guerrillas in El Salvador. In January 1982 President Reagan signed a directive giving the CIA the authority to recruit and support the rebels with $19 million in military aid, and in 1984 the United States Congress approved $24 million in Contra aid. When Congress learned of the CIA mining of Nicaragua ports, an international crime, it cut off all funds to the Contras by passing the third Boland Amendment which outlawed US assistance to the Contras "for the purpose of overthrowing the Nicaraguan government."

A secret Contra resistance program was run by the National Security Council, and with third-party funds, "The Enterprise" which served as the secret arm of the NSC Staff had its own equipment and secret Swiss bank account. Commander of the Contras was Enrique Bermudez. This operation functioned however without any of the accountability required of US government activities. The Enterprise's efforts ended up being the Iran-Contra Affair of 1986 and 1987, and was a political scandal in the United States that occurred during the second term of the Reagan Administration.During our days at the Inter- American Defense College in 1975-1976, Enrique Bermudez and I sat next to each other and had many conversations. He appeared to be a very busy man. I had a lot of respect for him. We were friends. On February 16, 1991, Enrique Bermudez was assassinated in Managua, Nicaragua by bitter political guerillas.The academic year of the Inter-American Defense College ended on an unhappy note for me. I was anxious to get back into professional work and hopefully that would be a command. When the time for assignments came, I was offered command of the Military Intelligence Brigade (MIB) in Korea. I was briefed that the army would be testing a new method of organizing the intelligence units within a command and in this case, all US Army units in Korea would be attached to the MIB. I also was well aware of the general opinion of most professional soldiers that professionally, an assignment to Korea was the best-kept secret in the army–meaning one will learn and do more soldiering there than anyplace else in the world. Also, I liked Korea and had a lot of respect for the Korean people. In all likelihood, if I did well, this could lead to a promotion, the big one. This would also be a big challenge filled with stress. I called my assignments officer and asked: "May my family accompanied me?" His response was a sharp," NO! This is a one-year assignment without dependents. If you take the assignment, the General wants to see you next week. If you decline the assignment, you must do so in writing within three days."

This was the most difficult decision of a personal nature that I had to make in my 27 ½ years of active duty. In short order, I realize that my love and concern for my family told me they needed me and at the same time I really needed them. I did not want to be away from my family for 365 days no matter what the reward to do so might be. Secondly, considering how I felt health-wise, I was sure I could not survive 365 days of stress. The next day I sent this message to United States Army MILPERCEN: "I decline the Command." Even today years later, once in a great while I'll awaken in the morning with the memory of this offer and spend a few minutes thinking of the "what if?'

Five Americans in the Class of the International Defense College 1975-1976
I am on the far right.

1975 – 1976 InterAmerican Defense College

Averell Harriman and I discuss Latin American Issues

Susan, Amy, Shellie, Jeff, Kip, Mike

Chapter 19
1976 – 1979 United States Southern Command

Having turned down the command assignment, I was quite sure that my chance of another promotion was nil. Having just completed a year of academics, I was obligated to remain in the army for two years. Knowing that my health was declining and that I had lost much stamina, I needed to find a staff assignment that would not be very stressful or demanding. When I was offered an assignment to the staff at SOUTHCOM, I happily accepted. Three days after my family and I arrived in Panama and were temporarily quartered at guest quarters at Quarry Heights, I was on my way to the Pentagon for several days with the SOUTHCOM Commander, Lieutenant General Dennis P. McAuliffe, and his staff. At the time I was the temporary J2 (intelligence) pending the arrival of the Air Force colonel who would fill that position, and I would be his deputy. (By agreements between the armed services, each senior officer position in a joint command is allocated to a specific service. In SOUTHCOM's case, the Commanding General was Army, his Deputy was Air Force, his Chief of Staff was Navy, J2 was Air Force, Deputy J2 was Army.) I was unhappy with the fact that I was not going to be the J2 because I was far more prepared for that position then the incoming Air Force colonel. In all fairness, I must admit that he proved to be an excellent J2 for the three years that we were together. Our business at the Pentagon was completed in several days, and we returned to SOUTHCOM HDQRS at Quarry Heights.

My first job was to get my family settled in our assigned quarters #10, Quarry Heights. It was a large, wooden structure built by the French in an advanced camp in the early 1900's, disassembled and reconstructed on Quarry Heights in 1918. It was a privilege and a pleasure to have that building as our residence, but as a structure, it and twenty other such quarters highly resembled one of the sheds or barns on a Nebraska farm. The walk to my office was less than two blocks away. The children's school bus stopped each day in front of our house. Rosa, who had been our maid previously, joined us and remained for three years.

We all missed Mike who remained at St. Bonaventure for a year of graduate school and then into the army for several years, including a tour in Korea. Kip came with us even though friends advised us that he would not be able to find a summer job because all of the jobs were taken. Within the week, Kip asked me to help him choose which of the three jobs he had been offered. He stayed very busy that summer. In the fall he entered Canal Zone College but soon decided to give that up and to join the Air Force. After training in Lackland Field, he served in Arizona, Alaska and lastly at Patrick Air Force Base in Florida.

Jeff did well in high school academics, excelled in sports, had a good circle of friends who tested the limits of society by such antics as painting the statue in front of the high school. He and his buddies got caught and had the pleasure of spending time cleaning the statue and learned that this fiasco was an annual event. The night he and his friend Carlton, along with a couple of other friends, rushed into our house after dark one evening looking very guilty; the thought occurred to me that maybe I had better pay more attention to this son of mine. Jeff told me that they had climbed over the fence around the swimming pool at Fort Clayton (the gate to the pool was locked for the night) and had gone swimming for the thrill of it until they saw the military police coming. They quickly climbed over the fence, got in the car and drove away. They hurried to our house but were not sure if the military police were following them, so he asked that his friends be allowed to stay for a while until everything calmed down. Frankly, I liked the gumption that he and his friend Carlton demonstrated. I also was thoroughly convinced that both of them were solid guys of sound character, even though Carlton's mother thought that Jeff was a bad influence. I told him they could stay awhile and gave all four of them a bit of parental advice. All the while thoughts passed through my mind of Hank and I and military police in Korea some sixteen years ago. Let's face it; there is something satisfying about being a young adult and being a little bit naughty.

Being the father of three sons is one thing. Being the father of three daughters is an entirely different thing. Michelle was the oldest of my three daughters, and therefore it was she who introduced me to the world of the growing up female. It is a beautiful, baffling and befuddling time. Simply stated, it is the "teenager." On October 17, 1977, Michelle became a teenager. She made sure that she developed every characteristic associated with being a teenager. And through it all, she and I developed a very close relationship, which we have maintained ever since.

Amy, as usual, was pleasant and independent. Her chief achievement was getting her arm broken. One of the neighborhood kids came to our door and excitedly informed me that Amy was lying in the street with a broken arm. A father's imagination has no bounds when it comes to such a notice. I dashed to Amy who was lying in the street surrounded by her friends who had been playing kickball in the street. As I reached for her arm, which was not straight, she hurriedly said, "No, don't touch it." She was not crying. She was calm and patiently awaiting the ambulance. In the days that followed, Amy, with her arm in a sling, continued life as though all was well with the world. She was always so kind, calm and patient; I could not imagine her as a teenager.

Susan was happy, bright and adventurous. Would she also have to become a teenager? She, and Amy seemed to raise themselves with very little fanfare. My fondest memory of Susan at this stage was watching her aggressively playing soccer with her blonde ponytail bouncing.

Since Darlene was a stay-home Mom and all was well at home, I was able to devote most of my time to my profession. Jim and Polly Bosch, longtime friends, lived in quarters #9 and Bob and Marilyn Waller in #11. Behind our house and across the alley were the Officers' Club and guest quarters. About 500 feet in front of quarters 10 was the headquarters building. Across the street was a two-hundred-foot tunnel with a wide corridor with large rooms on each side for staff elements of communications, intelligence, and operations. Quarry Heights is part way up Ancon Hill (654 feet high), overlooking land and water for many miles. The upper part of Ancon hill is a nature preserve packed with flora and fauna but limited by the fact that it is an "island" which is neither big enough nor rich enough to support a full complement of species. It was a pleasure to be awakened in the early morning by the sounds emanating from above. To some it was a cacophony, to others, including me, it was a symphony. And for visual entertainment, there was the "Panama Air Corps," the sight of large numbers of Black and Turkey Vultures making use of the updrafts from the hill.

Panama Canal Zone Treaty

The story behind the September 7, 1977, signing of the Panama Canal treaty by US Pres. Jimmy Carter and Panamanian head of state Omar Torrijos is complex. It all began in 1903 when the United States President, Theodore Roosevelt, supported the cause of Panamanian independence from Colombia and negotiated the entitlement of United States right to a strip of territory 10 miles wide and 50 miles long between the Atlantic and Pacific oceans, through the newly created country of Panama, to construct a water passage from one ocean to the other(a distance of 50 miles). A ship traveling from the Atlantic entrance of the Canal to the Pacific entrance of the Canal going around the southern tip of South America would travel 7872 miles. The Panama Canal was opened in 1914, whereupon the Panamanians questioned the validity of the original treaty in part because the man who negotiated the treaty of 1903 on behalf of the Panama Government did not have formal consent to do so. Furthermore, the Panamanians received what they saw as too small income from canal operations and frequently complained that the toll for passage of a ship through the canal was entirely too low, causing the United States to partially subsidize the canal and to pay Panama far less than they expected. News of the Suez crises of 1956 further stirred the sentiments of the Panamanian people. Eight years later Panamanian students entered the Canal Zone and raised the Panamanian flag alongside the American flag. This act, which was meant to soften contentions, resulted in the school officials and students taking negative action, which resulted in a torn Panamanian flag. Riots ensued, and 20 Panamanians died. Panama broke off diplomatic relations with the United States and demanded that a new treaty be negotiated. A new treaty was drafted in 1967 but was not ratified by the Panamanian government.

Here is a small story about the breach of diplomatic relations within the larger story of the treaty. In 1971 I began a three—year tour as commander of the 470th Military Intelligence Group located at Fort Amador, near Quarry Heights. Within a few days of my arrival, a senior civilian of the 470th gave me an in-depth briefing on some events of recent times. In 1968 Gen. Omar Torrijos of the Panamanian National Guard, in a coup, took over control of the Panamanian government. Gen. Torrijos was described as "a heavy drinker, drug dealer, rough around the edges and sort of a country bumpkin." He was not accustomed to diplomatic ways and was upset with the United States. He chose to seek advice and assistance in communicating with the United States through two members of the 470th with whom he socialized, while refusing to have anything to do with the United States Ambassador, or his staff, much to the Ambassador's embarrassment, who expressed animosity toward the 470th for involving itself in State Department matters. (In normal parlance this ignoring of an embassy by the host country would be described as "breaking off diplomatic relations.") A thorough investigation was conducted to determine if the two members of the 470th or any other members of that unit were guilty of misconduct. Apparently, none was found. Yet, the rumor occasionally came to light that the 470th was a real problem for the Ambassador. During my more than three years in the 470th, I do not recall a single time when I or anyone in my unit had what might be called a problem with the Ambassador or his staff. In 1976, when the new J2 arrived, and I accompanied him at times on his orientation visits with people with whom we would be doing business, we visited the office of a senior army officer who, according to him was acting part-time as the military attaché in the United States Embassy in Panama. After a friendly chat, as we were about to leave his office, he told us, in a very subdued voice, that we might want to keep a close eye on the 470th military intelligence unit, "which is apparently "on the loose and has proven to be a real menace for the Ambassador." Neither the J2 nor I said anything and left. I was so tempted to go back and have a few words with the man who was wearing the Army green yet aligning himself with those outside the Army who were spouting negatives about an Army unit that had faithfully and honorably served for more than fifty years in Panama.

Sometime after the coup, I don't remember the date, Torrijos was returning to Panama from an overseas trip when he was informed that a contra-coup was in the works and he would be arrested when he arrived at the airport. Torrijos took an airplane to Costa Rica and from there traveled overland to David, the first town inside Panama, where Captain Manuel Antonio Noriega commanded the Panama National Guard Detachment. Noriega had the choice to side with the contra-coup faction, arrest Torrijos and escort him to Panama City or side with Torrijos and sneak him quietly into the city. He chose the latter option. Over the years that followed Torrijos awarded Noriega with promotions and power. In 1981 Torrijos was killed in a plane crash, which was rumored to be caused by a bomb planted on the aircraft by Noriega. After that, Noriega rose to the position of chief of Panama National Guard intelligence, and from there he gained control of the government, becoming its dictator in 1983. Noriega was captured in 1989 by US armed forces, tried and convicted of numerous crimes, imprisoned for years in the United States, then tried and convicted and imprisoned in France and from there imprisoned in Panama until 2013 when I lost track of him. Since then I learned that he died in Panama City in 2017.

The upheavals in Panama's Government not only made negotiations difficult but also changed the subject matter. It should be noted that with all major decisions in government many interests are at work in molding a law. The Panama Canal Zone Treaty was much more involved than its title would imply. The Panama Canal negotiations became the most symbolic target of Latino nationalism and anti-Americanism. American banks and corporations concluded that turning the Canal over to Panama was essential if the United States was to maintain a climate conducive to continued American investments in Latin America. A deal had recently been made between leading New York banks and General Torrijos in which the General agreed to reorganize Panamanian banking laws. With that reorganization, the General made his tiny country a tax and regulation-free haven for foreign financial institutions along the lines of the Bahamas and Cayman Islands as an international refuge for the world's largest banks. So, the Banks were putting heavy pressure on the government to negotiate a treaty. Along the same lines, major corporations in the United States were putting pressure on the government to complete the treaty. The American people, by and large, did not favor "giving away our Canal." California Senator S.I. Hayakawa said, "We should keep [the Panama Canal]. After all, we stole it fair and square."

The media was saying that the President was losing his hold on the power and influence associated with being president and needed a major success. In the end, President Carter chose the Panama Canal Treaty to be the first big success of his administration and put his full effort into concluding a treaty using all the influence he could muster including a large-scale campaign allegedly using taxpayer money and government employees to convince the citizenry that the Treaty was in the country's best interests. Naysayers claimed that his methods were illegal, that he was an engineer, a micro-manager engaged in minutia, did not see the big picture, didn't have much of a relationship with Congress and didn't understand the politics of the treaty. After more than six months of deliberations, the Senate ratified the two treaties, with one vote to spare, in March and April 1978.

We at SOUTHCOM breathed a sigh of relief when the treaty was finally ratified. The circus was over. For months a large number of people: senators, congressman, VIPs, etc. paid us a visit to learn about the Panama Canal and the Canal Zone. Senators may have come to help themselves decide how they would vote on the bill for ratification. Members of Congress may have come to prepare for talks with their constituents. VIPs may have come to assess business potentials. Many of them came "just for the fun of it" which was understanding, given the fact that we offered them escorts, briefings and, most importantly, a helicopter ride, at a low level, down the full length (approximately 40 miles) of the Canal. All the important people were pleasant, informal and gregarious. A case in point: as I was walking toward the headquarters one-day, Lt. Gen. Dennis P. McAuliffe was greeting a gentleman who had just arrived by auto. When he noticed me, the general called out: "Hey, Fred! Come here! I want you to meet the Speaker of the House, Tip O' Neill."

For most of us at SOUTHCOM, the Panama Canal treaty matter was not our primary job. I was a senior military intelligence officer with the obligation to learn, know, and teach. As a matter of fact, The United States Army is one of the world's largest teaching and training organizations. Every weekday morning, we, the intelligence staff, presented a formal briefing to our commander and his staff. The briefing contained all matters that were of interest to the commander, to include an analysis of information where necessary. Junior officers normally do the contents of the brief and its presentation under the supervision and with the assistance of the Deputy Assistant Chief of Staff for Intelligence (me), or the Assistant Chief of Staff for Intelligence. A practice briefing is conducted an hour before the scheduled briefing to ensure that all is prepared and accurate. In addition to the preceding, staff members are prepared to provide information to members of the staff or the command provided they have the necessary security clearances and the need to know. This, then, is the major way in which I fulfilled my responsibility to teach.

The responsibility to know is satisfied first of all by one's background, the accumulation of knowledge over the years. Secondly, one needs to read a lot of incoming reports and data from many sources. The third and most important process is analysis to study the acquired information and to ascertain its veracity and significance. The responsibility to learn is comprehensive and continuous. Simply stated, as a senior intelligence officer I should be able to answer any question the commander in chief asks me or know how to find the answer quickly and with understanding. To find an answer quickly is quite easy because you have learned your way around over the years and know where to look. The "with understanding" means that you have to know a little bit about everything—foreign affairs, science, geography, history, etcetera. On my own time, I spent five years in college (BA and MA degrees), read many books, and took a lot of correspondence courses. I spent 8 of my 28 ½ years in the army as a student in a military school. As a result, I have an understanding (but not necessarily a knowledge of) a broad range of subjects.

To give you an understanding of what an intelligence briefing might be like, imagine that you are a senior United States government official who with a need to know asks me: "What is this Argentine dirty war all about?" This might be my answer:

The Dirty War

In the 1960s and 1970s, a flood of revolutions and civil wars arose throughout Latin America. To fully understand what was happening required a basic understanding of government and politics in the area. The fundamental form of government in both Latin America and North America is democracy–rule by the people through elected representatives. In the United States the military, in its entirety, is subject to the Commander-in-Chief—the President, and the mission to defend the nation against all enemies foreign and domestic. For the president and his administration to be removed from office, only the Congress and the Supreme Court can do so legally. In Argentina and many other Latin American states, the military's mission is to protect and defend the Constitution which means that if an administration is incompetent or not performing in the best interest of the country, the military (usually and ideally with a junta whose members include the senior officer of each service) has not only the right but the obligation to take control of the government and rule until a civilian government has been formed to their satisfaction. As strange as it may sound to Americans, the military takes over the federal government to save democracy.

Since colonial times, most Latin American countries were controlled by the elite: large landowners, senior military officers, wealthy and influential citizens, and the hierarchy of the Catholic Church. Each country had a very small middle-class but a huge powerless and poverty-stricken lower class. The conservation of the status quo was foremost in the minds of the elite who were alarmed by two developments: communism and liberation theology. In light of the events in Cuba and the efforts of Che Guevara, Soviet Communism was making its way into the populous. Meanwhile and unrelated to the communist threat was the growing popularity of liberation theology which advocated that the fundamental teaching in Christian Scripture is a focus on the well-being of the poor and downtrodden and was being taught by the priests and nuns to the predominately Catholic lower-class majority. It was Father Gutierrez's Book "A Theology of Liberation" (1971) that had a huge impact on Latin American thinking and an alarm to the elite who were dedicated to the status quo. Some insurgent organizations became active after the overthrow of Juan Peron in Argentina in 1955, and the traditional oligarchy was in power. These insurgent organizations grew in strength and began to form military units, which effectively engaged in armed conflict with the Argentine army. A seven-year campaign by the Argentine government ensued against suspected dissidents and subversives and had been known as The Dirty War (1976-1983). The military regime was ruthless, kidnapping, imprisoning, torturing, and killing without restraint. In a three-year period, allegedly 30,000 Argentines were killed. Human rights had run amuck in Argentina (and other places in Latin America).

On one occasion Gen. McAuliffe traveled to Uruguay and gave what some reporters termed as a "lecture on human rights." Some of my acquaintances in the Canal zone expressed surprise that the General would so endanger our relations with Latin Americans with such blunt criticism. His speech was in fact fully in step with President Carter who reversed long-standing United States policy of supporting military dictators in the name of anti-communism by embarking on a moralistic crusade. He appointed ambassadors who aggressively confronted the right-wing generals in Brazil, Chile, Argentina, Uruguay, El Salvador, Nicaragua, and Paraguay accused of alleged human rights violations, and curtailed or cut military aid to those countries. He also strained relationships with Brazil just weeks into his presidency in 1977 by condemning its nuclear program.

In 1978 the Beagle Conflict between Chile and Argentina over the possession of some islands and the scope of maritime jurisdiction associated with those islands brought Argentina to the brink of war. I was all set to visit the troops in the field of both countries to assess the situation, but my plans were overtaken by other matters, so someone else went in my place. I had looked forward to some discussions with Paul Coughlin, the Army Attaché in the US Embassy in Argentina and his deputy, Jack Bohach, both friends from previous assignments. The big question was to see why and how this conflict fit into the dirty war. My guess was this was nothing more than a decoy to distract public opinion from focusing on the atrocities taking place in Argentina. That technique was definitely in play in April 1982 when Argentina invaded and occupied the Falkland Islands in an attempt to establish the sovereignty it claimed over them. The world watched as the British fleet moved across the Atlantic, made war on the islands, decisively defeated the Argentines, and went home—all in 72 days. The embarrassment for the Argentines resulted in an intense protest against the ruling military government, hastened its downfall and the end to the Nazi-styled horror that proved once again that "absolute power corrupts absolutely." End of briefing.

For over a month I had been thinking about making a trip to the Three Guyanas since we had so little intelligence about them. On November 18th, 1978 I was working late in the alert center when information came in on what would become known as The Jonestown Massacre. During the next several weeks, SOUTHCOM elements as well as those from Stateside placed 918 bodies in body bags and returned them to the United States for burial.

The Peoples Temple, a religious cult, had established a compound deep in the jungles of Guyana. Their leader and founder, Jim Jones was a charismatic and deranged visionary, who wished to establish a communist community far away from any influence by the United States government. He surrounded the compound with armed guards and prohibited anyone from leaving. United States representative Leo Ryan from San Mateo, California heard of strange goings-on at this compound and decided to visit it. He took along his adviser, an NBC film crew, and a group of concerned relatives of The Peoples Temple. They were well received, but soon a message was secretly passed to Ryan. It contained a list of members who wanted to leave the compound but were not allowed to do so. The next day, before departing, Ryan announced that he would take with him anyone who wished to leave. When it came time to board the truck, many who had expressed a desire to leave had changed their minds for fear of repercussions from Jones. As the truck which was taking Ryan and his entourage to the airfield began to leave, some members scrambled aboard. Shortly after they arrived at the airfield a vehicle with armed men approached the truck, and the armed men rose up and shot and killed Ryan and a number of the other passengers on the truck. Back at the compound, Jones was panicking and convinced many of the people that American parachutes would soon fall from the sky and torture and kill babies and seniors and members. The only solution was to commit the "revolutionary act" of suicide. Large kettles were filled with grape flavored Flavor-Aid, cyanide, and Valium and were given to drink, first to the babies, then to the children, then to the mothers and then to the rest of the membership. Armed guards ensured compliance. Jones died from a shot to the head. Only a few members survived either by fleeing in the jungle or hiding in the compound. As with hurricanes, earthquakes, and many other tragedies, the United States military was asked to serve. In this case, to go into the hot steaming jungle and retrieve hundreds of bodies of well-meaning victims of evil. Would this have happened if we in the U.S. intelligence community had done our job?

Chapter 20
1979-1981 University of Mississippi

As I drove from Washington DC to Oxford, Mississippi, the location of the University of Mississippi (known to all as Ole Miss) I mentally reviewed the present situation and how things should evolve in the coming assignment. My first concern was for my family. Mike and Kip were each busy with their own life and work. Mike was in the Army and Kip was in the Air Force. They were doing fine. Jeff had decided to live with us for a while longer and attend college at Ole Miss. Michelle was doing well in high school and might continue to Ole Miss if we were still in Oxford. Amy and Susan were doing well both socially and academically so they would be okay. Darlene would have things under control at home. Hence, I could devote my working hours to commanding the ROTC detachment. Being a commander is the best job in the army. A commander can put to work all the things he has learned over the years to mold an effective team and carry out a mission in the finest and most successful way that is humanly possible. It is a pleasure and an honor to see a group of soldiers develop teamwork, know-how, efficiency, and unrestricted dedication to the team, the work, and the flag. I hoped that was or soon would be the nature and quality of the detachment at Ole Miss just as it was at St. Bonaventure. For myself, things did not look so bright. I felt like I was worn out. Recently I had another bout of "impending doom." I dreaded the idea of retiring. I cherished my career as a senior officer in the United States Army. I decided to do the best I could for a year or so, and then I would retire and move out West, maybe to Monterey California.

The first person I met at Ole Miss quickly became a valued friend and a great supporter of the ROTC detachment. Jack Savage was the Comptroller at Ole Miss and a Colonel in the Mississippi National Guard. He was very helpful in getting my family settled in a faculty house on Sorority Row on campus. He introduced me to many of the movers and shakers at Ole Miss and some of the officers in the Mississippi National Guard, including the State Adjutant General.

He was instrumental in getting Jeff an ROTC scholarship. Most of all, he clued me in on the state of affairs in the Army ROTC unit. Not surprisingly there were a few professors in the faculty who were anti-military. There were also rumors going around that the Administration was deeply concerned about the Army ROTC detachment. All in all, the Army ROTC detachment was not on the same level of popularity as the Air Force and Navy units on campus. Ouch! I suggested that we save the discussion on that subject until I had an opportunity to meet the cadre of the Army ROTC detachment.

Over the years I had learned to size up a group of soldiers quickly, whether in a command or a staff element, by observing individual military bearing, team spirit and morale. It would not be possible to do that for several weeks since much of the cadre was at summer camp or were newly assigned and busy getting the family settled and getting to know the staff and faculty at Ole Miss, as was I. At this time there was a lull between semesters; only a few ROTC cadre were on duty. The senior officer on duty with the rank of Major asked to meet with me. He began our meeting with a proposal that somewhat reorganized the detachment and that specified which officers and noncommissioned officers would hold down which jobs. He gave me a written copy of his proposal. I assured him that I would look it over. Next, he told me that they were preparing to have a private farewell party for the departing lieutenant colonel and that they were going to present him with a saber which is in the ROTC supply room. (This "telling the commander" is a common trick by someone who is intent on doing something against Army regulations, in this case, to misappropriate government property, but be able to avoid prosecution if he is caught by stating that his commander knew what he was doing and permitted him to proceed.) He added that I would not be invited to the party. He presented all of this in somewhat of a surly, arrogant way. Obviously, the Major was not well versed in Army protocol.

When I asked him several questions about the soon-to-depart officer, his final statement was in a scold mode. "I don't have anything negative to say about him. He's a personal friend of mine, and I don't want to talk about him." As we broke up the meeting, I told him that I had been to many private farewell parties and I thought they were a great tradition. I assured him (with a chuckle) that I would not crash his party. I did not comment about the saber.

I studied the proposal that the Major had given me. It started with the idea that he and one of the captains by name had been in the detachment for some time and were best prepared to bring continuity to the ROTC unit and, with the few changes spelled out in the proposal, the newly assigned personnel would more quickly contribute to the success that the unit has heretofore achieved. The proposal also contained a list of personnel and their respective duty assignments.

The Major and I had a very brief meeting to discuss his proposal. I pointed out to him that four years earlier I had completed a year as PMS at St. Bonaventure University in New York. I had been lucky in inheriting an excellent program run by a closely-knit team of dedicated and enthusiastic professionals which allowed me to do a variety of support activities for the team and ROTC in general. I intended to apply what I learned there to the detachment at Ole Miss. Shortly before the beginning of the fall semester, we would have a meeting in which we as a unit would go over the organization and operation of the unit, and all officers and NCOs will have an opportunity to speak up. Also, each will have a say in what his duties will be. A critical factor in any ROTC unit is recruitment. I said I wanted to talk with him sometime soon on making his primary duty recruitment given his extensive knowledge of the staff, faculty, and students and the way things are done at Ole Miss. Finally, I thanked him for his proposal, and said that I would hang on to it.

Several weeks before the fall semester all the members of the detachment were assembled for an hour of meet, greet and talk about the coming year. After the meeting, I gave thought to those who were not newly assigned to the detachment. I saw very little team spirit, enthusiasm, or interest. I concluded that, coupled with what I had learned from my conversations with the Major, whatever was holding back the Army ROTC unit might disappear with those who were leaving the detachment.

The fall semester got off to a good start. The returning cadets were many and were enthusiastic. The recruitment of new cadets at Ole Miss was a success thanks to the Major and two captains who worked on that issue. Each of the captains who was in charge of an ROTC program at one of the four extension schools seemed to be doing very well. The sergeants (Noncommissioned Officers, i.e., NCOs) with more years of experience than most of the officers and with extensive experience in training soldiers are a great asset in any ROTC unit, and most definitely at Ole Miss. The newly assigned lieutenant colonel was difficult for me to size up. He seemed very uneasy around me, and as time went on, he became very aloof. (His role would be similar to that of an executive officer: supervise and lead the primary function of the unit and develop significant activities.)

The work I programmed for myself was fourfold:1) observe and scrutinize the training at Ole Miss and the four extension colleges, and stay in contact with each member of the cadre, 2) participate in university activities and associated social events, 3) maintain contact with appropriate military organizations, and 4) work on project Expand the Base by contacting other colleges within our area to interest them in sponsoring an ROTC program.

I got to know many of the Ole Miss department chairs by being a member of the Sundowners Club, a self-imposed title of the department chairs' meetings once a month beginning at 4 pm and often lasting until the sun went down. Jack Savage and I made several trips to Jackson to meet National Guard members and to establish a good liaison whereby the Guard was very supportive of our Army ROTC program. I made contact with Mississippi Valley State University and with Delta State University. Each expressed interest in what I had to say about Army ROTC. By the end of the semester, I was pleased with the team spirit, enthusiasm, and fine work that the cadre displayed, but I felt that we still had room for improvement. Then I read an evaluation report relating to Army ROTC at the University of Mississippi written by the Commanding General of the Third ROTC Region, (which includes Ole Miss) and Brigadier General French, Deputy Chief of Staff/ ROTC at United States Army Training and Doctrine Command which included the following phrases: "cadets are top quality; training of those cadets is among the best we have in ROTC". "ROTC is the thing to do at the University of Mississippi." This was a big surprise, given what I was told and what I observed seven months ago. And best of all, the Officers, NCOs, and Cadets, through teamwork and personal hard work achieved this success without much involvement by me or anyone else. With the beginning of the second semester in January 1980 the Army ROTC unit began, in the words of one cadet, "the same thing all over again, only better."

Worthy of note was the acquisition of two more extension centers: Delta State University and Mississippi Valley State University. Once we had introduced ourselves to these institutions and they expressed interest in having ROTC on campus, I transferred Captain Thomas P Watts and Master Sergeant Lewis Pacsuta to the Area to see how well they could recruit students to enroll in ROTC. They greatly exceeded my expectations so that in January 1980 we had enough ROTC students to establish a temporary program on each campus. Of note was the fact that Oxford was two hours' drive from these universities and so these two men received less assistance at times than they may have needed from the cadre at Ole Miss.

I spent the month of February in Washington DC where I was on a selection board for officer promotion to lieutenant colonel regular army. It was a great experience. It was gratifying to see how thorough the files of every officer in the zone for promotion were scrutinized and the equity of the whole system of advancement in rank. When I returned to Ole Miss in early March, I was pleased to learn that the Army ROTC unit at Ole Miss had done very well without me, Thank you very much.

The rest of the semester was quite routine although I didn't see enough evidence of team spirit or enthusiasm within the cadre. The cadets performed very well at summer camp. In the fall semester, I team-taught a course entitled Philosophy of War with a professor from the Philosophy Department, worked on the extension courses at Delta and Mississippi Valley Universities, and at Ole Miss and two nearby extensions.

In October I received a letter from the President of Mississippi Valley State University, E.A. Boykins and a similar letter from the President of Delta State University, Kent Wyatt. Both letters offered kudos to the cadre of our detachment. President Wyatt requested the immediate establishment of Delta State University as a host institution for the Army senior ROTC program not later than the beginning of the fall semester, 1981 and that a cross-enrollment agreement be established with Mississippi Valley State University. President Boykins wholeheartedly concurred with President Wyatts' request and further requested that Mississippi Valley State University be designated as an extension center from the Delta State host program. In discussion with the Chancellor of the University of Mississippi, Porter L Fortune, he expressed extreme pleasure with the success of "our Military Science Department." and particularly the performance of Captain Thomas P Watts and Master Sergeant Lewis Pacsuta. He reminded me that he had presented our current arrangement to the Board of Trustees of State Institutions of Higher Learning and would now support immediate action to establish Delta State University as a host institution for advanced ROTC. It was indeed a pleasure and an honor for me to pass on to the officers and NCOs these kudos and to acknowledge the successes they had achieved in such a short time, and my gratitude for a job well done.

I never did succeed in reaching the level of esprit de corps that I had intended for the detachment and knew I had lost interest in trying. It was obvious that it was high time that I retired.

I submitted the necessary documentation to the Army Personnel Center with a proposed retirement date in late summer, 1981. In June I was assigned to the staff at the 1981 Summer Camp at Fort Riley, Kansas. While there I took the retirement physical examination and was found to be healthy (no disabilities). Since the examination did not include a stress test, I asked the examining physician for one and gave him my reasons, from the fact that my father had died of a massive heart attack at the age of 51 to how I felt physically and the "impending doom" attacks. He was adamant that I had no symptoms of heart disease and that the United States Army could not afford to grant stress tests to anyone with no symptoms to warrant one. The following Saturday I had dinner with my commanding general, and he bragged about how healthy he was, based on a recent stress test. (Most officers like to brag to one another about how physically fit they are, including me.) I told him my experience of the previous day, and he said he would look into it. On Monday morning at 7:30 AM, I received a call from the medical center and told to report there at 10 AM for a stress test. Later in the week, I got a call from the medical center informing me that the test results were being forwarded to the cardiology staff in Denver for review since the test results indicated several discrepancies and I would be informed of their findings. A few days later I received written orders to report to the Eisenhower clinic in Athens Georgia for further tests.

1979-1981 University of Mississippi

Jeff, Mike Shelly, me, Amy Darlene, Susan Kip

Susan, Amy, Shellie, Jeff, Kip, Mike

Chapter 21

1982 - 1990 Military Hospital to Retirement

I reported in at the Eisenhower clinic on Monday of the arranged date having taken a bus from Oxford to Athens, Georgia. We had only one car so I had to use public transportation and bus travel was the cheapest way to travel aside from hitchhiking which I had outgrown but enjoyed years ago.

Tuesday was devoted to taking some tests and Wednesday morning was the big test. I was taken to the examination room where a tube was inserted in an artery in my groin and passed up to the heart. Dye was put to the heart so that the cardiologist could see where there were constrictions or expanded areas of the heart vessels. After the tests I was returned to my hospital room, accompanied by a nurse who gave me strict orders not to move around for a few hours so that the incision in the groin had time to seal. As if by some comedian's act, 10 minutes after I had gotten into bed, in walked a cheerful medical person with a wheelchair and instructed me to get on board as we needed to be downstairs for some lab tests. I told the young lady that I wouldn't be going anywhere for a while. Somewhat shocked by the finality of my comment she began to preach to me that we had to go right now, they were waiting for me, and it was not up to me to make that decision. When she found out that I was a stubborn old bird she left with the promise that she would return with someone in authority. I never saw her again.

On Thursday at 10 AM I was scheduled to meet with the cardiologist, a Major, in a room near the examination room. As I waited there a couple of well-meaning staff members told me about the Major and how super dedicated and exacting he was. One of their tales involved an elderly lady whom he lectured severely and then refused to see again since she would not quit smoking. He had previously explained to her that she was wasting her time and above all else his time if she, with heart problems, continued to smoke. His scold was soon followed by a meeting of the minds between the Major, his superior, and the hospital director on how much authority the Major had. I was prepared for a tiger when the Major showed up at precisely 10 AM, asked a staff member if the tape was ready. It was, and I accompanied him into a 10 x 12 room which contained only two chairs, a table, a projector and a projection screen. Without saying a word, he started the projector and began talking in technical terms about what I gathered was a recording of my heart and vessels. I interrupted him to state that I had no idea what he was talking about. He stopped, dumbfounded, and asked if anyone had explained the heart and coronary arteries to me. With my response of no, he slowed down a bit and pointed out on the screen where the blockages were in the coronary arteries and their percentage of blockage. And he sped up again and rattled off that he couldn't get me into Walter Reed Hospital in DC for a month but he could get me into the Army teaching hospital at Fort Sam Houston, in San Antonio, Texas the following week. Again, I interrupted: "Major, what does all this mean and what are my options?"

He gave me the clearest and most concise answer I have ever had to any question I have ever asked: Colonel, you don't have any options. In fact, I cannot promise you that you will leave this hospital alive. Your best chances are in getting surgery to bypass those blockages just as soon as that can be done, which is at Fort Sam. Okay?" He looked at me expectantly. I said: "Let's do it." We shook hands hurriedly as he told the nurses what to do with me and he was gone.

I returned to my room somewhat befuddled. It was good news that the doctor had made a clear diagnosis and was taking care of my problem immediately. It was bad news that I had something horribly wrong with my body and did not know what that portended. A clerk interrupted my thoughts with the news that I would be staying in the hospital until Sunday at which time I would take the medevac plane to Denver, spend the night there, and arrive at Fort Sam on Monday. My operation was scheduled for Thursday morning. Frankly, I didn't like that schedule one bit but saw no point in discussing it with him. I definitely wanted to go home, get things settled there, and go to Fort Sam on my own. But the question was: how am I going to go contrary to the standard operating procedures of the Army medical system? I quickly found the answer. There is one person in this whole outfit that knows the rules but also knows how to do the impossible. I called the Command Sergeant Major's office and asked that he stop by and see me sometime that day if possible.

About a half hour later he walked in. After some chitchat about friends and acquaintances, we had a review of my problem. He said: "Colonel, it is now 1:30, I will get back to you before the end of the day." At 4:45 he walked in with some papers and said: "Colonel, here are your orders releasing you from this hospital as of tomorrow morning and ordering you to report to the hospital at Fort Sam on Monday. I talked with the Command Sergeant Major there, and he is ready to help you any way he can. Our driver will be waiting for you at the hospital entrance tomorrow morning at 7:30 and will take you to your bus on time." I thanked him with a smile. I knew what was coming. With a humorous smile, almost a smirk he said: "The difficult we do right away; the impossible takes a bit longer. Have a safe trip, sir."

When I got home, Darlene and I visited our next-door neighbors at their insistence. The man of the house knew exactly what I was going through and used his own experience as proof that one survives the operation. He had bypass surgery two years earlier. I appreciated the pep talk. He assured me that bypass surgery wasn't exactly routine on par with 'tonsillectomies or ingrown toenails" but it was an everyday event in many hospitals, and the survival rate for the operation was in the 90+ percentile. So, I settled down a little, thinking maybe this isn't the end of the line after all. Kip was summoned to come home on emergency leave and take care of the girls while Darlene and I drove to Fort Sam. Darlene got a room on post near the hospital. She quickly made friends with several other wives whose husbands were having bypass surgery. When I reported into the hospital on Monday, I met the chief surgeon who mentioned that he was a graduate of Creighton University medical school, which gave us a bond of sorts since I was a graduate of Creighton University. He also told me that patients are best served in a ward environment rather than a private room, which I was authorized if I so wished. He mentioned that at the moment they had only one patient in a private room and felt certain her isolation was very depressing.

The ward to which I was assigned was large and had two sections: one for those who were awaiting surgery and therefore were quiet and fearful, and one for those who were recovering from surgery who were talkative and in high spirits. One glitch that came up which worried me had to do with the video of my cardiogram, which was needed by the surgeon so that he could plan the operation. It was misplaced at Eisenhower Medical Center.

The nurse told me that it was my fault because I didn't follow the standard operating procedures, which would have had the video accompany me on the flight to Fort Sam. At the last moment, the video was found and was rushed to Fort Sam in time to keep me on schedule. The surgical preparation on the night before surgery was eerie–two surgeons examined my chest and left leg and made indelible ink markings where the incisions would be made the next morning. While they were doing that I got a clear mental picture of a movie scene in a western movie where the condemned who was to be hanged in the morning was being measured the night before by the undertaker for measurements needed to make the coffin. Weird! Eerie and Scary! On the evening before the surgery, I was joined by Mike, Jeff, Mary and Darlene in a group hug and prayer. It was indescribably consoling. In the operating room the next morning I was given some drugs and told to count backward from 100. Later I was told that I got all the way to 96.

"You are doing great, Fred. You're looking good. You are happy. Don't try to breathe! Let the machine do your breathing. You are happy, doing well. You can wake up now. Don't try to breathe!" The doctor was sitting by my side, a comforting hand on my shoulder, saying things that comforted me. So, as I awoke, I felt very happy. The big pumping device on my left was odd; the fact that I wasn't breathing and didn't have to because air was being pumped in and out of my lungs was strange, but I was okay with it. The doctor said that he was leaving, but two staff members were standing by and would take good care of me, and he would see me later in the day. I had a strong desire to tell him how happy I was and how thankful I felt for what he had done for me but since I couldn't speak, I smiled at him and squeezed his hand.

After a couple of very long hours, I was taken off of the breathing machine and moved to the recovery room. Most people react to this situation in one of two ways: either extremely anxious or very relaxed. I was fortunate to be in the latter category. The next day I was moved next to the nursing station in the recovery ward. I was still wired to a machine on wheels that gave off little beeps and flashes. I was treated with extreme kindness by all the staff, and I felt at peace, secure and happy. All of a sudden, the honeymoon ended. A male nurse came up with a ridiculous idea. He came to me and said:" Ok Colonel now you are going to get up and go to the bathroom." No way was I going to get out of bed and push that machine to which I was attached to with electronic wires and tubes anywhere! The persistent nurse first had me sitting, then standing, then shuffling one foot in front of the other while I pushed the machine slowly down a very long (20 feet) hall. The trip back to my bed seemed shorter. I smiled at the nurse with pride. I was mobile!

Most of us patients found that as fast as we mended, we became friskier. Several of us, the more imaginative patients, concocted a story that a deep cover mafia operation was going on here. We kept a keen eye on the gang of four (the surgical team) as they made their rounds each morning. Dr. Luigi was downright shifty-eyed. His compatriot, Dr. Goodfellow, was too kind and considerate. Inside he must be a cold and conniving hood. Dr. Colonel may be a real doctor, but he's no more military than Bugs Bunny. There is no doubt that all three are fine surgeons, but that is not what they really do for a living. They are making big money, and it has something to do with the coffee sales throughout the hospital, which patients have to pay. That money must size up to a considerable sum. We guess that every other day they spend the night gambling in Las Vegas. They are too happy and wide-awake when we first see them at 4:30 each morning on their way to the OR. They are probably returning from another success at Vegas. And what about "Dr. Mole?" Who do they think they are kidding? No female doctor I have ever seen looks that sexy! And those legs! And that flirtatious look of hers! Impossible! Probably she is the distraction that allows the other three to cheat at Vegas and thereby make lots of money. We talked about bringing some of the other guys on the ward into our work of observing and analyzing, and maybe publish a weekly expose that we would pass around the hospital. But then the Marine Sergeant Major arrived.

To meet a marine is to know one and so in practically no time at all after he took up residence, we all knew him. He wasn't very gregarious. Not that he was shy, an absurd thought; after all, he was a Marine. Nor was he rank conscious—the only three ranks here were doctor, staff, and patient. He was not very approachable, not that he was shy or aloof but because he was, as were we all, scared listless or some such cliché. Combat is bad, but this surgery business is horrible. We thought he was in fine order when, after he had stored his gear in the bedside chest, he pasted on its door, neatly and in the exact center, a large Marine Corps decal. We all looked upon it with great approval except one man, the Army Major who was the nurse in charge of the ward. He informed the Marine that what he had done by putting a decal on display on hospital furniture was against regulations and ordered him to remove it immediately, which the Marine did. Hallelujah! Forget the mafia thing. Now we had our cause celebre.

As ranking revolutionary, I assembled a motley contingent, and we planned a suitable solution to this onerous conflict between the United States Army and the United States Marine Corps. While the Marine was off getting his operation, we developed our own style of operation. We gathered up a toilet plunger, a broom, some masking tape, and a Marine Corps decal (thanks to a Marine on the outside who was clued in on our caper). We picked a spot on the very high ceiling directly over the Marine's bed. One evening when our favorite nurse was on duty; she being somewhat of a revolutionary herself and was somewhat interested in the Army Major and saw her participation in all this as a flirtatious joke on him. She made sure that the coast was clear for us to do our thing. We carefully placed the decal on the downside-up-plunger with the decal's sticky side up. One man stood on the bed and held the plunger high so a broom handle could be taped to the plunger handle, and then applied the decal firmly to the ceiling.

The next day the patients and even a couple of the nurses and staff took a peek at the ceiling. The Marine returned to this bed the following day and was most pleased to see what the heavens had brought. It was also noticed the day the doctors made their rounds when the chief surgeon whispered something to the others, and they all looked up to admire the heavens and then went about their rounds. I left for a month of convalescent leave, but before I left, I saw that the Marine was receiving many visitors, most of whom were patients from other wards of the hospital. Many of the visitors followed a routine: look up, smile, greet the Marine, and go on their merry way. A couple of weeks later when I returned from leave, I noted four things: The Marine was still there, the decal was still in place, the Marine continued to have many smiling visitors, and our cooperative nurse and the Army Major appeared to be on especially good terms.

I spent months of recuperation at Fort Sam awaiting orders to either return to active duty or retire. I took leave to be home in Oxford over the Christmas holiday and then returned to Fort Sam where I finally got orders to retire in January 1982. The day I exchanged my active-duty identification card, which I had carried for 27 years, was an emotional experience. My hand tightened up as I handed it to the clerk and accepted a retiree identification card. I turned down an invitation to be hosted with a retirement ceremony including a parade, instead I just "faded away" (from a famous quote from military history: "Old soldiers never die, they just fade away") to our home in Oxford.

It was a real joy being back with the family although I was troubled by the constant sensation that I should be accountable to somebody, to make sure they knew exactly where I was and what I was doing; which had been my state of affairs for the past 27 years. I liked walking and did a lot of it, trying to get back into better health through exercise. The 2½ foot long incision on my left leg and the incision on my chest were now tender scars. The wired-up sternum did not allow much for twisting and turning. On the other hand, the subject of this entire story, the heart, happily 'lubdubbed" along with a confident beat.

I needed to be under the care of a cardiologist, so I went to the Veterans' Administration Hospital in Memphis. There I followed Julius Caesar's actions at the Battle of Zela: Veni, vidi, vici (I came, I saw, I conquered). I conquered any will or reason to remain in that facility. I found a cardiologist in Oxford who agreed to take me on.

Besides being as active as my body would bear, walking and gym time, I did a lot of, reading, studying, planning, and exploring. After a month of this, I worked on preparing our house for sale. The previous owner had greatly increased the size of the family room by removing a wall between it and the garage. The garage area then became part of the family room although the garage floor was 3 feet lower than the family room. I reconstructed a wall dividing the garage from the family room. Next, I renovated the dining room and painted the living room and the bedrooms. Finally, I did some restructuring and re-flooring in the entryway and the front hall. I also did a great amount of gardening and repairs in the backyard. After I completed all of that, I felt very confident and ambitious but didn't know what to do. Darlene came up with the solution; we would buy the TV Tempo franchise from a young man who wished to sell his.

The TV Tempo was a free magazine that listed television channels and their programs for the next week and contained advertising space for local merchants. The selling of advertisements provided the income, part of which went to TV Tempo Inc. Each week a layout of the advertisements was prepared and sent to the TV Tempo printer with an order for the number of issues to be distributed. Each week the magazine is distributed to racks in Oxford and several nearby towns. I enjoyed doing the layout and the distribution. I did not like making sales calls, and I did not have faith in what I was selling. After 11 months we sold the franchise to a law professor who was highly educated and exceptionally bright but a real wacko who saw everything as a big deal and who was very unsure of himself. We had 11 extended conversations before he finally decided to buy. And even then, I tried to get him to understand the reality of things, but he kept on dreaming about how he was going to develop this into a major publishing firm. Six months later he took us to court for the fraudulent and evil things we had done in selling him this business. I began to worry that this guy would like to put me in prison for life. The judge ordered us to return his down payment. In the final analysis, I lost a thousand dollars but learned a priceless lesson: if you go to court, get the best lawyer you can afford. Inexpensive attorneys may prove to be incompetent and lose the case that you think is solidly in your favor.

In the summer of 1983, we decided to take a trip out west. Michelle was not with us since she had employment, but Susan and Amy went with us. We planned to find a place to retire and to visit Mike and family in Washington State. As it turned out, this was a really profitable idea. On July 13 we arrived in Las Vegas late in the afternoon and decided to spend the night and see the sights. Late in the evening, after we had put the girls to bed and they were sound asleep, Darlene and I walked to the Desert Inn Casino and tried our luck on the slot machines. I was having a lot of luck on the quarter machines, and my plastic cup was full, so I turned the quarters in for silver dollars. I was attracted by a set of five Machines tied together, which offered a super prize. One silver dollar would play the machine, but three silver dollars would include a chance to win the super prize. Since I had been lucky all evening and in my mind, I was playing with the house's money, I played three dollars each time I pulled the handle. The third time I did that whistles and bells began to play, and lights began to blink. I did not know what was going on. I looked about for help.

A croupier and the people sitting at his table were looking my way. He pointed excitedly to the top of the machines where the number in neon was flashing $211,044. I looked at it, and my brain went numb. I could not comprehend how much money that was. An employee came, wrote down my name, and told me that a vice president had to come in to approve my winning after a technician had checked the "call strips" to ensure that the machine was functioning properly. About an hour and a half later the Vice President arrived, affirmed that I had indeed won the money and asked how I would like to be paid: coins, bills, or check. I chose a check since their bank was a block away. Then we filled out federal Form W-2G, "Statement for Certain Gambling Winnings," which contained notice about the payer and payee and the amount of winnings. The original copy was immediately sent to the Internal Revenue Service, copy B went to the payer, and I received copy C as a certification that I had indeed won the money. We agreed to meet the next morning at 10 o'clock for a formal presentation of the award of the check and to pose for some pictures. It was about 3:30 AM when Darlene and I finally got back to our motel. I slept very poorly that night, waking up every hour or so trying to figure out how much our winnings were worth. Could we buy a new car or are we financially set for life? We went to the bank the next day, received the check, held a two by 6-foot prop of the check for the photographer, and then walked to their bank, all the time very mindful of that huge check in my pocket. We put most of the money in a CD account. We got a suite for three days at the Desert Inn, had a first-class formal, private dinner, saw the sites, did a little shopping, and did a little more (very little more) gambling and won an additional $400.

We headed west out of Las Vegas in high spirits. It was time to look ahead because our future might lie in Monterey. Since the first day I saw Monterey, a quarter century earlier, I pictured it as the ideal place to retire. Twenty years ago, I was stationed at the Army language school a second time and again, Darlene and I resolved that Monterey would definitely be our retirement home. Now, with our family finances greatly improved, we thought we might buy a house while we were visiting Monterey.

The Monterey Bay area was disappointing. It was very crowded, seemed to have lost some of its mystique, and was very expensive. In the coming years, I visited the Monterey Bay area every other year. It is one of my favorite places in the whole wide world, but I choose not to live there. After a couple of days in the Monterey Bay area, we drove up the coast of California and Oregon to Centralia, Washington, to the home of my son Mike, my daughter-in-law, Anchalee, and my first grandson, Matt, for a few days visit. Mike and I recounted our adventure three years earlier, after the eruption of Mount Saint Helens. We had rented a plane and pilot to fly over Mount Saint Helens for about an hour to view the extensive damage and for Mike, who was then a journalist, to take pictures. From Washington, we returned to Ole Miss in time for me to begin law school.

Many years earlier I was excited with the idea of attending law school, but now, after one semester at the University of Mississippi law school, I realized that I had lost that fervor. Our good friends Henry and Mary Richarde, who had retired in Florida convinced us to consider retiring there. After scouting out Tampa and Orlando, we bought a house in Orlando. Darlene and the girls returned to Oxford to complete the spring semester at school and then joined Kip and me in Orlando. Meanwhile Kip, who had recently left the Air Force, and I rented an apartment in Winter Park, Florida and began searching for a job. With the help of Henry Richarde's son-in-law who was on the board of directors of Employers Association of Florida (EAF), I was hired on as a consultant. Most of my work consisted of teaching leadership and management techniques to mid-level supervisors in member companies and to do company-wide employee surveys. For me, teaching leadership was easy; but selling myself to a company owner or manager was challenging since he would know much more than I about the current gurus who wrote books about leadership and management and could speak their lingo. Doing employee surveys was a pleasure and very useful for a company. Some companies that were members of EAF had multiple plants in states as far removed as California and Ohio. I especially enjoyed doing surveys for them since it meant that I had the opportunity to sit with the senior executives of the company and provide them with some meaningful and helpful information. After I had been with EAF for about 18 months, serious discrepancies in the handling of money by others were uncovered.

The Board of Directors of the Association found it necessary to reduce the number of employees and relieve the director. I had been one of the last to be hired, so I was one of the first to be fired. This gave me an opportunity to pursue my dream of teaching full time at a college. It also gave me the drive to readjust my private life. My marriage had not been a good match, and for the past fifteen years, my wife and I lived in estrangement. I loved my children and was determined to hold the family together until the children were adults. Now it seemed the time to separate had come even though my youngest daughter had not yet completed high school.

The world was changing for me in many ways. Leaving the army after nearly 28 years of service was a drastic change. As my children grew to adulthood and left home, I missed each of them intensely. The heart surgery and recovery affected me physically, and psychologically. When a cardiologist told me after my operation that I would probably be back for more surgery within five years and definitely within 20 years, I assumed that my life would be ending in a few years. I wanted those years to be happy years not sad ones living in estrangement. So, I moved into an apartment and notified the children that I was going to file for divorce. The months that followed were filled with surprises. Since we were a very close family, I assumed that the children would be very opposed to what I was doing. Early on, I resolved that I would not get involved in a discussion of why this was happening, other than to state that their mother and I were two very different people, that this is a very personal and final decision, and I hoped this would not change the close relationship they had with both their father and mother. My three sons seem to take it all in stride; my three daughters not so much at first but soon my relationship with them was back to normal.

Darlene surprised me the most. I assumed she wanted a separation as much as I. I was shocked and downhearted when I realized what this meant for her: embarrassment, feeling abandoned, frightened about her future, her source of income, being homeless and destitute. The attorney I hired to handle the divorce was a neighbor, a friend of ours, very compassionate and, as I requested of him, as fair to Darlene as to me. I was honestly trying to give Darlene a fair share of our assets. As it turned out, she got more than I did.

I began my quest for employment as a college teacher at Seminole Community College. As luck would have it, the geography professor had just resigned, so I was hired as the geography professor, and with a little bit of effort on my part, I also was hired to teach International Relations. The department chair, Dick Loper, told me that I might also be able to teach in the Honors Program. He said he would recommend me to the Director of the Honors Program, Lucinda Coulter (Cindy), who was looking for someone to teach an honors history class (Western Civilization). I did not hear from her for several days while she was offering the position to other people whom she knew well but who could not squeeze her course into their schedule. Probably out of sheer desperation she hired me. Some years later she admitted to me that at our first meeting she thought I was "a bit arrogant." I'm not surprised that a six-foot-four-inch 220-pound army colonel who is trying to sell himself as a teacher to a five-foot-eight-inch powerful faculty member with many years overseeing students might succumb to judging "this novice" as "too big for his britches." The first semester was very demanding. Honor students are by nature good students, meaning they actually study and read the textbook. Even though my major in college was history, I had to relearn all those many minor facts that are quickly forgotten over the years. A course outline had to be prepared, as well as tests, handouts and writing requirements. Also, a good teacher should have interesting tales and observations, which are not in the textbook but are appropriate and are appreciated by the students. All of these things are a lot of work but need to be done only for the first time a course is given.

Cindy and I were married in a formal ceremony at her church, Bear Lake United Methodist Church, before a gathering of members of our families and friends on July 4th 10 months later. Few knew that we had plans to leave on Tuesday on a military aircraft as retired military space available passengers out of a naval base in Jacksonville, Florida. Because Cindy would need documentation as my dependent (spouse) and since we were due to leave early Tuesday morning and since Monday was a holiday, and military support offices would be closed, we also had to get a military ID for her; therefore, we were legally married by the minister in the parsonage on July 2nd, so we could get a military dependent ID on the Second of July. We made the flight, which was headed for the US Naval Station in Sicily. We stopped to refuel at the US Navy base in Rota Spain much to our surprise. Cindy's response was "since we want to go to Europe, and this is Europe, let's get off." We unloaded our luggage, passed through customs, and went outside to breathe the open air. We were on the mainland of Europe, a first for each of us. We rented a car, drove to Granada to see the Alhambra, then on to Toledo, which is a must for tourists, then through Madrid where traffic was horrible and the temperature worse, and on to Barcelona. After seeing Gaudi's Cathedral and seeing the city and some flamingo nightlife we turned in the rental car and took a train to Geneva and after a day onward, to Payerne, Switzerland which we had picked out on a map when we were planning the trip. Much to our surprise, there were no mountains in view. We got a room in the railroad hotel for the night and, while having dinner, met the hotel manager. He was a relocated Serb, and we struck up a good conversation about Yugoslavia. At some point, we told him we had just recently married and would like to find a romantic spot in the mountains where we would spend a week. He recommended the Village of Rougemont. He told us how to get there by train and how to find bed and breakfast once there. He proved to be very helpful and an excellent conversationalist.

We arrived the next day in Rougemont, got a room in the railroad hotel, and received much help from the small but sufficient tour office about activities in the area. That evening, there was a knock on the door and a large package mailed to us by a sender whose name we could not read. It was a mystery since no one who knew us knew where we were. In the package was a box neatly tied with a colorful ribbon and inside the box was a dress that Cindy had left in the closet at the Payerne train station hotel. Obviously, the hotel manager thought that we had forgotten it and took great delight in sending it to us. What a guy! In truth, Cindy had intentionally left it for the maid or whoever. It is our practice when we travel to take old clothes and to leave them along the way. Henceforth we leave such in the wastebasket, so there is no doubt that we are abandoning them.

The next day we got a lovely bed and breakfast. In the village, we made purchases of bread, cheese, and wine for our trip up the funicular to a high trail for a hike down to Gstaad.

The choice of this vacation spot could not have been better. Our hosts spoke only French. Fortunately, Cindy spoke a little French so she could communicate a bit with the lady of the house. Our room had a View of the mountains, and the food was excellent (morning and evening meals). Our daily treks through the high plains needed only the music from the movie *The Sound of Music* to make it complete. The trails were generally flat, not muddy, although occasionally we would cross patches of snow. The ambient temperature was in the high 60s: quiet, clear sky, little wind. Sometimes we could see the fields hundreds of feet below us with herds of Swiss brown cattle with cowbells. One day we met only three people on the trails. It is one of those experiences where everything seems perfect, and the memories are clear and permanent.

Some local entertainment filled most evenings at Rochemont. One evening it was the local military band. The most memorable was a local Alpine horn band. The huge Alpine horn is played with one end on the ground and the other end held by the player who is standing, except for this evening. As a small crowd gathered around and had been entertained for some time, the red-headed and colorful player began sinking into a chair; then to the ground and finally off to sleep after copious amounts of his favorite libation, much to the crowd's amusement.

From Switzerland we took a train to the United States Air Force base at Frankfurt, Germany, hoping to catch a space available flight to the States. We waited for two days but no luck, and we had to get back to school, so we bought airline tickets. That was one of only two times in all of our space available travels that we could not get back to the states at a reasonable time via space available. This trip wetted our appetite for seeing Europe. Since then, through our many travels, we've probably spent nine or ten months total in Europe.

1982–1990 Military Hospital to Retirement

A lucky day.

Cindy and I wed.

Honeymoon in Trier, Germany

Susan, Amy, Shellie, Jeff, Kip, Mike

Chapter 22
1990 Sabbatical

The word Sabbath refers to the seventh day of the week, the day according to the Bible that the Lord rested after having created the world and all its contents. The third of the Ten Commandments states: "Keep holy the Sabbath." In academia, the sabbatical year is a special award, which provides that every seventh year a professor may obtain a leave of absence, often with pay, for travel, research, and rest. Seminole community college offered their professors sabbaticals for one semester or one-year subject to formal application and certain restrictions. Cindy had never applied for one during the more than 25 years she had been teaching. The idea of taking time off to explore and write about some part of the world intrigued us. Since the Soviet Union was collapsing, this would be a great time and opportunity to partake in the collapse of communist Europe and the excitement in Western Europe as the Iron Curtain ceased to exist. We planned on meeting with personnel from select US embassies and local universities to discuss events as they developed. Now our concentration would be on economics (Cindy's field of study) and foreign relations (my field of study). Both of us had studied and taught European history.

We planned to commence travel on the first of July and return from Europe about December the first for a total of five months of research and travel in mainland Europe. Our goal was to visit all the countries of Western Europe and as many of Eastern Europe as possible. In 1990, the general sentiment was that the Soviet Union was weakening under the stress of trying to keep up with the United States and that the anti-missile defense system which the United States was initiating would bankrupt the Soviet Union or bring her to her knees. We wanted to see Eastern Europe as it was under the communist regime. During the spring semester, we did a fair amount of individual study of Europe. Additionally, I encouraged my geography class to use that portion of the course which required students to write no less than 3000 words, to write what they would do if they were given a free five-month semester to tour and study Europe. Each student was asked to provide a sequence of countries to visit and the ideal time to be there. Student responses were exceptionally good. Most of them made a great effort to create an ideal itinerary, and several were so pleased with their work that they intended to follow their plan themselves if they could sell their idea to mom and dad. Throughout my time of teaching geography, I recommended to my students that they spend a semester overseas during their college years, preferably the second semester of their junior year. Some followed my suggestion, and either they or their parents gratefully acknowledged that it was an effective way for both learning and maturing.

The final plan for our trip was as follows: fly to Brussels, lease a car for five months. Drive to Bonn, Germany, pick up the camping gear which a student carried for us and left at her mother's. Camp our way through Scandinavia and take a five-day tour of St. Petersburg (Leningrad), Russia. Take a ferry to Sweden, ferry and drive through Sweden, Denmark, West and East Germany including Berlin to Poland. Head south through ten countries to Greece, interrupted midway with a drive to

Heidelberg, Germany for a five-day international conference on cooperation in improving the European Union with emphasis on education. From Greece, we planned to go through Yugoslavia to Italy, France, Spain, and Belgium and return Stateside. And in fact, we followed the plan quite closely. The weather was near perfect the entire trip, and our coverage of Europe could not have been more extensive or in depth.

Finances were a real concern, so we economized to the max. One of our daughters took care of our car. Dean and Mary Shirley, close family friends, lived in our house for five months, took care of our two dogs, and paid the bills. We leased a car in Brussels for the entire trip. We had our camping gear which we used from time to time as it was cheaper than B&Bs which are our preferred accommodations when traveling, and we made use of US military facilities whenever possible. We lived the life of blue-collar, middle-class people, which was food for the soul, the pocketbook and a way to meet interesting people who were forthcoming in their friendly and sincere conversations. The value of these five months was priceless. The total cost to us was $25,000. Cindy had purchased an early laptop computer and would write as we traveled. I would do most of the driving.

Five Months Exploring Europe

We arrived at the Orlando airport three hours early. I guess we were extra cautious so we wouldn't miss our flight to JFK airport in New York, where we had a departure time for Brussels at 7 PM. About an hour before our departure we were advised that weather would delay our departure for New York. Two and a half hours sitting on the runway later we finally departed, knowing that unless the overseas flight had been delayed, we missed our connecting flight to Brussels. This was bad news since I had purchased the tickets at a very good price, but our agreement stipulated that if we missed our flight, it would not be rescheduled nor reimbursed. Our five-month tour of Europe was not getting off to a good start. When we arrived in the vicinity of New York, the pilot informed that we would be delayed since so many commercial flights were ahead of us because of the weather. We now were concerned for another reason, our safety. Finally, our turn came, and we were on final approach when the pilot gunned it, and we went back up to get in line once more. The pilot gave the reason that a Chinese aircraft was on our runway. "This is going to be one exciting sabbatical," said Cindy.

When we got on the ground, we made a run for the desk to see if our connecting flight to Brussels had already gone. It had. Then we were second in line to speak with a very young-looking girl representing the airlines. She would talk with the older couple ahead of us, punch the keyboard of a computer terminal, talk with the couple and punch the keyboard. Then she went to talk with the clerk at the next station. There were now two lines before the airline reps. Our young Afro American clerk came back to our station and again talked with the older couple. Now there was a long line on our left before the other clerk and a long line behind us. The problem was that the long line to our left was moving right along, and our clerk was still talking with the couple ahead of us and punching a computer. Then she talked on the phone. Again, she went to talk with the other representative who was processing people expeditiously. Instead of getting peeved we laughed. We saw humor in this extreme fiasco and the events of the day. After all, we were free for the next five months. Our clerk came back to her station to tell us that she had to go to the office and would be gone for a bit, but she would be back. She returned after five or 10 minutes with a hand full of papers and said: "Here are your tickets for the flight at the same time tomorrow night; here is a voucher for a room at a nearby hotel for tonight. Here also is a voucher for limousine service to the hotel and back tomorrow, and also vouchers for dinners tonight and breakfast tomorrow. I am sorry for the delay. We are also upgrading your tickets to business class." Then she looked at us; a frown fluttered across her pretty face but quickly faded, and a smile lightened up her eyes.

"You'll have to forgive me for being so slow. I am just a trainee. I was supposed to come in to observe this evening, but because of the bad weather, many personnel couldn't make it in, and so they put me on this desk and told me to do the best I could. I hope you understand." Cindy and I were overjoyed with the good news of tickets and vouchers. We gave her a big smile and said: "Given the situation, you did an outstanding job. Thank you very much for your service." We headed for our luggage and the limousine.

The business class flight to Europe was excellent. We had terrific service, great food, and lots of room. We arrived in Brussels; picked up the Audi car we had leased with no trouble and left for Bonn where we picked up a suitcase of camping equipment, which a student had carried to Europe for us. Then we started north towards Scandinavia. We drove for about an hour, found a two-story Gasthaus and went to bed.

The next morning, I was a late riser whereas Cindy had been up for more than an hour. She told me she had repacked most of our things and was going down to pay our bill and check out. She was gone a few minutes when suddenly she rushed in and announced: "Hurry up and grab our things! This place is on fire." We put our things in the car and drove the car across the street to safety, and then joined the small crowd that had assembled to observe the smoke rising from the roof. About fifteen minutes later a fire truck with hoses arrived. By then flames began to come through the roof. About ten minutes later a fire truck with ladders arrived and began spraying the roof; at which time we hopped in the car and headed north and spent the next hour analyzing what we had just witnessed.

During a leisurely drive up the middle of the peninsula of Denmark, we stopped at Billund where we visited the world famous Legoland, which was developed on a grand scale. In one building a room full of gleeful children were putting together an assortment of contraptions using Legos taken from a mountainous pile. What a joyful place! In another building was a dollhouse museum with tiny ornate doll houses from many periods of time. Each room and piece of furniture had been created with amazing consideration to detail.

On the northern coast of Denmark, we took a ferry to Goteborg, Sweden and drove to Oslo, Norway. There we found delightful B&B hosts who were teachers. We walked all over Oslo, exploring. We found that from 5:00 p.m. on Friday until eight a.m. on Monday all stores except restaurants were closed. The Norwegian Museum of Cultural History was one of our favorite tourist's sites. We enjoyed the church with its intricate wood design and the exemplary houses built over many years. During the ten days that we spent in Norway, we explored many of the urban areas and talked with many people. We saw no evidence of poverty. We also saw no examples of great wealth. Even the Palace of the King and Queen was relatively modest by European standards. The diplomacy of the people who lived on the Scandinavian Peninsula was remarkable when they peacefully split their country into Norway and Sweden in 1905. (It should be noted that the same diplomacy divided Czechoslovakia into the Czech Republic and the Slovak Republic in 1993)

On a tram in Stavanger, we spoke with an older man about

why he thought Norway would never join the EU. He said he didn't trust the Germans: "When the band begins to play, the Hun will begin to march!" Our B&B host, a widow, told us how terrifying the German occupation of Norway during World War II had been. Her husband had fled across the mountains into Sweden for refuge. He may have been Jewish, but it didn't come up. After the war, he came home.

I should make it known that throughout Europe, we were mostly treated as relatives stopping for a brief visit. During our visit to the US Embassy, we were surprised to learn some interesting things, such as the major US export to Norway was entertainment. They love our records, movies, and television shows.

We drove north on a two-lane highway that wound around the fjords, the narrow road usually bounded on the cliff side by a low stone wall. Traffic was slow, and no one seemed to pass. We could see ships and boats and houses and mountains and cliffs like a constant changing mural. A special treat was a drive up and through an ice-strewn path. Twenty-foot walls of ice dwarfed our car as we drove through occasional cuts. It was treeless alpine meadows with unfenced sheep, usually a mother with bell and two lambs. They will pause in the middle of the road to observe us in the car as we stopped. And then the lambs would nudge close to their mother as she calmly picked her way off the road. We saw a long valley of ice with a small glacial lake and cross-country skiers in groups of two to ten making their way vigorously across the field of ice, their bright ski suits like tumbling flowers against glistening ice.

As we drove north from Bergen, the valleys became wider, farms larger, Fields flatter and farm machinery bigger. Fields of small grain stretched for hundreds of acres as we drove towards Trondheim. White houses and huge red barns dominated the rolling countryside. Trondheim was hosting a run when we arrived at the center of town. The first lackadaisical tourist information person we encountered on the trip wasn't too encouraging about the campgrounds because of the people in town for the run. Her directions to campground some ten kilometers away were excellent. We walked down to the docks and through several city streets noticing again that all stores were closed. We finally found a small grocery store open where we bought bread and cheese. The drive to the campground carried us along the fjord to a ferry stop.

We have camped in Canada, New England, Alaska, and over the United States, but none of those places are better than Norway. A real advantage of camping if you want to learn about a country and its people is the opportunity to have close contact in an informal setting.

On one side of our tent was a young couple with playful children. Their father was a mechanical engineer from Tampere. They were driving a large station wagon and had a neat tent with two compartments, one for the adults and one for the children. A young teacher from Norway came over to chat, and we enjoyed munching on a rather sparse breakfast as we talked with him. He had been trained as a journalist but was now teaching history and other social sciences. He had taught about seven years after working for a magazine. His wife was a nurse. His English was fluent. "Age," he explained: "strongly influences how Norwegians feel about the EC and Germany. The older people remember the World War, the German attacks, and are still bitter about the war and the Nazi occupation of their home front. They are still distrustful of the Germans, do not want a united Germany, and wish the Economic Community would go away."

At our next campground, we encountered a friendly international set with whom we shared the kitchen. It was a Dutch family living in Sweden, an older couple from Denmark, a German from Kiel, and a young couple from Switzerland busy writing postcards. The Dutchman, a young manager for Unilever and his beautiful blonde nurse wife, was analytical of the Swedes. He had been there three years, his children attended Swedish schools, and his wife worked in a Swedish nursing home. He was ambivalent about the Swedish system. According to him, about one-fourth of his workforce would be on vacation, sick leave, or not working for some reason on any given day. He didn't think much of their work ethic. On the other hand, if a worker was an alcoholic, he couldn't fire him or even threaten to fire him. He might have to pay for treatment or more leave and recovery time. If a worker had a strong disagreement with the supervisor, he might be sent home at full pay to cool off for two weeks. "The Swedish culture is a very caring one," he said. The children are provided a hot meal at school; there is childcare for working mothers and lavish vacation and sick leave. Taxes are very high, and there is the usual bureaucratic paperwork. The Swedes keep statistics on everything. "Unemployment is a big problem. "If my company dismissed the workers who aren't really working, there would be many more unemployed."

We crossed the border between Norway and Finland in the far north, above the Arctic Circle. It was the first time on sabbatical that we had crossed a European border where we didn't have to go through checkpoints. As we drove south through Finland, we found mostly small towns. In one, a resort area, we had dinner in a large, pleasant hotel. It was my first and only experience eating reindeer hamburger. We continued to camp, although the weather had become rainy with a light drizzle. The campground at Oulu on a small but pleasant beach on the Gulf of Bothnia had outdoor cubical saunas for men and women. The camping Finns looked prosperous with their trailers, huge tents with outdoor sitting rooms with painted on plastic windows with curtains. The Finns did not seem as gregarious as the Norwegians.

From the highway, we saw mostly forests with fir only or birch only trees with evidence of selective logging. In the morning Cindy cooked breakfast in the cook shed area, accompanied by six students from Poland. They spoke English poorly but enthusiastically. They had pooled their money and rented a car and come north for a holiday and a new taste of freedom. Two were in law school, and one had a degree in economics. Poland had just opened to the outside world after a heroic battle of political wheels between Lech Walesa and the Polish communist government. These students were breathing the free western air and exhilarating in each breath. They discussed economic issues, especially how industrial wages were set in the United States. They were bounding with enthusiasm to go home and change their country. Three were planning to return and create a private school, which would openly teach capitalism and freedom. Cindy was preaching and pontificating, pointing with pride and viewing with alarm in her most professorial way when it dawned on her that maybe it was time to head down the road. That night ended our 13 straight nights in a tent, three in the rain. What a relief to leave the countryside and reach Helsinki. We had driven into town on a highway titled, Mannerheimvägen. To get to the tourist office, we needed street Norra Esplanaden. Suddenly we found ourselves, I know not how or why, at the tourist office. In the coming weeks, I would discover what a remarkable navigator Cindy is. The tourist office directed us to a business-like, reasonable Hotel where we relaxed for three days before undertaking the only prearranged tour of our trip. To get a visa for Russia required so much red tape that we simply booked a five-day train tour from Helsinki into Leningrad.

Since we had some time in Helsinki, we decided to try getting a visa for several of the Eastern bloc countries we hoped to visit soon. We went to the Bulgarian embassy and left our passports for two days and got a visa. Next, we tried the Polish Embassy for a Visa and had one the next day. The Czechoslovakian embassy told us that we would not need a visa for Czechoslovakia. They seemed very uncertain as to the situation. The bureaucrats didn't seem to know any more about visas than we tourists.

In our exploration of Helsinki, one of the most interesting and unusual places we visited was the Helsinki Worker Housing Museum. It had some of the world's first public housing in 1909. Each unit was a two-room apartment which had an average of five people per room. A unit represented each decade; telling the life story of a family that had lived there. The apartments were made up to look as much as possible as they had looked when that family lived in them. Former residents donated some of the objects in the exhibition. Each unit had running water and a toilet. After 1918, the apartments had electricity.

We visited the Bank of Finland Museum, which had exhibits showing the history of money and the role of the Central Bank of Finland in the European system of central banks. We also saw the Sebelius monument, a tribute to the great Finnish composer. The monument, one of the most memorable of our travels, consisted of about 600 steel pipes altogether which brought memories of all the pipe organs we had seen in numerous churches and cathedrals during our travels. We also enjoyed the classical buildings with their columns and statutes reminiscent of ancient Rome and Greece and gave the city a stately, formal air.

Finally, the day came to board the train and venture into the mysterious land known as the USSR. Immediately our expectations came to life as a stern looking uniformed official examined our passports and visas. A stout, dough-faced woman in uniform searched our train compartment, even standing on the bench seat to examine the overhead compartment and hidden narrow ledge above the door. Out the window, we watched as a dreary, monotonous landscape of dark green punctuated by rough looking tan buildings sped past. We arrived in Leningrad in good time and were housed in a bleak, multistory rectangle hotel of gray concrete. The furnishings looked cheap. Our room was small and austere. There was a television in the room. It was playing early our first morning. On the small black and white screen were young women exercising. They all dressed alike, in something like a ballerina warm-up. It went on and on. I had the TV on probably 40 minutes, and that was what was on the one available channel. Boring!

Our guide for the tour was a pleasant woman about 40 who was an English professor at the University of Leningrad. She spoke excellent English and was cheerful and friendly. We did the usual tourist things: The Hermitage Museum, the summer and winter palaces, the Aurora, the bridges, the Smolny Cathedral, parks, ballet, and folk dances crowded into five full days.

I was impressed with the subway. We descended on the longest escalator I had ever seen deep into the bowls of the earth. There were beautiful chandeliers, ornate marble floors, alabaster friezes, vaulted ceilings, and hordes of grim-faced people all rushing through the environment. The subway was started in 1940 and partially completed after the war. Since most of the construction occurred during the Cold War, the subways were built to double as nuclear bomb shelters.

We left on the train returning to Helsinki. At the outskirts of Leningrad, we saw acres and acres of small garden plots, each with a shed. We learned later that most communist countries had such plots around cities where city people could grow vegetables privately. In some cases, the shed was said to become virtual summer homes where people could get away from the stifling cities. Again, the train was searched before we passed the Finland border, only this time even more thoroughly. A stern, uniformed woman stood on a seat to closely examine the upper luggage storage to be sure no one was escaping the workers' paradise. We were glad to be leaving. For me, it was especially enlightening to travel with Cindy who has long studied Russian history.

We spent one more night in Finland before driving to Turku where we got the ferry to Stockholm. We had called ahead and booked a room in a moderately priced hotel. When we found it, we discovered that they had no hotel parking and that the hotel began on the second floor of the building. A clerk advised that we could park our car in a public garage across the street. We got three small suitcases from our car and went to our room and went to sleep. The following morning, we discovered that someone smashed a window of the car and much had been stolen. The thief had taken a cigar box containing three pairs of prescription glasses of each of us, traveler's checks, a personal checkbook, a suitcase full of clothing, and worst of all our 35-mm camera with a roll of film from Russia and Finland. Our insurance covered all of our losses except for the film.

The next day we moved to the outskirts of Stockholm to stay at a B&B run by a lovely lady we came to call Glinda the Good after the good witch of the South in the movie *Wizard of Oz*. Like Glinda, she spoke in a giggly, high pitched voice. She was blond, and very beautiful, in her late forties. Like many of our B&B hostesses, she and Cindy hit it off well. She explained that Americans were very uptight about sex, while Swedes were uptight about alcohol. According to her, Sweden had some of the world's highest taxes on alcohol, which would give them a problem entering the EU where import duties on alcohol are lower or non-existent. She said that the reason so many Swedes were on the ferries on the Baltic was that they took the weekend off to drink. On the other hand, she said, when she was 16 her parents didn't want her out driving with her boyfriend, so they let the boyfriend move into their house, and they were allowed to sleep together for a couple of years until they became bored with each other. One of the things I learned from our world travels is that different societies and cultures have different ways of looking at the world, some very surprising.

One of the most interesting things we saw in Stockholm was the Vasa, a huge Swedish warship constructed between 1626 and 1628 for the Swedish king, Gustavus Adolphus to join his fleet for the Thirty Years' War. His advisers and shipbuilders were too frightened to tell him that the ship had structural problems. The result was, when the 1200 tons, 226 feet long behemoth was launched, the top-heavy ship lumbered out of the homeport and sank within a mile. In the 1950s she was discovered just outside Stockholm Harbor and raised, mostly intact. Now she is housed in the Vasa Museum which had just opened when we visited.

Later as we returned from Sweden by ferry from Malmo to Copenhagen, we enjoyed this delightful city built on an island in the Kattegat, the narrow isthmus between Denmark and Sweden. Soon after our trip, the Oresund Bridge and tunnel were built joining the two countries. It is the longest road and rail bridge and tunnel in Europe.

Cindy and I grew up Reading the beloved tales of Hans Christian Andersen. The movie featuring Danny Kaye made Copenhagen a magical city, and it truly is. When we were there in the summer of 1990, it was filled with young people from all over Europe and from many other places in the world. We stayed at a delightful B&B at the edge of the city; while the youth hostels overflowed with laughing, backpacking teenagers, and twentysomes. Many bathed in the train station, which had lots of showers at cheap rates. There were parks in which to sleep. It is easy to see why Copenhagen attracts the young and the young at heart. The center of the city contains Tivoli Gardens one of the two oldest amusement parks in the world. Tivoli was begun in 1843, and the other is Dyrehavsbakken, nearby in Denmark, which began as a royal deer park but was opened to the public in the early 1600s. We spent an afternoon and evening in Tivoli. The painted boats, an exaggerated Japanese pagoda, a very old wooden roller coaster, and street magicians added to the festive atmosphere. There were small duck houses at the edge of the water, with little-inclined bridges. The ducks would walk up the boards with small planks attached and enter the elaborate houses. By evening, the lights, music, and laughter made this one of our favorite spots in Europe. It should be noted that street performers are a delight all over Europe. Mimes are our favorite. Cindy liked most of the musicians such as the lawn violinist who said she spends hours a day practicing and does it on the street where her open violin case attracts a groovy sum of money each day, where she "blends the mood of the violin with the mood of the street." We engaged a number of the adventurers in conversation. Each of them was exploring Europe alone but teamed up with a couple of other interesting persons for a while, before finding new friends and new places. Many were on tight budgets. So, an offer to buy them a drink and a bite is almost always accepted with enthusiasm and hearty conversation.

The drive from Copenhagen to Hamburg and then across northern Germany was a study in agriculture. The countryside was much more densely populated than in Cedar County, Nebraska where I grew up. It seemed more modern as most of the roads had hard surfaces, The fields were smaller, and the farm places (most often two or three would be clustered at a road junction) would have large, brick buildings; giving one the sense of stability and permanency of the family on the farm. This is in deep contrast with what I see or don't see when I return to Cedar County each year. My grandfather began farming on his own late in the 19th-century on land several miles south of Wynot, Nebraska. He and a brother built a small house. When I was a boy that house was then used as a cow barn since a large wooden house had been built. I had a special attachment to the home place where I worked several summers during my high school years. It was large, had a lot of memories for many relatives, and had lots of wooden structures: house, barn, hog barn, car barn corncrib, smokehouse, outhouse, tool shop, etc. It was a sad day indeed when the day came that I drove by the home place where now only rows of corn met the eye.

We had the run of Berlin for three days. The Berlin wall had been breached, and Checkpoint Charlie was now a tourist attraction and passage, although still manned by East Berlin guards. US military (including retirees) could ride the public transportation for free, and tours of the city were plentiful and excellent. Everywhere we looked we saw familiar features since the city had figured so prominently in our memories of news clips and movies of World War II and the Cold War era.

While in East Berlin we looked for old currencies for souvenirs. We wanted to exchange American money for East German coins and carried a sign for people to read. To our surprise almost immediately, a few young people searched their pockets and bags, and we got a handful of coins for our collection. We had seen very few smiles in East Germany, but we saw a lot on that day. Then we moved on to Potsdam where we were able to go into the small museum and touch the tables where Truman, Churchill, and Stalin had sat to restructure much of the postwar world.

On to Poland. The first things we noticed about Poland were its ugly buildings, especially houses, which were built of masonry and had large areas of exposed rubble. We concluded after some discussion that it was so because of two factors. First, stucco costs money and money was very scarce, therefore "looks" would be a foolish consideration in spending the precious zloty, and secondly, since no one else had stucco applied to their house repairs or modifications, neither should anyone else.

On our way to Warsaw, I learned an interesting fact about humans. We came to a crossroad, but there were no signs. I thought we must turn left to go to Warsaw, but I was not sure. An elderly couple was walking to our left. There was no traffic, so I waved them down and in my warmest voice asked: "Warsaw?" as I pointed. And I did it again. The couple said a lot in Polish to each other, and they became somewhat upset. Then I remembered that W is V in German. So, I said to them in an inquisitive voice: "Varsa?" and pointed left. You would have thought we won the jackpot. Varsava!, Varsava! As we thanked them and drove left, I looked at the old man's solemn face. Without a word, his face said loud and clear: "Why in Hades didn't you say so in the first place?"

We got a room in a large, old fashion, spacious hotel in Warsaw and much to our surprise we paid only $29 a night. Apparently, they had not yet received the word that for American Tourists the charge in most places was $100 a night for Americans. The accommodations were excellent. Few spoke English. In the dining room, we looked about for a dish we recognized and pointed at it when we ordered, not very polite but effective. When we had crossed the border and presented our visas at a checkpoint, we also exchanged money. It took some effort on the part of the exchange clerk to explain that the old currency is worth 10% of the new currency. We needed to cash a check to get local money. There was no convenient American Express office, so we went to a large bank downtown. There we joined in the line in front of the building. Poland still had a communist government although the leadership of Lech Walesa had moved the country towards a little liberalization. The big question was how to change communism into something else. When our position in line got into the building, we were given a number, so that we could mill around until our number was called. Cindy began talking with a tourist from South Africa on the difficulties of coping with the local systems. After about 15 minutes, our number was called, and we went to a window and told the teller that we wanted to cash traveler checks for $200. We were told that we would be called at a window further back in the building. I assumed that this office of the bank only handled the exchange of checks and notes. The receiving clerk called our number. She inspected both of the American Express checks thoroughly and motioned for us to return to our seats and then placed the papers in the box of what I assumed was the office supervisor's. The supervisor sat transfixed in her small cubicle across the narrow hallway from the receiving clerk. The cubicle was small. She did not move a muscle for a few minutes when she picked up our papers, examined them thoroughly and attached them to a paper of her own and then placed them in what I presumed was her outbox. A few minutes later a clerk came in, picked up the bundle and took it to her cubicle, which was immediately behind the supervisor. She prepared an original and proceeded to type fill the form. Once finished she took the growing bundle and delivered it to form-filler-outer Number two who had a cubicle immediately next to her.

 The bundle sat untouched for five or ten minutes when clerk number two laid out the contents of the bundle on her desk and examined each document carefully. Then she took a colored document form from one of the boxes in the beehive boxes sitting on her desk and the three white forms from another beehive box, separated them with carbon paper, combined them with the colored form, rolled them into her antiquated manual typewriter and began to type. About midway through the form, she stopped typing and carefully examined the form previously filled out by filler-out number one. Then she proceeded to remove the papers from the typewriter and slowly and deliberately removed all carbon paper and methodically erased some spot on each of the forms. I like to think that maybe she misspelled. Then she reassembled the ensemble, rolled it back into her antiquated manual typewriter and continued to complete the forms. Once finished with the said forms, she got out five copies of a small form, covered each with a small carbon sheet and a blue form, and filled it out. She delivered the bundle to the gentleman who sat in a cubicle between the receiving clerk and the dispatch clerk. It would appear that his cubicle was originally meant to be for a clerk since the glass window fronted it along with the two clerk cubicles and a passage slot was cut in the glass for each clerk. They probably put the man, the stamper, here for efficiency because it certainly gave the flow of paperwork an efficient route and as we will see, it gave the office a sense of industry in progress.

    The stamper had two desks, one on the side of the dispatcher cubicle. Here he had a beehive of shelves only this time instead of taking; he was giving back to the boxes of carbons the used carbon sheets. Then he inspected our passports with interest, the first forms with aplomb and the letterforms with professional fastidiousness. Once convinced that all was in order he carefully laid out the forms in one stack, evenly aligned on the top and left side and place them on the desk on the side of the cubicle towards the receiving clerk. Then he got out two ink pads and place them 'just so' on his desk. And finally came to the three stampers, one large and two small ones and placed them in precise locations. Then he began what I would describe as a methodical, melodious and staccato rendition that would have given Chopin a headache as bad as mine as he tried to beat the life out of his inkpad, alternating with a beat on each sheet of paper, precisely in the upper left-hand corner as he flipped each page to its execution. It was a performance of the cacophony and choreography that any communist would be proud to claim as a product of their superior system. This whole performance has entertained Cindy and me so much over the years that it was well worth the two hours it took to exchange American Express traveler checks for local currency. At the time Cindy summed it up so well when she said as we walked out "Just think! Somewhere in this country, there are warehouses employing thousands of people where our papers will be stored along with billions of others until the end of time or this regime." A few weeks later we went into the American Express office in Vienna to cash some checks. We exited with our money in four minutes flat. Cindy mused as we exited the office: "Remember what one of the Poles told us? "We pretend to work, and they pretend to pay us."

We visited the economics department at the University of Warsaw and had a long discussion with one of the professors. (Cindy was well qualified to discuss; I was well qualified to listen and learn.) This is a sample of the discussion: Polish output had been so communized that all the industrial production of the country was organized into about 75 companies owned by the state. There were some problems. The companies belonged to the state, that is, the people. People working in the industries felt they should have a share of each business as it was privatized. Jeffrey

Sachs, a brilliant young Harvard economist, proposed shock therapy for the Polish economy designed to privatize, deregulate, and liberate the national economy. This is what they tried. The economists Cindy spoke with in 1990 said that the first thing he had noted in the early stage of liberalization was that there were bananas sold for the first time in the open market. Before that, he had heard that bananas were only in the stores for the communist bigwigs. Now there were bananas in the market for everyone. Apparently, those who could access a car were driving down to Yugoslavia or Greece, filling up the car with bananas and bringing them back to trade in the market. We saw an interesting future for Poland. Our next country was Czechoslovakia.

On Sunday, October 14, after a short stretch of beautiful countryside, we began to see smoke stacks all belching putrid, purple, poisonous filth from their tops. As we drove east, we went through dirty, factory towns with a pall of the heavy solution poisoning the air and view. When going through a woodsy area, the air had been crisp with the sky clear and blue, but suddenly, the smog settled over everything, blotting out the sun at 4 o'clock in the afternoon.

We felt so sorry for the people who had to live there. We blamed it on the system. In our form of government, we have several forces that lead to environmental protection. First, there was capitalism; then there was the wealth and technology that created the consumer goods and the pollution, but also the technology and wealth to control the pollution. Then there was a democratic system that gave the population the voice to express opposition to pollution and the force to make industry pay the costs to protect the environment. Then there were the newspapers that told people about the problem and informed them as to what the representatives were voting on to solve the problem.

When given information, power and wealth, society found ways to reduce the pollution that is a corollary with economic growth. Under the state system of Eastern Europe, the people had neither the knowledge nor the power. Since they were denied travel and thus exposure to the rest of the world, they had no basis for comparison. The result was that the Soviet, Socialist, Republics (SSRs) found themselves with lower income then capitalism can produce and a dirty, polluted, environment.

It was getting very late in the day, and we were struggling with navigation. Roads were poorly marked or not marked at all. I asked a young man with a motorcycle how to get to the next town and showed him on our map. He gave me a big smile and motioned for me to follow him. He guided us through town and then pointed the way ahead on another road. The next town was very small, and so we decided to go on to a bigger city nearby. The city was mostly dark when we arrived, so we needed someone to tell us where to go. Cindy spotted a watchman who approached us and seemed willing to help us. Unfortunately, he spoke only one language, which we did not understand. Since Cindy is a master at charades, this would be no problem. Between an imaginative watchman and an actress of renown (in charades only), we had our directions: "go back two streets, turn left, go over three bridges, continue for a long way to a big intersection, turn left, drive a ways out of town and on the right, is a motel for important people". Bingo! That is where we had our dinner of apples, dried soup and tea and a good night's sleep (I believe we were the only guests). Late the next morning we excitedly headed for Prague.

We arrived in Prague to discover that the tourist office was closed. I found what looked like a deserted shopping mall. Cindy looked for people and finally found a pay phone on the wall and with the help of an operator who spoke English she called the American

Embassy to ask for advice. The woman who answered the phone told her immediately, "no one comes to Prague without reservation. Wait a moment. Try this number." She gave Cindy a number and hung up. Cindy called the number. A woman's voice who spoke passable English told Cindy that they had a room and gave excellent directions to the B&B, which was near downtown. We were surprised and pleased that the B&B was a very nice modern home.

Our hostess was a dentist; her husband was a professional, and their son was studying architecture. They were a delightful family and our stay with them was a joy even though language was a problem. Their house and its furnishings, of which they were proud, were impressive and on par with a middle-class home in America. In the backyard was a garage that contained a modern German car and an impressive vacation trailer which they had constructed from parts they were able to find locally. The car and trailer allowed them to vacation frequently in Dubrovnik, Yugoslavia.

We enjoyed the charm of the old city with its astronomical clock and Prague Castle. We enjoyed wandering the streets, and we had a good visit with US embassy personnel who filled us in on some of the current economic and foreign affairs.

We entered Italy through the Brenner pass. Immediately we were struck by the ruggedness of the mountains. The contrast between Austria and Italy was striking. In one valley, we admired white or old occasionally cream Tyrolean houses trimmed in wood with cascading red geraniums. Every town seemed clean, neat, and filled with flowerpots and window boxes overflowing everywhere. In the next valley after the pass, old, stucco buildings, gray or tan, took on an Italian style – grayer, older, occasionally shabby, yet noble. The Italian guards nodded at our passports as we drove on the road twisted through tiny, one road towns, with nearly empty streets and occasional parked cars. The isolation of their existence was wondrous, yet the beauty of their environment compensated. It was a charming road and a beautiful valley, and we were both happy that we had missed the autobahn that might have sped through such a lovely area. We coasted most of the way down the mountain in second gear.

Driving in Italy unnerved Cindy, and she tells why: "I am just not an aggressive enough driver to cope with Italians. I don't move or think fast enough, so they cut in front of me or threaten to run over me. Also, stoplights are anathema. Fred honed his driving skills in Argentina where the Italians taught the Argentines to drive. I realized after three days in Italy that Fred drives like an Italian. That left me with a real dilemma. If Fred drives, I am constantly terrified that he will run over someone. If I drive, I am equally afraid that someone will run over me. Italy was very stressful."

We drove across the Grand St. Bernard pass where we saw the home of the St. Bernards and I had a chance to admire the dogs. Then we drove down and through the Petite Grand St. Bernard pass. The road was one hairpin curve after another and Cindy drove almost all of it in second gear. There was little traffic, but the view was consistently spectacular.

If there is a site close to heaven, it is the camping park high in the French Alps on the road between Italy and France. We had covered the kilometers with Cindy driving curve after hairpin curves, zigzag up the mountain never passing, dreading to be passed, always in second gear. There were rails occasionally, and the road was good, but visibility was usually about 35 yards or less before the next curve, and Cindy was always nervous when she can't see the road a good distance ahead. The top of the pass had a splendid view with mountains rising like cards and retreating in the distance, each layer distinct with darkening hues of blue-grey. We stopped to admire the scenery. We started down the mountain on the French side. All guardrails had disappeared, the road narrowed and became rougher as numerous patches appeared like a gray patchwork quilt. Suddenly we passed a sign," Camping." Cindy made a remarkably quick U-turn, and we drove into the campground. There was a Crêperie sign, a small restaurant, an office, all seen through the window over the back of a monstrous and interested German Shepherd watchdog. There were no people. We drove up into the campground. Campsites had been painstakingly laid out and flattened surrounded by the stately trees. We pitched our tent in an ideal place, whereupon the pleasant manager arrived and charged us the equivalent of nine dollars for the most attractive campsite I have ever seen. Our tent faced a towering snow-covered peak framed between the tall pines that we thought might be Mount Blanc. Adjoining a bit to the right was another more rounded and lower peak, still snow-covered. The setting sun hit the two mountains making them shine above the rising darkness. Overhead a half moon took on brighter glow through the trees. As we lay on our air mattresses, snug in our sleeping bags, we looked through the mosquito screen at the mountain peak framed between the trees hoping to fix the view forever in our memories. The crisp, clean night air filled our lungs, and the rustling wind among the treetops lulled us to sleep. The next morning, I drove the rest of the way down the mountain, marveling all the while at the beauty of the French Alps. We entered the city of Grenoble, where we knew there was an outstanding university. Cindy contacted the economics department, and with some skill and lots of luck, she arranged for Professor Vladimir to spend some time with us. He was fluent in English, was a handsome young technocrat who was the epitome of the desirable college professor: articulate, observant calm and witty. He described his qualifications, of Russian ancestry, he was an expert in Eastern European economics, having published several books on the subject. He had visited all the eastern economies numerous times as well as Japan and the United States. Another of his interests was petroleum. Shell oil had met him and members of his group to make projections of the Eastern economies at a one-day workshop. He described this as simply projections for Poland and Hungary. He described how Czechoslovakia was different and gave generalized projections for East Germany and Czechoslovakia. When asked about EU matters he pointed out that this was not his specialty but proceeded to describe the internal relationships. We were particularly interested in his opinion of Britain's role and the EU. He noted that Britain had closer ties with the United States and was not really a continental country, At least not until the channel, the tunnel now bridging the English Channel, is complete. Like the Scandinavians, he was somewhat awed at the potential economic power of a United Germany, possibly as great as the United States, but felt that a Germany, folded into Europe, was not so threatening. Forty-five years of West Germany democracy should ensure that. One of his more interesting comments was concerning an upcoming conference in Moscow. For the first time, he had been advised to bring food. The Soviet economy he saw as facing enormous problems. They may have the will, and two dynamic leaders in Yeltsin and Gorbachev, but the people know nothing of entrepreneurship, nothing of the market system. He pointed out that a colleague who was in accounting spoke fluent Russian and was knowledgeable of the Soviet system but found it almost impossible to communicate with them because they had no internalized concept of costs and profits. West Germany would provide a crash course for East Germany. Poland, Czechoslovakia, and Hungary had never been as communized as the USSR. Furthermore, with free travel, their young people would learn rapidly. After more than an hour of discussion, we parted. He echoed our thoughts throughout our travels. This is a most interesting time in Europe. Changes, great, meaningful changes are everywhere. I was thinking about that as we left when Cindy remembered an ancient Chinese proverb," Lord, protect me from living in interesting times."

From here we altered our sabbatical tour somewhat so that we could attend a conference in Heidelberg, Germany, which Cindy had signed up for the previous year. It was a great interlude. We stayed in a small hotel within walking distance to the conference center and had the luxury of staying in one place for almost a week with a group of English-speaking people from the United States and Europe. The conference was excellent, covering such social subjects as European economics and German educational system. The most informative sessions for me were on the opportunities of education in Germany versus the United States. In Germany, children were divided by tests at about age 13. The top third would go to academic high schools destine for higher education. The middle third was going to apprentice schooling programs, and the bottom third would get training for menial jobs. There was nothing like our community colleges offering advanced education and training for everyone. We spoke with a graduate student in economics studying at Heidelberg University to be a business economist. When asked if she had thought about teaching, she told us that the program track she was on would not prepare her to teach, only to consult for large businesses.

The Workshop took us to the Porsche assembly plant. There we saw young students who spent half a day and classes in the factory and half a day working in the plant. Through their apprentice period, they would work in every part of the plant, while getting the equivalent of an American high school, non-academic education. We were told that when the students completed the program, they would have good, well-paying jobs with a month summer vacation. Germany provides healthcare through taxpayers supplied programs. One would have to be impressed with the program, but imagine, locking in a student at age 13, based on one test, to a lifetime track.

The Heidelberg workshop also took us by bus to Strasbourg, France where we learned about the European Parliament, the parliamentary body of the European Union.

With the completion of the Heidelberg Workshop, we drove to Munich. We saw the Marienplatz and the famed Glockenspiel. We explored the Dachau concentration camp of World War II, which had been built to hold 5,000, but held about 27,400 when the American army liberated it in April 1945. Some 50,000 prisoners were murdered there. They were the victims of medical experiments, torture, and brutality, rarely equaled in this world. Only in the killing fields of Cambodia in 1975 to 1979 where the Khmer Rouge murdered an estimated two million were helpless victims so mesmerized by horror and cruelty.

En route to Austria, we visited several other German sites. Berchtesgaden is where Hitler and others of his inter-party once entertained at the luxurious Platterhof Hotel. It was bombed in 1945, and after the war, the US Army commandeered it and turned it into a recreation center for US troops in Europe. We stayed at the Skytop Lodge, which had once been part of the farm where vegetables for Hitler's table were grown. Nearby was the Eagles nest or Kehlsteinhaus where Hitler and Eva Braun and their Shepherd dog once frolicked with their guests.

We visited the American military recreation center at Garmisch Partenkirchen and Mad Ludwig's Castles at Neuschwanstein and Linderhof. It is said that the Neuschwanstein Castle influenced

Cinderella's Castle at Disney World. It is beautiful, and now a major tourist attraction. We also visited a salt mine where we dressed in miner's clothes and rode a small train into the mine. We learned of the history of mining salt there.

We entered Austria by way of Salzburg, a beautiful, colorful, exciting, and amazing city. This is where we (and probably most tourists) relived the classic story of the von Trapp family, immortalized by the *Sound of Music*, and visited some of the film locations. We enjoyed Salzburg, the beautiful interior of Austria, Innsbruck, which is a beautiful medieval town with stunning contemporary architecture, surrounded by the majestic Alps, and the magnificent and imperial Vienna where we stayed four days and wished it could be four months.

Across the Danube and approximately 40 km east of Vienna is the city of Bratislava, Capital of Slovakia as of 1993. In June 1990 the Velvet Revolution (so named because the revolution was "soft," without warfare) brought a peaceful end to communism in Czechoslovakia, and Vaclav Havel, the hero of the revolution, became President of the Czech Republic. In 1993 these so-called Velvet Divorce took place when Slovakia became independent, free from the Czech Republic. Cindy and I found all this very interesting, and when we count the number of countries we visited in our sabbatical, this one is two.

We knew little about Hungary when we arrived in Budapest except that at one time, Buddha was on one side of the Danube and Pest was on the other. Through the visitor's center, we found a B&B with a friendly widow who spoke a little German. She and Cindy sat up late with pantomime and a little understanding of German, Cindy learning that our host at one time owned a big house on a farm in the country until the Communists took over, land and all. Then she moved into the apartment, which was spacious. She had big, carved wooden furniture that they had brought with them. She showed a picture of her daughter in ballet costume and told Cindy she had found a job in Belgium and that she sends money home.

Cindy and I bought a boat trip with dinner on the Danube from where we were surprised and elated to see the huge, beautiful Parliament buildings that had escaped bombing during the war. We enjoyed a goulash dinner heavily flavored with locally produced paprika. The small band onboard played the themes from a couple of Hungarian Rhapsodies by Franz Liszt per Cindy's request. We saw the Kings' Palace, the Concert Hall, the Chain Bridge, and walked the grounds of the Fisherman's Bastion.

The next day I was very sick. Our hostess, filled with compassion, took us to a nearby hospital. She obviously had some clout because the medical people walked us past a long line of patients in the hall—in wheelchairs, on canes, in casts, and we went immediately into a small examining room where a doctor checked me over and diagnosed a urinary tract infection. He gave me some pills and said that there would be no charge. I gave him a $20 American bill, which he appreciated. I felt much better the next day, so we moved on to our next country, Yugoslavia. As for the pills, several weeks later I asked an American Dr. what he thought of the pills. He smiled and said that American doctors had not been using those pills in the United States for some years, but he wasn't surprised that they worked fine.

We approached Yugoslavia with some trepidation. It was still a communist country, but not part of the collapsing Soviet system. We passed through the border checkpoint with only a cursory glance of our passports. The guard mumbled something and pointed to his left. I was elated to be in Yugoslavia and drove down the road ahead. Cindy explained to me that there was a long line of cars to our left and that was probably where we would get our passports stamped. I said: "Nah, the guard let us in."

With a little looking, we found a B&B—an attractive, middle-class looking house in a very nice neighborhood of two-story, well kept, homes with small but beautiful lawns. I went to bed early. Cindy ended up in the kitchen, drinking tea, and talking with our hostess, an earthy, attractive blonde of about 45, her daughter, and a neighbor; all of whom were eager to try out their English. The most fluent was the daughter, about 14. She immediately began explaining to Cindy Croatia's conflicts with Serbia. She pointed to a map of Yugoslavia on the wall with outlines between Croatia, Bosnia, Serbia, and the much-contested area north of Greece near Albania. The lines had been added to the map. While we knew that after the death of Tito in 1980, there was political and ethnic conflict in Yugoslavia, we did not understand how near the country was to civil war in 1990.

Our ride the next day to Beograd (Belgrade) was one of the most nerve-racking of our trip. At the tourist center, we got a room and directions to a hotel but were advised that it was at some distance and maybe somewhat difficult to find. We missed a turn, asked directions about six times, always showing the map and name of the hotel. Each time we were given directions we were also given assurance, "You can't miss it," and we always did. Finally, we found the hotel off the busy highway. While the room was small, it was nice, reasonable, and had a private bath. The major disadvantage, which wasn't apparent at first, was that the restaurant on the ground floor had a band and lots of customers each night. The band played very loud music, some rock, jazz, golden oldies from our high school days, rock versions of Beethoven, Hungarian Rhapsodies, the Beatles, and we guessed current music. We spent the next day downtown going by bus.

I met a friendly civil engineering student on the bus who had studied English for five years and seem to want to practice it. He told us where the Economics University was, and several things to see. At the US Embassy, Cindy discussed Yugoslavian development and trade relations with the US with the economic adviser. I spoke with the Political Officer about driving through the rest of Yugoslavia. He said that the Embassy had a travel advisory against driving in the area bordering Albania, our planned route back from Greece. He explained that there was growing tension in the area bordering with Albania and the advisory really pertained to Americans of Albanian ancestry or Albanian names. He thought we would have no problems, but we should be aware of the high tension and should avoid crowds.

We went by the economics department at the University of Belgrade where a friendly professor spent some time with us discussing the Yugoslav economy without Tito. In the research Cindy had done before the trip, Yugoslavia was grouped with moderately developing countries. He pointed out that as long as the per capita income was under a set amount the country qualified for aid. He implied that the government fudges the figures to keep the country eligible for assistance. We also discussed the Dalmatian coast.

"Yugoslavia," he said: "had been encouraged to develop tourism along the coast. It had not worked out well. Europeans tend to all take their vacations in August. You can't build a tourism industry on one month a year." Later in October as we drove along the lovely Dalmatian coast, we found all the hotels and recreation areas closed. Europeans vacation in August.

As we left Yugoslavia to enter Romania, we drove into the Yugoslavian border checkpoint to be greeted by the ugliest, meanest—looking, stocky Serb. He obviously had imbibed the night before and was enjoying a hangover of the highest order. He thumbed through each passport. He did it a second time. Then he glared at me who was behind the steering wheel. "No have stamp," he thundered in angry English. I gulped: "I don't understand." With emphasis, he repeated: "No have stamp." I began to perspire. Cindy and I remembered that line at the border when we entered the country, the line that I had bypassed. Thoughts were flashing through my brain. This is a communist country. I have studied Serbo-Croatian at the Army language school. I am in Army intelligence. I am a senior military officer. I have no proof that I entered Yugoslavia legally. Cindy and I may be in a really serious predicament. Then I had a stroke of genius made for this, the idiot salute. So, I tightened my lips, raised my eyebrows, raised my shoulders as high as I could, looked him in the eyes, turned my hands palms up and raised them slightly and waited. He stared at me in surprise, hesitated a moment as his face relaxed, he handed me the passports and with a twinkle in his eyes and the beginning of a smile he returned the idiot salute and waved us onward. I like to think I did him a favor that day.

We entered Romania greatly relieved with our idiot salute. We spent our first night in a five-story hotel at the edge of the city of Timisoara. As we entered the hotel, we found that we could read most of the printing on placards, signs, and pamphlets. We were overjoyed. Until then we had not given a thought to the fact that the Romanian language is a romance language similar to Spanish and, which each of us spoke and had studied.

Our room was on the third-floor, but we could hear clearly, hubcaps crashing to the ground one by one as they were being removed. We could also hear what we were told were demonstrations by students and workers hoping to influence the government. I chose to ignore whatever was going on outside and went to sleep. The next morning, we found that our hubcaps were missing, but nothing had been stolen from the car. We told the hotel manager about the theft, and soon two armed policemen came to interview us. We assumed that they would give us paperwork to show that the hubcaps have been stolen so that when we turned in the car in Brussels; our insurance company would cover the loss. A young man from the hotel acted as interpreter in our conversation with the policemen. The police made a mockery of the whole situation and were beginning to scowl and glare at us to the point that it appeared to me that we were going to be accused of a crime. So, I told them that it would be OK, "We'll just go, let's forget the whole thing," and we got in our car and drove away. Weeks later when we reached Brussels and were turning in the car at the car rental, Cindy told the clerk that the missing hubcaps were stolen in Romania.

The polite young clerk smiled and said, "and they wouldn't give you paperwork from the police. We understand."

In 1989, a year before our visit to Romania, students at the University rose up and in union with workers from the factories overthrew Communist dictator, Nicolae Ceausescu. After a brief trial, he and his wife were executed by firing squad. Then the citizens of Bucharest were allowed to walk through some of the elaborate palaces and see the luxurious living quarters constructed for the communist elite.

We reached the tourist office in Bucharest, which sent us to an apartment near one of the main streets of the city. A well-educated, retired lady graciously made us comfortable in her tiny apartment. We were given her bedroom which had substantial, but old and well-worn furniture crowded into a space about 10' x 10'. She had a kitchen one half that size. The living room had two chairs, a thread worn area rug, and a love seat sized sofa. We paid $15 for the B&B. Cindy and the hostess talked well into the night. The hostess spoke some French, Russian, as well as Romanian and had read a lot of English literature.

She told Cindy that she stood in line, sometimes seven days a week, for an hour or more to buy bread, a dress, potatoes, whatever. People had been afraid to speak out because of the government. She was pleased that the dictator was gone but afraid for the future. The following day we headed for Bulgaria.

The world was getting ready for the Gulf War when we left Romania and entered Bulgaria. We knew little about this communist country for so many years behind the Iron Curtain, except that they nod sideways to indicate yes, and up-and-down to indicate no. The tourist office in downtown Sophia made a reservation for us at a bed-and-breakfast and wrote the address on a card. Imagine our dismay when we arrived at the address to see typical Eastern bloc identical five-story apartment buildings, One after another. Cindy could not find any numbers or names and couldn't read the written note. Finally, an elderly man, gray and poorly shaven, led Cindy to one of the buildings and pushed a button, whereupon an older woman met her and showed their apartment. She spoke very little English. The apartment had two bedrooms, was dark and forbidding.

It was very cold inside. We learned that oil is almost the sole source of energy in Bulgaria and that oil came from Iraq. Trying to curry favor with the West, Bulgaria was obeying the embargo on Iraq oil, designed to force Saddam Hussein to withdraw from Kuwait. Our hostess' daughter, a nurse, told us that kerosene was to be used for the hospitals and orphanages first. It was rumored that there was cholera near the Black Sea. The apartments had electricity and heat only a little through the day. There was no hot water. We dressed warmly, even inside. We were afraid that if someone stole our gas, we would never get out of Bulgaria. Fortunately, no one did, so we had enough gas to get to Greece.

We walked over much of Sophia. We saw the beautiful St. Alexander Nevsky Patriarchal Cathedral with its arches and wedding cake exterior, and the much simpler Church of St. George, which dates from the 4th-century.

As we walked through a small urban Park, we admired a large interesting series of statutes. They were rough and dark, as though carved of dark and gray concrete. They were stooping, contoured, miserable men, reaching out to touch the one ahead as if blind. The effect was stunning. Cindy stopped a well-dressed young man walking through and inquired if he could speak English. He could. When we asked about the statue, he told us it reminded the people of a war between Turks and Bogarts. In 1014 after the battle of Belasitsa, the Byzantines captured 15,000 Bulgars. Ninety-nine of every 100 men were blinded. One was left with one eye to lead the others home.

Several months after we arrived home, Cindy received a lovely small book of the artist who created the statuary from the young man Cindy had stopped in the park. I think he was just a kind Bulgarian, proud of his country and of the artists he wanted to share. Our drive was uneventful until we reached the bridge that spans the Nestos River that divides Bulgaria and Greece. We encountered a line of transport trucks that went on for miles. Fortunately, they let the few cars go ahead. The bridge was narrow, and it took more than an hour to get across it.

When we arrived in Thessalonica in northern Greece, we headed first for the American Express office where we received a couple of welcomed letters from home. While there we ate our first Greek moussaka, a delicious dish of ground beef, goat or lamb, eggplant, and various other ingredients. In Thessalonica, we called ahead for a bed and breakfast in Athens to make one of the few advanced reservations we were to have on our five-month trip. When we arrived in Athens, we found a plain, but comfortable establishment run by a partly retired sea captain. Our companions in the B&B were an assortment of British expatriates, backpacking but affluent College students, tired travelers, and a tiny staff of helpful Greeks.

We discovered that apparently few tourists visit Greece in October, so none of the attractions were crowded. On our first day we walked up to the Acropolis to visit the Parthenon, the tiny shops along the way had few customers.

We admired the architectural work of the ancient Greeks, marveling over the subtle adjustments to symmetry that create the illusion of floating as one gazes at the delicate beauty of the huge building. We took the obligatory pictures of the Doric columns and found an obliging tourist to take a picture of us together in front of the edifice. It is one of our favorite pictures from our travels. It was a glorious day, clear, crisp, cloudless sky. We were surprised at how friendly, personable, and mirthful the Greeks are.

We walked down the back of the Acropolis, a wide and dusty path. We had gone only a few yards when we came upon a small Orthodox Church, a pearl of a building. There was a group of about 30 obvious relatives gathered for a celebration, a baptismal. A jolly, plump, bearded Priest took a chubby baby girl of about two months and held the squirming naked infant high above his head. He brought her down below the surface of a huge vat of water and immediately raised her, as the crowd oohed, and the baby sputtered but did not cry; then twice more as the crowd's oohs became louder and higher. Through gestures, we were invited to stay and partake of the meal to follow the ceremony, but we declined. We continued down the path to the city.

One of the more amusing sites of our five days in Athens was the changing of the guard at the Greek Tomb of the Unknown Soldier. The costumes of the soldiers, brief white tutu-like skirts, puffed sleeves, and French couture-like hats elicited chuckles, but the handsome, serious young men and the earnestness with which they performed their routine brought well-deserved applause at the end of the ceremony.

On the advice of our host, we left Athens for the Peloponnesian Peninsula over a bridge from the mainland and stayed at an austere but comfortable B&B at a coastal fishing village. The weather had turned almost frigid, but our room had lots of cover for the beds. Cindy walked out on a pier and met a wrinkled old man. She tried to engage him in conversation, but he wasn't speaking.

We visited an open-air Greek Theatre, with seats carved into a natural bowl, and of acoustics so perfect that we could hear a penny dropped from the top stone seat. One could almost hear the voices from ancient times and Greek theater. Comedy and tragedy heralded the birth of drama. Visiting a statuary shop and watching carvers do copies of ancient statues, driving around the island, wondering at the land of the Spartans, marveling at the creation of the steep sides of the canal at the isthmus of Corinth, we delighted at each discovery.

Back at the mainland, we spent an afternoon on Mount Olympus enjoying the haunts of the Grecian Vestal Virgins. As we neared the border of Yugoslavia, we began to again become nervous. We must be sure not to enter any part of Albania, which was under the dictator, Enver Hoxha.

We entered Macedonia and had an uneventful drive to the city of Skopje. Some miles beyond Skopje, through a mostly barren countryside on a traffic-less two-lane road, we were stopped by the gendarme. There were six men dressed in dusty dark blue nondescript uniforms and carrying rifles and large walkie-talkies. None seemed to speak English. They took our passports and looked at them while talking on the walkie-talkies. Then they gave the car a perfunctory search. Finally, after a half hour, they let us go. We drove about 10 km along a houseless road where there was still no traffic. Again, we were stopped by the gendarme. They were armed with rifles and again spent most of the time talking on large bulky walkie-talkies. Again, they searched the car, pawing through our camping equipment and pulling out a few of the things in the backseat. Finally, they let us go. The third time we were stopped, about 5 to 10 km along the road, they again looked at our passports, looked over the back seat and the stuff piled in the trunk. One of the men told us in English to go on. Later we learned that about 15 men had been killed just north of where we were in one of the first clashes between Serbia, Montenegro, Kosovo, and Albania. We reached Titograd, now Podgorica, where we found a bank open to get local money with our travel checks. A little later on the coast, we found a B&B with a hand-lettered sign in front. After examining our room, we walked to a tiny store, which was in one room of a small house and bought bread, cheese, and some wine. The next day we drove north on the Dalmatian Coast Highway. It was paradise: blue Adriatic, mountains with orange trees and olives and grapevines, red tile roofs, stucco, and lots of flowers. It was the tourist coast, but there were few tourists. At one city we saw a big, beautiful hotel at the beach. It was closed as were the restaurants and tourists' stores nearby. Obviously, it was not August. A young man asked me if we were looking for a place to stay. When we said we were, he told us that his parents had a B&B. He led us to their neat, clean but modest home. They gave us a bedroom in the attic, a room with rafters overhead, a pleasant, comfortable bed and lace curtain windows. We reached Dubrovnik, a university town since medieval times. We found a hotel room with hot water and spent the day exploring the beautiful walled city with its Romanesque arches, tiled streets, red tile roofs, and sun-kissed fountains. There were college students aplenty. Later, as Yugoslavia broke into civil war, parts of the city, which had escaped destruction in World War II, were bombed. As we left Yugoslavia, we visited the Lipica Stud Farm for Lipizzaner horses. There we got to admire those beautiful animals. Sometime later the farm was bombed by the Serbs, and many of the horses were stolen.

We headed to Aviano where there was a large American military base. We got a room on base, ate at the mess hall, mailed a package with all our films and souvenirs, shopped at the commissary and PX and planned our drive to Venice. Early the next morning, as we prepared to continue to Venice, we looked at each other and in unison said: "Let's stay." We got the room for another day, checked out two VCR movies to watch in our room, had a big breakfast, and wasted much of the day relaxing in our room. Sometimes one just needs a break.

The next day we got to Venice very early and explored the city. We walked along the canals, admired the glass bead necklaces, watched the glassblowers in the shops, fed the pigeons in St. Marcos Square, and climbed to the top of the Campanile for a spectacular view of the splendid city. We splurged on a meal in a small restaurant with tablecloths and all, only to discover that we liked our American spaghetti better.

The drive south was very interesting. Recently a superhighway was built through mountains, but not up-and-down. It was bridge and tunnel, bridge and tunnel so that the road was almost straight and level but also very expensive. We drove down the east coast of Italy to San Marino, one of the ten mini-states of Europe: Vatican City, Monaco, San Marino, Liechtenstein, Malta, Andorra, Luxembourg, Cyprus, Kosovo, and Montenegro. We visited all except Malta and Cyprus. San Marino claimed to be the world's smallest republic. It is an independent country belonging to the United Nations. It was hard to believe that such a small country managed to keep its independence since the year 301. We spent the night there and enjoyed walking the hilly streets. From San Marino, we went to Naples where we found a lovely hotel overlooking the harbor. The next day we explored Pompeii with much interest since each of us had spent a lot of our school days studying Roman history.

In 79 A. D., Pompeii and its sister city, Herculaneum were destroyed and completely buried during a long catastrophic eruption spanning two days. The eruption buried Pompeii under 4 to 6 meters of ash and pumice, and it was lost for over 1500 years before its accidental rediscovery in 1599. We walked through the streets admiring the frescoes on the walls, the mosaics, the statutes, and the plumbing. We were there on a pleasant fall sunny day with the great mountain watching over us and its handiwork. There were no crowds so that we could linger over all. A satisfying experience

Our guidebook on Rome said that if we went on a Tuesday up two flights of stairs, at a certain address that we could get special tickets for an audience with the Pope on Wednesday if he were in town. He was in town. Since it was a couple of days until Tuesday, we explored Rome: The Coliseum, Trevi Fountains, the catacombs, the Pantheon, the Spanish steps, Victor Emmanuelle's monument, and triumph arches of Titus, Constantine, and others.

We arrived Wednesday morning and wandered the Vatican library admiring beautiful pages of Bibles scribed by medieval monks, examined the Pieta by Michelangelo in St. Peter's, and admired the ceiling of the Sistine Chapel but were not able to see the altar in front because it was hidden behind drapes for restoration. The time came for our audience with the Pope. We showed our tickets to one of the Swiss guards who directed us to a huge auditorium. There we found seats way back towards the entrance. Sure, that there must be a mistake, I showed our tickets to another guard who pointed out to me that six nuns and several priests were even further back behind us. It wasn't exactly a private audience. We estimated that there were several thousand people in the auditorium. We saw and heard John Paul II, formerly Cardinal Wojtyla of Poland, who greeted the quiet crowd in a number of languages. Some nuns in the crowd sang, the Pope spoke for about 15 minutes. It was an interesting experience, and we both enjoyed it.

At Pisa we made funny pictures of each of us holding up the Leaning Tower and marveled that it is still standing. On the way to Florence, we stopped at the Carrara mines where the beautiful white marble is cut from the earth. I got a piece to use as a bookend. It is like a mountain range of the glistening white stone that has been used for buildings and statuary for thousands of years. In Florence, we saw the David by Michelangelo and spent an afternoon in the Uffizi Gallery, which featured Botticelli's birth of Venus and la Primavera which we loved, and Caravaggio's happy paintings. We both were excited to see Ghiberti's Bronze Doors.

From Florence, we explored France beginning with the French Riviera, a fabulous place. We did a bit of shopping and sped through the cities of Nice and Marseille, gambled a little (very little if Cindy was about) and enjoyed entertainment in Cannes. From there we entered the Pyrenees Mountains, the border between France and Spain. Several times we came upon a group of wild horses, which was exciting.

The next day we arrived in Lourdes, France. According to

believers, the Virgin Mary appeared to Bernadette Soubirous on a total of 18 occasions at Lourdes. Lourdes has become a major place of Roman Catholic pilgrimage and miraculous healings. People come by the thousands, in wheelchairs, on gurneys, on crutches, faces full of hope and anticipation. Can the mind cure? Can hopes and dreams, and meditation or prayer? We watched the parade of the sick and injured with their attendance accompanied by priests and nuns. They moved by and were touched by the holy water, and some appeared to have been cured. They threw down their crutches and walked off, while others waited and cried, apparently feeling the lack of faith that prevented their cure. It is a magnificent scene, full of wonder and puzzlement. Did Cindy and I believe? No, not really. But we wanted to believe as we felt so did many others. One must be there to experience the mystic. We did feel a sense of awe.

After leaving Lourdes, we visited Bordeaux ('the city of arts and history) and headed for Mont San Michelle. We stopped at a campground that had a deep base of sand. There was a strong, chilly breeze which made it almost impossible to put up our tent. We finally found a few large rocks to anchor the tent. We built a little fire near our tent and had a small meal and complimented ourselves for succeeding in pitching our tent for the last time and in having a successful sabbatical so far. The next day we spent at Mount San Michele, the impressive structure that appears on so many photos and paintings. Puffing, we climbed the 900 steps to the Abbey, wandered through the cloisters, and thought of medieval times when monks labored, placing the stones that form the towering edifice. The next day we visited Nantes and then on to Normandy.

It was about 10 PM when we finally found the pizza restaurant on the dark, lonely road in western France. It looked slummy, but we were starved, and this was what the B&B hostess had said was the only nearby restaurant. There were only a few customers, most of whom looked like field hands or cowboys. After ordering, Cindy followed the server's directions to a poorly lit hallway and two restrooms, labeled "Hommes" and "Femmes." Here is how she told me the rest of the story: "I opened the door to the ladies and felt inside for the light switch. I found nothing on either side of the door. Opening the door further, I looked in the dim light from the hall at the area over the sink and felt along the dark wall, but I found no cord or switch. As I stood puzzled, a man came out of the Hommes. I enquired in my rusty high school French, interspersed with my college Spanish, "Ou est la "luz"? He rattled off an answer in French no word of which I understood. I stood there with my mouth open when, to my horror, he pushed me into the dark Femmes toilet and slammed the door behind him. I suddenly realize that if I screamed my husband probably wouldn't hear me over the music. I froze as the bolt was thrown behind him–and the light came on. The gentleman threw open the bolt, and the light went off, and he left down the hall. I stood in the bathroom, relieved, shut the door, threw the bold, and relaxed as the light came on again. I was too stunned to say, Merci.

It was a windy, gray, dingy day when we drove into a little French Village in Normandy. We got out of the car and began to walk around a small Gothic church. As we rounded the back of the church, I suddenly remembered that in World War II this was the town where the American parachutists accidentally dropped in the center of town, and the Nazis shott many. Suddenly we saw a white parachute waving in the breeze around the steeple, and our hearts rose in our throat. What an effective symbol! We thought of the movie, *The Longest Day*. We remembered what a price so many paid in the D-Day invasion.

We spent the next day exploring the beaches, museums,

and cemetery of Normandy. The Americans landed on Omaha and Utah Beaches. There is a fine Memorial museum of Omaha Beach. There was the detritus of the invasion along the beaches. There were excellent dioramas, photos, and maps. We took our time and thought of those thousands of young men on both sides that gave their lives. Later on, Cindy told me that the experience she remembered the most of that day at Normandy was our stroll through the crosses at de Colville-sur-Mer cemetery, which contains graves of over 9000 American soldiers.

She said that as she walked into the cemetery, an older Frenchman approached her: "Merci beaucoup, merci beaucoup. Thank you, Thank you." He said to her and lifted his arm and waved it in front of the field of crosses. She said: "Our eyes met, and we both nodded. We shared the freedom those lives had bought. There has always been a special place in my heart for France and England."

Other points of interest we visited were the Chartres Cathedral, allegedly the most beautiful cathedral in France; the cave paintings of Lascaux estimated to be of Paleolithic times; the Limoges porcelain factory; the Bayeux tapestry, hand stitched, telling the story of the Normandy invasion of England in 1066 (the battle of Hastings) and Versailles, once the center of the absolute monarchy, today a wealthy suburb of Paris.

"I Love Paris" is a popular song written by Cole Porter and published in 1953. It is also an expression of my sentiment and many millions of other people around the world. I view Paris as the greatest city on earth. We visited the Cathedral of Notre Dame, the banks of the Seine, the Louvre art gallery (which includes the Mona Lisa and the Venus de Milo), Paris-Sorbonne University, the Basilica Sacre Coeur, the Champs Elysees, the Eiffel Tower, and the Marc Chagall Paris Opera Ceiling.

From Paris, we drove north to Brugge, Rotterdam, The Hague, and Amsterdam where we visited the Anne Frank House, and the Van Gogh Museum. From the Netherlands, we drove to Belgium, to Brussels, returned our leased car, and took the train to Frankfurt, Germany. We spent two days at the United States Air Force Base at Frankfurt seeking a space available flight to the States with no luck so on the third day we bought commercial flight since we were due back to classes in a few days. Of the many flights we have flown after that, only one other time did we fail to get a space available flight back to the States.

German Gasthaus burning on first morning of Sabbatical.

1990 Sabbatical

Sebelius Monument in Helsinki.

I photograph St. Isaac's Cathedral in Leningrad.

I stand behind long desk at Potsdam where
Truman, Churchill, and Stalin met.

1990 Sabbatical

Berlin Checkpoint Charlie.

Kehlsteinhaus, Hitler's eagle nest retreat.

A lovely day in October near Athens. Note the lack of crowds.

Chapter 23
1991 - 2018   Retirement

Retirement is an enjoyable part of life if you take advantage of the release from most responsibilities and enjoy the freedom it gives. For most people, it is that time when you give up your job and do as you please. For me, it is to do as I please to create many projects and commitments to the point that, at times, I work harder, am more stressed and more committed than when I was employed. I retired from the army in 1982 at the age of 49. It took me until the year 2000 when I stopped teaching that I worked my way into believing that I was a retiree, free and ambitious, enjoying doing projects. In the early part of the year 2003 Cindy talked with me about the things we might do once she retires: travel, write, dabble in real estate, spend lots of time with our children and grandchildren, and engage in projects we might dream up. All of that sounded doable to me, but I cringed as we approached the month of May when she came up with many more ideas: learn to train dogs, develop a canine act and take it to elementary schools, play the piano more, go to the theater more often, and volunteer more at her church. And so, retirement for the two of us began, but soon we found that we didn't have time for many of our intentions.

In the fall of 2004 four hurricanes and a tropical storm did extensive damage in parts of Florida. Hurricane Charles waltzed up the center of the state with the eye coming a mile or so from our house with 90 mile an hour winds ripping 100-year-old oaks up and toppling trees everywhere

Also, in 2004, my oldest grandson, Matt Burbach, became the first published author in the family. I was so proud when Matt presented me with his book, *Gym Climbing: Maximizing Your Indoor Experience.*

Cindy and I found something far more adventurous after retirement. I sat in the pilot seat of a Cessna airplane with an instructor beside me, and Cindy in a seat behind me as I practiced the maneuvers by orders from the instructor. All was going well with my training to become a pilot until I took the required physical exam, which I flunked. Commercial travel will have to do.

Grandparents in general and we in particular really enjoy our grandchildren, yet most of them live hundreds of miles away. Fortunately, three attractions cause them to yearn to come to Florida: Disney, the beach, and grandparents. Cindy and her son Charles decided that a house on the beach was a necessity (we live 50 miles from the beach). After much searching and evaluating beach houses we came upon one built by the owner/occupant who was under pressure to sell his house soon. The two-story house was on a half-acre lot, in good condition, with five bedrooms, attached three-car garages, a kitchen and sitting room on each floor, a billiard table, ping-pong table, and three bathrooms. It was bought to be a vacation rental which the internet had made renting possible. Cindy had the enjoyable task of decorating and furnishing the house throughout. I helped with some of the repairs and maintenance. The price of the house was under $520,000. The value of the house had those three characteristics which realtors love to repeat: location, location, location; and was later appraised at over $1 million. Cindy and Charlie have been very generous letting relatives and friends use the house.

Cindy had consulted the hurricane records, and no hurricane had struck Melbourne Beach for 105 years. But Hurricane Frances came ashore a few miles south of there with 110 miles an hour winds. Hurricane Jeanne followed close to Frances path a few days later and tropical storm Bonnie passed through Florida. Insurance companies paid a heavy price that season, including $150,000 plus damage to Cindy's properties. Camaraderie and teamwork cleaned up a lot of debris. Bright blue tarps on the roofs of many houses attested to the chaos, and because of their multitudes, repairs came slowly.

In 2005, I had helped with some of the repair and maintenance when I came upon a great opportunity to take on a challenging project. Mark and Susan and their children Sadie, Sam, and soon-to-be-born Marley were moving to Atlanta. One of Susan's very close friends lived in an ideal neighborhood where a comfortable house at a fair price was found. When Susan called me and happily told me of the wonders of her new location, she ended the description of the place with the words "there is no place for Sadie's swing set and no way to have one since the backyard is very steep." I told her I was anxious to see her new home the following week and especially that backyard.

Now here was a time when I needed to do some quick thinking. I have three daughters, each of whom has been brainwashed by their Dad that he can do anything. Secondly, each of my daughters learned with the first time I saw them smile and definitely the first time I heard them chuckle, that she has dominion over me. Also, as Army brats, they had too often heard the Army brag – "the difficult we do immediately, the impossible takes a little longer."

Mark Stovin and I took a good look at the backyard and side yards of the lot. I was flabbergasted by the challenge at hand.

Mark is my kind of optimist. There was no doubt on our part that we could have a flat area for Sadie's swing. All we needed to do was to figure out how. There was not enough room on either side of the house to bring in motorized equipment. Dirt would have to be brought in by trucks, dumped on the driveway and then brought to the site with day laborers and wheelbarrows. About 40 feet from the house down a very steep, ivy covered, incline was a less steep- inclined space, about 12 by 12 feet square, where we could construct a retention wall made with timbers and bring in enough dirt to make a flat surface for the swing. After that, a lot of work had to be put into building access to this site, including decking, fencing, retention walls, steps. Etcetera. By Army standards may we say that: "this project could not be done immediately, so it must have been impossible. So, it took us a little (several years) longer. (If you think what I wrote makes no sense at all, you are beginning to understand Army lingo.)

Another project grew out of that one. At the time, Sadie was six years old, and Susan thought it would be interesting if I wrote a couple of pages telling what my life was like when I was her age. I did that. Susan liked what I wrote. In fact, she came up with the idea that I should write the story of my life. I disagreed to no avail. Since writing my autobiography was not one of my favorite projects, I often set it aside to do projects that I enjoyed more. As you can see, I am now in my eleventh year and, hopefully, last year of this project.

The first years after Cindy and I wed were spent working at the college and struggling to keep five of the nine children in advanced education. Cindy's son Charles was doing undergraduate work at Vanderbilt until he graduated as an engineer and later got a masters at Georgia Tech. Alix worked for a while and then got a Law Degree from Vanderbilt University where she met Tom

Cross, also a Lawyer and they married. Amy did undergraduate work in psychology and then earned a Master's program at the Pennsylvania College of Optometry in counseling for the visually handicapped. Stacey graduated as an optometrist and began work teaching at Nova Southeastern University in Florida. Amy got a job counseling for the VA.

Susan got a degree in Marketing. Jeff got two Masters on his own. And then they all were out. For a few years, it was like funding the national debt, although all helped by working full or part-time and some got student loans. Cindy had some insurance money and investments which helped.

Then, one by one they married, and we were rewarded with grandchildren. Son Jeff and daughter-in-law Mary had sons Jeffrey Michael and James before Cindy and I were married. Mike and daughter-in-law Anchalee had Matt and then Joe and Jessica. Some of our happiest times were visiting when the children were young.

We especially enjoyed visiting Jeff and family in Alaska when he was stationed there. Jeffery Michael and James were very young and so funny and fun. Later, son, Jeff was in the Khobar Towers bombing in Saudi Arabia in 1996 where he got a purple heart. And son Mike was in the Pentagon when it was hit on 9/11. Both sons achieved full Colonel in the army.

We were in Germany for Christmas with Jeff and Mary when we were told they were expecting again, and last year we had the pleasure of being at their son Johnathan's high school graduation. We were fortunate to have him spend a week with us once before he grew up.

One year I built a very elaborate dollhouse for Jessica, my first granddaughter. When we reached their home in Kentucky where Mike was stationed at that time, they had lit candles in paper bags (luminarias) leading up to the house, and there was deep snow. Anchalee cooked her delicious Thai food. Mike and Matt and I built a fort, and when we were opening presents, Jessica was reluctant to take time away from the dollhouse to open her other presents. In July of 1997, Mike, Jessica 8, Joe 9, and I visited Cedar County, NE, and environs and I told them all about the family and growing up there. The girls and Kip are planning on going in spring of 2018.

Amy and son-in-law Tim had a fine wedding. We enjoyed watching their three, Sarah, Ben and Jack grow up. Sarah has begun college, but I am convinced that she could be a terrific comedian. She is so funny. We had the pleasure of seeing Ben and Jack play basketball. Both boys are very tall and athletic as well as smart and popular.

Susan and son-in-law Mark Stovin have Sadie, Sam, Marley, and Charlie. In addition to being pretty, Sadie has her mother's winning personality. Twice she came in first place in an Atlanta equestrian competition. We went to Michigan to see Sam compete in the International Odyssey of the Mind. Marley has always been my butterfly, a nickname I coined for her. Marley and Mattie Coulter spent ten days with us one summer, and we marveled that never a cross word was heard between the two. Charlie has impressed us with how he speaks up and holds an audience. At his grandmother Darlene's funeral, he demonstrated a lot of poise and confidence. Maybe the family will have a politician there.

We are so fortunate to have son Kip, daughter Michelle (Shelly) and granddaughter Hannah living close to us. They are constantly around when us old people need attention. Hannah is currently in college and just moved out on her own. It was always so much fun to watch her play volleyball. Shelly and I have coffee at Starbucks most Saturday mornings, and Kip helped me for years schlepping concrete as I built ponds and walks and gardens around the property. We are especially close to daughter-in-law

Elsie and her son Aaron. Aaron recently began a new job with Amazon in Seattle, and it was fun last Christmas to hear about the amazing things going on in that tech ripe company. Elsie and Kip have moved from house to house where they bought and remodeled and sold. Elsie is very artistic. She paints and enjoys interior design.

I have been very close to Alix and Tom's sons Will and Cole, attending many soccer and baseball games as both boys excel in sports and academically. Will and I played Risk for years until he had the joy of beating me. Tom and I once constructed a screened-in porch.

We spent a week in London with Stacey's husband, Jim Barrett, and grandson Riley as we took Riley to museums while Jim attended meetings. Later we went with Riley to the international robotics competition where his team was a finalist. Stacey and Jim were invited to Renaissance Weekends in Savannah and Colorado where Cindy and I enjoyed the ambiance and babysitting. We remember how much fun Liam was as a red-headed, laughing, affectionate two-year-old.

Charles Coulter and daughter-in-law Malinda have Alix, Mattie, and Harvey. I especially appreciate how Harvey draws, creates stuff and plays the ukulele. Alix and Mattie excel academically and play the piano. The two girls spent a week with us riding Cindy's horses, Romeo and Juliet at her farm recently. Fun. Both girls are very fond of animals.

Stacey, Alix, and Charlie gave their Mom a splendid retirement party to which she invited many, and as a result, there was a big turnout. The three also gave her a significant and appropriate gift, considering that she taught for over 40 years, an endowed economics scholarship in her name at Seminole Community College. Later in the month, we joined Stacey and Jim and their young sons at a rural vacation in New Hampshire. One June we explored Utah and its beautiful canyons with Dottie and Earl Holtgrefe.

On the homefront, we entertained some of our grandchildren with rides on Jasmin, our Shetland pony. In 2004 I bought an iMac Desktop Apple Computer. That opened up a whole new way of life for me. Previously my projects were mostly physical labor outdoors.

2007 was a very eventful year for Cindy and me. In January, the long-expected word arrived that my aunt Gert, the closest person I had for a mother image as I grew up, was declining fast. She was 97 years old. She passed away peacefully. With all of her living children and grandchildren and many great-grandchildren, other relatives and friends gathered in Hartington Nebraska for her burial alongside her husband in the Catholic cemetery. It was a great disappointment that my younger sister Della broke her ankle two days before the funeral and couldn't attend. To console her, Cindy and I drove to Minneapolis after the funeral to visit Della and Al. We had a pleasant visit, but it was obvious that Della was in pain, so we didn't stay long. We drove to Atlanta to visit Mark and Susan Stovin's and Charlie and Malinda Coulter's families. A day later a call came that Della had died suddenly. We drove back to Minnesota, attended her funeral, commiserated with Al and their four sons and, with heavy hearts, returned home.

Three-quarters of a century! The Burbach family thought that anyone who lives that long deserves a party so on Father's Day in June, my six children, their spouses, and our 14 grandchildren gathered at the home of Tim and Amy Jensen's, in Fairfax, Virginia, and celebrated my 75th birthday. It was one of my happiest days. I cherish the many formal and informal photographs we have of the attendees.

I have often claimed that the silence in a monastery is far more than merely the absence of noise. It is a therapeutic setting for meditation, peace, and contentment, which I experienced when I lived in the environs of Conception in high school and junior college. Cindy, along with our traveling companions Steve and Barbara Greenwell got a taste of that silence at the Franciscan monastery in Guadalupe, Spain during our exploration of east-central Spain in July 2007. The monastery is huge, ancient, and grand; the village is small, colorful and interesting. Our trip also included a few days in Seville, always a delight, and Merida, with its museum and archaeological finds - possibly the best Roman ruins outside of Italy.

Our biggest excursion of the year began in September of 2010 when we drove to Atlanta to Charlie and Melinda's home for a week where I helped Charlie build a lengthy block wall, and Cindy delighted in helping care for Ali and the twins Harvey and Mattie. Also, we had a fun visit with Susan and Mark, Sadie, Sam, Marley, and Charlie. From there we drove to Nashville to the home of Tom and Alex Cross and their bright and athletic sons, Will and Cole. Next, we drove to our humble abode in Cindy's hometown of Halls, Tennessee. We upgraded our residence by selling our cheap cottage and buying a much newer and nicer house across the street, which we refer to as "The Retreat." After arranging things to our satisfaction inside the house and the yard, we drove to Fairfax, Virginia by way of Gatlinburg. Cindy was driving and thought it would be fun to drive the Blue Ridge Parkway; but after an hour during which we traveled 35 miles, only 10 miles as the crow flies, she opted for the interstate while we commented on roads in general. The annual Army Ten-Miler was that weekend. Our entrants this year were Tim, Amy, Shellie, Mike, and Kip.

In 2007 after a visit at the home of the Jensen's: Amy and Tim, daughter Sarah and sons Ben and Jack; home of the Burbachs: Anchalee and Mike, daughter Jessica and son Joseph; and: another Burbach home: Jeff and Mary, sons Mike, James, and John; we boarded a British Airways plane for a flight from Dulles to London and a train to Salisbury, England. We enjoyed seeing Stonehenge and the Salisbury cathedral and returned to London for a week stay at the Intercontinental near Hyde Park. The plane ride was a birthday gift from Alix and Tom for Cindy's 70th birthday, and Stacy and Jim provided the London hotel stay, theatre tickets, and the London Eye (stories-high, with enclosed-capsules) Ferris wheel with an extensive vista of early evening London.

We were very appreciative of both gifts. From London, we traveled to Derbyshire, from which Cindy's ancestors came three hundred and fifty some years ago. Cindy spent a week exploring the area where the Alsobrook family is first recorded. Meanwhile, I visited another famous wall (Hadrian's). So far, I have also visited the great walls of China and the Berlin wall. I have built a few walls in our yard at home. Cindy has hopes that I don't get the idea of competing at a higher level.

Our final two days in England were spent at Windsor, visiting the castle and its environs and staying at a B&B whose hostess is the mother of all B&B hostesses. When we arrived, she greeted us with a half hour of gossip about the royal family and the goings-on at the castle. It seems that several years ago she actually got into the private quarters of the Queen and also met her; so, part of the accounting was "me and the Queen" and what "we" think. The likes of Charles Dickens could not have improved on her presentation.

When we returned stateside, we visited Cindy's brother Cary in Murfreesboro, Tennessee and then to home sweet home. We enjoyed a week at the beach house during Thanksgiving with Charlie's and Alex's families. We finished the year in the holiday season with Shellie and her daughter Hannah, and Kip and Elsie. We are so happy that they live near us. We six are the only Floridians in our extended family of 40.

In 2008 we visited Santiago, Valparaiso, and Puerto Montt, Chile, and Bariloche and Buenos Aires, Argentina. It was an excellent trip except for my lamenting the changes that had taken place since I had last been there 40 some years ago. My memory of Chile and Argentina was not the Argentina and Chile that we were visiting.

When we got back to the states, we visited Cindy's uncle, Joe, where they discussed the original handwritten diary of her great-grandfather from the Civil War. Cindy values that document greatly and is indexing and annotating it for publication. I was impressed visiting uncle Joe and realizing that I was talking to a man whose grandfather fought in the Civil War. Suddenly it seemed that the Civil War took place in my real world rather than in the distant days of history.

The year of 2009, we watched a new president (Barack Obama) take office and try to cope with two wars and an international Great Recession while Senator Mitch McConnell gathered members of Congress to attempt to ensure that this African-American would be a one-term president. The ambitious multimillionaire Donald Trump was trying to convince the world that Barack Obama was not a citizen, did not have a birth certificate and therefore could not possibly be the President of the United States. Since that time, I have taken a very big interest in national politics and the activities of the two aforementioned men.

The Great Recession was especially disruptive in real estate. Cindy had helped me buy two houses from her daughters before we married. When the houses tripled in value, I sold them at the suggestion and with the help of Mark Kimble, a real estate agent. At the time he was buying houses that were for sale but which were in dire need of repair. He had a small crew who did fine work. He invited Cindy and me to join him in his business, which we did. For a brief time, we did very well but then the recession hit and drove us out of business. Fortunately, we have remained good friends, and each of us is doing well and living a good life.

During these times Cindy and I have had three great tours. The first was to Southeast Asia (Thailand, Cambodia, Laos, and Vietnam) with our favorite travel agency. Touring India was magnificent. It has been a lifetime dream for both of us to visit the Taj Mahal, which is just as beautiful and awe-inspiring as it is supposed to be. It is an exquisite creation, delicate yet massive. We rode an elephant through one of the gates in Cambodia near Angkor Wat and loved the view from on high. We rode camels in India. We watched as the dead were cremated on the banks downstream as pilgrims bathed in the waters of the Ganges upstream. What an interesting world. Vietnam is enjoyable with no one shooting at us, and we were happy to see that their economy is growing and the people seem to be well fed. A boat ride on the Mekong to Cambodia, again with no one shooting at us, was very enjoyable. India, in spite of the failure of a year's monsoon, seemed to be experiencing economic growth and development. All five countries we visited are desperately poor, and if you think American education has problems, you should see young, intense Indian and Cambodian students trying to learn in crowded classrooms, sometimes sitting on the floor with little more than a book and a dedicated teacher. If our grandchildren and all Americans could really understand how much we have to be thankful for, we would be happier people.

Our next trip was Costa Rica. The highlight of the trip for me was touring the cloud forest and spotting a Quetzal with its very bright colors of red and green, and a very long tail feather. Next, we had a stateside trip beginning with a visit to Branson Missouri, Denver, where Kip joined us, onward to South Dakota to see Crazy Horse and Rushmore monuments, through Wyoming to see Yellowstone Park and the Grand Teton mountains, Then we dropped down into Colorado to see the Air Force Academy and many other sites. In Denver Kip left and we continued to the west coast.

In 2011, on a cool, crisp morning in late May, ten other tour friends and we were drifting lazily across the rugged, cave-pocked dusty brown landscape of Cappadocia, Turkey, awed by 59 other colorful, silent airships (hot air balloons) that soared with us. It was a sight to photograph and store in our memories for the rest of our days. We were amazed that the pilot seemed to steer our balloon at will. He explained that on most any beautiful and peaceful morning there were numerous air currents and one could choose the direction of flight by choosing the right attitude. Remarkable! This quiet, colorful balloon ride was one of those times in life when all one could do was to enjoy the moment and remember the sight and thrill, which too quickly vanishes. For an example of a thrill, we did not experience a takeoff, rather Mother earth slowly sank away from our ship.

My grandson, James Paul Davis Burbach, died in May 2012. Grandfathers undergo a great sense of sorrow when a grandchild dies. It's not nearly as intense as it is for the parents and siblings but it must be next in line. It's a harsh sense of guilt, of loss and a hollow in the chest. When I learned of James' death, I retrieved a gift of years ago from James and his brother Mike, a simulated newspaper in a frame with headlines asserting to the greatness of their grandfather and I hung it on a wall in my office. I placed a picture of James in the right lower corner of the frame and a copy of a poem in the left lower corner.

With the poem in my hand and with no one around, I sat in my favorite chair, and I cried. As I recuperated, I began to read the poem and felt a bonding with James, a feeling that he was with me, and that we were of one mind, one spirit and deducing what the poem meant to us. Afterward, I sat for a while at peace, feeling a spiritual presence of James. The poem was "The Little Boy and The Old Man" by Shel Silverstein. Most often when James and I got together, we usually did a lot of bantering. The very last time we were together, he began in the role of an elderly father finding faults with my conduct and giving me advice. I responded by playing a role of an obstreperous teenager. I loved him. An endearing memory. At one time in his childhood, we had proudly professed to the world that he and I were bums.

In June 2012, Cindy was informed that she had breast cancer. Bravely and with my full support she calmly went through therapy. When those months passed, Cindy treated herself and me to a New York theater production of *Book of Mormon*. Two years later, she joined her son Charles and family on a trip to China.

In May 2013, at the end of Cindy's radiation treatment, we chose to experience our favorite vacation scheme—military space available to wherever the first flight out of Dover Delaware would take us. The first flight was to England, so we explored the south coast of England: Dover to Lands End, including the Isle of Wight. Our return flight to the states was aboard a noisy, cold and uncomfortable military KC 135 to a small air force base near Boston. From there we drove a rented car to Dover, got our car and drove home. All the while Cindy was aware that she was ill. When we finally reached her medical team; she was diagnosed with pneumonia. One of the nurses told Cindy that if she did not go immediately to the hospital, she could die. Cindy responded that she might die, but not in the hospital. It would have to be at home near her garden. She survived.

In June 2013, Jerry Burbach died at age 77. Jerry, his brothers Don (died June 1997) and Richard, "double first cousins," have been very close since our childhood. The love, compassion, and respect that filled the many attendees at Jerry's funeral was also a tribute to his impressive wife Marilyn and their two sons Matt and Chris.

All of our sons and daughters (in-laws and outlaws alike) are doing well. Each of them enjoys their work and live active and productive lives. We bite our lip to keep from bragging about them on an individual basis. Not so for the grandchildren! Each of them provides us with many bragging rights, which we feel obligated to pass on. It is a grandparents' duty. Our experience with the psychology of grandchildren runs something like this: when they reach 18 years of age, grandparents fall off the planet. 13 to 18-year-olds are non-laboring intellectuals who have huge social responsibilities and little time for old people chatter, and those younger than 13 come running when we arrive, give us a big hug and unknowingly disclose what they think of each of us: Papa is funny and fun, Gam is interesting and smart.

Early in 2016, Cindy was operated on for uterine cancer followed by weeks of chemotherapy and radiation. She came through it all very well. Some weeks later she joined Charlie and family on a trip to London.

Darlene Petersen Burbach, my former wife, and mother of our six children died peacefully in early October 2016 with most of her children and grandchildren in attendance. She had been declining in health for several years. Heartfelt acknowledgment of memories of her life was voiced at graveside by the attending children and grandchildren, led by grandson Charlie Stovin.

Recently, my daughter, Susan introduced me to her neighbor, Dr. Hanna, an expert in knee replacement operations. Once I had a conference with him, I knew he was what I had been looking for, and the operation was simple and effective. Also, Cindy and I are grateful that Charlie, Malinda, and their kids invited us to stay with them for my four weeks of therapy and recuperation after the operation.

Our retirement years today are truly blessed by our outstanding relatives and friends, and because Cindy and I have each other. We notice that we have a growing number of new friends who are physicians and pharmacists. With that in mind, we remember the title of a song: "Accentuate the Positive, Eliminate the Negative!"

1991 - 2018   Retirement

Stacey Coulter, Charles Coulter, Cindy, Alix Coulter.

Alix and Tom Cross and sons Cole and Will

Scholar, Father, Soldier, *Wynot!*

Jim Barrett and Stacey Coulter
sons, Liam and Riley Barrett

1991 - 2018   Retirement

Harvey, Charles, Alix Coulter, Malinda and Mattie below

Chapter 24
Thoughts & Memories

Ever since I became an army officer, I have looked forward to the summertime when I would pick a subject to explore. The first several years, I subscribed to a correspondence course. In subsequent years, I satisfied my curiosity about some field of study, event, or happening without any obligation to account for my time or effort – no tests, no queries by others, and no agenda for myself. Just delve in and follow my curiosities. One summer the subject was philosophy, which I had minored in in college but had not learned much about philosophers of the 20th Century such as Camus, Kierkegaard, etc. The courses seemed more indoctrinating then informing. Admittedly the best course I had in college was a philosophy course entitled logic, which today is receiving a revival under the words 'critical thinking.'

Another summer I chose communication with some attention to other means of conveying ideas (e.g., print and writing, art, code (for the blind) and my favorite at which Cindy is very adept, charades. As for my studying spoken languages which I had studied previously, I wanted to see how well I could do with them and see if I wanted to work on improving any. A quick review of Latin and Greek confirmed that I had forgotten much and had no interest in the study. The same was true of Serbo-Croatian which I had studied intensely for one year at the Army language school and had passed a fluency test, but within a couple of years of zero use, I had no fluency in Serbo-Croatian, it was as though I had never studied it. When I hear German spoken, it sounds very familiar, but I lacked a sizable vocabulary to claim much fluency in, speaking it. In my youth, it was a household language preferred by many older adults including my grandparents with whom I lived, and I had studied it is in college and at the intelligence school. I brushed up on German over the ensuing months as well as Spanish which is the only foreign language I can speak with fluency, and of course I also studied English by extending my vocabulary and applying punctuation marks properly.

The biological sciences are teeming with interesting facts, but I have never taken to them. A course in zoology in high school was informative, especially the labs, but it didn't lead to further study. The summer I chose biological sciences for study was the year that the genome was completed. I did a quick survey of medical science breakthroughs, health and longevity, DNA, viruses and bacteria, the mitochondria, the arguments over stem cell research, abortions, medical ethics and that splendid computer the brain. It was an informative and fun summer.

One summer I studied earth sciences which turned out to be both boring and rewarding. Boring to the extent that I already have a superficial understanding of some of the subjects because of the duplication in the study of geography. I am first of all a student of geography, starting in the fourth grade. Over the years I have taught various courses in geography with a specialization in area studies as the discipline and Latin America as the concentration. I found this summer, as I read books on geology, climatology, sociology, etc., which I had long ago learned the fundamentals of the subjects and knew where to find the specifics if needed. For me, further study of these subjects was not interesting. On the other hand, the greening of the earth became an issue for the world to pay heed. Local environmental studies are often boring, but a worldview of the environmental impacts of man's actions or inactions are quite another matter.

The preceding summer studies were obviously more academic than involving. The final five subjects of my summer studies bring about not only study but action. They are the arts, economics, genealogy, theoretical physics and religion. The several summers that I engaged in the arts was a reflection of previous experiences, much reading and research, and the resolve that materialize in some actions after that. Music. I have gathered some classical music recordings, and I have a couple of music appreciation study guides which I plan to enjoy when I get time. I began lessons several times under Cindy's tutelage to learn to play a musical instrument but soon lost the willpower to practice. In other words, I am an active listener of music but a worthless producer thereof.

Painting. Many years ago, Cindy and I spent several weeks in Ireland seeing the sights. One day, as we toured the west coast, we spotted what we each thought was an ideal picture of an Irish home, and so we took many photographs. When we got home, I was still impressed by the scene, so I began to put on canvas what I saw in the photograph. When my daughter Susie saw what I was doing, she insisted that when that painting was finished, it would be hers (and so it was). With humor, I announced that I am now an artist in great demand. Soon after that my son Mike saw the painting and said that the next painting I did was his. It would be of his favorite mountain, Mount Reiner. When the painting was completed, Mike showed his appreciation by displaying it above the fireplace in his living room. I have never told him how amateurish it is for fear that he might agree with me and dispose of it. I trust this is a case of "honor thy father," and so I am satisfied and gratefully silent. Since then I have completed a few other paintings and hope to do much more as soon as I complete writing this book. An appealing factor about painting is that the eye and the brain often find features on the canvas that the painter suddenly notices but never intended.

Sculpturing. Cindy owns the vacant lot adjoining her property all of which incline graciously to Mirror Lake. When we married, we agreed to bring all her land together into a Japanese-like landscape. First, we learned how to make boulders, thanks to some people in a museum in Vancouver Canada and by a hit or miss technique of our own using concrete, hardware cloth, stucco, and dyes. With the boulder concept, we built a 15-foot-high, 20-foot-wide "mountain" on the upper edge of the vacant lot and included pumped-in water that flowed down three waterfalls which fed a six by 15-foot concrete-based pond after passing under a Japanese styled, high arched wooden bridge with rails and painted in bright red. Next, step sized waterfalls on both ends of a crooked 12-foot-long creek reached the Plum Tree Puddle which was another pond in the center of which was a small island holding a tall wild plum tree. Water flows over a fall on the lower end of this pond, then under a white, low surfaced, low railed bridge, and via a long meandering creek, under the Chinese bridge, and into the lake.

The six-foot-long, three-foot-wide, brightly painted Chinese bridge has panels engraved with Chinese Characters for Long Life, Double Happiness, Prosperity, and Good Luck. We have often talked of building a teahouse somewhere on our grounds. The finest example of a teahouse we found was in a Japanese Garden in Ireland. We took photos of that teahouse, and I crafted a cubic foot- sized model. The miniature is now ten years old and has passed through so many playful hands of grandchildren that it hardly is a true replica of itself.

Woodworking has been a hobby for much of my life. Most military bases have a well-furnished craft shop that military personnel may use, and I have often availed myself of that privilege. At Fort Ord I built a coffee table, at Fort Sill a tv stand, in Korea, with the help of the skilled hands of a Korean, we built a set of highly crafted speaker boxes which I donated to the base recreation Center. At Fort Amador in the Canal zone I designed a frame within a frame for displaying molas and gave it to a local merchant who then began selling framed molas with great success, or so I was told several years after I had left the Canal Zone. I dreamt of the day when I could have my own workshop. My brother-in-law Al Bruns had an ideal shop and was producing many admirable pieces for family members. He was truly a skilled craftsman. My day finally came after I retired when I could have a permanent residence. Over the years I developed a good shop, but for the past ten years, I have had little time for woodworking. So many other projects took precedent that I have put most of my woodworking tools in storage. I am having the workshop cleaned up, debugged, renovated and renamed the Art Studio. I intend to cover the walls with framed pictures and paintings from family members and from what we have gathered over the years from our travels abroad. By January 2018 I hope to be using the studio for paintings by me and by visiting grandchildren, for calisthenics, for desk work and for constructing model airplanes, ships, and the like.

First come will be a balsa wood and paper model of a Cessna 150 which I bought a few years ago when I was taking flying lessons in a Cessna 150 but stopped when I failed the flight physical medical exam), In the lower part of the shed, I will have a workshop for woodworking. I still have some of the lumber from an old walnut tree that we harvested from Cindy's parents' backyard and still dream of making some fine pieces of polished walnut, which I have thought about for years. This is also my 'handyman' workshop where anything that needs doing gets done.

Religion

In Father Lawrence's literature class in my senior year at Conception Monastery boarding high school, we memorized much poetry and many speeches and delivered them at our Saturday evening entertainment, which was attended by all students and some faculty and monks. I delivered a memorized piece from Shakespeare's King Lear where a father is giving his son, who is leaving soon, some advice on how he should live his life. The advice ends with "And this above all, to thine own self be true and it shall follow as the night the day, thou canst not then be false to any man." That concept internalized in me and at the same time, I had a burning desire to know, to understand precisely what is important. What is 'Truth'? What does "to know God" mean? I know what 'to know' means, but I don't know God, nor does any of my schoolmates nor any of the monks. And what does 'to believe' mean? I must believe in God, but he is described only by absolutes such as 'perfect' and 'eternal.' My imperfect and temporary brain cannot comprehend them. All my life I had accepted Catholicism and all that it entailed, but I resolved that henceforth I would pay more attention to the 'real world' thoughts of honored men and try to understand fully what 'to thine own self be true "entails.

I came to realize that there was no own self'. For years I had been a victim of intense indoctrination so that my basic convictions and attitudes fixated on an unquestioned set of beliefs and that my mind and my body were devoid of freedom that would allow me to grow into a man who could be self-sustaining, could be 'his own self.' Outwardly my way of life continued as it had been for the past ten years. I completed two years of college in Catholic boarding schools where my apparent intentions would lead me to the priesthood. Inwardly I struggled with the idea of a 100% change in my convictions and attitudes. My first action in that change was to spend my third year of college at Creighton University. I believe it was the worst year of my life psychologically. I was alone, lost in an unknown world, and destitute. I rescued myself by joining the army. Some years later a chaplain asked me to help in establishing catechism classes for teenagers. I agreed to help in providing the facilities but declined to teach classes. It had surprised me that I did not think it would be ethical to get involved in teaching something that included things that I did not believe. Today I am a Catholic and an agnostic. After observing many contradictions and discrepancies in seeking a marriage annulment, after many scandals by members of the clergy, and after much of the dictates and voids emanating from the Vatican, I believe the Catholic Church hierarchy will wake up someday to find that the Church (the true Church) has passed them by.

The Family

Soon after I retired from Seminole, my daughter, Susan sent me a book called *Legacy* by Linda Spence about writing a personal history. She said something like this, "Write it down dad. For the grandchildren. Tell us about your life. So, I started 14 years ago. I've had a long life. I am 86 years old now. I've had a career in the military and a half career teaching. I think I've discovered what is important to me, family. What gives me joy are my six children and their 14 children. My wife and her three children and their seven children, which makes 21 grandchildren. Grandma Wieseler would be so proud and agree.

Words of Wisdom
Advice from Uncle Art: "Life is what you make it."
Observation from Uncle Mark: "It's never as bad as it seems."
From a western movie: "A man's gotta do what a man's gotta do."
An old Army motto: "Be all that you can be."
Advice from Russ: "Just show up."
My advice: "Live until you die."

The Extended Family
The Coulter-Burbach Extended Family came to be when Cindy and I married in 1987. I was the father of three sons and three daughters, and Cindy was the mother of 2 daughters and one son. Those nine offspring never melded into a close family, but varying degrees of friendship developed between individuals. On the other hand, every grandchild, in its earliest age of recognizing, saw each of us as a grandparent. Cindy and I were most concerned about being accepted by each other's children. It was obvious to me that Cindy's children greatly cherished their father (Harvey Ransom Coulter) who had died two years earlier. Would they see me as some intruder who would try to be a replacement for their Father? I was overjoyed when I found solid evidence that I was accepted. When Cindy's first grandchild (William Ransom Cross) was born, I quietly and hopefully asked his mother (Alix): "May I be Will's grandfather?" she looked at me with a quizzical expression and asked: "Why? What else would you be?" And immediately after that Will had three grandfathers: Papa Cross, Papa Harvey, and Papa Fred. I was confident that I was welcomed into the Coulter family. Cindy had a tougher obstacle than I, but with patience, kindness, and understanding she has been welcomed by the Burbachs.

In our extended family, there are ten families containing 21 grandchildren. Each of the families is splendid, and every grandchild is above average!

Top Row- Jessica, Matt, Joe, James, Michael Burbach
Row 2, Ben and Sarah holding Jack Jensen, Sadie, Marley and Charles Stovin, Hannah Springer, John Burbach with hand on Sam Stovin

Cindy, Alix Coulter Cross, Cole Cross, Alix Coulter, Will Cross, Harvey Coulter, Liam Barrett, Stacey Coulter, Riley Barrett, Charles and Mattie Coulter

When, What, Where

Feb '37 - Aug '46	Elementary School	Hartington, NE
Aug '46 - Jun '50	High School	Conception, MO
Jun *50- Aug '53	College	Conception, MO Fond du Lac, WI Omaha, NE
Aug'53- Feb'54	Army Basic Training	Ft. Leonardwood, MO
Feb'54- Aug'54	Officer Candidate School	Ft. Sill, OK
Aug'54- Dec'55	C Battery, 548 FA BN	Ft. Sill, OK
Jan '56-Dec '56	Army Language School	Monterey, CA
Jan'57- Aug'57	Army Intelligence School	Ft. Holabird, MD
Aug'57- Jun'58	45th Army Intelligence Company	Ft. Holabird, MD
Jul '58 - Jan '60	Army Staff, Pentagon	Arlington, VA
Jan '60 - Aug '60	Creighton University	Omaha, NE
Aug '60 - May '61	Artillery Officer Career Course	Ft. Sill, OK
Jun'61- Sep'62	502nd Army Intelligence Battalion	Seoul, South Korea
Oct'62-Jul '63	Army Language School	Monterey, CA
Aug '63 - Aug '64	University of Oklahoma	Norman, OK

Aug '64 - Dec '64	Army Command & General Staff College	Ft. Leavenworth, KS
Jan '65 - Mar '66	Foreign Area Studies	Buenos Aires, Argentina
Mar '66-Dec '67	Army Southern Command	Canal Zone, Panama
Jan'68-Jan'69	HQS, Military Assistance Command	Saigon, South Vietnam
Jan'69-May '71	Defense Intelligence Agency	Arlington, VA
May'71-Jun'74	470th Military Intelligence Group	Canal Zone, Panama
Jul'74-Aug'75	St Bonaventure University ROTC	Allegany, NY
Aug '75 - Jul '76	Inter-American Defense College	Ft. McNair; Washington, DC
Jul '76-Jul'79	Southern Command	Canal Zone, Panama
Jul '79-Aug'81	University of Mississippi ROTC	Oxford, MS
Aug '81 - Jan '82	Fort Sam Houston Hospital	San Antonio, TX
Jan'82-Dec'83	Retired	Oxford, MS
Jan '84 - Jul '85	Consultant, EAF	Orlando, FL
Aug'86-Jun '90	Faculty, Seminole Community College	Orlando, FL
Jul '90-Dec '90	5-Month Sabbatical	Europe

| Jan'91-Jun'01 | Faculty, Seminole Community College | Orlando, FL |
| Jun '01 - Present | Full Retirement | Orlando, FL |

www.ingramcontent.com/pod-product-compliance
Lightning Source LLC
Chambersburg PA
CBHW052006070526
44584CB00016B/1640